979.00497
R45f

130045

Th

DATE DUE			

THE FRONTIER PEOPLE

THE GREATER SOUTHWEST IN THE
PROTOHISTORIC PERIOD

BY

CARROLL L. RILEY

CENTER FOR ARCHAEOLOGICAL INVESTIGATIONS

OCCASIONAL PAPER NO. 1

CENTER FOR ARCHAEOLOGICAL INVESTIGATIONS
SOUTHERN ILLINOIS UNIVERSITY AT CARBONDALE
APRIL 1982

Standard Book Number: 0-88104-000-2
Library of Congress Catalog Card Number: 82-050284

CONTENTS

FIGURES

[1]Figure 9 is reproduced by permission, adapted from Kelly (1977); copyright, Regents of the University of Arizona. Figures 11, 12, and 15 have been conceptually influenced by Dutton (1963a); Montgomery et al. (1949); and Kidder (1932), respectively. Figure 13 is largely drawn from Schroeder (1964), and is reprinted with the author's permission.

FOREWORD

This volume marks a new phase in anthropological studies of the Greater Southwest simply because it is an ethnohistorical study of great scholarly value in its own right. Traditionally, ethnohistorical studies of the Southwest have been used in two ways. Ethnohistory has been a means of testing archaeological "truth" and putting human behavioral flesh on cultural material bones. On the other hand, historical documents have been used to enhance descriptions and offer explanations about what used to be called "the ethnographic present." It is not suprising that southwestern ethnohistory as a handmaiden to archaeology and ethnography was less than successful, its data suspect, and its collaborative value dubious.

Professor Riley has convincingly demonstrated that a judicious and conservative use of historical documents permits an understanding of the protohistoric period. Instead of using historical accounts to understand the archaeological record or flesh out the early ethnographies, he has used the results of these anthropological subdisciplines to provide a better perspective on the very important sixteenth century.

The goal of Professor Riley is not simply to describe the Greater Southwest in the 1500s but to come to an understanding of the cultural subunits of the region at the time of the Spanish entradas and the interaction that existed between them. He demonstrates the unity of the cultural subunits and the interaction between subunits of the Greater Southwest and those peripheral to the study area. In short, he is concerned with relationships on a local, regional, and superregional basis. Prior to this publication the majority of ethnohistorical studies have dealt with "tribes," individual pueblos, or, at the most, populations of river valleys. Few attempts were made to comprehend the essence of unity and interaction between what Professor Riley calls provinces.

This study marks the first successful attempt to view the Southwest as an entity, a systemic whole, at the time of Spanish northward incursions—and with it southwestern ethnohistory has come of age.

George J. Gumerman

ACKNOWLEDGMENTS

I have been drawing together materials for this volume for several years. In that time, a number of my ideas concerning the late pre-Spanish and early historic Southwest have been given in symposia at various professional meetings and published in scholarly journals. I have had a great deal of input from colleagues both in the United States and in Mexico, many of whom have been generous with their suggestions and constructive criticisms. I thank them all.

I am especially grateful to colleagues here at Southern Illinois University. George J. Gumerman and W. Bruce Masse read the manuscript in detail and had many important suggestions. Donna Dickerson Rabinowitz, Helmut Publ, and Lee E. Holland all worked with the manuscript and all contributed timely ideas. Karen A. Schmidt and Thomas W. Gatlin prepared maps and charts. Donna E. Butler, John M. Coggeshall, and Lee H. Hill helped with editorial matters, as did Robert W. Layhe and Ernest E. May. Sandra K. Spezia, Tedi L. Thomas, and Jodie A. Misch typed, and Dawn M. Larsen computer-scripted portions of the manuscript at various stages of production. Joni L. Manson served as my research assistant during the final stages; her meticulous editorial work and valuable substantive comments have enriched the publication. My wife, Brent Locke Riley, herself an expert in southwestern ethnohistory, shared insights and knowledge of the area with me from the very beginning of the project.

The shortcomings of this volume are my own.

CHAPTER I

INTRODUCTION

In this publication I examine protohistoric (A.D. 1400-1700) contacts among various peoples of Mesoamerica and the complex societies to the north and west. I have used the term Greater Southwest for this frontier of Mesoamerica because it is, indeed, the southwesternmost portion of the continent of North America. At the hinge of my Greater Southwest, the lower Colorado River area, the continent falls off sharply to the east. Panama and Colon, the southernmost cities of what is traditionally considered North America, both lie east of Miami, Florida, and virtually all of Latin America is both east and south of the Greater Southwest.

Although my Greater Southwest is in part a cultural construct and includes neither the two Californias nor culturally primitive portions of northwest Mexico, those areas are geographically part of a greater Greater Southwest.

Other names for this general area include the Southwest, a word I prefer not to use because it traditionally refers to only the American portion of the area. The term Arid America is far too general, and Gran Chichimeca is somewhat misleading since the word Chichimec in its original meaning designated the hunting-gathering and low-level agriculturalists of northwest Mexico. The Northwest Frontier of Mesoamerica might do, except there is more than one "northwest frontier," and, in any case, I hesitate to introduce still another term into the literature.

The research design of this project is the deceptively simple one of interdigitating five "information pools" to reconstruct the cultural subsystems of the Greater Southwest, to relate them to their environmental bases, and to examine various kinds of interaction within the Greater Southwest as a whole.

The five types of materials that provide a data base for this project are:

(1) Contemporary, firsthand, documentary accounts of the sixteenth century Southwest.

(2) Historical, derived accounts of various kinds, especially from the sixteenth to eighteenth centuries, which deal in one way or another with the Greater Southwest.

(3) Ethnographic material from the eighteenth to twentieth centuries that allows us to say something about the sixteenth.

(4) Archaeological data, as appropriate, especially the archaeology of the sixteenth century sites.

(5) Information from cultural and physical geography, ethnobotany, and ethnozoology, insofar as these materials provide information on the cultural and natural environmental conditions in the sixteenth century.

The approach taken here is a very conservative one and will, as far as possible, stay within the parameters of the actual data. It would be, of course, very tempting to relate the cultural activities of--let us say--the nineteenth century Rio Grande pueblos as seen by Bandelier to Tiguex in the sixteenth century or to describe Zuni as observed by Stevenson in the later 1800s as if it were Cibola in the early 1500s. Unfortunately, reconstructions from contemporary data are almost never able to make proper allowances for the most profound cultural and biological event of the New World culture history--the massive and rapid impingement of Euro-Asia and Africa on the Americas, beginning around A.D. 1500.

In this study, I suggest the following model. The Greater Southwest, at the time of first Spanish contact, formed an interaction sphere in which the major linkages were those of trade but which included other kinds of sociopolitical and religious contacts. What I present here can be considered as both an explication of this model and an attempt to analyze the implications of its various manifestations, particularly the nature of relationships of the various subsystems discussed below.

To demonstrate the model, three hypotheses need to be tested, to the extent that the diverse but often inadequate materials allow for such testing. These are: (1) the Greater Southwest was, at contact time, an internal interacting area; (2) the Southwest oikoumene was, at least in part, fashioned out of the trade necessities of civilized peoples to the south and east; and (3) relationships in the Southwest, both internal and external, at least by A.D. 1500, extended well beyond mere trade contacts.

These hypotheses are obviously interrelated, and, in a sense, proposition (2) forms the core from which (1) and (3) draw their meaning. That is to say, certain events that helped influence and shape the Greater Southwest were external to the Southwest and had their genesis in the great civilizations to the south. A frontier is meaningful only in relation to the heartland at its back.

CHAPTER II

THE GREATER SOUTHWEST: A DIVERSE UNITY

A study of the Greater Southwest as of the beginning of historic times (c. A.D. 1500 to 1550) presents certain problems but also advantages over the purely archaeological prehistoric reconstructions of the area. The sixteenth century lacks the large amount of archaeological work that has been lavished on such pre-Spanish peoples as the Hohokam, the Mogollon, and various branches of the Anasazi. On the other hand, the sixteenth century was one of far-ranging Spanish expeditions, planned and unplanned, which often give rich insights into aspects of culture that can broaden and amplify the archaeological picture. Unfortunately, the documentary evidence is somewhat disconnected. Often, in fact, we do not know the exact areas for which we have large pockets of cultural information. In addition, there are striking gaps in the data. It is not so much that these data are slanted or even that they particularly represent one aspect of culture over another. Rather, information is tossed helter-skelter into the reports, chronicles, trial hearings, letters, etc. An author may introduce a mention of women's costume, trade habits, linguistic distributions, or a description of local biota into an account that has as its major purpose the Spanish treatment of Indians. The diffuse nature of this ethnohistorical information, even though much of it is easily available, has led to its underutilization.

The historical archaeology of the Greater Southwest, which could answer at least some of the questions posed by the historical documents, lies mainly in the future. There are notable exceptions: the excavations at Hawikuh, Kuaua, Pecos, historic Awatovi, the Tewa and eastern Keres area, Piman mission sites, and, more recently, in the Sonora River area and at Casas Grandes. Of course, many of the earlier excavations do not address themselves very efficiently to problems of sociopolitical, economic, and religious organization, systematic trade, and the like.

Certainly, the decade of the 1980s will see a considerable increase not only in the amount but also in the sophistication of archaeological work in the late prehistoric and early historic Southwest. In addition, work now underway to computerize far-flung archival sources for the Greater Southwest for easy retrieval under various subject headings (see Polzer et al. 1977; Barnes et al. 1981) will surely add a great deal to our historical knowledge.

It seems to me that the Greater Southwest in the transitional sixteenth century can best be studied in terms of "provinces," with the understanding that the term does not necessarily have implications of political unity and corresponds more to what an older generation of anthropologists would call "culture areas." In an emic sense, provinces are those regions where people had a sense of identity, a kind of "us" versus "them" feeling. I shall try to demonstrate that these provinces are valid for the sixteenth century--or perhaps for a period stretching from the late fifteenth century to the early parts of the seventeenth. Before that time the large and diverse populations of the Greater Southwest, the major and still somewhat puzzling shifts of peoples (desertion of the San Juan area and of much of central Arizona, for example), and the incomplete nature of archaeological evidence make it impossible to organize data in the way proposed here. After about 1620 or 1630, Spanish intrusion into the Greater Southwest had diluted the native way of life and had certainly compromised the autonomic cultural mechanisms that gave meaning to Indian life in the Greater Southwest. In other words, after the early decades of the seventeenth century, we are dealing largely with Spanish culture and history in much of the Greater Southwest. It is true that the Indian groups still maintained part of their traditional culture, but in the major subregions of the Southwest this native culture was already in thrall to the Spanish Great Tradition. Even those regions not immediately and directly affected by the Spaniards (the Gila-Salt and lower Colorado rivers) were no longer part of a pan-southwestern tradition; their functions in terms of the larger system had been subverted.

As stated above, the hypothetical position taken in this work and the major raison d'être for its production is that in the sixteenth century the entire Greater Southwest operated as an interacting entity with trade relationships and specialist productions and ties of a sociopolitical and religious nature. The various parts of the Southwest did not share equally in this policy. It seems clear, for example, that the lower Colorado and lower Gila River peoples were somewhat peripheral to the Greater Southwest. Indeed, properly speaking, there was no center, rather a group of autonomous but interlocking regions (provinces) that had greater or lesser effect on the Southwest as a whole. The Little Colorado province, because of its geographically central position, probably had the largest amount of interprovince interaction. In addition to contacts within the Greater Southwest, all the provinces of the Greater Southwest had contacts outside it. For example, Pecos and, to a lesser degree, the Rio

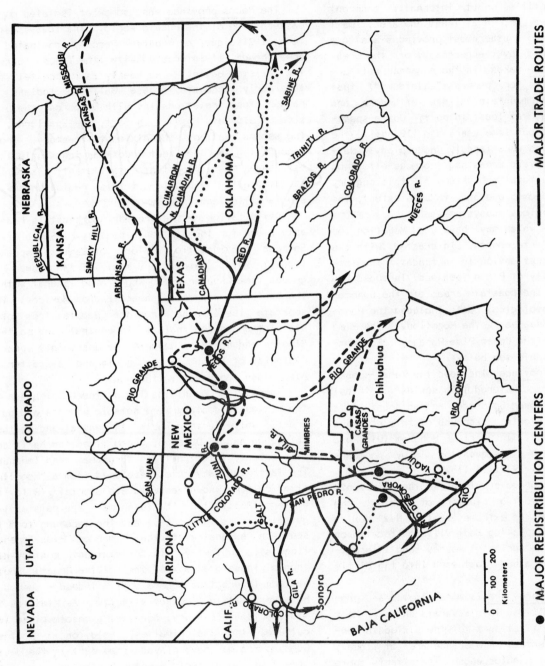

Figure 1. Trade Routes in the Greater Southwest, A.D. 1500.

Grande pueblos had firm lines of communications to the Plains and beyond. The lower Colorado region maintained trade links with the Pacific Coast, and of course the Serrana and Desert provinces were middlemen for the elaborate and important trade routes to Mesoamerica.

The six provinces proposed here represent, then, not political entities but internally coherent units--tribal, town, or, in at least one area, small statelets. The two southernmost provinces are to a large degree defined by the geography of the area. The Serrana province takes in those rather well-organized small states (or perhaps "chiefdoms") that flourished in the mountain valleys of Sonora and Chihuahua and were, at least in part, Opata-speaking. As I pointed out some years ago (1976b:1), the mountains themselves were largely unoccupied. Nevertheless, the mountain areas had enormous effect on several of the cultural subsystems of this region, especially the economic one and, to some extent, the political and religious subsystems.

The Serrana, which may have had Mogollon (or "Mogollon-like") antecedents, interacted with the Desert province, most obviously in trade. The latter province, mainly of Piman speakers, included the valley, monte, and coastal areas of the Sonoran Desert. Its archaeological roots included the Hohokam and, to some degree, the Mogollon. The Pima spoken of here are the Upper Pima-Papago. For comments on the Pima Bajo see below.

The Colorado province included the Yuman-speaking villagers that clustered in a series of tribal units along the lower Colorado and adjacent Gila rivers. The prehistoric background of this province may also have been, in part, Hohokam (Di Peso 1956:252), although this question is by no means settled (see Huckell 1979:133-138).

The Little Colorado province in the sixteenth century had shrunk to two clusters of pueblos, the Zuni-speaking group in extreme western New Mexico and the Shoshonean-speaking Hopi villages located on mesas adjacent to a series of washes and intermittent streams that drained southward into the Little Colorado.

The Rio Grande province is more complex and probably should be divided into several units. Most information in the first part of the sixteenth century is from the central Rio Grande area of Tiguex, a large cluster of pueblos whose inhabitants spoke Tiwa. People speaking kindred dialects (Piro, Tompiro) stretched southward along the Rio Grande, perhaps as far as the Las Cruces area, and in a parallel line along the east flank of the Sandias and Manzano ranges through the Salines. North of the Tiwa speakers were users of Keresan languages who also extended westward to the San Jose-Puerco

drainage and included the pueblo of Acoma. Tewa- and Tano-speaking Indians lived generally to the north and east of the Tiwa, although the northern-most pueblo in the Rio Grande basin, Braba or Valladolid (Taos), was Tiwa-speaking. The isolated pueblos that I will collectively call Jemez used the Towa language.

The Pecos province was somewhat isolated on the eastern edge of the Pueblo world. The Towa-speaking town of Ciquique, or Pequish (Pecos), dominated the area though it interacted with the Tanos towns of the Galisteo Basin. As nearly as I can tell from the early accounts, these Galisteo Indians had rather close relationships with Pecos on the other side of Glorieta Pass. In fact, the Spaniards, in the second half of the sixteenth century, though recognizing the fact that Pecos was the single largest and most important settlement, sometimes included all the people of this region under the single title Tanos, or Tamos.

Delimitation of the Greater Southwest is reasonably clear for the sixteenth century. South of the Serrana province lie a block of Cahitan speakers (Yaqui, Mayo, etc.) and most of the lower Pima groups (see Chapter VI), who are peripheral both to the Southwest and to the heartland of Mexico. They separate the Serrana province peoples from other statelet-organized Indians in central and southern Sinaloa and northern Nayarit, groups mainly speaking dialects of Tahue in the north and a scatter of Aztecoidan languages in the south.

Across the mountains in northern Chihuahua in the sixteenth century were nomadic hunters and gatherers, while further south in central and southern Chihuahua and in Durango, there lived rancheria peoples known historically as Tarahumar and Tepehuan. The latter, at any rate, developed from a "Mogollon-like" culture known as Loma San Gabriel (Riley and Winters 1963:184). The Tarahumar are related linguistically to the Opata, and the Tepehuan form the southern extension of the Piman or Pima-Tepehuan linguistic subfamily. In the sixteenth century neither of these groups was part of the Greater Southwestern interaction sphere and, indeed, seemed to have very little contact with it. As late as the mid-fourteenth century, however, a mesoamerican subculture, the Chalchihuites, held on in southern Durango and may have played some part in the development of the historic Greater Southwest.

Around the northern and eastern peripheries of the Greater Southwest and also interspersed with its agricultural populations were hunting peoples who traded with the Southwesterners. These hunting groups were given names such as Jumano, Tejas, Rayados, and Querechos by the early Spanish explorers. Some of the nomadic hunters--those internally

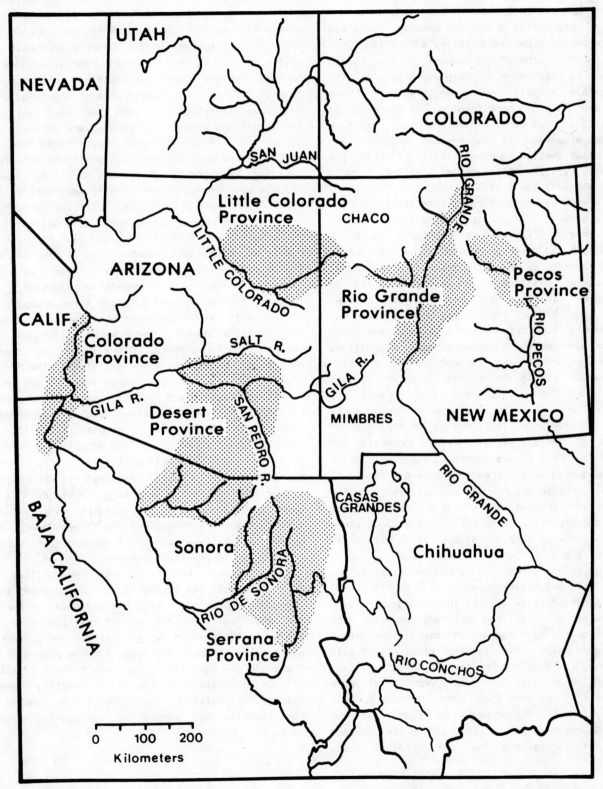

Figure 2.   Provinces of the Greater Southwest, A.D. 1500.

marginal ones and ones to the north--were ancestral to modern Apaches, Navajos, and perhaps Utes. Others, on the eastern fringe of the Southwest and eastward, may have spoken Caddoan, Apachean, Coahuiltecan, or even conceivably Kiowan languages. An especially interesting group (or groups) contacted somewhere in the upper Verde Valley and called "Cruzados," or "Querechos," by members of the Espejo expedition of 1583 and the Oñate expedition of 1598 were possibly Yavapais (Schroeder 1974:76). These Indians seem to have been involved in the trade of pigments to various parts of the Southwest, and they were also middlemen in the movement of Gulf and Pacific Ocean shells and pearls (Riley 1976b:38; see also Cuevas 1924:295-296; Bartlett 1942:25; Hammond and Rey 1953:327, 396 ff.).

There were major cultural similarities throughout this area. All of the southwestern peoples lived in more or less well-defined towns, although in the Desert and Colorado provinces these tended to be of an advanced rancheria pattern with the actual units somewhat dispersed. House types varied to some degree. In the Desert and Colorado provinces there is some evidence for massive adobe structures, but certainly more common was a light frame construction sometimes on a stone or adobe foundation. The same kind of dwelling is described for the Serrana groups, but in the Serrana it occurs side by side with substantial stone and adobe houses. In the Anasazi areas were multi-storied stone and adobe beehive type towns--in fact, mention of this type of building in the sixteenth century documents for northern New Spain always refers to the Pueblo area. All the peoples of the Greater Southwest made pottery; all practiced agriculture, usually intensive and often with irrigation systems; all were involved in an elaborate trade network in which various items (turquoise, shell, parrot feathers, bison skins, to mention only a few) were in demand from one end of the region to the other. There was political interaction within and between provinces, but it is not well understood today. The interchange included alliances for political and military purposes, the latter involving both aggression and various defensive strategies. There is also considerable evidence that, within the Greater Southwest, travel over very large distances was common. We have accounts of trips from the lower Colorado to Hopi and Zuni, from the latter pueblo to Pecos, and from the Rio Grande area to the Colorado on the one hand and the Buffalo Plains on the other. Indians in the

Serrana province were well acquainted with both the Little Colorado and the Rio Grande areas and, of course, with the Desert and lower Colorado regions. In other words, the "world view" of the Indians of the Greater Southwest definitely encompassed the entire Southwest and, indeed, areas well beyond.

Political systems in the Greater Southwest were mostly of the "tribal council" type with only the Serrana province clearly exhibiting something more complex. There was, however, a strong infusion of religious functionaries into the political life throughout the area. All groups were warlike, and, in most or all of the provinces, formalized war officers were part of the sociopolitical structure. Religion had strong astral and fertility aspects and, in most areas, a considerable mesoamerican flavor. There were priesthoods (that is, structural organizations whose duties were to propitiate and manipulate supernatural forces) in the several Pueblo provinces and probably also in the Serrana. The Desert province peoples had, at least, an organized, functionally differentiated shamanism, and this was likely the case with the Yuman groups.

Although the Greater Southwest can be considered a cultural macrounit, there were differences from one province to another. Overall, it seems reasonable to speak of three major divisions. The Serrana province was the most complex in terms of sociopolitical organization and probably of economic organization as well. The various Pueblo groups represented a somewhat less complex situation in sociopolitical terms, and the Desert and Colorado provinces, the simplest culturally, were to some degree a rancheria people and thus differed only in degree from the rancheria-living Cahitans. In the case of the lower Colorado Indians it is justifiable to treat them as part of the Greater Southwest mainly because they were such an important part of the trading interaction patterns.

The various hunting groups that filled the interstices of the Greater Southwest present something of a problem. They did function as part of the larger polity to the extent that they were middlemen in the trade network. Unfortunately, we know all too little about any one of these peoples. On the basis of such scanty evidence I feel justified (if not entirely comfortable) in treating them as essentially outsiders in terms of the complex of relationships that linked the various Southwesterners.

CHAPTER III

CONTACT HISTORY

The Greater Southwest remained terra incognita to the Spaniards for the first four decades after Columbus' first voyage. In the period 1519-1523 Spanish control in North America suddenly and dramatically extended itself from a power base in the Antilles to include much of the central and southern Mexican area. This was brought about by the conquest of Anahuac and the Mexica by Hernán Cortés and by the subsequent investment of Colima, parts of Jalisco, and Michoacan by Cristóbal de Olid. This general westward movement involved contact with and conquest of the Tarascan kingdom of Michoacan which became--for a short time--a client kingdom of Cortés. By 1523 Cortés had also heard of an island of women somewhere off the west coast of Mexico (Cortés 1971:298-300). This Amazon legend and the legend of the Seven Cities, both part of the Old World heritage of the Spaniards, dominated the planning and execution of Spanish explorations for the next two decades. Following up this Amazon dream, Hernán Cortés, in 1524, sent Francisco Cortés de Buenoventura northward from Colima to Tepic and perhaps as far as southern Sinaloa.

The first real contact with the Greater Southwest, however, came with the conquest of west Mexico by Nuño Beltrán de Guzmán. This adventurer was made governor of the east coast province of Panuco in 1527 and president of the First Audencia of Mexico in 1528. The following year Guzmán began an expedition westward, overrunning the Tarascan area. In 1530 and 1531 Guzmán conducted a long, bloodthirsty raid up the west coast of Mexico. Nuño de Guzmán himself only reached as far as the Culiacan River and established a settlement (San Miguel de Culiacan) on the San Lorenzo River immediately to the south. However, elements of his army continued probing to the north, engaged mainly in slave-hunting expeditions.

As early as the 1520s there were a number of vague stories of fabulously rich lands to the west and north of central Mexico. I have mentioned the rumor that Cortés heard of an Amazon land somewhere off the west coast. Guzmán also heard of an Amazon country and believed that it was about 40° latitude north (Pacheco and Cárdenas 1864-1884:Vol. 13, 408-409). However, the most definite information on the northwestern area was obtained by Guzmán in 1530, or before, from an Indian named Tejo. This man, who lived in the Valles area of eastern Mexico, told Guzmán of trading voyages to a land forty days' journey northward where rich plumes were traded for gold and silver. The land described by Tejo had seven large towns, each the size of Mexico City.

Members of the Guzmán expedition and Spanish parties sent by sea continued to press northward up the west coast of Mexico. By 1532 an encomienda had been awarded on the Mocorito River to one Sebastián de Ebora. That same year a sea expedition launched by Hernán Cortés from Acapulco was sent north under the command of Diego Hurtado de Mendoza. Under circumstances not entirely clear, one of the ships was seized by mutineers and seems subsequently to have been lost. Hurtado and a number of survivors from the other ship reached the Fuerte River in extreme northern Sinaloa, the northernmost penetration by the Spaniards to that time. All the Hurtado party were killed by Indians in the Fuerte River area.

The following year a land party under the command of Diego de Guzmán worked its way north, probably as far as the Yaqui River and so to the very edge of the Greater Southwest. For the next three years a series of slaving parties seem to have been operating in the region between San Miguel and the Yaqui.

The year 1536 saw the end of a long journey by Alvar Nuñez Cabeza de Vaca and three companions, sole survivors of the Narváez expedition to Florida that began in 1528. Cabeza de Vaca and his party entered the Greater Southwest from the east, crossing the Sierra Madre Occidental and reaching the upper drainage of either the Sonora River or the Yaqui. While in Sonora the Spaniards heard of fellow countrymen who were ravaging the land to the south. They pushed on and at some point, possibly as far north as the lower Yaqui Valley (DRH), made contact with a Spanish slaving expedition (Riley 1974:34, n.2).

The story told by Cabeza de Vaca and his companions, especially accounts of riches in the northern portions of the Southwest, was a stimulus for two major expeditions launched within the next few years. The De Soto expedition to the Southeast, setting out from Cuba in 1539, was little short of a complete disaster and had collapsed by 1543. One of De Soto's captains, Luis de Moscoso, in 1542 penetrated into eastern Texas and received some information on the Pueblo country; other than that, the De Soto expedition impinged only slightly on the Southwest.

A more successful and much better planned expedition was that of Francisco Vásquez de Coronado, governor of the recently founded Nueva Galicia in west-central Mexico. Coronado was commissioned by the viceroy, Antonio de Mendoza, to explore the region of the Seven Cities and to incorporate them

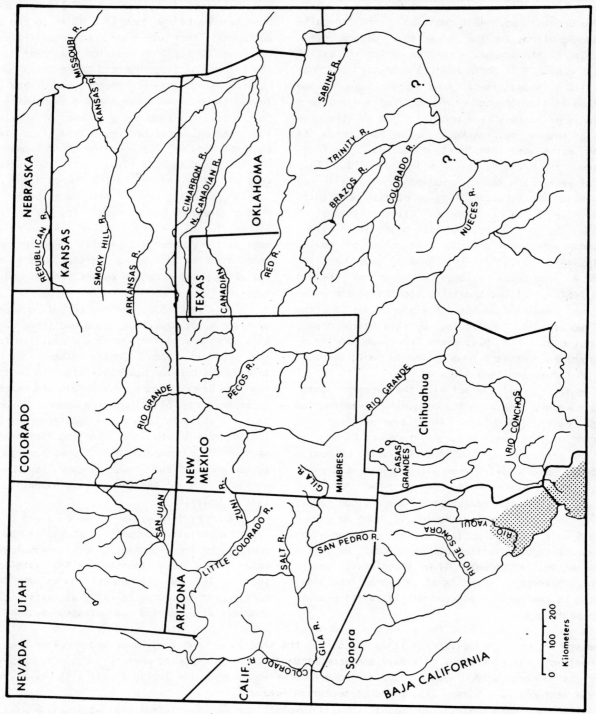

Figure 3. Spanish Penetration of the Southwest, A.D. 1533.

into the Spanish Crown.

The Coronado undertaking was actually a conger-
ies of expeditions beginning early in 1539. In
March of that year a Franciscan friar, Marcos de
Niza, with the Black slave Esteban de Dorantes from
the Vaca party and a number of Indians, set out from
San Miguel. The two leaders traveled together as
far as Vacapa, a settlement probably in the Altar-
Magdalena region of northwest Sonora. Esteban then
went ahead to the Seven Cities which Marcos learned
were collectively called Cibola. Esteban never
returned; he was killed in front of the westernmost
Cibolan town, the Zuni pueblo of Hawikuh. Marcos
pushed on northward and perhaps viewed Hawikuh from
a distance before retreating to Mexico. His stories
of the wealth of the area created a climate of
excitement in Mexico, and plans were made for the
departure of a major expedition the following year.
Still cautious, however, Coronado and Mendoza sent
another party, this time a military group under Melchior Díaz, to check the stories of Marcos. Díaz
left San Miguel in the fall of 1539 and did not
return till the following spring, meeting Coronado
and the main expedition already en route.

Coronado advanced on the Southwest in two parties: a vanguard of some hundred Spaniards plus a
number of Indian allies and the main army of perhaps
250 Spaniards and several hundred Indians, bringing
large herds of cattle and sheep. The advance party
reached Cibola in the summer of 1540, the main army
arriving in the late fall. By this time Coronado
had already shifted headquarters to the Rio Grande
area, after sending parties under Pedro de Tovar to
Tusayan (Hopi), García López de Cárdenas to the
Grand Canyon, and Pedro de Alvarado to the Buffalo
Plains. Melchior Díaz, after going with the vanguard to Cibola, was sent back to the Sonoran town
of Corazones (first contacted by Cabeza de Vaca) to
establish a Spanish settlement that would guard
Coronado's lines of communications to Mexico. Following that, Díaz went with a small party to the
Colorado River where he was to contact Captain Hernando de Alarcón.

The latter individual led still another segment
of the Coronado expedition. Alarcón with three
ships in the late spring and summer of 1540 sailed
up the Gulf of California carrying supplies for the
army and planning a rendezvous with Coronado at or
near Cibola. Captain Alarcón reached the Colorado
in late summer and explored to about its junction
with the Gila River. Finding himself unable to
reach Cibola, Alarcón retreated to west Mexico,
planning another trip later that year. He was immediately caught up in the Mixtón War and never
returned (Mendoza 1542). Díaz, meanwhile, missed
Alarcón by only a few days. While in the area of

the Colorado River, Díaz was badly injured and died
on the return to Corazones. This left the incompetent Diego de Alcaráz in charge at that important
way station. Alcaráz blundered into provoking an
Indian uprising sometime late in 1541; he was killed
and his forces scattered. This military setback
greatly weakened Coronado's lines of communication
with Mexico and was one of the factors that led to
the failure of the Cibolan expedition.

Even before these events, in the winter of
1540-1541, Coronado was forced to put down a serious
Indian uprising in the Rio Grande Valley, largely
destroying Tiguex in the process (Riley 1981a:209).
Restoring a very brittle peace by the spring of
1541, the commander felt secure enough to venture
into the Plains looking for what was to be still
another chimera, Golden Quivira. After marching the
full army into the Llanos Estacados, Coronado sent
most of his men back to Tiguex and with thirty
horsemen and a few foot soldiers pushed on to Quivira and Harahay. Finding these "kingdoms" to be
nothing but villages of Wichita- or Pawnee-speaking
Indians, Coronado returned to Tiguex in the fall of
1541. Now, realizing that the expedition was a
costly failure, shaken by the news from Corazones,
and injured in a fall from his horse, Coronado opted
for retreat and began the voyage home in April 1542.
Left behind was a Franciscan lay brother, Luis de
Ubeda, who remained in Ciquique. With Ubeda was a
Mexican or Tarascan Indian boy named Cristóbal
and--perhaps--two Black slaves, one of them with a
wife and children. The fate of this group is
unknown (Riley 1972:253, 1974:29).

One of the priests on the expedition, Father
Juan de Padilla, chose to return to Quivira in company with a Portuguese soldier named Andrés Do
Campo, two Tarascan brothers who were "donados"
(that is, given from childhood to religious service), and a Black freeman who served as interpreter
(Riley 1972:253, 1974:29-30; Chavez 1968:68-72).
Padilla was killed in Quivira, but the soldier and
the donados escaped to return to Mexico. The fate
of the Black interpreter is unknown. In addition to
the above, a number of Mexican Indians stayed in the
Southwest, and members of this group were still
alive forty years later (Riley 1974:30-32).

The failure of the Coronado expedition and the
discovery a few years after Coronado's return to
Mexico of rich silver deposits in the northern
interior of New Spain led to a decline in interest
in the west coast area. One other expedition was
mounted, however. In the period 1564-1565 Francisco
de Ibarra, governor of the newly founded province of
Nueva Vizcaya, organized an expedition to the north
and west. Moving north from San Miguel de Culiacan,
the Spaniards founded a new settlement named San

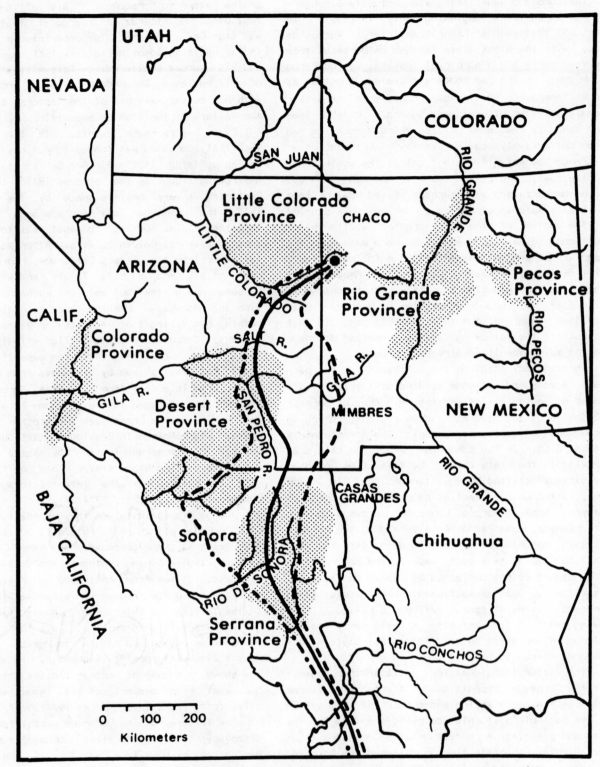

UTAH

NEVADA

COLORADO

SAN JUAN

Little Colorado
Province

CHACO

ARIZONA

LITTLE COLORADO

Rio Grande
Province

Pecos
Province

RIO GRANDE

RIO PECOS

CALIF.

Colorado
Province

SALT R.

GILA R.

GILA R.

MIMBRES

NEW MEXICO

Desert
Province

SAN PEDRO R.

RIO DE SONORA

CASAS
GRANDES

RIO GRANDE

BAJA CALIFORNIA

Sonora

Chihuahua

Serrana
Province

RIO CONCHOS

0   100   200
Kilometers

PROPOSED ROUTE ESTEBAN - MARCOS, 1539 ·—·—·

POSSIBLE ROUTES FOR CORONADO, 1540
PROPOSED ROUTE 1 ———
PROPOSED ROUTE 2 — — —

Figure 4.   Early Spanish Routes to Cibola.

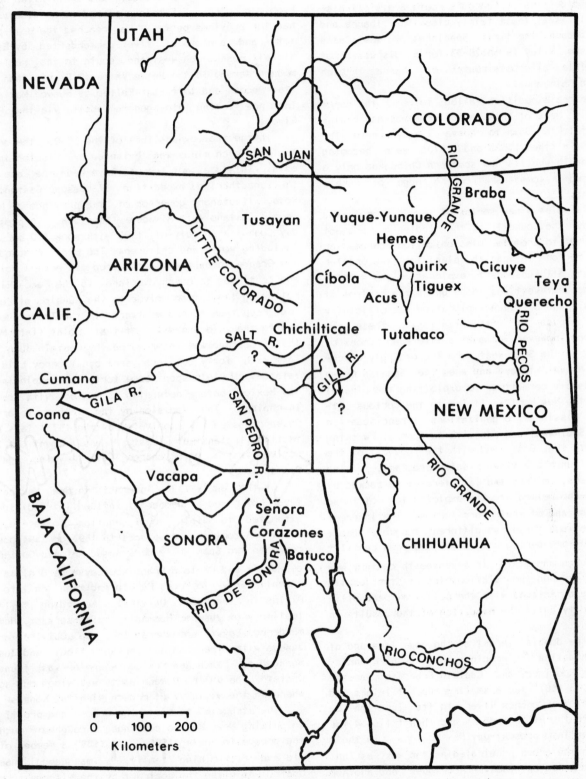

Figure 5.   Major Centers Visited by Coronado Parties, A.D. 1539-1542.

Juan in the Fuerte Valley. They then pushed on into Sonora, but like the Coronado route many of the topographic details of Ibarra's route are still disputed. It is at least fairly clear that Ibarra and his men became the first Spaniards to see Casas Grandes (see Riley 1976b:28-33 for a discussion of the possible alternate routes of Ibarra through Sonora and Chihuahua).

The Ibarra expedition failed to reach the upper Southwest. News of this latter area was now beginning to trickle down to Nueva Vizcaya where the Spaniards in the 1560s and 1570s were becoming established in what is now southern Chihuahua only a few hundred kilometers from the edge of Pueblo Indian land.

At this point a new series of laws, promulgated in 1573 by the Council of the Indies to protect Indians and to promote missionization became an important factor in Spanish plans for the Greater Southwest. All subsequent exploration and settlement of the Southwest was done under the control of these laws, and all such exploration was officially for the purpose of missionization. These new restrictions, however, came at a time when rumors of rich mines in the Southwest were increasingly circulating in Nueva Vizcaya and when the Spanish Crown was also deeply committed to exploiting the mineral wealth of the New World. It led to the curious situation of missionary organizations (Franciscans in the upper Southwest and Jesuits in Sonora) working closely with the Crown and with the Council of the Indies to launch ambitious mission programs, joining with soldiers, miners and settlers--also backed by the Crown--who aimed at the exploitation of these same Indians and of their territories. The inherent conflict between these two different conquest ideologies caused smoldering and sometimes open conflict between Church and State in seventeenth century New Mexico and shaped the relationships of the Jesuits of Sonora and Arizona with the political and military authority until the expulsion of the Jesuits in 1767.

Under the double thrust of the new laws and of the Spanish desire for precious metals, the Franciscan Agustín Rodríguez and Captain Francisco Sánchez Chamuscado in 1581 led a small group of friars and soldiers up the Conchos River to its junction (La Junta) with the Rio Grande, and then followed the latter river into present-day New Mexico. In their exploration the group penetrated as far west as Zuni and as far north as Taos. Rodríguez and another friar remained in Puaray, a Tiguex town, perhaps the "Arenal" of Coronado (Riley 1981a:210), and were killed soon after the soldiers of the expedition returned to Mexico. Concern over their fate was the excuse for another expedition in 1582, this one led

by Antonio de Espejo. Again the Rio Conchos was followed to the Rio Grande, and that river to the Pueblo country. Espejo explored more widely than had the previous party. He reached the Hopi pueblos, and a group of five Spaniards led by Espejo himself pushed on west and south to the region of modern Jerome in the Verde Valley. Espejo then visited Pecos and left San Felipe de Nuevo Mexico (a term now coming into general use) via the Pecos River.

In the two expeditions of the 1580s the desire to find rich mines was balanced by mission interests. This does not seem to have been the case with the unauthorized expedition of Gaspar Castaño de Sosa, lieutenant governor of the province of Nueva Leon. Castaño left Almaden (Monclova) in present-day Coahuila in July of 1590 with some 170 persons, including women and children. The party reached the Rio Grande somewhere in the area of modern Del Rio and continued to march overland to the Pecos River. Following the latter river to the pueblo of Pecos, the group then turned westward to the Tanos pueblos and to the Rio Grande. At that point (late March 1591) Castaño was intercepted by Captain Juan Morlete with forty soldiers sent by Viceroy Luis de Velasco. Morlete spent some forty days exploring in New Mexico before returning to Mexico with Castaño in chains. The decision by the viceroy to arrest Castaño was partly motivated by the 1573 laws protecting Indians--at least, enslavement of the natives was a major charge later leveled against Castaño.

By the early 1590s interest in New Mexico was fever hot, and a number of influential individuals attempted to obtain royal sanction to settle the area. A comi-tragic episode in 1593 or 1594 occurred when two Spanish leaders named Antonio Gutiérrez de Humaña and Captain Francisco Leyva de Bonilla led a small party to Pecos Pueblo and then on into the Plains in search of Quivira. According to later testimony of Jusepe, Humaña's Indian servant, Humaña murdered Leyva somewhere in the Quivira area. Jusepe with other Indian servants fled, and Jusepe managed to reach New Mexico where he was found by Oñate. The entire Humaña party was wiped out somewhere in the vicinity of modern Wichita, Kansas.

The struggle to have the honor and profit of colonizing New Mexico continued throughout much of the decade following 1590. In 1595 a member of an old and rich mining family, a man named Juan de Oñate, was given the contract by the viceroy to colonize and missionize the new land. Political maneuvering and pressure from a rival claimant delayed final approval, but finally in late Jaunary of 1598 Oñate set out with some 200 men, women, and children, large numbers of livestock, and other supplies. Unlike earlier ones this expedition did not follow the Conchos River but struck out north-westwardly, roughly following the line of modern Mexican National Highway 45 but intercepting the Rio Grande somewhat to the south and east of modern El Paso. Reaching the Rio Grande on the 20th of April, the expedition continued upriver and on May 4 marched through the El Paso-Ciudad Juarez area. On the 28th of May it reached the Piro pueblo of Qualacu in the San Marcial area, and on June 30, Santo Domingo (Castaño's old headquarters).

The latter part of 1598 saw a flurry of activity. The expedition established headquarters at the Pueblo of San Juan near the junction of the Chama and Rio Grande rivers. Parties of soldiers and missionaries visited Jemez, Taos, Tano, Pecos, Acoma, Zuni, and Hopi. The sargento mayor, Vicente de Zaldívar Mendoza, was sent with an exploring party to the Plains, and Captain Marcos Farfán de los Godos was dispatched from Hopi to the Rio Verde mining area previously explored by Espejo. A rebellion at Acoma and various logistic problems caused Oñate to cancel a trip to the lower Colorado River. In 1601 the governor undertook a major expedition to Quivira, roughly following the routes of Coronado, Humaña and Leyva, and Zaldívar. Finally in 1604-1605 he made the long-planned trip from Hopi to the lower Colorado and the Gulf of California.

With the settlement of Oñate the independent culture of the northern Southwest comes to an end. All major Pueblo groups had received resident priests within approximately thirty years of the entrada, and massive and forced acculturation began immediately. Drastic changes in the religious, economic, political and social life of the Pueblo Indians followed very rapidly, and this seems to have been coupled with a steady depopulation, a population decline that probably had begun by the mid-sixteenth century (see Dobyns 1966). Except for a brief interregnum in the late seventeenth century the heavy hand of Spanish domination was never again lifted from New Mexico until the end of New Spain itself.

Following the rather pointless expedition of Ibarra, Spanish interest in the Mexican west coast waned, the European-controlled areas of southern and central Sinaloa became Spanish settlement backwaters, and the regions still further north were left to their own devices. Probably the sophisticated statelets of the Sonoran area had some indication of Spanish activity around them, but they gained a half century of peace. The northern thrust of Spanish imperialism interfered with the aboriginal trade network; after about A.D. 1600 the trade to the upper Southwest was considerably disrupted, though contact with the western pueblos continued on a sporadic level into the eighteenth century. There may have been depopulation due to Spanish-introduced diseases, at least such would fit the general patterns of decline in native population throughout New Spain. Such a population decline may well have weakened the various north Mexican groups. At any rate the next wave of Spanish conquerors did not meet the powerful and organized resistance that was faced by Ibarra and Coronado.

In the year 1591 two Jesuit missionaries, Fathers Gonzalo de Tapia and Martín Pérez, visited the northwest frontier, reaching San Felipe on the Sinaloa--the relocated and renamed successor to Ibarra's San Juan. At a time when Spanish authorities were talking seriously of retreating to the Culiacan River, the enthusiastic reports of those missionaries led the Crown to authorize a Jesuit Mission Province along the northwest coast of the Gulf of California. Slowly, over the next forty years, the Blackrobes moved valley by valley into the heart of Sonora. In 1604 Jesuits were on the Fuerte and by 1614 on the line of the Mayo. Attempts to move to the Yaqui River met furious resistance by the warlike Yaqui Indians, and Diego Martínez de Hurdaide, military commander in the area, met with a number of defeats. A truce allowed the Jesuits, now led by Andrés Pérez de Ribas, to reach the Yaqui in 1617. The decade of the 1620s saw further spread up the Yaqui River system, and then in 1638 Father Lorenzo de Cárdenas spearheaded a missionary effort into the Sonora Valley. In the next two decades the Sonora, the lower San Miguel, and the upper Yaqui drainages were missionized. Still another major thrust came after 1687 when Father Eusebio Francisco Kino became the leading missionary spirit of the northwest frontier. Under Kino the Altar-Magdalena area of western Sonora and the upper Pimeria of southern Arizona were missionized. Kino visited and established visitas as far west as the Yuma Indian territory on the lower Colorado River, a region uncontacted by the Spaniards since the Oñate expedition a century before. In making these discoveries Kino also rediscovered the fact that Baja California was a long peninsula and not an island, a fact demonstrated by Alarcón but forgotten for a century and a half. This amazing gap in the cartographic knowledge of the Spaniards is perhaps the best single demonstration of the lack of interest in the northwest coast of Mexico from the time of Ibarra.

In spite of occasional exploration by such missionaries as Sedelmayr, the lower Colorado area remained very peripheral for over a half century after Kino's contact around 1700. Much of the Sonoran and Arizonan southwest, however, remained firmly tied to New Spain. In the last third of the eighteenth century, the Spanish Crown and Franciscan missionaries (who replaced the Jesuits in 1768) established a land route to upper California via Yuman territory. This last outpost of the Greater Southwest was now subject to continuous contact and to outside control.

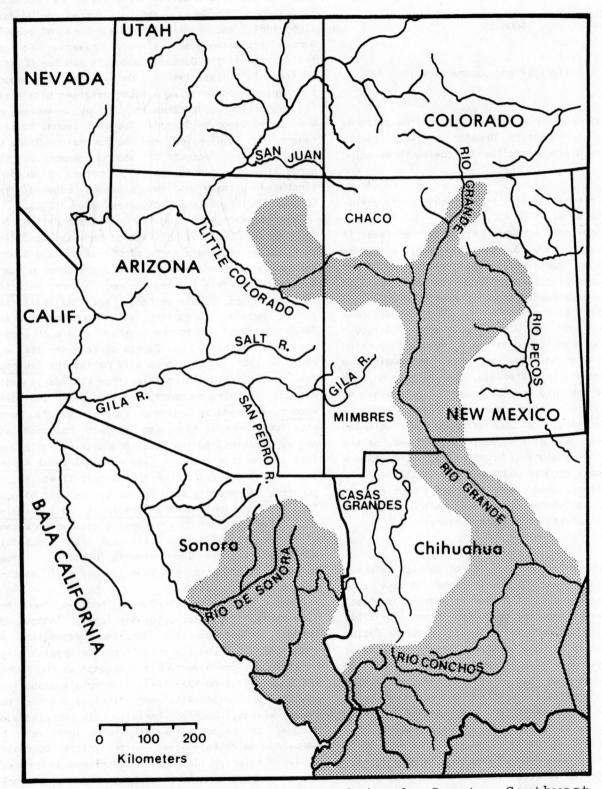

Figure 6.   Areas of Spanish Control in the Greater Southwest, A.D. 1650.

CHAPTER IV

SOURCES

Historical and Documentary

The historical sources that bear on the cultures of the sixteenth century Greater Southwest can be conveniently divided into the following three major groups:

(1) Primary accounts by sixteenth century visitors to the area.

(2) Secondary accounts that draw, at least in part, from primary documents. Many of these accounts are themselves sixteenth century, but important ones utilizing primary materials appear as late as the seventeenth and eighteenth centuries.

(3) Firsthand seventeenth and eighteenth century documents on the Greater Southwest. Although they must be used with great care because they refer to an acculturation situation, these documents have enormous amounts of materials, especially on the Indians of the Rio Grande area, the Indians of Sonora, and to a lesser degree the western Pueblos. On the other hand, documentation on lower Colorado tribes comes only at the beginning and end of the period. The regions of central and northwestern Arizona remain largely undocumented until the nineteenth century, and there is hardly a scrap of information on northwestern New Mexico until the last quarter of the eighteenth century.

(1) Primary accounts. First Spanish information on the Greater Southwest seems to have come with the vague rumors of Amazon Islands off the west coast of Mexico reported by Cortés in the mid-1520s. These stories and parallel tales of the Seven Cities probably motivated Nuño de Guzmán in his conquest of west Mexico. For example, an Indian from Valles in the Panuco drainage told Guzmán of seven great cities and much wealth in gold and silver somewhere in the northern region. The only source for this story, Pedro de Castañeda de Najera, states that Guzmán heard the story in 1530, but the date 1527, when Guzmán was governor of Panuco, is more likely. In any case the various documents from the Guzmán period give us the first firm knowledge of the west coast of Mexico. In the latter part of the nineteenth century, edited versions of the Guzmán entrada data, including the various hearings after Guzmán's arrest, became available, partly due to the

publication of the Colección de documentos inéditos from the Seville archives by Joaquín F. Pacheco, Francisco de Cárdenas, and Luis Torres de Mendoza (1864-1884) and partly from the labors of Joaquín García Icazbalceta and Alfredo Chavero. For an Indian view of the Guzmán conquests see the "Lienzo de Tlaxcala" (Glass 1964). Perhaps the most important Guzmán documents were those relating to a slaving expedition undertaken in 1533 by a nephew of Nuño named Diego de Guzmán. The party seems to have reached the Yaqui River, and the journal of Diego de Guzmán and the account of another member of the party (the "Second Anonymous" reporter) give us a firsthand glimpse of the southern edge of the Greater Southwest (see Hedrick and Riley 1976).

Three years following the Guzmán expedition, the four survivors of the Pánfilo de Narváez expedition crossed the northern parts of Chihuahua and Sonora and reached western Mexico. There are three primary documents for this journey. One, a short Relación of Alvar Nuñez Cabeza de Vaca, head of the little party, relates to earlier years somewhere on the Texas coast and not to the Southwest. A much longer document, published by Cabeza de Vaca in 1542 and again in 1555 and now generally called the Naufragios, covers the entire trip from Florida to west Mexico. A third document, usually called the Joint Report, was made by Cabeza de Vaca and his two European companions, Alonso de Castillo Maldonado and Andrés Dorantes, to the Royal Audencia of Santo Domingo in the late 1530s. The original Joint Report document is now lost, but fortunately it was incorporated, apparently word for word, as part of book 35 of the Historia general y natural de las Indias of G. Fernando Oviedo y Valdés, a massive work compiled in the 1530s and 1540s but only completely published in the mid-nineteenth century. Other material relating to the Vaca journey will be discussed under (2) below.

As a result of information received from the Vaca party, the viceroy of New Spain, Antonio de Mendoza, launched the Coronado expedition of 1539-1542, and under a writ from the Spanish king, Hernando de Soto undertook a conquest of the American Southeast from 1539-1543. De Soto's expedition was well documented with narratives by the "Gentleman of Elvas," Rodrigo Ranjel, Luis Hernandez de Biedma, and an account written many years later by Garcilaso de la Vega based on the written documents of two soldiers, Juan Coles and Alonso de Carmona, and of a noble member of the De Soto party, probably a man named Gonzalo Silvestre (see Lewis 1907; Bourne 1904; Garcilaso 1951). Unfortunately, the De Soto expedition never reached far enough west to obtain any significant information on the Greater Southwest. Only in 1542 when Luis de Moscoso, successor to De Soto, found himself in the Trinity River area of eastern Texas did the Spaniards receive a certain amount of information on the Pueblo area and see actual trade goods from that region.

The narratives of the Coronado expedition, on the other hand, form a major corpus for any study of the sixteenth century Greater Southwest. The published Coronado material can be divided into three major parts. The first of these are accounts of the preliminary expeditions of Marcos and of Melchior Díaz in 1539. A second group has to do with the main expedition. Of this group the two most important single documents are the account of the expedition given by Pedro de Castañeda de Najera, written, or at least finished, sometime around 1563, and a long letter from Coronado to Viceroy Mendoza dated August 3, 1540. Other short accounts include that of Juan de Jaramillo; an anonymous "Relación de suceso"; a letter of Coronado to King Charles dated October 20, 1541; a "Traslado de las nuevas," perhaps composed by García López de Cárdenas; a very short "Relación postrera de Cibola," conceivably written by Father Motolinía; and the report of the discovery of Tiguex by Captain Hernando de Alvarado and Father Juan de Padilla, probably composed mainly by the latter. The third group of documents consists of a journal and auxiliary letters reporting the sea voyage of Captain Hernando de Alarcón to the lower Colorado River.

A definitive critical edition of the Coronado materials, including all the accounts listed above plus a muster roll of the soldiers and documents on the Coronado residencia and the trial of García López, was published by George P. Hammond and Agapito Rey in 1940. There is a scattering of other published data, including the Coronado testimony in the Mendoza residencia published in part by A. S. Aiton and Agapito Rey in 1937. Other documents, mainly subsequent petitions to the Crown by members of the Coronado group, have been collected by A. F. and F. Bandelier and included as part of volume 1 of the publication of this Bandelier material by C. W. Hackett (1923-1937).

There is of course a considerable amount of documentary material in Seville and other archives. Commonly known but still unpublished archival sources from the Archivo General de las Indias include the Información contra Coronado and various other materials on the investigations of Coronado and García López following the return of the Cibola expedition.

Several narrative sources for the Coronado period have not yet come to light. A comprehensive list of these can be found in Bolton (1964:472-475). Especially tantalizing ones include the reports of

Pedro de Sotomayor, the chronicler of the army, and the papers of Pedro de Tovar, commander of the small party that first contacted the Hopi. It is possible that Castañeda used some of the Sotomayor materials, and probably he did draw from Tovar, whose writings were also utilized in both the seventeenth and the eighteenth centuries (see below).

After the return of Coronado there is no information on the northern regions until the expedition of Francisco de Ibarra in 1564-1565. A major discovery in the 1920s of a lost narrative of Baltazar de Obregón (one of Ibarra's soldiers), written in 1584, provides most of our information on this particular expedition. Obregón's work, entitled Historia de descubrimientos antiguos y modernos de la Nueva España, not only contains his eyewitness account of the Ibarra expedition but also includes accounts of the Chamuscado and Espejo expeditions. A second chronicle by a member of the Ibarra party, that of Antonio Ruíz, is known from abstracts in the Punctos sacados, Archivo General de Mexico, volume 25 Misiones (see Sauer 1932:52-58). It is much shorter than Obregón's narrative, but it is very useful as a contemporary account.

Materials for the expeditions to San Felipe de Nuevo Mexico of Chamuscado and Rodríguez and of Espejo in the period 1581-1583 were published in translation in 1966 by Hammond and Rey. They include the Hernán Gallegos Relación, the testimony of Pedro de Bustamante and Hernando Barrado, the accounts of Antonio de Espejo (there are two slightly variant forms in volume 15 of the Colección de documentos inéditos from the Archivo General de las Indias, Pacheco and Cárdenas 1864-1884) and Diego Pérez de Luxán, and other shorter documents. The only other major source for these expeditions is that of Obregón mentioned above, taken from interviews with members of the two parties. Parenthetically, the Espejo account was incorporated--with other documents on New Mexico--in the 1586 edition of Historia de las cosas mas notables, ritos, y costumbres del Gran Reyno de la China by the Augustinian friar Juan González de Mendoza who was in the Nueva Viscaya area sometime before 1573 (Wagner 1937:Vol. 1, 151).

The Gaspar Castaño de Sosa journey into New Mexico in 1590-1591 and the expedition of Juan Morlete to arrest Castaño in 1591 are mainly known through the Castaño Memoria (a kind of field journal of the trip) and from portions of a letter from Morlete to Viceroy Velasco reporting his activities. The Castaño Memoria was published in two slightly differing forms in Pacheco and Cárdenas (1864-1884), and the Castaño, Morlete, and Humaña-Leyva materials were brought together by Hammond and Rey in 1966. A detailed analysis of the Castaño journey with a translation of the text was done by A. H. Schroeder and D. S. Matson in 1965.

The vast amount of data concerning the Oñate expedition which began in 1598 has also been edited and translated in highly usable form by Hammond and Rey (1953), drawing from previously published materials from Documentos inéditos and elsewhere and adding material from the Seville Archives (AGI). This includes essentially all the available textual materials of the conquest period of New Mexico with the exception of Gaspar Pérez de Villagra's epic poem, entitled Historia de la Nueva México, printed in Alcala in 1610. The Relación de descubrimientos de Nuevo México by Juan de Montoya, printed in Rome in 1602, does not appear as such, but Montoya's material (at least that relating to Oñate) is found in the Hammond and Rey corpus or in Bolton (1916), taken from archival sources. The Oñate documents give us another look at the Buffalo Plains, the Quivira area, the central Arizona (Verde Valley) region, and the lower Colorado River. Documentation on the regions of southern Arizona, southwestern New Mexico, and Sonora, however, comes only after the beginning of the seventeenth century (see below).

It might be well to point out that the basic documents of the sixteenth century in the Greater Southwest often come to us in very roundabout ways. I have mentioned above that one of the two major Cabeza de Vaca documents is known only because of its inclusion in Oviedo's Historia general. Two crucial documents for understanding the Coronado expedition, the Coronado letter to Mendoza from Cibola and the report of Alarcón's expedition to the lower Colorado River, are presently available only in the Italian translation of Giovanni Battista Ramusio, Terzo volume delle navigationi et viaggi, published in Venice in 1556. Although Herrera in the early seventeenth century had available the Spanish text of Alarcón and summarized it in his massive Historia general (see below), both the early English (Hakluyt) and French (Ternaux-Compans) texts of Alarcón are drawn from Ramusio. The Spanish document has been lost. The same situation exists for the Coronado letter; both the earliest English and French translations are taken from Ramusio. This Italian compiler also gives a version of the Marcos journal that contains materials not found in the two essentially identical AGI copies. In addition, a slightly different version of this Marcos journal is to be found in a manuscript now in the Library of Congress, Washington, D.C.

(2) Secondary accounts. For the Coronado period in the Greater Southwest the sections on Cibola and Quivira by Francisco López de Gómara represented

consultation of contemporary or near-contemporary documents. Gómara's Historia general de las Indias, published in Anvera in 1554, contains details of the Coronado journey, including the name of the Quiviran chief, Tatarrax (a word meaning "chief" or "head man" in Wichita), and details of his appearance. Gómara (1922) also gives specific population figures for Cibola that do not appear in other accounts.

A more intriguing account of the regions of the Greater Southwest comes from Bartolomé de Las Casas, Apologética historia sumaria. This document was completed around 1560 and existed in a series of differing holograph manuscripts both in Spain and in the New World. In two separate sections of the Apologética historia are bits of information on the Corazones area, Cibola, the Rio Grande towns, Pecos, and Quivira. The report of Las Casas describes sophisticated and well-organized chiefdoms or primitive states that, at least for the New Mexican area, seem unlikely. Las Casas' information, however, does tend to parallel that given by Obregón for the region of north and central Sonora. I am not very clear on the sources of Las Casas. Some of his information may have come from Marcos de Niza, but whether Marcos acted as an informant or whether a lost document of Marcos—perhaps a letter—was used is unknown. As I demonstrated some years ago (1973), a portion of the Benavides Memorial of 1630 essentially duplicates Las Casas, and from internal evidence a common source seems a real possibility. Probably Marcos was not the only source for Las Casas. The latter indicates that some material was drawn from Cabeza de Vaca (perhaps from an interview), and various of the Coronado documents may have been used. For a reevaluation of the Las Casas materials see Riley (1976a).

Mission activity in northwest New Spain was mainly the concern of Franciscan missionaries in the sixteenth century; only toward the end of the century was there a surge in Jesuit activities. Franciscan reports, therefore, give a considerable amount of information on the area, some of it primary data. The important work of Father Toribio de Motolinía, Historia de los indios de Nueva España, was actually sent to a patron, Antonio Pimentel, sixth count of Benavente, in the year 1541, at a time when Coronado's army was in the Greater Southwest. The account given by Motolinía (1541) of Coronado is surprisingly garbled, but it does contain rather interesting information on the differing routes taken by Coronado and by Marcos. A rich series of sources, still not completely evaluated, can be found in the collections of documents submitted to Minister General Franciscus Gonzaga of the Franciscan order for his universal history of that order (De Origine Seraphicae Religionis

Franciscanae.) published in 1587. Documents from the New World collected from Fathers Pedro Oroz, Gerónimo de Mendieta, Diego Muñoz, and Francisco Suárez went into the Gonzaga compilation. Some of the material was published in the early seventeenth century by the Franciscan Juan de Torquemada (Monarquia indiana), and other portions were rediscovered in the nineteenth and early twentieth centuries (for example, the Mendieta Historia eclesiastica indiana published by Joaquín García Icazbalceta in 1870 and the Oroz, Mendieta, and Suárez Relación de la descripción de la provincia del Sancto Evangelio published by Father Fidel de J. Chauvet in 1947). The Relación de la descripción de la provincia del Sancto Evangelio que es en las Indias Occidentales by Father Oroz was translated by Angelico Chavez in 1972 under the title The Oroz Codex.

To what extent the Historia of Antonio de Herrera y Tordesillas (publication of which began in 1601) draws from documents now lost is unclear, but Herrera did have rather free use of archival materials. His material on the Alarcón voyage is based on the original account and perhaps on other lost documents relating to the Alarcón expedition. The short section of the Coronado journey seems to be taken in part from the Jaramillo narrative but contains other materials as well. Herrera's summary statement on the Vaca journey seems generally to have been taken from the Naufragios.

There are a number of Jesuit documents from the seventeenth century that reproduce or summarize earlier materials on the northwest Mexican area (for examples, see Sauer 1932:51-58; Riley 1974:34, 36). A closer examination of various Jesuit archives and collections (e.g., the Pastells collection, cited as DRH in this volume) may be useful in producing new source materials.

In the seventeenth century the Franciscan priest Antonio Tello, who in 1653 wrote the Cronica miscelanea . . . de la santa provincia de Xalisco, drew extensively on the sixteenth century Franciscans but also included now lost materials from Pedro de Tovar, discussed above. In 1742 Matías de la Mota Padilla, a native of Guadalajara, wrote a Historia de la conquista de la provincia de la Nueva Galicia that makes extensive use of the Tovar papers and perhaps of other lost eyewitness accounts (see Day 1940b). Also in the eighteenth century the Jesuit Father Francisco Xavier Alegre in his Historia de la Compañía de Jesus gives a novel place identification of Corazones, utilizing documents that seem to be now lost.

Other documents that have some value in an ethnohistorical study of the Greater Southwest include the official Geografía y descripción natural de las Indias recopilada . . . desde el año de 1571 al de 1574 by Juan López de Velasco (1971), who preceded Herrera as official chronicler of the Indies. This work gives a few cultural and geographical details but nothing that does not appear in other documents known to us. On the other hand, the Compendio y descripción de las Indias Occidentalis by Antonio Vázquez de Espinosa compiled during the 1620s has locations of certain southwestern groups as of Coronado's time that differ from any other known source. Another considerably later publication that gives bits of information, drawing perhaps on lost sixteenth century sources, is the Historia de Nueva España of Archbishop Francisco Antonio Lorenzana, published in Mexico in 1770.

(3) Seventeenth and eighteenth century documents. The documentation for the history of New Mexico in the seventeenth and eighteenth centuries is extremely diverse, and only a general indication of the sources will be given here. Among the most significant documents of the earlier period is the Memorial of Fray Alonso de Benavides published in two versions in 1630 and 1634. Benavides was the Franciscan custos of the mission in New Mexico from 1623 to 1629, and his Memorial gives a considerable amount of documentation on the numbers and locations of various Indian groups. Another important Franciscan source is a document of one of the earliest New Mexican missionaries, Father Gerónimo de Zárate Salmerón (see Bolton 1916). Also important for seventeenth century studies is the group of articles published by France V. Scholes on the early mission church and the provincial government in early New Mexico. Scholes includes transcripts of the documents from which he worked.

One curious account from the seventeenth century is the story of Father Nicholas de Freytas of a supposed voyage to Quivira in the mid-seventeenth century by Governor Diego Dionisia de Peñalosa (Shea 1882). It is now reasonably certain that Peñalosa faked the expedition and the account. It is drawn from accounts of previous expeditions and may possibly contain some material now lost.

In 1680 the Pueblo Indians revolted and drove the Spanish soldiers, missionaries, and settlers southward to the El Paso area. The documentation of this period and of the Spanish return, beginning with Otermín in 1681 and culminating under De Vargas in the 1690s, is quite extensive. For the eighteenth century there are a number of rich sources; important ones include the report of Fray Francisco Atanasio Domínguez of his inspections of the New Mexican missions in 1776 and the accounts of Domínguez and Father Velez de Escalante of their trip of that same year to the Ute country and the western

Pueblos. In addition to these various inspection and expeditionary reports, there are such accounts as that of Father Agustín de Vetancurt, Teatro Mexicano (1698), which contains information up to the period of the Pueblo Revolt. Another useful source is the Cronica de . . . Michoacán of Father Pablo Beaumont written in the late eighteenth century and organized year-by-year for our period. An invaluable source for materials especially on New Mexico is to be found in Henry R. Wagner's two volume work, The Spanish Southwest 1542-1794: An Annotated Bibliography. Also very useful are guides to historical materials by F.B. Steck, H.P. Beers, and T.C. Barnes et al.

Historical materials for the northwestern Mexican area in the seventeenth and eighteenth centuries come mainly from Jesuit sources until the 1760s, though there are secular sources as well--for example, Domingo Lázaro de Arregui, whose Descripción de la Nueva Galicia was completed in 1621. Tello and Mota Padilla have been discussed above in terms of the Coronado expedition, but their works have material on the north of Mexico for later times as well.

A massive amount of Jesuit documents--mission inspections, reports, apologies, "rudo ensayos," vocabularies, and the like--some published but many still in manuscript form, give rich information on Sonora in the seventeenth century and on the southern Arizona area from about 1700 (see Beers 1979; Polzer 1972). Especially important works include the synthesis, Historia de los triunfos de nuestra Santa Fe, by Father Andrés Pérez de Ribas, published in 1645. Missionary reports by men such as Lombardo, Kino, Pfefferkorn, and Nentvig among others; accounts of laymen such as Manje, Kino's military companion; and works of compilers such as Alegre and Clavigero give a rich though not complete picture of mission Sonora, Arizona, and California.

After the expulsion of the Jesuits, a number of Franciscan missionaries moved into the Sonoran and Arizonan regions. Under the Franciscans the contacts with the lower Colorado River, made three-quarters of a century earlier by Kino, were reestablished. The reports of Fathers Francisco Garcés and Pedro Font and the diaries of Captain Juan Bautista de Anza and a number of other sources, both published and unpublished, give a picture of the Sonoran, the Gila-Salt, and the lower Colorado River areas for the last third of the eighteenth century. By this time, of course, Indian acculturation had proceeded very far indeed.

Ethnological

There is no doubt that, for all the areas of the Greater Southwest, the ones that have seen the greatest amount of ethnological fieldwork are the Little Colorado and the Rio Grande drainages. These portions of the Southwest passed to American political control in 1846, and within a generation American scientific institutions and to some degree the American public had become interested in the exotic native peoples of the region. The period from about 1880 to the beginning of World War I was one of extensive field study of southwestern Indians. In 1880 James Stevenson of the Smithsonian Institution and his wife, Matilda Cox Stevenson, began a study of Zuni Pueblo. That same year Frank H. Cushing, a member of the Stevenson expedition, established residence at Zuni and over the next few years actively participated in the religious life, actually serving as Elder Bow Priest. In the 1880s, Dr. Washington Matthews, an army surgeon and self-taught ethnologist, began a study of the Navajo Indians, and in the next decade J. Walter Fewkes, like Stevenson sponsored by the Smithsonian Institution, began his archaeological fieldwork at Hopi. The year 1880 saw Adolph F. Bandelier, under the auspices of the Archaeological Institute of America, begin fieldwork at Cochiti in the Rio Grande Valley. A little later Bandelier, Cushing, Fewkes, and others would be involved in the Hemenway expedition to the Southwest. Matilda Cox Stevenson, who carried through the study at Zuni after her husband's death in 1888, also worked in the Rio Grande, producing a major report on Zia and doing some of the early research on Taos Pueblo. Other early fieldworkers, most of them combining archaeology and ethnology, were Cosmos and Victor Mindeleff in Zuni, Hopi, and Jemez; A.M. Stephen in Hopi; and W.H. Holmes at Jemez (mostly archaeology, however). In 1907-1910 the monumental Handbook of North American Indians, edited by F.W. Hodge, was released by the Smithsonian Institution. Between 1907 and 1920 Edward S. Curtis compiled his twenty-volume The North American Indian, several volumes of which concerned the Southwest.

Following a lull in the period of the First World War, there was a strong pickup of activities in the 1920s and 1930s. Elsie Clews Parsons did studies on the Tewa towns, Isleta, Taos, Hopi, and Jemez. Leslie White did a series of ethnographic sketches on the Keresan villages of Santo Domingo, Acoma, San Felipe, and Zia. E.S. Goldfrank studied Cochiti, and J.T. Hack, L. Thompson, Fred Eggan, and C.D. Forde worked at Hopi.

Even when the first generation of researchers

was in the field, the cultural situation of Indians on the Little Colorado and the Rio Grande was changing. As early as September 1906, Mrs. Stevenson reported to W.H. Holmes, chief of the Bureau of American Ethnology, some disturbing observations on a revisit to Zuni. According to Holmes:

> A number of changes were noted in the dramas and other ceremonies since her last visit, and Zuñi, heretofore presented at night the quiet somberness of an aboriginal village, has now, when dusk falls, the appearance of an eastern town with many lighted windows. Mrs. Stevenson notes that changes are creeping steadily into all the pueblos, Taos perhaps excepted, and is led to express the earnest hope that the work of investigating the town-building tribes of the Southwest be carried forward with all possible energy [italics mine] (1912:11).

The field reports of the post-World War I period were already of Pueblo Indians undergoing a massive acculturation. Workers in the post-World War II period faced groups in even more advanced stages of acculturation. Although the research of E.P. Dozier on First Mesa Hopi-Tewa, Charles H. Lange on Cochiti, and A. Ortiz on the Tewa (to mention only a few) are painstaking and perceptive, they represent studies of cultures still another long generation from the equilibrium obtained by the Pueblo Indians in Spanish-Mexican times. To talk of an aboriginal situation as far as the Pueblo Indians are concerned is pointless.

Ethnology in the other southwestern provinces is much more sketchy than in the Little Colorado and the Rio Grande. Pecos and the Tanos region, in fact, have no ethnology. The Galisteo area was essentially deserted by Pueblo Indians before 1800, and the last remnant population at Pecos had migrated to Jemez by 1840. We are not even sure of the sociopolitical system at Pecos. Anthropologists generally make the gratuitous assumption that it was similar to Jemez, but this cannot be demonstrated. A recent study based on cranial indices from various archaeological populations of the Southwest, including ones from Pecos and Jemez, advances the bold proposition that the Pecos people did not even speak Towa (Mackey 1977). In the face of rather clear historical evidence to the contrary, it is difficult to take this particular study very seriously, but it does point out that our knowledge of Pecos has a striking number of gaps.

The contemporary ethnology of the Serrana province, like that of Pecos-Tanos, is largely absent.

Fortunately, the seventeenth and eighteenth century sources on the Opata contain rich ethnological detail. The Opata as a cultural and linguistic entity were in drastic decline by the nineteenth century, and investigators such as Bandelier who visited the area in 1884 and Lumholtz who was in the region in 1890 and again in 1909-1910 received only disjointed scraps of information.

For the Desert province we are a bit more fortunate, mainly because of the ethnological work of Frank Russell. Studying the Pima in the first years of the twentieth century, Russell attempted to reconstruct lifeways which were already disappearing and which related to the time of the first major American contact with the area. It seems reasonable to believe that some of Russell's data may have validity for even earlier periods, although it is difficult to evaluate the amount of American and Spanish-Mexican influence and the changes in Pima life brought about by eighteenth and early nineteenth century pressure from the Apache. There is useful later work—for example, that done on the Papago by Ruth M. Underhill who, of course, deals with Indians in highly acculturative situations.

The Colorado peoples are the subject of a number of studies including ones by Daryll Forde, E.W. Gifford, William Kelly, Edward S. Curtis, A.L. Kroeber, and Leslie Spier, among others. A useful survey of the culture history of the river Yumans was published by Jack D. Forbes in 1965.

Apart from the more-or-less standard ethnological studies in various parts of the Southwest, there are also series of geographical, botanical, and zoological studies, often of great value. One of the most important of these is the work of John P. Harrington in the early 1900s, published in the twenty-ninth Annual Report of the Bureau of American Ethnology as The Ethnogeography of the Tewa Indians. Junius Henderson and Harrington also published an Ethnozoology of the Tewa Indians in 1914, and Mrs. Stevenson (1915) did an Ethnobotany of the Zuni Indians. The works of E.F. Castetter and W.H. Bell on the agricultural systems of the Piman and Yuman peoples are also very useful, especially since these two latter authors were themselves interested in ethnohistorical reconstruction.

In the 1950s and 1960s a great deal of work was done in the aboriginal Southwest and elsewhere in the United States as part of the Indian Claims Commission hearings. Various kinds of research on southwestern Indians were involved, including archaeology, ethnohistory, ethnology, ethnobotany, and ethnozoology. Much of this material has now been published by Garland Press, New York.

Archaeological

Although there has been a scattering of historic archaeology in the Greater Southwest, most of the archaeological concentration to date is on prehistoric Indians. In part this is because archaeologically rich portions of the Southwest were deserted before the appearance of Europeans. For example, the extensive Anasazi occupation of the San Juan drainage had come to an end by about A.D. 1300. The various intermixed traditions of central Arizona--Sinagua, Anasazi, Salado--also had ended by the end of the fifteenth century. Farther south the Hohokam of the Gila-Salt area disappeared well before Spanish contact times as--probably--had the remnant Mogollon peoples of the Mimbres and Gila areas. In Chihuahua, the great sub-Mexican center of Casas Grandes was a ruin by the time of first Spanish penetration into the Greater Southwest. The situation in the Sonoran northern sierra and desert is less clear; the problem there is that very little archaeology of any sort has been done to date.

Nevertheless, for the Pueblo area in general--descendants of the Anasazi--there is significant archaeological work in all three provinces, and the listing below does not pretend to be exhaustive (see Ford et al. 1972 for further discussion). The most famous and far-reaching exploration of an early historic site is the excavation of Pecos Pueblo by A.V. Kidder in field seasons from 1915 through 1929 and published in a series of monographs (see Kidder 1932, 1958; Kidder and Shepard 1936; Hooton 1930). Not only was the excavation of Pecos one of the most extensive efforts in the Southwest on a historic site, but it also became an archaeological, professional, and cultural event of the first importance. The first annual Pecos Conference was held in 1927, and major decisions for classification, terminology, and future directions for archaeological research in the Southwest were made (Schroeder 1979a:9). Additional work at Pecos was done from 1938 to 1940 by E.N. Ferdon and W.B. Witkind, though this was never published. In 1966 the National Park Service began new excavations under the direction of Jean M. Pinkley and following Pinkley's death in 1969 by R.S. Richert and A.C. Hayes, (see Hayes 1974 for details of work on Pecos).

There was excavation of the Salinas (Piro) site of Gran Quivira south of Pecos in the mid-1960s by Hayes, but this work remains largely unpublished. In addition, various of the Tano sites of the Galisteo Basin have been surveyed or excavated (Nelson 1914, 1916, 1917).

More spectacular were the excavations of the Tiwa towns of "Bandelier's Puaray" and Kuaua, one or the other possibly to be identified with Coofer, or Alcanfor, the headquarters of Coronado in the winter of 1540-1541. The excavation of both Bandelier's Puaray and, more ambitiously, Kuaua was a combined effort of the School of American Research, the Museum of New Mexico, and the University of New Mexico. Work continued on the latter site from 1934 to 1939. A major publication on Kuaua is Sun Father's Way (Dutton 1963b), which contains an analysis of the numerous layers of mural paintings dating from the fifteenth and sixteenth centuries found on two of the kivas. A second site with murals dating almost to the historic period is that of Pottery Mound near Los Lunas south of Albuquerque, New Mexico (Hibben 1955, 1960).

In the Jemez area Paul Reiter and associates of the University of New Mexico and the School of American Research excavated the historic (largely fifteenth and sixteenth century) site of Unshagi from 1928 to 1934, building on earlier excavations by the School of American Research of the mission site of Giuseya near Jemez Springs. A series of other historic excavations in various Rio Grande sites have been carried on over the years, including work by Charles H. Lange and others in the Cochiti Dam area. Excavated sites that stretch to the very edge of historic times are the pueblos in Frijoles Canyon and Puye near modern Santa Clara. In fact Tyuonyi in Frijoles seems to have been occupied until about 1550 although there is no evidence that the Spaniards ever visited it. Another site that overlaps the historic period is Paa-ko on the east side of the Sandia Mountains northeast of Albuquerque (see Lambert 1954).

In the Little Colorado a major historic archaeological project was the excavation of Hawikuh by F.W. Hodge in the period 1917 to 1923 but mainly published by Smith et al. in 1966. Hawikuh was founded in the fourteenth century and became the first point of contact of Spaniards coming into the Southwest in 1539 and 1540. It was visited sporadically by Spanish exploring parties and finally received a resident priest in 1630. The town was deserted sometime around 1700.

Another significant excavation of a historic pueblo was that on post-Spanish portions of the Hopi pueblo of Awatovi near Jeddito Wash east of the three major Hopi mesas. This excavation, undertaken by architectural historian Ross Montgomery and archaeologists Watson Smith and John O. Brew, was sponsored by Peabody Museum of Harvard and conducted over five field seasons from 1935 to 1939 (see Montgomery et al. 1949).

Historic archaeology in the Desert province includes the excavations of what Charles C. Di Peso considers to be historic Piman mission sites (see especially Di Peso 1953, 1956). There has also been work in the middle Santa Cruz (Doyel 1977) and at one of the Sobaipuri settlements visited by Kino in the San Pedro (Masse 1980). For an up-to-date summary of the final prehistoric manifestations of the Hohokam see Gumerman and Haury (1979:86-88). Farther to the south, work in the Trincheras area (which may have a historic component) by Braniff, Oliveros, and others has been going on sporadically for a number of years. See Sauer and Brand (1932) and Johnson (1963).

The Serrana province, for all its vast importance to any understanding of the sixteenth century Greater Southwest, has been a virtual archaeological no-man's-land. The work of Di Peso at Paquimé or Casas Grandes on the eastern fringe of the area is useful in working out trade networks across the Sierra Madre. Archaeological materials for Di Peso's late prehistoric and early historic Tardio phase, however, are very scanty, and Paquimé itself seems to have been deserted by at least the mid-fourteenth century. Di Peso sees a series of small "kingdoms" in the very northern Sierra—statelets such as Chichilticale, Marata, and Totonteac, some or all of which may have received population from Paquimé. It is significant that recent work by Richard A. Pailes and his students indicates that the densely occupied Sonora Valley, whose sites date from the Medio phase at Casas Grandes up into historic times (sixteenth century), seems to have strong contacts with Casas Grandes and perhaps with the Trincheras region as well.

The archaeology of the Colorado province is still somewhat confused. This is due partly to the fact that sites were often built in the river floodplain and many may have been washed away or covered with alluvium. Two major schema for the prehistoric and early historic archaeology have been worked out for the lower Colorado. That of Malcolm J. Rogers (1945:184-190) sees a sequence which he calls Yuman (a name first used archaeologically by Gladwin and Gladwin 1930, 1934; see also Colton 1945:119). Rogers postulates a formative period beginning sometime after A.D. 800. With a second phase (Yuman II) beginning about A.D. 1050 there was a considerable upriver movement. Yuman III, beginning about 1500, saw a further expansion up the Gila River (Rogers 1945:193-194).

A.H. Schroeder (1960), on the other hand, has suggested that a Hakataya (Yuman) culture developed along the Gila under strong Hohokam influence and was eventually diluted and submerged by the Hohokam and later Sinagua. A modified form of Hakataya continued into Spanish times as the historic Yuman culture (see also the comments of Forbes 1965 and Huckell 1979).

It is clear that a great deal more archaeology in the lower Colorado and adjacent areas needs to be done. There is, for example, tantalizing mention of "Mexican"-type ruins in the lower river area as early as the 1775 De Anza trip (Forbes 1965:20). In 1826 a British naval officer, R.W. Hardy, mentioned a "Casas Grandes" some 2 or 3 km from where the Hardy River joins the main Colorado (1829:333, 335). In 1903 a cowboy ran across adobe somewhere near the junction of the Colorado and Hardy rivers and described walls "eight feet thick and ten feet high" (Kniffen 1931:46-48). To date, these have not been found.

In this chapter I am attempting only a broad summary of archaeology. For additional detail see the discussion of archaeology for individual provinces.

CHAPTER V

NATURAL FEATURES

Several different kinds of geographical regions are involved in the Greater Southwest, all of which extend beyond its boundaries as defined here. There are, however, certain generalizations that can be made about the area as a whole. The Southwest is a land of alternating mountain ranges and basins, plateaus, and valleys. It is generally dry except in the higher elevations, and especially characteristic is a scrub or xerophytic vegetation. On the aesthetic side, the area abounds with magnificent scenery. The Greater Southwest is typically a land of color--harsh reds of the barren deserts and mesas sometimes dominate and, elsewhere, desert pastels or, in the mountains, forest greens.

I shall briefly consider the Greater Southwest in terms of seven major regions or subregions: the Basin and Range; its southern outflank the Sonoran Desert; the Colorado Plateaus; the Southern Rockies; the southwestern fringe of the High Plains; the Sierra Madre Occidental; and the North Mexican Basins.

The great physiographic region called the Basin and Range is characterized by hundreds of isolated mountain ranges, oriented for the most part on a north-south axis and commonly separated by broad upland valleys. The province is quite high; elevations even of the valley floors are often 1500 m or more. The northern and higher portion of the area is formed by the Great Basin of Utah, Idaho, and Nevada, one of the largest internally draining areas in North America. This is an arid region with only the higher slopes receiving any large amount of rainfall. Following periods of rainfall there appear large numbers of temporary lakes in the basins, some only a few centimeters in depth. In addition there are a few more-or-less permanent lakes. The largest of these is the Great Salt Lake, a remnant of Pleistocene Lake Bonneville, formerly covering a large portion of northern Utah. The permanent lakes of the Great Basin tend to be saline since, in many cases, they have no outlet and lose water only by evaporation.

The valleys of the Great Basin are so dry that they can support at most a scrub vegetation, typically sagebrush, with willow, cottonwood, and other trees along the watercourses. In parts of the area, there is such a concentration of salt that vegetation is essentially lacking. In the mountains, the hardy juniper is sometimes found as low as 1650 m and, with the pinyon, may form considerable forests at higher elevations. Temperatures show considerable annual variation in the Basin, and, due to its continental position and absence of cloud cover, there is appreciable fluctuation from day to night. Summers are very hot in the lower valleys, and winters are normally quite cold (though this depends to some extent on altitude, latitude, and the degree of protection provided by adjacent mountain ranges).

The southern part of the Basin and Range includes the drylands of southern California, southern Arizona, and parts of southern New Mexico. The largest component is the Sonoran Desert which, including the Mojave Desert, extends from California to southern Arizona and much of Sonora (an area important enough to warrant separate treatment here). To the east are the mountains of the Arizona-New Mexico border, the relatively low plateau of southern New Mexico, and still farther east a series of north-south ranges separated by such valleys as that of the Rio Grande. The entire region is one of dry, often extensive valleys interspersed with a series of north-south faulted and tilted ranges. The higher mountains generally have considerable precipitation which drains to the valleys in the form of ground water or intermittent and, in a few cases, permanent streams. In some parts of the region, especially in southern Arizona, even the mountains are deficient in rainfall. In southwestern Arizona, the percentage of plain to mountain is quite high, thus providing a situation where evaporation is intense and condensation and accumulation of water is relatively slight. There are sharp temperature differentials between day and night, and the summers are extremely hot. Winters, however, in the lower elevations are much milder than in the Great Basin--so much so that some localities in southern Arizona have become popular winter recreation areas.

The vegetation of the Basin and Range varies with altitude. Only in the mountains is a forest cover found; sometimes, as in the higher New Mexico mountains, this may be rather extensive. In the foothills and upper reaches of the valleys there are often sparse juniper stands, and scattered deciduous trees frequently follow drainage courses. Along the valley floors there is sage, and in the south occur vast numbers of xerophytic plants, especially cacti.

In the northern portions of the Basin and Range and in the Colorado Plateaus there are a number of large mammals, including foxes, wolves, deer, mountain lions, and bears. Formerly, elk and mountain sheep were plentiful but are now rarely, if ever, seen. Smaller fur-bearing animals are common in the mountains, and several varieties of rabbits and other rodents abound in virtually all areas.

The Basin and Range subprovinces are partially

separated by the high plateau country of the Colorado River. This area was occupied by the northernmost Anasazi peoples a thousand years ago but in the sixteenth century was occupied by hunting peoples except for the two clusters of the Little Colorado province, Cibola and Tusayan. Roughly circular in outline, the Colorado Plateaus include portions of four modern states: Colorado, Utah, Arizona, and New Mexico. This is a complex area; drained by the Colorado River, it comprises dissected tablelands, or mesas, flanked by deep canyons in which early geologic strata are often exposed. The Colorado Plateaus are generally high with some mesas above 3500 m. In the higher elevations there is considerable rainfall--500 mm per year or more--and a considerable growth of conifers. Lower, these forests dwindle into sparse stands of juniper, and this, in turn, gives way to sagebrush and various dry-weather grasses. A few true mountains, volcanic or laccolithic in nature, appear in the area. Certain of these, especially Mount Taylor and the San Francisco Mountains, are important in the religious life of some of the native peoples. The area is also one of extensive archaeological ruins.

East of the Colorado Plateaus are the Southern Rockies, a series of north-south ranges interspersed with broad parklands. These mountains extend through Colorado and, in a narrow band, into central New Mexico. Climatically, this area resembles the northern portion of the Range but because of higher altitudes and latitude even the valleys or parks receive more moisture. Individual peaks of the Southern Rockies may rise 4000 m or more in New Mexico and southern Colorado and 4300 m or more in central Colorado. The mountain slopes are covered with coniferous forests, and the valleys with sage and scrub grass. The mountains also support large numbers of fur-bearing animals.

East of the Pecos River are the High Plains, formed by the deposition of hundreds of meters of alluvium on an older plain surface. The southern portion of this region includes the famous Staked Plains (Llanos Estacados) of New Mexico and Texas and also the Edwards Plateau of west-central Texas. The altitude of the High Plains reaches some 2000 m in central Colorado but is considerably lower (ranging between 700 and 1500 m) in west Texas. Except in certain locally favored areas, such as the Edwards Plateau, the High Plains are treeless and rather arid. The commonest vegetation is bunch grass, and the most important animals were bison and antelope. The effect of the High Plains upon southwestern culture has been varied, but for peoples of the Pecos and Rio Grande provinces they were of very great importance from the late fourteenth century till Spanish conquest times at the end of the sixteenth.

Within the political boundary of present-day Mexico there are three physiographic areas that lie, in part, within the boundaries of the sixteenth century Greater Southwestern interaction sphere. In the west, bordering the Gulf of California and including both Baja California and much of Sonora, is the Sonoran Desert subprovince of the Basin and Range. The center of the Sonoran Desert is a downwarp, the great rift or trough of the Gulf of California which stretches for some 1000 km and, as a structural feature, extends to the Salton Sea area of southern California. West of the Gulf the land rises abruptly, with a high fault block that reaches elevations of 2000 m or more. East of the Gulf in Sonora and in northern and central Sinaloa, there is a gentle slope from the coast upward to the foothills of the Sierra Madre Occidental. The area is crosscut by streams draining mainly southwestward from these mountains. This coastal strip is relatively flat and is partially composed of alluvial fans, the rich alluvium deposited when swiftly flowing streams reach the flat coastal lands.

The region is quite deficient in rainfall; parts of northern Sonora rank among the driest portions of the Earth. Due to rains in the Sierra Madres, however, the larger rivers bring considerable water to the arid coast.

At higher elevations, the Sonoran and Sinaloan rivers have cut deep channels, or barrancas, some of which extend far into the Sierra Madre Occidental. This range begins approximately at the international boundary (at about the New Mexico-Arizona state line) and extends in a southeastward direction to the Rio Grande de Santiago where it joins the central mountains of Mexico. An old, deeply dissected plateau in which considerable volcanic activity has altered the landscape, the Sierra Madres present a formidable barrier between coastal and interior Mexico, but one that was breached by a series of important trails that carried trading, diplomatic, and military parties throughout this portion of the Greater Southwest. The upper reaches of the Sierra Madres are fairly well watered, being in some cases over 3000 m, and are heavily forested.

East of the Sierra Madre Occidental are the Northern Basins. These are areas of detrital-filled valleys with bolsones, or dry lake beds, in the center; many of these are completely landlocked. Interspersed among the valleys are a series of basaltic and volcanic masses. Because of the rain shadow produced by the Sierra Madre Occidental, the region is one of great dryness and of xerophytic vegetation. The desertlike aspect of the Northern Basins is modified by a few streams, two of which merit mention: the Rio Conchos, a tributary of the

Rio Grande; and the Rio Nazas, a stream which loses its waters in the Coahuilan Desert.

On the east (and well beyond the boundaries of the Greater Southwest) the Interior Basins are bordered by the Sierra Madre Oriental, structurally similar to the basin country but much higher. Southward there is a gradual rise of land leading to the wetter highlands of central Mexico.

In the province chapters below, I shall discuss the natural landscape in some detail for each group. This information should be read in the context of man-land interaction. It is clear that to some degree the peoples of the Greater Southwest were shaped by their particular, largely arid, environment. The distribution of certain domesticated plants, the development of irrigation systems, of various house types, and of clothing styles and related weaving and skin-working techniques obviously need to be seen in their environmental setting. The meagerness of Colorado River native culture (in southwestern terms) surely relates to some degree to the warm, dry environment and to the bounty of the great river itself. Conversely, one cannot hope to understand completely the Little Colorado peoples without an awareness of the harsh climate with its burning summers and bitter winters and of the moisture budget, seemingly inadequate but with a seasonal rhythm that maximized certain kinds of agricultural activities.

Trade in the various provinces also relates directly and importantly to the natural landscape. The fingering of the Sonoran Desert up river valleys into the Sierra Madre not only offered the Serrana peoples a variety of environments (desert, mountain slope, forested uplands, high parklands) within a matter of kilometers, but also provided natural highways north and south. Pecos, at the other end of the Greater Southwest, lay across the most natural route from the vast reaches of the plains to the Rio Grande Valley and beyond. In addition, Pecos controlled rich forest products from the mountains to the north. Mines containing various mineral ores and, most important of all, turquoise lay within one or two days' journey of the pueblo as did rich outcroppings of fibrolite.

Throughout all of the Greater Southwest, length of growing season, intensity and seasonality of stream flow, rainfall patterns, and availability of natural resources were of constant concern to the people involved. To give one example, peoples of the southwest have, throughout the centuries, been voracious consumers of wood for house building, water control projects, and most especially for firewood. The desertion of entire pueblos or even groups of pueblos (as happened in the Cibola area in late prehistoric times) may well have been due to the depletion of nearby wood supplies.

Each chapter below will, then, provide an environmental setting to give greater depth and meaning to the cultural systems being examined. No ideas of "environmental determinism" are implied; interaction of man with his physical environment is the key concept.

CHAPTER VI

THE SERRANA PROVINCE

The rather sophisticated Indian groups that lived in the flanks of the Sonoran and Chihuahuan sierras in the sixteenth century were described sufficiently by a number of exploring parties for the outlines of their cultures to appear. Unfortunately, however, the descriptions fail to give us any really significant data on many of the cultural subsystems. We know something about economic organization and trade, about distributions of towns, and a little about urban organization. There are intriguing hints of the political and social life. Only one author writing on this early period gives any amount of information on religion.

In the seventeenth and eighteenth centuries, Spanish priests of the Jesuit order, with the backing of the military, made their way northward and slowly infiltrated the area of the Sonoran highlands. Their data on Indians, especially during the first half of the seventeenth century, sometimes seem to relate to the realities of the sixteenth. Unfortunately, there is no way of telling to what extent such factors as disease and disturbances brought about by the introduction of Spanish lifeways, directly or indirectly, may have changed the life of the sierra people. There seem very good reasons to believe that the changes were in the direction of impoverishment, both demographic and cultural. In the seventeenth century the Serrana groups were already a barbarized remnant from the flourishing statelets of the previous century. For example, the sixteenth century was a period of town living, but by the seventeenth the Indians had already returned to a rancheria life (Riley 1978c; Spicer 1962:12-13).

Natural Features

The area here called "Serrana" corresponds to a large degree with the intermediate Serrana zone of Braniff (1978:74). The aboriginal populations of the Serrana province were distributed along the streams that drain out of the mountains of Sonora, streams that eventually reach the Gulf of California in some cases and in others disappear into the lowlands of the Sonoran Desert.

Only the middle and upper portions of the valleys and stretches of broad upland, where there was some settlement, can be treated as Serrana country proper, and geographically much of this represents a montane penetration by the desert. Nevertheless, those Indian populations were dominated in an environmental sense by mountain topography.

The Sonoran Desert portions of eastern and central Sonora (from a vegetational and climatic point of view) include the course of the Sonora River to a point north of Arizpe--that is to say, roughly to the 1000 m contour of elevation. These riverine fingers of the desert take in most of the valley floor and slopes of the Moctezuma River drainage to about the same contour, north of Cumpas. The same is true of the other major north drainage of the Yaqui River, the Bavispe-Bacamuchi. Much of the main Yaqui lies in the desert zone, including the important Nuri Chico River area, as does the entire drainage of the Matape.

Relief in this area is considerable. The valleys for the most part are under 1000 m; in the middle range of the Sonora and Yaqui rivers they are considerably lower. For example, Ures, one of the regions that is a serious candidate for sixteenth century Corazones, is about 425 m in altitude. As one goes up the Sonora River the land rises to around 550 m at Baviacora, to roughly 600 m at Aconchi, and to about 800 m at Arizpe. In the Moctezuma Valley, the town of Moctezuma is about 600 m, while Nacozari at the very northern end of the valley is a bit above 850 m. The easternmost river basins are higher; for example, Bavispe on the north-flowing loop of the Bavispe River is around 1100 m in altitude, although Oputo on the south loop of the same river is only 665 m. Of course, beyond the valley country the land rises very sharply, for this region is one of very high relief.

South of the main Yaqui drainage the rivers that drain into the Yaqui are somewhat lower. Sahuaripa, for example, is only some 450 m in altitude, while further west on the Rio Chico the important valley of Nuri averages about 15 m lower than Sahuaripa in the valley floor. On the other hand, the land rises sharply as one goes south on the Rio Sahuaripa, and at Yecora is about 1645 m.

The San Miguel River joins the Sonora a few kilometers north and east of present-day Hermosillo. It forms the western edge of the Serrana province and is somewhat lower in general topography than the Sonora River proper. Rayon, in the middle valley of the San Miguel, is under 600 m, while Opodepe, some 25 km to the north, is under 650 m. The mountain areas rise very sharply from these valley floors. The Sierra Aconchi, which divides the middle San Miguel and the middle Sonora drainages, rises to well over 2000 m; the Sierra Azul at the headwaters of the San Miguel drainage reaches almost 2500 m. As one goes eastward the land rises toward the crest of the Sierra Madre. A few kilometers east of the valley of the Sonora there are ridges that run between 1500 and 2000 m. East of the Moctezuma and in the drainage areas of the Bavispe, the Aros, and the Sahuaripa, elevations of 2500 m are not uncommon. The highest point in this portion of the Sierra Madre Occidental is a peak of 2770 m in extreme western Chihuahua some 32 km almost directly east of the town of Bavispe.

One dominating feature of the mountains is a sharp western escarpment. The Sierra Madre itself is largely of volcanic formation, mainly rhyolite and andesite, and its western escarpment gives, within a matter of 50 km, a relief difference of 2000 m or more. The same kind of dramatic variation in elevation is also true of the middle and upper river valleys. The two great river systems of northern Sonora, the Sonora and the Yaqui, both flow through structural basins in their middle courses, eventually devolving onto the Sonoran lowlands. The Yaqui also forms a series of barrancas in its upper valleys, actually capturing streams that at one time drained eastward. Barrancas, in the upper Yaqui drainage, may be hundreds of meters in depth, and they produce an almost unbelievably rugged terrain. Indeed, Sauer describes the Aros and Papigochic drainages as "being as nearly impassable a barrier as exists in North America" (1932:45). Nevertheless, the uplands of the upper Sonora and Yaqui drainage also contain high rolling meadowlands, important in channeling the various trails and utilized because of their wealth in animal and plant life, although not permanently settled.

The rainfall patterns of the Serrana area in many ways differ only in degree from those of the Sonoran Desert itself. The mean annual rainfall generally increases as one moves from the desert to the higher reaches of the Sierra Madre; however, the amount and distribution of rainfall varies with latitude and the various elements of local topography. Generally speaking, both the middle and upper courses of the Sonora and the Yaqui lie in the 350 to 500 mm annual rainfall zone. Only in a roughly triangular zone that includes the upper portions of the Moctezuma, Sonora, and San Miguel rivers does rainfall go much over 500 mm annually (where in the Sierra Azul and Sierra de Madera areas it may reach 650 mm or more). Another area of relatively high rainfall lies in the high country near the confluence of the Papigochic and the main Yaqui rivers. The highest annual rainfall in the Sierra area, however, lies in the rugged zone of Chihuahua and Sonora, south and east of Yecora, where the fall may exceed 900 mm.

Most rain in the Serrana zone falls in the summer months, normally from late June through September. For example, at Baviacora in the middle Sonoran drainage there are approximately 210 mm of summer rain and only some 110 mm of winter rain, the latter falling in showers from December through February. At Moctezuma, across the mountains to the east, this disparity is even greater—300 mm as compared to 84 mm. The ratio of summer rain to winter rain holds throughout the Serrana region. At Bavispe it is 295 and 110, respectively; at Nacozari, 355 and 137; at Ures, 384 and 115; and at Nuri on the Rio Chico, 490 and 120 mm. Rainfall in summer normally takes place between noon and midnight with mornings apt to be clear. Winter rains are somewhat more sporadic but also tend to fall in the afternoon.

Summer rainfall in the Serrana zone of Sonora is due to penetration of the Gulf summer anticyclone which brings moist Atlantic air across the Sierra Madre Occidental. The scanty winter rainfall is due to the southern movement of the Pacific subtropical anticyclone which produces the "Mediterranean" rainfall patterns of California. These winter rains, though declining drastically as one goes from north to south, afford the Sierra in general more rainfall than they do the desert to the west. Available moisture is carried by western winds across the warm Gulf of California, where the air takes on more moisture and expands. As a result such desert stations as Hermosillo receive only about 35 mm of winter rainfall. As the air builds up on the west flank of the sierras, it cools and loses some of its moisture load. Ures, only 100 km east of Hermosillo, though still deficient in winter rainfall, receives about three times as much as does the capital. Yecora, still farther from the direct effects of the California winter anticyclone but at an altitude of over 1600 m, receives over seven times as much winter rainfall as does Hermosillo.

The relatively barren northern sierra and the tongues of the Sonoran Desert that run into the mountains have high percolation into the rhyolitic and granitic gravels and soils. There is xerophytic and semixerophytic vegetation over much of the mountain pediments, the valley floors, and the adjacent desert. With low humidity, large amounts of sunlight, and high evaporation rate, the Sonoran rivers flow intermittantly over their lower watercourses. The Sonora River, with its basin area of 21,560 km^2, does not normally flow at Hermosillo, and at the measuring station of El Oregano, a few kilometers upstream from the junction with the San Miguel, streamflow averages less than 10 mm over the basin area. The Yaqui, with a much larger basin (69,960 km^2), has a watershed yield of only about 35 mm. The yield is much higher in the south tributaries of the Yaqui than in the north ones. For example, the

Bavispe yields only 22 mm, and the Moctezuma about 12.7 mm. On the other hand, the north-draining Papigochic yields more than 75 mm at its junction with the the Yaqui (Dunbier 1968:90, 92, 399; Tamayo and West 1964:117). The small watershed of the Matape-Guaymas (some 5160 km^2) is restricted to the western slopes of the Sierra Madre, the drainage farther east going mainly into the Yaqui. The Matape seems to have played only a small part in the development of the Serrana peoples, though future archaeology may modify this picture.

The watershed figures quoted above for the Sonora and Yaqui basins are, of course, for modern times, and factors of water control, especially for the lower Yaqui, mean that the aboriginal situation has been considerably altered. On the other hand, the modern figures probably reflect something nearer the aboriginal situation in the middle and upper valleys of both river systems.

Climatically, the Sierra/Serrana zone of Sonora lies almost entirely within Köppen's BSh, a warm steppe climate marked by scrub vegetation and inter-mittant streams but with sufficient rainfall for dry farming (Vivo Escoto 1964:207-208). Of course, the temperature in this region varies with altitude, but in the valleys the climate is mild with relatively few killing frosts. For example, at Bavispe the January mean temperature is about 10°C and the July mean about 29.5^{o}C. At Suaqui, in the middle Sonora River, the January mean is approximately 14.5^{o}C, and the July mean 30.5^{o}C. Ures, farther downstream on the Sonora, and Nuri, in the middle Yaqui Valley, have virtually identical averages, a January mean of 15°C and a July mean of 30°C. There is considerable absolute variation, but even the variation is roughly the same for the two stations. The lowest recorded temperature at both Ures and at Nuri is about -7°C. The highest temperature at Ures is about 48°C, while at Nuri it is 46°C (Dunbier 1968:397-398).

Vegetation in the Serrana area varies considera-bly with elevation and to some minor degree with latitude, the latter variation due, in part, to an increase in summer rainfall. The desert fringes and river valleys of the middle Sonora, Matape, and Yaqui have a vegetation consisting of mesquite (Pro-sopis), and various cacti including the cholla (Opuntia fulgida), tree cactus (Pachycereus), and sahuaro (Carnegiea gigantea). The latter, however, grows mainly on the eastern and southern fringes of the area. The pochote (Ceiba acuminata) also appears, as do certain of the palo verdes (species of Cercidium). There are also various species of Acacia, for example the huisache and palo blanco, and varieties of Ipomoea, including the palo santo. Other common plants include the ocotillo (species of Fouquieria) and, in the compositae, species of Franseria.

Up-country from the flatland and hill vegetation in the higher elevations are stands of oak (Quercus sp.), and on the ridges, summits, and high plains are various conifers interspersed with llanolike areas of grama grass (Bouteloua). Stands of oak may start as low as 1000 m, but the heavier oak forests appear around 1500 m, replacing mesquite and creo-sote bush (Larrea). Yuccas and opuntias continue up the slopes to 1800 m or more; at that elevation the junipers, agaves, and oaks also begin to be replaced by pine (Brand 1936:21-22; Dunbier 1968:66-67; Shreve and Wiggins 1964:Vol. 1, 143-186; Wagner 1964: 254-255; Shreve 1934:373-380).

Fauna varies with altitude, but rodents are especially common and were utilized in the native diet. There are a number of squirrels including the ubiquitous tree squirrel (Sciurus). Among the rodents are such forms as mice, rats, gophers, and prairie dogs. Lagomorphs such as the cottontail and the hare appear in the area. The hystricomorphs include various porcupines, and artiodactyls are represented by the deer, mountain sheep, and prong-horn. Deer was of tremendous importance not only as a food animal but also for ceremonial purposes. The first European contact with Serrana peoples involved the giving of deer hearts, and early accounts describe the ritual sacrifice of deer hearts to native deities. The cult of the deer is still known through much of northern Mexico; modern examples of the ceremonial importance of the deer include the Yaqui and Mayo (Beals 1945:122-123, 126-131); the Southern Tepehuan (Riley, Tepehuan fieldnotes); and the Huichol (Lumholtz 1902:2, 154-155). Among the deer group the white-tailed deer is most common, but the mule deer also appears. Mountain sheep and antelope occur in the higher elevations.

There are a number of carnivores. The Canidae are represented by the grey and kit fox, the coyote, and the wolf; and the Felidae by the lynx, or bob-cat, and the mountain lion. Both of these major groups of animals are found mainly in the mountains. There are also reports of jaguars and ocelots; these felines are basically animals of the warm lowlands, but jaguars do occur in the mountains at least as far as northern Chihuahua (Brand 1937:55). Bears, on the other hand, were common throughout the high-lands and can still be found in remoter areas. Par-enthetically, a sinister vector of disease is the bat. Large numbers of bats seasonally inhabit caves in the Sierra Madre. They are of no importance as a food source, but many carry rabies and so present an ever-present danger. Even so, the bat had and still has economic value in terms of insect control.

A number of birds were important to the

aboriginal groups in the Serrana. They include the wild turkey, duck, quail, woodpecker, parrot, macaw, and many others. Amphibians and reptiles were of no great importance as a human resource (though the Crotalidae did represent a certain threat). Fish from the various streams were eaten; indeed, fish consumption is documented for the Serrana as early as the mid-sixteenth century, and fish poison was also used. Shellfish were of tremendous importance not only in the Serrana but also throughout the Southwest, not so much for food but because the shells helped fuel the widespread trade routes that ran through and out of the area.

Some use was probably made of nonvertebrates for food, including grasshoppers and locusts, grubs, and such caterpillars as the maguey worm. Honey from wild bees was a much sought-after food in historic times; it was probably utilized in the Serrana area aboriginally, though a more widespread use came with the Spaniards who introduced advanced techniques of bee culture. Indeed, bee domestication in a rudimentary way may have predated the Spaniards; at least it did so in the Nayarit area (Oviedo y Valdés 1959: Vol. 4, Lib. XXXIV:270). However, Pfefferkorn (Treutlein 1949:139-140), writing in the eighteenth century, believed that only wild honey was collected in Sonora, at least in his time. The Serrana peoples had the usual inventory of unpleasant insects and arachnids including cockroaches, at least two major varieties of ticks, mosquitos, red bugs, and jijenes (pp. 135-139). There was also the common scorpion of the genus Centruroides. Although local varieties are somewhat dangerous, especially to children, Sonora does not have the truly malignant types of scorpions that abound in Durango, Jalisco, and Nayarit to the south.

Some of the insects were, of course, vectors of disease, but in the absence of paleoepidemiological studies, relatively little can be said about the disease situation. Although the evidence from this area is scanty, there seems little doubt that one of the legacies of the Spaniards was the introduction of Euro-African diseases. Malaria seems to have been unknown in pre-Spanish days although the malarial mosquito, Anopheles quadrimaculatus, presumably was native to the New World. The actual malarial parasite (species of Plasmodium) came with Euro-Africans to the New World and was probably introduced to the mainland of North America sometime in the very early sixteenth century. It was surely a factor in the drastic depopulation of the Nayarit-Sinaloa areas and must have reached Sonora in relatively early times. Other European diseases, such as smallpox, measles, whooping cough, and virulent syphilis, were also introduced at an early time, at least some of them during the sixteenth century. We have little direct information on disease for any part of the Greater Southwest, but the steady decline in populations, more or less documented during the seventeenth century for the area, was certainly due in part to introduced disease (see also Treutlein 1949:105-143; Stuart 1964: 316-362; Dobyns 1966:403-404; Guiteras 1951:28-35; Nentvig 1971:73-83).

Language

The major language in the Serrana area in the sixteenth century was very likely Opata as it certainly was a few generations later. A more difficult question is whether the Opateria (in the sixteenth century) was coterminous with the Serrana itself--that is, with the interacting, squabbling statelets, their good-sized towns, irrigation agriculture, and extensive trade. If Sauer's ideas concerning the distribution of irrigation agriculture and of languages in the sixteenth century are correct, the southern portion of the Serrana may have been Piman-speaking. Sauer also points out that the deeper Sierra people, the Jova, although speaking a language similar to that of the Opata, were at a somewhat lower level of economic and political development. It may be that the Opata, in the sixteenth century, were in the process of subjugating the cruder Jova (Sauer 1934:50).

Sauer has pointed out that almost certainly irrigation was practiced at Ures in the middle San Miguel region and in the Yaqui Valley as far south as Onavas and Nuri, and he believes that all these people were Piman-speaking, though obviously interacting with the Opata (1935:Map 1).

I have suggested elsewhere (1978c, 1979) that the Opata may represent an intrusive sophisticated people from the Casas Grandes region who settled the northern Sonoran sierra and opened or reopened major trade routes from Mesoamerica to the Southwest sometime in the period around A.D. 1400. This Casas Grandes origin for the Opata, though not the dating, was also suggested by Bandelier (1890-1892:Vol. 1, 59; Lange and Riley 1970:276, 278). For another view of Casas Grandes-Opata interaction see Di Peso (1968a:32-33).

The Pima, on the other hand, may represent an indigenous rancheria people, perhaps a remnant of the old Sonoran culture (Pailes 1972). The town-dwelling Pima of the sixteenth century seem to have been highly acculturatively influenced by Opata neighbors and formed part of the Serrana world. Those Pima Bajo who were not acculturated and/or absorbed by the Opata probably were peripheral to the more complex cultures of the Greater Southwest. For that reason I do not include the Lower Pima as a whole in the Greater Southwestern interaction sphere.

There is a little information on the actual names of the languages. According to Cabeza de Vaca:

> Those who spoke that tongue we properly call Primahaitu (which is like saying Vascongados). We found it spoken over more than four hundred leagues of our journey without another over all that territory (1555:fol. xlix).

This statement cannot, of course, be taken at face value. Four hundred leagues is more-or-less 1700 km, and there was no native North American language spoken exclusively over such a distance in the sixteenth century. If Vaca meant forty leagues, that would be the approximate distance through Lower Pima territory from the Opata towns to the Cahitan area.

In the Diego de Guzmán expedition of 1533, both Guzmán and the Second Anonymous reporter indicate that the language changed at the Sinaloa River from Tahue to another unintelligible tongue and that this language stretched to the Yaqui River (Hedrick and Riley 1976:17, 51). There seems no reason to doubt that this language was Cahita (Sauer 1934:23-24). Castañeda, describing the country from Culiacan to Cibola, indicates that Tahu, or Tahue, was spoken in the Culiacan area as far north as the Sinaloa River. Farther north, he mentions groups who seemed to live in the area between the Sinaloa and Yaqui rivers. These rivers, according to Castañeda, were settled by peoples "of the same type" (Hammond and Rey 1940:250). The Corazones and Señora valleys contained another kind of population, and the Suya Valley still farther north had peoples who were the same type as those of Señora. "They have the same dress, language, ceremonies, and customs and all else found up to the despoblado of Chichilticale" (pp. 250-251).

The comments of Obregón in this regard are rather curious. According to this member of the Ibarra expedition:

> The regions extending from Petlatlán to the last inhabited area of the mountain range and the slopes toward the South Sea comprise over three hundred leagues of Caitas and Pimahitos, which is the same as to say Mexicans and Otomites. They are found in many places all mixed together and intermarried among themselves. These two words, Pimahito and Caita, mean no

hay, and Alvar Nuñez Cabeza de Vaca says in his history that Pimahito alone extends over four hundred leagues. In this he was mistaken, for even in the regions near them are other people using different languages, such as those of the coast, at Uparo bapucar [Seri], and in the heart of the mountain range who are of different languages. He was wrong in regard to the number of leagues because he had traversed the territory on foot, making many turns. He was also in error concerning the language because he did not go down to the coast nor did he travel through the mountains as we did (Cuevas 1924:173).

A little later on, Obregón speaks of "the provinces and regions of the valleys and districts of Señora (languages of Caitas and Pimaitos)" (p. 176).

In point of fact, the word Pima (Obregón's Pimaito) probably meant something like "I don't understand" in the Pima language (Russell 1975:19). It has sometimes been assumed that Caita means "Cahita" (see, for example, Pennington 1980:6), but instead it is probably related to the Opata verb cai which also means "to understand." The tribal name Opata itself is a Pima word or phrase O-op o-otam, "enemy people" (Hodge 1907-1910:Vol. 2, 138).

The most detailed work on the aboriginal language distribution in northwest Mexico is that of Sauer (1934), who places the Opata in a compact distribution from the middle and upper San Miguel River in the west through the Sonora Valley from about the Ures Gorge northward and through much of the north drainage of the Yaqui River. A shatter zone with Pima Bajo extends from Matape to Sahuaripa. The Jova--related to the Opata--are given the Papigochic River Valley. The Pima Bajo lie mainly east and south of the Opata-Jova.

This seems to have been the situation in the early seventeenth century, but there is some evidence that the Ures Basin (considered by Sauer to be Piman) was occupied by Opata in the sixteenth century. In any case, the Ures area, as well as part of the San Miguel Valley and especially the Nuri region of the Yaqui Valley, was part of the town-dwelling Serrana during the first part of the sixteenth century. The rancheria dwellers off to the south and east, whether Pima Bajo- or even Jova-speaking, did not belong to the polity of the Greater Southwest.

The Pima Alto, however, were part of the Southwest interaction sphere. They were irrigation-using, agricultural groups that in the sixteenth century were involved in the west coast shell trade to the Southwest and in fact functioned as a very important part of it, though perhaps not as important overall as the Serrana or the Pueblo area. Such groups of Pima Alto may have included the Piato and Himeri who in the seventeenth century were found in the Altar-Magdalena region and the Sobaipuri who were located in the seventeenth century on the San Pedro. The roots of these groups probably go back into the Hohokam culture. I will discuss them in greater detail in Chapter VII.

Population

Detailed and quantified studies of the Serrana populations in the sixteenth century are, at present, quite impossible. Not only are we uncertain as to the actual locations of the large populated valleys, but there are only the most general estimates of population, either of specific "provinces" and towns or of the area as a whole. Eventually, a combination of archaeology and documentary history should allow scholars to make sophisticated studies of population size. For the moment we must make the most of insufficient and sometimes conflicting data.

The first European visitors to the Serrana region, members of the Cabeza de Vaca party, gave no firm population figures. Vaca does speak of marching through a hundred leagues of country with permanent habitations, where the people gave the Spaniards deer hides and cotton clothing, turquoises, corals, beads, and food supplies (1555:fol.xlv). The "Pueblo de los Corazones" where the party received presents of 600 split and dried deer hearts is mentioned, but no population figures are given. He adds, rather puzzlingly, "We think that near the coast by way of the towns through which we traveled, are more than a thousand leagues of populated area with much food" (fol.xlvi). The figures here are not very meaningful, but Vaca seems to be saying that the party was in a rich area.

The Joint Report gives more specific information on Corazones, saying that there were "three small towns that were close together in which there were about twenty houses that were like the previous ones and were close together (there being none scattered about here and there as they were in the peaceful land which they later saw)" (Hedrick and Riley 1974:62). Somewhere in the Corazones area the towns of flat-roofed houses came to an end, and there were houses of matting and straw (pp. 62-63).

Contrary to what is commonly believed, there is good reason to doubt that Marcos de Niza actually visited the Serrana area during his 1539 trip to Cibola. The following three years, however, saw a number of expeditions to and through the area and an actual series of Spanish settlements. The accounts of members of the Coronado expedition, the records of the trials of Francisco Vásquez de Coronado and García López de Cárdenas, and the residencias of Coronado and of Viceroy Antonio de Mendoza give various, though somewhat conflicting, descriptions of peoples, places, and populations in the Serrana.

Most of these accounts are generalized and give relatively little population information. For example, in the testimony of Domingo Martín during the Coronado trials, the witness says that when Coronado visited the area:

> The people of the valley of Corazones as well as the valley of Señora and of Cicique and of Fuoyas [probably Suya], and all the rest whom they saw until they arrived at Cibola came out peacefully . . . invited them to their houses, gave them necessary food according to their ability, especially in the province of Señora where they obtained large supplies, loading horses and mules with them although some were obtained in exchange for goods (ICC:23).

The maestro de campo, Tristán de Luna y Arellano, was ordered to establish a town in "these valleys," and Melchior Díaz was sent "to reside in these pueblos and provinces." Díaz arrived in "the valley of los Corazones y Señora" but left shortly afterwards for the fatal trip to the lower Colorado River, leaving the incompetent Diego de Alcaráz in charge. A number of other witnesses spoke of receiving supplies from the Indians in Corazones or in Señora (pp. 23-24 ff.).

Coronado himself gives very little information on the Corazones region. He does say, however, that at Corazones "we found extensive planted fields and more people than anywhere in the country which we had left behind" (Hammond and Rey 1940:164). There were no provisions to be had (the crops were still green in early June), but maize was found in the nearby Señora Valley (p. 164). Curiously enough, the Relación postrera de Cíbola, the Relación del suceso, and the Traslado de las Nuevas give very little significant information on the Corazones and Señora areas. Indeed, the Relación postrera denies that there is any significant settlement between the Culiacan area and Cibola: "It is more than three hundred leagues from Culiacán to Cíbola, and little of the way is inhabited. There are very few people, the land is sterile, and the roads are wretched" (p. 308).

As I suggested in Chapter IV, this brief account may have been written by Father Toribio de

Motolinía. It certainly betrays a lack of firsthand knowledge of the area. The Relación del suceso does give some geographical information. Señora is a valley ten leagues beyond Corazones. The peoples of the area have maize and cotton, though not great amounts of either. Coronado did get "a little" maize from the valley of Señora (pp. 284-285). The Traslado de las nuevas contributes only the curious comment that on the whole trip from Culiacan to Cibola "not a single peck of maize was obtained" (p. 179).

The best informants for the Corazones-Señora area are Jaramillo and Castañeda. According to Jaramillo, the "arroyo" and the town of Corazones had irrigation, mat houses, and "maize, beans, and calabashes, in abundance" (p. 297). In another valley, or perhaps in another section of the same valley, was Señora, which extended for six or seven leagues and also had irrigation. Another day's journey led to the settlement of Ispa. Then there was a four-day despoblado, and at Nexpa (in the San Pedro Valley?) one came on Indians of a somewhat more primitive type.

Castañeda has more details. Corazones was "down the valley of Señora" (p. 250). The latter was a river and valley thickly settled with towns that contained temples. Castañeda goes on to say:

> Around this province, toward the sierras, there are large settlements forming separate small provinces. They are composed of ten or twelve pueblos. Seven or eight of them whose names I know are Comu, Patrico, Mochil, Agua, Arispa, and Vallecillo. There are others which we did not visit.
>
> From Señora to the valley of Suya there is a distance of forty leagues . . . . Round about this valley there are many pueblos. The people are of the type as those of Señora. They have the same dress, language, ceremonies, and customs and all else found up to the despoblado of Chichilticale (pp. 250-251).

From the Coronado accounts alone it would be difficult to draw any sort of complete picture of the area and its population. The report of Bartolomé de Las Casas, on the other hand, gives a wealth of detail as to population and other aspects of culture. According to Las Casas (who wrote about 1560) this information, or at least part of it, came from Marcos de Niza. Las Casas states that the valley of Señora was sixty leagues by ten leagues and very flat:

The whole valley is heavily populated with towns and large places and full of cultivated fields, because the land is admirable beyond comparison. Our Christians named the first town, the Pueblo of Corazones . . . .This town had 800 very well-executed houses . . . .

From there, six leagues further on in the valley was another town larger than Corazones which the Indians in their language called Agastán . . . well aranged and well done like the other. The principal city and government center of this region was comprised of three thousand very good houses and rather large in the majority . . . . This city was named, or they called it, Señora or Senora. There were many other towns, and in some of them were very tall stone and mud temples for idols and for the entombment of principal personages (Riley 1976a:19-20).

Such an area as described here obviously had a rather large population, certainly on the order of tens of thousands in the Señora Valley alone.

After the Coronado party returned to New Spain, the northern Mexican area was left alone for approximately twenty years. Eventually, however, in 1564-1565, another exploration party was mounted, this one led by Francisco de Ibarra, governor of the newly founded province of Nueva Vizcaya. As is the case with Coronado, we cannot be absolutely sure where Ibarra traveled. He seems to have entered the Serrana via the Nuri Chico Valley, the site of Oera which some believe to have been the location of one of the Spanish settlements of San Gerónimo (Di Peso 1974:Vol. 3, 810). Oera consisted of a town of 1000 houses and 2000 inhabitants. The Oera people were in contact, often hostile contact, with the peoples of Cinaro, Corazones, Guaraspi, and Batuco. From Oera there was a four-day march to two beautiful valleys five and six leagues long, crisscrossed by many streams (Cuevas 1924:147). These were the valleys of Corazones and Señora, where the third Spanish town of San Gerónimo de los Corazones had been founded over twenty years before. The "province" of Señora had over 20,000 people in an area thirty leagues long and twenty wide. They were enemies of the people of Oera, Uparo (probably the Seri), and the Yaquini, or Yaqui (p. 148). From the Señora Valley the army marched another three days to small towns with terraced houses and on the fourth day reached Guaraspi, a town with 600 to 700 terraced houses, irrigation, and "well planned" streets. From Guaraspi, the army continued on through small towns of 100 to 200 terraced houses. A five-day journey brought Ibarra to Cumupa, a town of 500 houses that resembled Guaraspi. Cumupa was in a valley, one league long, all in irrigated fields (labores de regadio), and in its neighborhood were four small towns from one to two leagues apart, whose columns of smoke could be seen (p. 158).

Leaving Cumupa the party marched for a day through three small towns resembling those of the Cumupa area. This part of the march from the Señora Valley to Sahuaripa was through the best populated part of the whole area (p. 158; Hammond and Rey 1928:175). At that point, the army went over a high mountain where, apparently the next day, Sahuaripa was reached.

Meanwhile the inhabitants of the valleys of Señora, Cumupa, Guaraspi, "and the other pueblos" decided to mass a united attack in the valley of Sahuaripa. The latter was a valley stronghold town at the side of a very steep ravine, manned by 600 fighting men with their women and children. The allies planned to field some 15,000 warriors from all the neighboring valleys (Cuevas 1924:168). News of the battle (in which the Spaniards held their own) was flashed by signal fire, reaching Cinaro on the Fuerte River within two days (pp. 171-172).

The Ibarra party traveled on to the eastern side of the Sierra Madre, where they met hundreds of hunting Querecho Indians, heard news of Cibola, and examined the ruins of Paquimé (Casas Grandes). Returning over the mountains after great hardships, the army found a pass where, according to Obregón:

> From this point I could ascertain where the lands and valleys of Señora were located and that the way through was in the direction of the towns of Guaraspi, Zaguaripa, and Cumupa, which are near the town of Señora [italics in original] (p. 219).

Ibarra continued his march and two days later arrived at a small town. A day farther on they reached another tiny village of five houses but with "grandes cantidad de maiz, frijol y calabaza" enough to feed the entire army, it would seem (p. 221). Señora was only three days' march away at this point (p. 220).

Continuing the journey, the general skirted the settlements of Señora and lost several horses in a skirmish. He marched slowly onward for two days, then suddenly turned back at night and attacked one of the Señoran towns, killing a number of people and capturing an Indian to be a guide. With this guide Ibarra managed to reach the friendly settlement of Batuco (p. 230) which earlier had helped the Coronado party (see below). The location of this town

is uncertain, like most places in the Serrana area, but there was a later town with that name in the Moctezuma Valley. Such a location would fit the comments of Obregón, who talked about the valleys of Pinebaroca and Paibatuco (apparently in the Batuco area) that are on the Yaqui River and whose inhabitants were enemies of both the Señora and the Yaquimi peoples.

From Batuco the Spaniards marched four days to the town of the wild Huparo, or Uparo, (p. 230) who also were enemies of both the Señoran and Yaquimi peoples. One is tempted to locate this settlement somewhere in the lower Matape area. At any rate, from Huparo Ibarra sent messengers to the people of Yaquimi and on their return reached the Yaquimi country in one day. On the lower Yaqui Obregón noted 15,000 Indians (p. 230).

It is obviously impossible to draw accurate population estimates from this kind of information. For example, when Obregón talks of the province of Señora having 20,000 inhabitants in an area thirty by twenty leagues, what exactly is he saying? He cannot actually be talking about a river valley for nowhere in this part of northern Mexico are there valleys with a significant section anywhere near 80 km across. Obregón must, therefore, be including the mountain areas that parallel whatever river system is involved. This overall region, which is roughly 10,500 km^2, had, if Obregón's figures are used, a population density of about two persons per km^2. If we follow Sauer (1934:46-51, map) in the general outlines of the Opata area but add the region of Nuri which he lists as Pima Bajo, we have an elongated territory of some 45,000 km^2 (see Figure 8). Applying the Obregón formula (two persons per km^2) there would be a population of some 90,000 which is likely too high, for Obregón and others in the sixteenth century indicated that there was much unsettled country. Probably the best approach is that of Sauer (1935:5), who gives approximately 42,500 km^2 to the Opata and estimates 1.5 persons per square kilometer, or about 60,000. If the Nuri and Ures areas are added, there would be perhaps an additional 5000 to 7000 people. Sauer, incidentally, treats the Jova separately, considering them to be a somewhat more primitive people who lived in the uplands of the Papigochic and Aros rivers. Their lands covered about 7800 km^2, and their population, according to Sauer, was some 5000 souls. I agree with Sauer that the Jova were not part of the Serrana polity, as discussed above.

Sauer's population estimates for the Opata are based in part on the population of the Opateria in 1920, a time when agricultural production and distribution techniques probably were not significantly advanced over those of the Serrana statelets. In

1920 the population density for the old Opateria was 1.7 per km^2 (p. 5). In Sauer's words:

> Present rural numbers are, at least in this region, a useful guide in such interpolation. In very many areas the people are settled in the same villages which were inhabited at the coming of the whites, they have the same fixed area of land from which to draw their support, and the manner of subsistence either has not changed or the changes have been of a determinable degree and direction. Almost all the land farmed, and it is farming land which determines density primarily, is either alluvial or colluvial, and was equally available to the tools, crops, and tillage of the aboriginal and the present inhabitants. The crop system and dietary of the population today are not altered significantly from aboriginal conditions (p. 4).

Parenthetically, Doolittle (1979:9, 1980:340) has estimated the late pre-Hispanic population of the central Sonora Valley (an area of less than 2000 km^2) as possibly 10,000.

Only three generations after the Ibarra expedition, the Jesuits were beginning to move into the territory of the Opata. Even earlier, in 1603, the Ordiñola inquiry gave information on the Opata towns (Sauer 1934:46). The Jesuit Añuas indicate that as of 1620 there were some hundred "towns" on the Moctezuma River alone and seventy settlements in the Sahuaripa region, the latter all under the control of one Sisibotari (AGN:Añuas, tomo 15; see also Pérez de Ribas 1944:tomo 2, lib. vi, caps 13-21, pp. 173-203).

Whatever the population of the Serrana area in the sixteenth century, it declined at least from the early seventeenth century on. As of around 1675, a half century after the beginnings of missionization in the Opateria, the population of the Opata was listed as less than 9000 with the "Indios serranos," perhaps mostly Jova, another 4000. The Pima Bajo, including the Nebome, were listed as about 7600 souls (Navarro García 1967:70-71). This is a far cry from the estimates of Arregui (1946:111) of 200,000 Indians in 1620, although he probably included the lower Sonoran area and Ostimuri to the south.

The Opata as a recognizable ethnic entity continued to decline during the eighteenth and nineteenth centuries. In the mid-1820s Hardy (1829:437) gave the Opata population as about 10,000 collected in thirty-two towns, mainly in the Sonora and Yaqui drainages. About sixty years later, in 1884, Adolph F. Bandelier made a trip through Opata country and referred to these Indians as "a formerly important group, now so completely 'Hispanicised' as to have almost forgotten their native tongue" (1890-1892:Vol. 1, 56). However, Hrdlička (1904:72), who visited the Opata in 1902, reported pockets of Indians who continued to use the native language. Today, there are isolated reports of Opatan speakers, but Opata as a language and culture has essentially disappeared.

Subsistence

The Serrana area in the sixteenth century had an economy based firmly on irrigation agriculture. This is indicated by every major Spanish party that visited the area, and the still rather scanty archaeological evidence tends to support it (Doolittle 1980:335). The type of irrigation system is not actually well described in any of the sixteenth century accounts. As yet the archaeology of the area is not extensive enough to give much information on the matter, but in the nineteenth century Bandelier (1890-1892:Vol. 1, 60-62) described both the use of artificial tanks on the hills and extensive agricultural terraces, the latter probably utilizing runoff water. A few years later Lumholtz (1902:Vol. 1, 21-22) also reported extensive "trincheras" in the Nacori area, some as high as 2000 m, usually associated with ruins.

Certainly for the sixteenth century a number of Spanish accounts indicate considerable agriculture. Coronado's mention of "extensive planted fields" (Hammond and Rey 1940:164); Jaramillo's "maize, beans, and calabashes in abundance" (p. 297); the statements of Obregón about marching through league after league of richly planted irrigated fields (Cuevas 1924:145-59); and his comment that the people of Oera "gathered much maize, Castilian beans, melons, calabashes, and other vegetables" (p. 146) are all indications of this. Added evidence comes from statements of Ruíz that Corazones and Señora were "fertile valleys with abundant supplies of maize, beans, and calabashes" (PSM; see also Sauer 1932:55) and the earlier observation of Cabeza de Vaca (1555:fol. xlv) that there were long stretches of planted fields.

Virtually all of the accounts mention irrigation, but there is very little in the way of detail. Jaramillo talks of an irrigation arroyo (arroyo de riego) in the Corazones Valley (Pacheco and Cárdenas 1870:Vol. 14, 306). Obregón mentions "irrigation canals for their fields" (acequias de regadio para sus labores) at Guaraspi (Cuevas 1924:157).

It is quite clear that the basic food crops were maize, beans, some kind(s) of squash, and perhaps gourds. There are, as yet, no archaeological data for the actual races of corn, and the chronicles are not informative on this point. It seems likely that lowland strains of Zea mays, perhaps resembling those of the Gila-Salt area to the north, were utilized. Beans, again, are usually given simply as a generic term. As a guess we might suppose that both the common bean (Phaseolus vulgaris) and the tepary (Phaseolus acutifolius) were present, but at this time we cannot say for certain. In any case the tepary was cultivated in Jesuit mission times (Johnson 1971:173).

The squash/gourd certainly was present. Castañeda describes a "melon" so large that one person had trouble carrying a single specimen. These melons were cut into pieces and dried and could be eaten either raw or cooked. They were sweet "like dried figs" (Hammond and Rey 1940:251). Jaramillo mentions calabashes (p. 297), a term also used by Obregón (Cuevas 1924:149) and by Cabeza de Vaca. According to the latter, "y de su harina nos dieron mucha cántidad, y de calabaças y frijoles y mantas de algodón, y de todo cargamos" (1555:fol. xlv). What these various "melones" and "calabazas" actually were is impossible to say with certainty. Both Cucurbita and Lagenaria were found archaeologically in the Hohokam area, and it seems likely that both would have been present in the Serrana.

Cotton is also mentioned in a number of the accounts. Beginning with the comment by Cabeza de Vaca (see above) about cotton mantas, a number of chroniclers touch on the use of cotton. For example, Castañeda indicates that clothing in this region included "small tunics" (Hammond and Rey 1940:250), which, from the Obregón accounts, seem to have been made of cotton. Obregón, in several areas of Sonora, mentions that clothing of cotton and pita or agave fiber (Cuevas 1924:144-145, 157) was worn and also that there were cotton blankets (p. 146). Pita alone was used for heavy blankets which, according to Obregón, "las cuales nos servían de tiendas a falta de anjeo" (p. 157).

The variety (or varieties) of cotton is unknown. In view of the distribution studies of Volney Jones (1936:56), one would suspect that the Serrana area used Gossypium hopi, but until we obtain actual specimens, this must remain conjectural.

Native domesticated animals probably included the turkey, though the evidence for it is not very clear at this point. At any rate turkeys were common at Casas Grandes (Di Peso 1974:Vol. 2, 469), and Lombardo (1702:fol. 15) gives an Opata name for turkey, chigui. We can suspect that the domesticated

dog was also present, in view of the known aboriginal distribution of this animal, but there is little or no indication of it in the sources. Two types of wild birds were tamed. Castañeda (Hammond and Rey 1940:251) speaks of "royal eagles" kept by dignitaries, and Obregón mentions "large numbers of eagles and parrots, great and small, in cages" (Cuevas 1924:147). We do not know if the cages were like the macaw cages found at Casas Grandes by Di Peso (1974:Vol. 2, 468).

There was a considerable utilization of wild plants and animals. I have already mentioned agave fiber in weaving (Cuevas 924:144-145). Castañeda (Hammond and Rey 1940:251) mentions the use of pitahaya fruit in making an alcoholic drink. Prickly pear, one or another of the tuna producing Opuntia, was made into preserves and "mesquite [bean] bread, in loaves resembling cheeses, which keeps for a whole year" (p. 251). Parenthetically, these three wild foods are all from summer-ripening plants, utilized mainly in June and July. A root, probably Yucca elata, was used by women for washing clothing (Cabeza de Vaca 1555:fol. xlv).

As usual Obregón gives the most detailed information about foods. Of the Señora-Corazones area he says:

> There are good fields of maize, beans, calabashes, and melons. The fruits that they have are tunas, pitahayas, and chile. The melons are of seeds that were left when Alcaráz was killed [in 1541], they having grown and harvested them. They pick quantities of tunas and pitahayas and dry the insides. The seeds are kept to be eaten in times of necessity. It is a good food and in the same way they slice and dry melons and calabashes which last all year and which are carried as provisions in warfare. They have little salt, and to get it and to obtain women as slaves and as wives, they fight with their neighboring enemies, as I have mentioned (Cuevas 1924:149).

The wild chile referred to by Obregón was most likely chiltepin or chile del monte (Capsicum annuum) which grows throughout much of the Serrana country and today remains a favorite condiment in the region (Nabhan 1978:30-34). The mention of dried and stored calabashes probably refers to the same species as described by Castañeda (Hammond and Rey 1940:251; see also above). This likely was the camot which, according to the eighteenth century Rudo ensayo, was "put to dry in the sun, and then cut in slices and kept throughout the year"

(Guiteras 1951:23). The word camot is likely a corruption of the Aztec-Spanish camote (which in Spanish usually means "sweet potato"). This is also
probably the same plant--yellowish fruit, sweet,
dried for storage--that Pfefferkorn (Treutlein
1949:58) calls the seguelca. Whatever the name, the
plant is almost certainly a species of Cucurbita.

Obregón also mentions a curious use of alum as
some sort of condiment in Oera and in Batuco. The
alum, which was made into small loaves of a pound
and a half by the Batucoans, was desired not only by
the Oerans but also by those "who live on the coast
of the sea although it is more than 25 leagues from
Oera " (Cuevas 1924:146). Wars were fought over the
alum (pp. 146-147).

There was a variety of wild animal foods. Obregón mentions receiving game at Oera (p. 146). The
very name Corazones, of course, came from the fact
that Cabeza de Vaca received 600 split, dried deer
hearts from the natives of that valley (1555:fol.
xlv). According to Cabeza de Vaca, "deer are of
three kinds; one is the size of a small steer in
Spain" (fol. xlvi). Las Casas (Riley 1976a:20) mentions that not only deer hearts were important ceremonially but also those of wolves, hares, and birds;
and an eighteenth century writer, Beaumont, adds the
information that the Vaca party received "three baskets filled with animal hearts" (1932:Vol. 2, 396).
Castañeda also states that the natives had offered
Cabeza de Vaca "many hearts of animals" (Hammond and
Rey 1940:209).

Later accounts of the Opata indicate that they
hunted rabbit, mountain sheep, birds, and deer and
that rabbits were killed with sticks or light arrows
in community drives (Johnson 1971:174). Bandelier,
while traveling through the Sonora Valley in 1884,
records a former "great rabbit hunt" held each year
in May (Lange and Riley 1970:236).

Obregón indicates that the Serrana people
fished, using sap of the famous poison tree (see
below) as a fish stupifier. When branches were
thrown into "rivers, streams, ponds, and lakes," the
poison killed both fish and game (Cuevas 1924:155).
Obregón makes the further point that the Indians
around Oera caught "fish of all kinds" (p. 142).
Fishing remained important into the seventeenth and
eighteenth centuries. At least in Jesuit mission
times fish were caught by hand, in weirs, with hook
and line, with nets, and by use of poison (Johnson
1971:175). Of course some of these techniques may
have been introduced by the Spaniards, but Lombardo
(1702: fol. 11) does give a number of Opata names of
individual varieties of fish including both fresh-
and salt-water species. There is no sixteenth century indication of watercraft in the area, but the
anonymous Arte y vocabulario de la lingua Dohema,

Heve, o Eudeva, which seems to be seventeenth century in date, has a vocabulary item for "canoe,"
vvasguasiuen (Smith 1861:25). In the eighteenth
century, Alegre (1841-1842:Vol. 2, 93) states that
the people of Sahuaripa were clever at making and
using balsas. One suspects, however, that even if
present in the sixteenth century, boating can never
have been important in the Serrana.

One very interesting point concerning the economy of the Serrana area is that Spanish plants and
animals very quickly made their way into the region.
In 1540 Castañeda already noted "gallinas como las
de castilla" and was puzzled as to how European
chickens could have reached the northern Sonoran
area (Winship 1896:449). Twenty years later, as
noted above, Obregón is interested in melons that
"son de la semilla que les quedó de cuando mataron a
los de Alcaráz que los sembraban y cogían" (Cuevas
1924:149). At Oera Obregón also speaks of "frijol
de Castilla" (p. 146) which Hammond and Rey
(1928:160) translate as "chick peas" (Cicer arieti-
num). Actually, of course, the bare mention by
Obregón does not make it clear if the beans were
indeed chick peas (garbanzos). There is the obvious
implication, however, that they were an introduced
European crop.

Obregón also mentions "fruit trees" (árboles
frutales), making a distinction between them and
"wild trees" (árboles silvestres) (Cuevas 1924:161).
It is not at all clear what is being referred to
here, but probably Obregón is talking about some of
the native fruit-bearing cacti.

The significant thing in all this is not the
certain identification of a given plant or animal
but the indication that new domesticates entered the
Serrana economic picture with great ease. As I will
discuss below, one reason seems to have been the
great importance of trade and the middleman position
of the Serrana people and their dependence on trade
for basic items. This would be expected to make
them receptive to outside influences as, indeed,
seems to have been the case.

The historic accounts, information from archaeology, and comparisons with modern farming and collecting patterns give insight into at least the
broad details of Serrana subsistence. The contemporary picture gives some idea of what must have been
the case in pre-Spanish and early contact times.
Today, in parts of the middle and upper Sonoran
river valleys where agromechanization and factory
farming techniques have not yet been introduced,
irrigation is almost entirely of a very simple variety. Fields are spread out along the river beds,
and ditches serve individual plots or, more commonly, are utilized by a number of landowners under
the supervision of "commissioners." The ditches are

seldom more than 1 or 2 km in length (Dunbier 1968:283-284). The actual settlements tend to be on terraces, and recent archaeological work (at least for the Sonora Valley) has demonstrated that this was the case aboriginally.

The twentieth century system was and is not optimal. Because of the restricted size of the various irrigation systems, there is little overall planning, and upriver towns tend to siphon off water so that, in dry years, the downstream settlements are sometimes left without sufficient runoff.

There is some seasonal dry farming in the lower reaches of arroyos that drain down to the main rivers. In modern times wheat has become an important crop--so much so that today, in the central Sonora River settlements, the wheat tortilla has become basic to the diet. Maize is put in, usually in June, and receives the benefit of the July and August runoff as the rivers rise during the rainy season. Today, maize is also the most common dry-farmed crop. Beans are usually planted in late winter and harvested before the summer planting of corn. Wheat is sown in the fall and early winter months (October to January) and harvested in June. Double cropping is then practiced with the maize planted in the same fields and harvested in the dry, cool months of late autumn (Hewes 1935:289). Other crops, squash, melons, etc., are usually interspersed with maize in the small river plots (Dunbier 1968:286).

The ecosystem in the sixteenth century is not very well known, but double cropping seems certain. For example, when Coronado reached the valley of Corazones around the 7th of May, 1540 (Gregorian), he found "extensive planted fields." There was no eating corn, however (the maize not being ripe), and Coronado had to obtain supplies from the nearby valley of Señora (Hammond and Rey 1940:164). As Señora seems to have been a bit higher than Corazones, it is improbable that the corn there had ripened, and most likely Coronado drew on supplies stored from the previous year. The description of the Corazones fields suggests a winter planting, perhaps the same pattern as the sowing of wheat in modern times. In such a case, a second maize crop would be planted in June, as it is today, and harvested in October or early November. According to Pennington (1980:148-149), the Nevome, or Pima Bajo, double cropped maize until a generation or so ago. At Onavas the winter maize was planted in January or February. Curiously enough, Cabeza de Vaca, while in the Corazones area, states:

We think that near the coast by way of the pueblos through which we came, there is more than a thousand leagues of inhabited country with much subsistence because three times a year [emphasis mine] they plant beans and maize (1555:fol. xlvi).

Today, summer planting of maize often extends beyond the irrigated areas, for the light summer rains are generally sufficient to bring in a crop in the margins of river valleys and on dry arroyos. In recent times, yields have been rather low for irrigated crops, about 1000 kg of unshelled corn per hectare. Around 1930 at Huepac in the middle Sonora Valley, land holdings were about half a hectare per individual with only 60% of the land being fully irrigated (Hewes 1935:290-291). If one assumes, with Sauer, a rough equivalence of population in 1540 and in 1930--taking double cropping into account--the annual yield then was some 1000 kg of unshelled maize, or about 400 kg of shelled maize per hectare (the equivalent of 3500 to 4000 daily calories per capita). Admittedly the bases for this computation are very narrow, and the number of variables is great (for further discussion, see Riley 1979).

It may be that agriculture was somewhat more extensive in the sixteenth century. Hewes' study of Huepac in the period around 1930 indicated that a large amount of bottomland had been abandoned because of sand deposition and the reduced flow of the Sonora River. Even so, the Huepac area at the time of Hewes' survey was more than self-sufficient in grain (1935:291). This situation of sufficiency seems to hold for the entire Serrana country (Dunbier 1968:282-283). Parenthetically, the Rudo ensayo of Juan Nentvig, written in the mid-eighteenth century, speaks of a return--it would seem from the Opata--of 100 to 300 times per fanega of maize and prolific returns in "beans, lentils and other vegetables" (Guitéras 1951:23; see also Pradeau and Rasmusson 1980:23).

Another important source of food that Pennington (personal communication) believes was once common to the entire Serrana area is quelites, or field greens. Quelites, used as potherbs and for flavoring, included various of the Chenopodiaceae, the Amaranthaceae, and the leaves of numerous other trees and shrubs. We have no actual evidence that the Serrana people used quelites in the sixteenth century, but in view of the extensive use in other parts of the northern Sierra Madre, it seems very likely indeed. For the seventeenth century, Lombardo (1702) lists large numbers of quelites as well as medicinal herbs. The same situation holds for a number of roots (see Pennington 1963:124-129, 1969:138-140; 1980:168-169). The caloric importance of these foods to the diet cannot, of course, be estimated, but they would supply vitamin C and several of the vitamin B group as well as trace minerals.

From the various bits of evidence it seems a fair conclusion that the Serrana peoples had ample food. How much surplus was available is unknown, but in the Coronado testimony of Cristóbal de Escobar (ICC) it is stated that the Indians of Corazones, Señora, and Suya were willing to give up two-thirds of their harvest to the Spanish settlement of San Gerónimo, rebelling when the Spanish commander, Alcaráz, also took wives and daughters. In addition, it should be remembered that the Coronado party went through a largely ruined and deserted area that seemed to have stretched from near San Miguel de Culiacan to Corazones, a distance of 700 to 800 km. The advance party at any rate got little or no supplies until it reached the Corazones-Señora area (Hammond and Rey 1940:164). The Coronado party as a whole contained some 340 Spaniards and a large number of Indian allies, servants, and slaves. Viceroy Mendoza, at his residencia in 1547, stated that some 1300 Indian allies plus over a thousand horses and mules had accompanied the army (Aiton and Rey 1937:314). The statement of Archbishop of Mexico Francisco Antonio Lorenzana (1770:325) that there were 2000 men on the expedition is probably very near to being correct, though one should treat the figures with some caution. For example, another Mendoza residencia document says 300 Indians, "a few more or less" (García Icazbalceta 1866:118-119). In addition, there were many hundred head of cattle and sheep (and also probably goats, although they are never mentioned in any extant account).

The major part of this army and most of the livestock reached the Corazones-Señora area in July 1540 and remained there until the latter part of September. When the main army left the Serrana region, its commander, Tristán de Luna Arellano, left a party variously estimated at eighty to a hundred men to colonize the area. As far as is known, all sections of the Spanish army depended on Indian food when in northern Sonora. The drain on local food supplies must have been tremendous, but the Indians seem to have met Spanish demands without undue hardship. As previously mentioned, the revolt that destroyed the Spanish settlement of San Gerónimo a year later seemed to be more related to bad treatment of the Indians than to lack of food.

Not only does there seem to have been a surplus, but the food variety was considerable. All indications are that game was important in the diet, as was fish. The food animals would supply both protein and fat, and in addition there was plant protein from cultivated maize, legumes, and the wild mesquite bean. There were ample carbohydrates; if any food balance was lacking, it may have been in vegetable fat. Vitamins and trace minerals could be had in the various quelites and in the variety of wild fruits, including tunas.

Information from early Jesuit documents (though admittedly they represent a time of lowered population) indicate that the seventeenth century Opata lived quite well. It is clear enough that in the sixteenth century the Serrana groups had a considerable surplus of foodstuffs. This fits the general sociopolitical and economic picture to be discussed below.

Settlement Patterns

The important distinction between the Sonoran statelets and the regions both to the north (the Gila-Salt area) and to the south (the Pima Bajo and Cahita area) was that the Serrana peoples were town living whereas all surrounding groups were ranchería peoples. This is indicated by both archaeological and documentary evidence. In the area of the middle Sonora Valley, Pailes (1978, 1980) has found closely built stone and adobe surface houses superimposed on earlier scattered pithouse structures. I suggested above that this older occupation may have been one of Piman speakers who were overrun by Opatan speakers coming from the east. The date of the Opatan intrusion is very much open to question, but I believe it may have been around A.D. 1300 or a little before. This date is suggested by Pailes' archaeological materials, and it fits the sequence of events in the Casas Grandes area. In the sixteenth century the Serrana area was still expanding, as the accounts of the Ibarra party about the aggressive nature of the Serrana peoples would indicate. By that time the Serrana urban way of life was not exclusively Opata. It was shared with a fringe of Pima Bajo speakers in the middle Yaqui Valley and perhaps at Ures in the Sonora Valley and with groups in the San Miguel region. By the seventeenth century, however, the region was in a serious decline, and the town populations seem to have given way to ranchería populations (Spicer 1962:13).

The various Spanish accounts indicate that the Serrana area was organized into towns and also into what are called "provinces" or "nations." At times the two terms "province" and "town" seem to be interchangeable, but some accounts indicate clearly that a province might have a number of towns.

Descriptions of the towns are not entirely satisfactory, but these entities seem to be of close-together, though not necessarily contiguous, houses of mud and stone and also of jacal or of mats (the latter far commoner in the rancheria country to the south). One strongly suspects that these are references to substantial winter houses and somewhat lighter summer ones. Of course there are other explanations (for example, social differentiation reflected by house type).

The earliest account of Corazones, that of Cabeza de Vaca, is not very informative, but he talks of permanent habitations--some houses of earth, the rest all of cane mats (1555:fol. xlv). Over a hundred leagues of territory the party "continually found settlements with much maize and beans and where they received many deer and cotton mantas, beads, corals from the Gulf of California, and turquoise from the north" (fol. xlv). In the Vaca narrative a few lines later is the comment that "there are solid houses that are called buhios" (fol. xlvi).

In the Joint Report of the Vaca expedition (Hedrick and Riley 1974:146) there is a mention of three small towns of some twenty houses. It is difficult to reconcile these two accounts even if the publication meant that there were twenty houses in each town. I should point out, however, that the Joint Report is known only from its inclusion in the Historia general y natural of Gonzalo Fernández de Oviedo y Valdés and could have been somewhat edited. Oviedo is, in fact, not overly reliable when reporting on Indians, particularly when his sources might indicate any amount of Indian sophistication.

The Vaca party does make one distinction that is important. At Corazones the houses were "close together," instead of being scattered about "as they were in the peaceful land which [the party] later saw" (pp. 62, 146). This "peaceful land" was the Cahitan and northern Tahue country. A little later in the Oviedo account, it is suggested that the flat-roofed houses and "modestly dressed" women at Corazones represented traits taken over from the Pueblo area, because from Corazones to the south the houses were of matting and straw and the women much more scantily dressed (pp. 63-64, 147).

Melchior Díaz, who visited the Serrana in 1539, gives some information on house types in "a small valley located 150 leagues from Culiacán, and which is well settled and has terraced houses" (Hammond and Rey 1940:160). This distance from Culiacan suggests either the valley of Corazones or that of Señora.

Other members of the Coronado party give bits of information. According to Castañeda, the "pueblo called Valle de los Vellacos" was on a prominence, and the town of Suya "was situated near a small river" (pp. 232, 269). The Relación del suceso indicates that towns in the area were made of mat

houses, some on low terraces (p. 284). Jaramillo describes the houses of Corazones as follows: "Their houses consist of huts. After setting up poles in the shape of ovens, although much larger, they cover them with mats" (pp. 296-297).

The Relación postrera also speaks of houses "built of reed mats, and are round and small, a man being hardly able to stand up inside" (p. 308). This description, however, covers the whole route from Culiacan to Cibola and probably really refers to the Cahitan house types. Castañeda (p. 209) calls Corazones "a province." He also speaks of Señora as a "river and valley thickly settled with comely people" (p. 250). To this information Castañeda adds the list of province names: Comu, Patrico, Mochil, Agua, Arispa, and Vallecillo (p. 250; also see above).

Of this list, Arispa is likely the Guaraspi of Obregón and perhaps the Ispa of Jaramilla (p. 297), and Comu might be the Cumupa of Obregón (Cuevas 1924:168). The other names are Spanish, though Agua and Vallecillo might be translations of native names, and Patrico and Mochil possibly attempts to pronounce Opata names by using similar-sounding Spanish words. In this regard, it might be pointed out that, being with the main army, Castañeda actually spent some two months in the Serrana area. Jaramillo, with Coronado's vanguard, passed through the region in a matter of a few days, waiting only for supplies from Señora while camping at Corazones. In addition, Coronado had strictly forbidden his men to enter native towns, and one suspects that Jaramillo got very little chance to observe the uses of town life in the Serrana area. This would explain his lack of detailed knowledge about house types in that region.

The various witnesses in the Coronado and López de Cárdenas hearings made a number of references to Corazones, Señora, and Suya. In a number of testimonies Corazones is referred to as a "province," and Señora and Suya as "valleys" (see the testimonies of Juan Troyano, Rodrigo de Frías, Cristóbal de Escobar, and Domingo Martín in ICC). Others speak of Corazones, Señora, and sometimes Suya as "provinces" (Cristobal de Escobar) or "pueblos and provinces" (Rodrigo Ximón and Juan de Zaldívar). Domingo Martín also specifically refers to Señora as a province, and makes the statement quoted above about the Spaniards loading horses and mules with supplies. To some degree this fits the Coronado statement about trading maize with the people of Señora "which relieved the friendly Indians and some Spaniards" (Hammond and Rey 1940:164). Coronado may have been trying to downplay his dependency on the Indians of Señora for food supplies. Later testimonies vary a great deal in the amount of food actually obtained, but we do know that the Coronado party ran out of food again in the mountainous country south of Cibola. Nor for that matter are we certain of the size of Coronado's advance party. There seem to have been about 100 Spaniards, both horsemen and foot soldiers, plus a number of Indian allies and Black servants. Before reaching Corazones "some of our negroes and several of the Indians deserted, which was not a slight loss for the expedition" (p. 164). Later, in the final despoblado before reaching Cibola, the party also lost "several Indian allies and a Spaniard named Espinosa, besides two negroes, who died from eating some herbs because they were out of food" (p. 166).

These statements indicate that a fair number of non-Spaniards were with the party, but the idea of Day that the advance party contained "most of the Indian allies" (1940a:97) simply cannot be true. Any actual figure is bound to be a mere guess, but if one said that allies and servants made up half the party, it would probably not be too far wrong.

The account of Las Casas, included in the Apologética historia sumaria, claims to have drawn its information from both Cabeza de Vaca and Marcos de Niza. As quoted above, Las Casas talks of "towns and large places." Corazones had 800 houses, both mat covered and adobe. The town of Agastan was even larger than Corazones, while the government center for the region, a city named Señora, had 3000 houses. There were many other towns, some of them with "very tall stone and mud temples" (Riley 1976a:20).

Las Casas describes a somewhat more elaborate culture in the Serrana area than one might suspect from the Coronado documents alone (if one leaves out the account of Marcos de Niza). However, the Ibarra expedition of 1564-1565 reports a situation that sounds very much like that described by Las Casas. I have already surveyed the account of Obregón, but to summarize, Oera (probably in the Nuri Chico Valley) had 1000 "good flat-roofed houses about an estado and a half [c. 3 m] in height, and grouped in good order" (Cuevas 1924:146). The people of Oera were very warlike and fought with the Indians of Cinaro, Corazones, Guaraspi, Cumupa, and especially with those of Batuco. In the Señora, Corazones, and nearby areas, Obregón found towns with high adobe walls, terraced houses, well-planned streets, and irrigation canals. Small towns had from 100 to 200 houses; larger ones, like Cumupa and Guaraspi, 500 to 600. At Sahuaripa, a fortified town on the edge of the plains, the Ibarra group encountered a force of 600 warriors, who, with their women and children, made up perhaps 2000 individuals. Sahuaripa was a strong town built with the east and west sides surrounded by deep ravines. According to Obregón, "at

the end of this barranca there is a fortress of four houses in a large square with large strong mud walls surrounding a large patio" (p. 161). Another member of the Ibarra party, Antonio Ruíz (PSM), also speaks of many flat-roofed (or terraced) houses ("mucho caseria toda de terrado") with square narrow streets and defensive walls.

On his return trip to the coast, Ibarra visited the valleys of Pinebaroca and Paibatuco "which are on the upriver portion of the Yaquimi and border on those of Huparo" (p. 230). These valleys contain "numerous towns [pueblos] and a settled and friendly people" (p. 230). The people of Pinebaroca and Paibatuco (their valley seems also to have been called Pipa) were enemies both of the valley of Señora group and of the Yaqui (p. 230). This statement suggests that these places should be located somewhere in the middle Yaqui, perhaps along the Moctezuma River (which the word Paibatuco also suggests).

Following the retreat of Ibarra, there is no information on the Serrana area until the early seventeenth century. By that time the population seems to have gone back to living in rancherias (Spicer 1962:91-93). What caused this change is unclear, but as I noted earlier, population decline was surely an important factor. The warlike statelets of the sixteenth century are simply not found in the seventeenth century when valley after valley of Opata and Pima Bajo Indians eagerly accepted the Jesuits and all that missionization implied. By the mid-eighteenth century, Pfefferkorn, a perceptive Jesuit observer, could say the following about the natives of Sonora:

The unconverted Sonorans did not lead a community life. Even those who belonged to a tribe and spoke the same language had no formal and true villages, but lived scattered throughout vast regions. Only the nearest of kin associated with one another. Here and there a few households lived together, depending upon the fertility of the region. However, no one had pre-eminence in these societies, none had the right to command, and none could punish. All were equal in rank, and each managed according to his pleasure. This is still true of the unconverted Sonorans (Treutlein 1949:174).

This is a far cry from the sophisticated Sonoran statelets of the mid-sixteenth century. By Pfefferkorn's time even the memory of a Sonora of towns and provinces and of far-flung trade routes and relations with other peoples of the Southwest and beyond seems to have disappeared.

Trade

The importance of trade in the Serrana area was noted by the first Spaniards and commented on by every known expedition which visited the area in the sixteenth century. The reason is clear enough. The statelets lay across the major northern route from western Mesoamerica to the upper Southwest and were, in some ways, the most important part in the redistribution network. The Serrana area came to Spanish attention early in time, in part because of the trade routes. These were followed by Nuño Beltrán de Guzmán in the early 1530s and especially by Guzmán's kinsman, Diego de Guzmán, who in 1533 extended Spanish contact as far as the middle Yaqui River. According to the short accounts left by Diego de Guzmán and by the Second Anonymous reporter (one of the soldiers on the Diego de Guzmán expedition), the Guzmán party followed well-known trails and everywhere was able to obtain guides. On or near the Yaqui River Guzmán was offered clubs set with turquoises and "some bone beads that they trade" (Hedrick and Riley 1976:25). European goods already had entered the trade routes northward; in the Yaqui area, Guzmán found a Huraba- or Tahue-speaking Indian with a Spanish crossbow and various other things, unspecified. This individual may have lived in the Culiacan area, and he seems to have been on some sort of expedition of his own but had been detained by the local natives. The Guzmán party also found Spanish cloth and metal accoutrements called clavos de cintas, which were strung and worn as necklaces and armlets. What these were is unclear. One possibility is horseshoe nails; another is belt buckle pins or studs or possibly even the "jangles" on the fringes of European war-horse armor (p. 37; Di Peso, personal communication). These goods seem to have been taken from the Diego Hurtado de Mendoza party whose vessel had been wrecked in the Fuerte area and whose company, trying to go inland, had been killed (Hedrick and Riley 1976:37). The Guzmán party also found among the Indians of the Sinaloa River a knife, punch, poinard, hammer, file and rasp, and a string of clavos de cintas, presumably all from the Hurtado group (p. 32). On the Fuerte River, swords without handguards, knives, clavos de cintas, cloth, and other things were found. The interesting thing is that Hurtado and his party had been killed only a few months before; yet by the fall of 1533 goods taken from them were spread at least from the Mayo to the Sinaloa rivers, a distance of well over 100 km. The Spanish material continued to spread. In 1536 the Cabeza de Vaca (1555:fol. xlvi) party, somewhere in the Sonora or Yaqui drainage, saw an Indian with a necklace made up of a sword belt buckle and a horseshoe nail.

In spite of a deep penetration the Guzmán party accomplished very little, for basically it was a slaving operation, and contact with the Indians was hostile. The slaving groups continued their activities for some years, and in the period between 1533 and 1536 there was a considerable depopulation of the northern Tahue and Cahitan areas because of slave raids.

In the year 1536 Alvar Nuñez Cabeza de Vaca and his three companions entered northwest Mexico from the east, crossing the Sierra Madre Occidental and reaching either the middle Sonora or the middle Yaqui Valley. There the group discovered the town(s) and province of Corazones and also clearly intersected (and certainly traveled for some distance along) the major trade route from western Mesoamerica to the Southwest. In the Corazones area, as we have seen, Cabeza de Vaca found towns with considerable populations. At Corazones the party was given cotton mantas, beads, and corals, all from the South Sea (Gulf of California), and "fine turquoises" from the north as well as five "emerald" arrowheads used in ceremonials. The arrowheads and turquoise came from a mountainous area to the north where there were populous towns and very large houses. Vaca also received a bison hide from this area (Hammond and Rey 1940:149). The people at Corazones traded parrot plumes and feathers for the northern materials (Cabeza de Vaca 1555:fol. xlv). In the Joint Report it is stated that "many turquoises" came through barter. The Indians of the north had much food and cotton. The Vaca party received a rattle and cotton blankets that had been traded from the Pueblo area (Hedrick and Riley 1974:63).

According to Tello (1891:324-325), the Vaca party spoke of a very large province of Tzibola with seven cities of six or seven stories and doors adorned with jeweled stones. It seems likely that Tello is mixing up the accounts of Vaca and of Marcos de Niza--the latter man seems to have actually introduced the name "Cibola"--but the point is that Vaca in the Serrana area did get a fairly accurate account of the Pueblo country several hundred kilometers away.

The "emeralds" given Vaca at Corazones have long intrigued scholars (unfortunately, they were lost on the trip to Culiacan). Elsewhere (1976b:26), I have suggested that they were probably made of peridot from the Zuni area.

The Vaca trip led to an increased interest in the north of New Spain, especially the region of emeralds and turquoise. In 1539 Father Marcos de Niza and the Black slave from the Vaca party, Esteban de Dorantes, led a party, which certainly

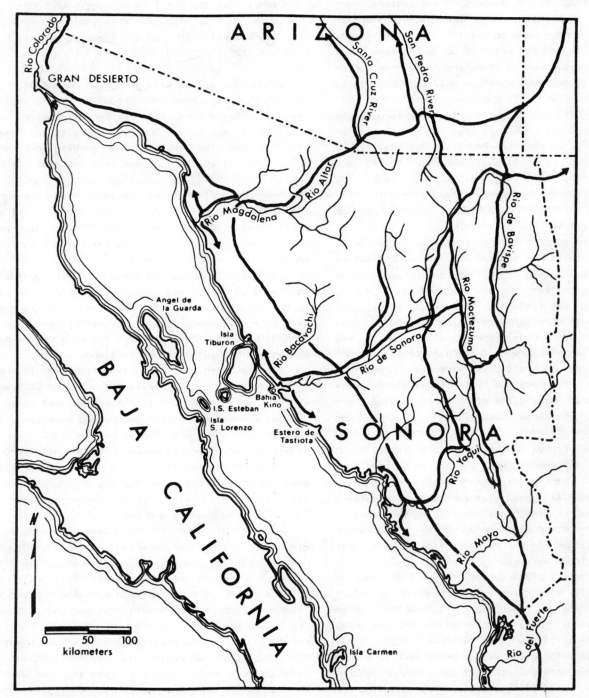

Figure 7.   Major Trade Routes in Sonora, A.D. 1500.

included some Pima Bajo Indians (Riley 1971:293), into the Southwest. My own analysis of the Marcos journey has Marcos traveling near the coast and eventually reaching the Piman-speaking Indians, perhaps Hímeri or Piato, in the Altar-Magdelena drainage, where Marcos came across the "town" of Vacapa. Marcos intercepted the trail from the Serrana country to the Pueblo region somewhere in extreme northern Sonora or extreme southern Arizona, perhaps in the San Pedro River Valley (Riley 1980a:44-45). On his trip to Cibola, Marcos journeyed on through the Pima Alto country, perhaps visiting rancherias of the Sobaipuri on the San Pedro. Eventually, he reached Cibola, or at least came near to it, and then retreated, following the same trail back. On his return journey Marcos may have reached the middle section of the Sonora River, but he did not investigate it for any distance.

Though he skirted the Serrana region, Marcos in his account tells us a great deal about the active trade that was moving north from the Serrana country and south into that region. According to Marcos (Hammond and Rey 1940:68), his first significant news of Cibola came three days' journey from Vacapa. Then, for an additional six-day journey, Marcos was among the Pima of extreme southern Arizona, and during those days he heard of a very rich trade from Cibola with turquoises and bison hides going south. He was offered many gifts of both items plus "very fine vases" ("xicaras muy lindas") (Pacheco and Cárdenas 1864-1884:Vol. 3, 337). Marcos continued to see these riches in turquoises and tanned bison hides, "two thousand" of the latter, as he continued northward. It is unfortunate that Marcos only reported materials going southward and southwestward on the trade routes, not mentioning the shells, feathers, and other items going north. Of course he was commissioned to report on cities in the north and not on trade as such.

The Melchior Díaz journey of the same year as Marcos' (1539) also gives a certain amount of information on trade and other contacts from the Cibolan area southward. Díaz went beyond the Serrana area, reaching Chichilticale (ICC testimony of Zaldívar). However, the information Díaz brought back to Mexico may well have been collected at Corazones or Señora. Wherever he was, Díaz received very detailed and strikingly correct accounts of Cibola. He talked to people who had lived at Cibola for fifteen or twenty years. He had circumstantial reports of the death of Esteban which had happened only a few months before. In fact, one of the Indians who had been with Esteban and who was a captive at Cibola had returned from that land and was interviewed by Díaz. One curious fact that Díaz mentioned was

"animals resembling large Castilian hounds. These they shear, and with their hair they make colored wigs, which they wear, like the one I am sending your Lordship. They also use this hair in the clothes which they make" (Hammond and Rey 1940:158).

Since Díaz was able to get hold of one of these "wigs," they may have been traded. It is unclear what they really were (for further discussion, see Chapters VII and IX). The Cibolans also had "small glassy stones like the one I am sending your lordship, and of which you have seen so many in New Spain" (p. 159). Perhaps Díaz here is talking of the "emeralds" like those traded in from the north that were collected by Vaca in Corazones. If so, Díaz' "glassy stones," like Vaca's "emeralds," were most likely pieces of peridot working their way south along the trade routes.

In 1540 Coronado followed the trade routes northward to Cibola and beyond. In Señora he collected an interpreter who could speak the language of Cibola and used him in the latter province to demand that the Cibolans accept the rule of the King of Spain (ICC, Juan Troyano testimony).

What the Spaniards clearly established in their first decade of contact with the Greater Southwest was that well-marked trails ran up the west coast of Mexico, across the Sonoran desert and mountains, and through southern New Mexico and Arizona to the Pueblo area. The old Hohokam region also entered into this trade partnership, and in the Gila-Salt area the trade routes split; one major one ran to the Gulf of California, while another continued on to the Serrana country and beyond.

Other trails ran to the lower Colorado area. Alarcón, on the lower Colorado River in 1540, had news of Cibola, found people with whom his Piman interpreters could converse (Riley 1971:302), and noted a number of trade materials that connected the lower Colorado not only with the Serrana but with the upper Southwest and with the Pacific Coast of California. For a detailed treatment of trade in the lower Colorado region and its implications for interaction with the Greater Southwest, see Chapter VIII. Let me say here, however, that I have demonstrated the existence of trails from the Serrana to and from the lower Colorado (1976b:24, Map 1). The major trail is generally considered to have crossed the northwest Sonoran Desert (Ives 1936:89, 1959:33), but I have suggested that this major route probably ran from the Sonora-Yaqui Valley region northward to the San Pedro and/or the Santa Cruz, to the Gila, and then westward (1976b:24-25).

Archaeological evidence for the use of major

trade routes through the Serrana country comes from various directions. In the region itself archaeological projects are in their beginning stages, but already Pailes (1978:140, 1980:35) is able to document the movement of trade into the San José site in the upper middle Sonora Valley, trade that includes wares from southern Arizona and from Casas Grandes--paint cloisonné, marine shell, and copper objects, as well as turquoise from Cerrillos and the Azure site, both in New Mexico. These have not been firmly dated, but a post-A.D. 1300 date for at least some of the material is feasible (Pailes, personal communication). At Hawikuh, a parrot burial and the utilization of parrot and macaw motifs on late prehistoric pottery (Riley 1975b:148) indicate contact with the south--an archaeological demonstration of the Cabeza de Vaca information of parrot feathers traded for turquoise. Parrots and macaws, or representations of these birds, are found at other sites that date from the fourteenth through the sixteenth centuries, at Pottery Mound (Hibben 1966:526-527), at Kuaua (Dutton 1963b:116 ff.), at Pecos (Kidder 1932:196), and at Pindi (Stubbs and Stallings 1953:126-127), among others. On the other side of the Serrana area, turquoise has been reported from Guasave (Ekholm 1942:100), though here the supplier may have been Casas Grandes rather than the Serrana area. More intriguing is Largo Glaze on Yellow, a Glaze B type from the middle Rio Grande found at the citadel of the Atitlan-Las Cuevas site in the Etzatlan area of western Jalisco. This glazed pottery dates from about A.D. 1400 to 1450 (Weigand 1976:3-5, 1980). The Etzatlan area lies across the major late pre-Spanish and early contact trail that led from Tarascan country and the region of Jalisco and Colima through Nayarit, Sinaloa, and Sonora to the Serrana area and the Pueblo world beyond.

Perhaps with the exception of the Las Casas account, the most detailed information on the Serrana area comes from the reports of Baltasar de Obregón and Antonio Ruíz, members of the Ibarra expedition of 1564-1565, accounts which I have used very extensively above. The Ruíz account is rather short, but it speaks in some detail of the richness of the Señora and Corazones area (PSM) though it has very little information on trade as such. Obregón, on the other hand, gives a great deal of information. Beginning at Oera in the southern portion of the Serrana region, Obregón says:

They have many slaves imprisoned in wooden stocks [con armas de madera]. They barter these slaves for others and sell them for mantas, salt, feathers, and for provisions, especially salt which they do not possess . . . . They have large

numbers of large and small parrots and large eagles and eaglets in cages (Cuevas 1924:146-147).

The people of Oera were involved in various kinds of relationships with neighboring groups. They were intermittently at war with the peoples of Cinaro (in the Fuerte Valley), Corazones, Guaraspi, and Cumupa. There were obviously other kinds of relationships, for the people of Oera supplied guides and provisions as far as Cinaro to the south and Señora to the north. The statelets could also unite militarily. From Oera, Ibarra's party followed the trail to Señora. Along the way in this four-day journey people from towns and villages on or near the route swarmed to barter food for glass and iron objects (p. 145). The Señorans were enemies of the people of Oera and of the Uparo (Seri) Indians of the coast. They especially desired salt and female slaves and carried on wars to get these items. No doubt, like the Oerans, they also traded for them; in fact, trade for salt survived the Jesuit occupation of Sonora and continued to be important into the eighteenth century (Riley 1976b:32).

The exact relation of the warlike Uparo with the Serrana peoples is not very clear. The two areas may well have been involved in a salt and shell trade as well as in warfare. In 1540, when Coronado was at Corazones, he was told that the sea was five days' journey to the west. Coronado summoned Indians from the coastal area and obtained information about coastal lands. When the main Coronado army reached the Corazones-Señora region later in that same year, a party was sent out to the Gulf and brought back an enormous Indian who was probably a Seri (Hammond and Rey 1940:209). Though the comments of Coronado and his captains are not very informative, they do indicate that there was a well-marked trail from Corazones and Señora to the Seri country on the coast.

By Ibarra's time, at any rate, the Uparo had a bad reputation for mistreating war captives. As his information came from the Serrana area, it is obvious that interaction between the coast and inland was common enough, albeit often unfriendly. Ibarra's men, probably while in the Señora Valley, learned that the famous "poison tree" (see Warfare, below) was known as far as the Mayo River on the south and as far as Cibola and Chichilticale on the north (Cuevas 1924:155; Hammond and Rey 1928:170-171). This is an indication of contact and interchange of knowledge, not of botanical distribution, for the tree seems to have grown only in the Serrana area.

As the Ibarra party advanced to Guaraspi and then on eastward, its members continued to barter with the townspeople on the way (Cuevas 1924:157). Both Guaraspi and Cumupa, five days' march to the east, were in touch with the Querechos, bison-hunting peoples who lived east of the mountains (that is, on the plains of northern Chihuahua). At Cumupa the party found that the inhabitants had just defeated a party of Querechos and had taken booty and slaves (pp. 157-158). Later in the Sahuaripa area a federation of Serrana statelets gathered 2000 warriors, the advance guard of some 15,000 which they had planned to throw against the Ibarra party. The Indians were defeated (p. 168), but news of the battle was carried by signal fire, reaching Cinaro (which Obregón overestimated as 300 leagues from Sahuaripa) within two days (pp. 171-172).

The Ibarra expedition represented the last Spanish contact with the Sonoran statelets. When the Jesuits pushed northward into Sonora in the first decades of the seventeenth century there seems to have been a return to a somewhat simpler rancheria life. It is clear from the seventeenth century records that there was still a great deal of contact up and down the sierra and between the sierra groups and those of the coast. Evidence for the warlike Serrana groups, however, is largely lacking. It is the Yaqui and other coastal peoples who struggled with the Spaniards--a struggle that the Yaqui especially carried on with considerable success. The groups in the mountain valleys of the Sonora and Yaqui rivers welcomed priests, and, during the seventeenth and eighteenth centuries, the Opata became model converts. The drastic change over a period of little more than half a century may have more than one explanation, but as I have noted (see Population, above), the drop-off in numbers was real and surely was an important factor. Another contributing situation very likely was that Spanish impingement to the east and especially to the Pueblo area to the north disrupted the trade routes. These routes, in any case, had been largely "beheaded" by the Spanish destruction of the native civilizations of Mesoamerica.

All this, of course, was in the future in Ibarra's day. From the Obregón information one can form a reasonably accurate picture of the trade patterns in the Serrana. In the 1560s Oera was an important center. The town and its surrounding valley were well known at least as far south as Cinaro in the Fuerte Valley (Cuevas 1924:139-145). Oera not only acted as a redistribution center for trade but, clearly, was in the business of manufacturing parrot and macaw feathers for the trade northward. From Oera, slaves were bought and sold, some of them probably coming from Cumupa and Guaraspi. Cotton garments were common and certainly part of the trade picture. At Oera the Indians were richly dressed

with beads (shell? turquoise?), feather crests, conches (carocoles), and pearl-bearing shell-- the latter two items traded from the sea, presumably the Gulf of California. The trade in foodstuffs is documented for Oera (p. 146), and indeed the eagerness of the Indians to trade food to the Spaniards for exotic goods suggests that this may have been a common practice. Desire of the Indians specifically for iron articles suggests that iron had already entered the trade network from the south. It is interesting that iron was found a generation later by Chamuscado's party near La Junta at the junction of the Conchos and Rio Grande (Hammond and Rey 1966:77). Chamuscado also found red and white coral and turquoise at La Junta which, according to the natives, came "from the direction of the sea," that is, from the west (p. 76). I have suggested elsewhere (1976b:34) that these items perhaps came through middlemen from the Pueblo region, but for the coral, at any rate, trade from the Serrana area is a strong possibility. The same is true of the piece of copper and the copper bead found in this area (Hammond and Rey 1966:76). Of course the copper may have been retraded from Ibarra who had a variety of gift and trade items including glass beads, iron articles, blankets, and "trinkets," or dijes (Cuevas 1924:142, 145, 147).

While at Oera, Ibarra received news of the Pueblo area (p. 146), and at Paquimé on the northeastern fringe of the Serrana country he was again told of Pueblo Indians (p. 186).

Other important centers for trade were Guaraspi and Cumupa, both of which were in or near the Señora Valley. Like the people of Oera, those of the Señora region traded for salt and for slaves and carried on wars for these commodities (p. 149). The Señorans were able to provide a guide and interpreter when Ibarra moved onto the plains somewhere in the region of Casas Grandes. This man, according to Obregón (p. 177), could also understand the language(s) of the Pueblo Indians; his flight was one of the reasons why Ibarra turned back to the coast. On the return voyage Ibarra reached Batuco where the army obtained a great quantity of salt, their supply having given out (p. 230).

The picture, then, is one of a very active trading area and one in which the Pueblo Indians continued to be important as they had been in the days of Cabeza de Vaca thirty years before. The interaction network was still very much in operation in Ibarra's day.

It would be of immense value to a study of sixteenth century trade if we could make out the mechanics of the trading operation. Unfortunately, the Serrana area, even more than some parts of the upper Southwest, has information that is either equivocal or missing altogether. We do know that traders and/or trading parties reached the Serrana from farther north (Cabeza de Vaca 1555:fol. xlv). It seems likely also that parties from the south regularly reached the Serrana, though by the time we have documentary evidence the rich southern area had been wantonly disrupted by the Spaniards. There are, of course, many indications of contacts between the Serrana and west Mexico: the appearance of Spanish chickens in early Sonora; Indian traders from Culiacan found in the Yaqui area (Hedrick and Riley 1976:24); archaeological discovery of southwestern trade goods in Jalisco (Weigand 1976:3-4) and in Sinaloa (Ekholm 1942:100, 111); the gifts of beads, turquoise, and feathers given the Vaca party in the Petatlán area; and the obvious, close personal contacts between the Serrana peoples and those to the south (Cabeza de Vaca 1555:fol. xlix). It is clear that the trade route was flourishing—indeed was a kind of "camino real"—well beyond the time of first Spanish contact.

In the ethnohistorical sources there are no indications of barrios, or special sections of towns given over to traders, as was the case in parts of Mesoamerica. We should, of course, not depend too much on negative evidence. Towns like Oera, Guaraspi, and Cumupa were certainly large enough to have separate quarters for trade parties, and, indeed, such special areas are documented for the sixteenth century pueblo of Pecos—though the situation there was somewhat special (see Chapter XI). Hopefully, the future archaeology of the Serrana sites will shed some light on this situation.

The social organization of the trading parties is not known. The description of trade at Oera makes one suspect that the province leaders may have had a hand in the operation, but it would be chancy to draw on the conventional chiefdomship-redistribution model, especially since the Serrana trading partners to the north (the Pueblo area) certainly utilized an entrepreneurial redistribution system where there were no chiefdoms but where individuals, families, clans, or societal groups, as well as pueblos as a whole, seem to have engaged in trade (Riley 1975b, 1976b, 1978a, 1980a). A possible argument for centralized control in the Serrana area might be the range of materials traded; it included basic foodstuffs, manufactured goods, esoteric ceremonial and luxury items, and slaves. The trading of slaves usually (or always?) obtained in warfare suggests a close link between the political and economic subsystems in the Serrana, but the nature of that link remains quite obscure.

In examining and applying trade models taken from the historic literature we need be very cautious indeed. A great many scholars describe trading activities in the prehistoric and early historic Greater Southwest by using the word pochteca, or puchteca. The pochteca were, of course, a complex and still incompletely understood guild or class of traders among the Aztecs. There is very little evidence that peoples from Anahuac were involved in southwestern trade in the sixteenth century though they may have been so involved at an earlier time. The Tejo story (Hammond and Rey 1940:195) of Castañeda sounds a bit pochteca-like, and it might actually be a distorted memory of a trade route to Casas Grandes—or even Chaco Canyon—from the east of Mexico (see also Riley 1976b:13-14 and Chapter III, this volume).

All mesoamerican trade to the Southwest in the sixteenth century came via western Mexico, and Tarascans may have had an important hand. In this regard it would be well to consider the comments of Lumholtz (1902:Vol. 2, 368-369) concerning Tarascans trading in the nineteenth century. These traders developed a vast network; Lumholtz met a Tarascan trader among the northern Tepehuan of Chihuahua. In former times the Tarascans made their way as far north as New Mexico and Arizona and as far south and east as Guatemala and Yucatan. The traders traveled in groups of from two or three to as many as thirty individuals, especially in the sierra. Goods were transported on the back, and the traders always carried a staff. This latter practice is interesting, for pochteca traders always carried ceremonial staffs, and pre-Columbian depictions of traders in the Southwest often show staffs. As Lister (1978:238) points out, some 375 canes were found in one room at Pueblo Bonito in Chaco Canyon. The Tarascan traders of the nineteenth century traded a great variety of objects, including live birds, cotton cloth, foodstuffs, maguey-fiber rope, manufactured items, etc. (Lumholtz 1902:Vol. 2, 367-370).

I suspect that the trade in the sixteenth century Greater Southwest was somewhat closer to the entrepreneurial Tarascan model, or perhaps the rather informal pueblo-wide organization described by Bandelier for the nineteenth century Rio Grande pueblos (Lange and Riley 1966:99-102), than to the more formalized pochteca. Eventually, archaeology and perhaps the discovery of new archival or other documentary sources will clarify and add information about the widespread implications—economic, religious, political, social, technological, perhaps even linguistic—of mesoamerican-southwestern trade.

Sociopolitical Organization

There is only scattered information on the social and political uses of the Serrana. In some cases the Spaniards were very observant as to social customs. For example, a number of explorers starting with Cabeza de Vaca (1555:fol. xlv) point out that women in this region were dressed quite modestly in long garments of cotton and deer skin in contrast to the nudity found in the rancheria area farther south. These same Spaniards, however, tended to ignore family, town, and state organization.

Marcos' account has a fair amount of information on the political organization of the Cibola, Marata, Totonteac, and Acus areas. His information is certainly incorrect for the Pueblo area, but if Marcos is actually reporting the situation of the Serrana region (as I have suggested, 1976a:28-29), his information may be useful. Marcos talks of independent kingdoms, often at war with one another. Of these, Totonteac, toward the southwest, was the largest. In the various provinces there were lords who appointed rulers for the various cities contained in their domains (Hammond and Rey 1940:71-74).

There is no great amount of information from the Díaz expedition of 1539. Díaz himself says very little of the Serrana where he spent the winter of 1539-1540. During the Coronado expedition proper, Castañeda as usual gives the largest amount of information. He talks of the "principal men" of the towns in the province of Señora (p. 232). Also in Señora "the dignitaries of the pueblos stand on some terraces which they have for that purpose and remain there for one hour, calling like town criers, instructing the people in what they are to do" (p. 250).

Las Casas and Obregón give the most information generally on both the social and political organization of the Serrana. Las Casas speaks of a "lord and King" of Señora who also was involved in temple sacrifices at the main temple of the kingdom. In this large stone and adobe structure there were dessicated bodies of dead rulers (see below). This temple was in the city of Señora which was the political capital in the valley of Señora (Riley 1976a:20-21).

When the Ibarra party was approaching Oera, they received a delegation of twenty well-dressed Indians who spoke "in the names of the inhabitants and head men [vecinos y mandones] of Oera" (Cuevas 1924:145). This group was authorized to commit both supplies and warriors (the latter to be used to attack people of Cinaro with whom the Oerans were often at war).

When Ibarra reached Oera, he was met by a party of 400 Indians dressed in ceremonial clothing who exchanged gifts with the Spaniards. Another 400 Indians met the Ibarra party when, led by Oeran guides, it entered the valley of Señora (pp. 146-148). In the next few days the Indians demonstrated a high level of political organization when they plotted against Ibarra and were able to raise 15,000 men, drawn from various towns and provinces (p. 168). "The league and assembly of Indians was called with many messengers and a number of high smoke columns" (p. 171).

There seems to have been some interdigitation of the religious and the political leadership. According to Obregón:

> They have their preachers and persuaders [predicadores y movedores] of their idolatries and wars. They do this with such attention, ferver and shouting, that many times it happens that they fall to the ground, fainting from their zeal, concentration and shouting. This office is given to the most important captains and leaders [capitanes y mandones] (p. 174).

This comment is rather interesting for it seems to parallel the strong influence of native shamans in the slightly later Indian rebellions farther south in the Sierra Madre Occidental. See for example the account of the Tepehuan War of 1616-1618 (Hackett 1923-1937:Vol. 2, 100-114). I am not at all sure that the situations are parallel, however, and indeed the context of Obregón suggests that instead of religious leaders of the shaman type serving a military function, they may have been civil and military leaders serving a religious function.

Unfortunately we have all too little sixteenth century information on political organization in the Serrana. Data on such things as kinship organization and marriage patterns are even more scanty. Obregon does make a few observations at Oera: "They have four and five wives and do not use those who are pregnant or nursing babies until the child is two years of age. They punish those who break this law" (Cuevas 1924:146).

There are other scattered indications of sexual mores. In the seventeenth century Father Antonio Tello, utilizing the Coronado-period Tovar account (now lost), does mention that in the valleys of Corazones and Sonora (Señora) are found transvestites, "boys in women's dress with their eyes painted" (1891:414). Transvestites are also mentioned by Castañeda (Hammond and Rey 1940:251), though without detail. Obregón believed that there

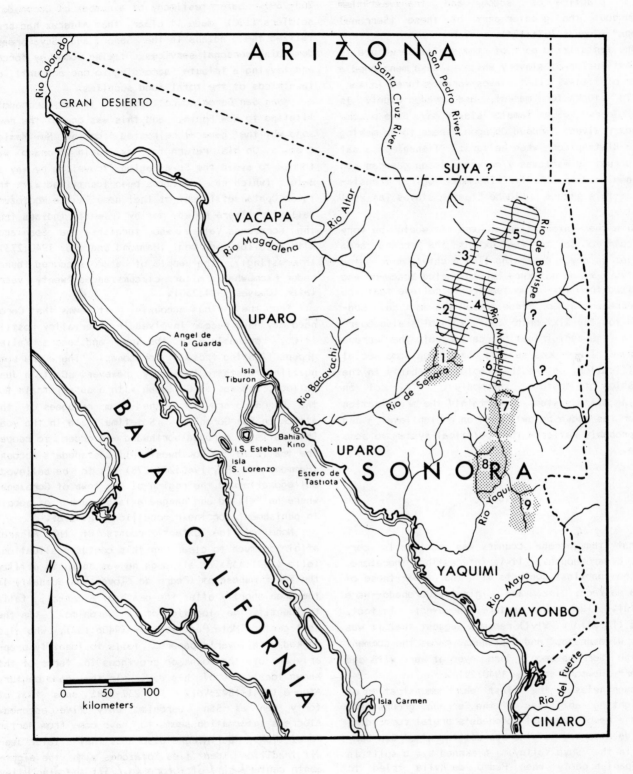

STATELETS *

1 Corazones	4 Cumupa	7 Pinebaroca
2 Señora	5 Sahuaripa	8 Paibatuco
3 Guaraspi	6 Batuco	9 Oera

* Boundaries arbitrary

⧄ Opata speaking

▨ Mixed Opata-Pima
or Pima speaking

Figure 8. Possible Location of the Sonoran Statelets, A.D. 1500.

was a practice of sodomy and transvestitism "throughout the greater part of these [Serrana] regions" (Cuevas 1924:174).

One tantalizing part of the social structure is the institution of slavery which I have mentioned a number of times. That slaves were captured in war, held in stocks for market, and traded widely is quite clear. Some female slaves may have become secondary wives; indeed Obregón seems to be making such a distinction when he says: "Tienen poca sal por la cual y esclavas y mujeres traen guerras con sus enemigos" (p. 149). The most logical translation of this phrase would be "female slaves [as well as] wives."

With the information at hand it would be very difficult to say to what extent the Serrana area had, let us say, something like a chiefdom-oriented society. We do not know who directed trade or who benefited from it. I am tempted to believe that the "entrepreneurial" or "free trade" system I have suggested for the sixteenth century Pueblos also operated in the redistribution centers of the Serrana country. There does seem to have been some social stratification, unlike the Pueblos, and hints in the discussion of costume, ceremonies, etc., of an emerging class system. Certainly the organization for war (as shown below) was on a high level, and this probably reflects the political system to some degree.

Warfare

That the Serrana country was warlike is certainly clear enough. It is interesting, therefore, that the earliest contacts with the area--those of Cabeza de Vaca, Díaz, and originally Coronado--were peaceful. There was warfare, however; in fact, Vaca's (1555:fol. xlvi) remarks suggest that it was rather widespread, and Castañeda makes the comment that the Serrana people "are ever at war with one another" (Hammond and Rey 1940:251).

Nevertheless, the first real demonstration of the fighting abilities of the Serrana groups came with the revolt against Coronado's brutal commander, Diego de Alcaráz, at the new settlement of San Gerónimo in the Suya Valley. Weakened by a split in the Spanish party when Pedro de Avila tried to return to San Miguel de Culiacan, Alcaráz lost several of his men to hostile Indian activity in certain unidentified "pueblos" presumably somewhere in the Serrana area. Alcaráz was then attacked and killed by the Suya Indians, and survivors fled to Corazones, where they were helped with provisions allowing them to escape southward to San Miguel (pp.

268-269). Later testimony of a number of Coronado's soldiers (ICC) made it clear that Alcaráz had brutalized the Indians in the Señora and Suya areas, demanding personal services, taking women by force, and levying a tribute (according to one account) of two-thirds of the total food supplies.

When San Gerónimo collapsed, it cut Coronado's lifeline to New Spain, and this was one of the reasons why the general retreated from the New Mexico area. On his return to New Spain Coronado was forced to avoid the Suya region, traveling by way of Batuco (which has sometimes been identified with the later Opata settlement of that name in the Moctezuma Valley). There he was met by friendly Indians from the Corazones Valley who furnished the Spaniards with supplies and men (Hammond and Rey 1940:273). Interestingly, the people of Batuco succored Ibarra under somewhat similar circumstances twenty years later (Cuevas 1924:230).

From the various accounts, it seems that Coronado may have become involved in intervalley hostilities, probably with the Suya and Señora Valley groups fighting those of Corazones. There are some puzzling twists to the story, however. Captain Juan Gallego, who was at Culiacan with a supply train for the Coronado army, learned from refugees of the attack on San Gerónimo. Sometime late in the year 1541 Gallego marched northward in order to reopen the trails to the Southwest. If Castañeda's account (Hammond and Rey 1940:277-278) is to be believed, Gallego attacked the region of the town of Corazones where he "killed and hanged a large number of people in punishment for their rebellion" (p. 278).

None of the extant accounts of the Alcaráz affair do much to clear up this confused situation. Tello (1891:438), although he was able to utilize the Tovar manuscipt (Pedro de Tovar was actually in the area shortly after the death of Alcaráz), fails to identify the location of San Gerónimo. In the next century Mota Padilla (Day 1940b:107), who also worked with Tovar's papers, fails to identify properly any of the towns or provinces in terms of the known localities of his day. In the same century Alegre (1841-1842:Vol. 1, 237-238) says that of forty men at San Gerónimo only five escaped. Alegre's information seems to have come from Martín Pérez (PSM), but Alegre also adds that a later Jesuit tradition identifies Corazones with the eighteenth century site of Yecora (p. 237; see also Riley and Hedrick 1976:247-248). Obregón, who actually saw the ruins of San Gerónimo, states that Diego de Alcaráz had 100 settlers, most of whom apparently were killed. San Gerónimo was "in the province of the valleys of Señora and Corazones," and a few lines later Obregón seems to locate the settlement in the Señora Valley (Cuevas 1924:147-148). The inhabitants of the valley of Señora, intoxicated by their victory over Alcaráz, now wished (according to Obregón) to attack and loot the Ibarra party (p. 151).

In all this confusion of identities, what seems to emerge is that Alcaráz, by his outrageous behavior, did indeed trigger a rebellion in the Suya and/or Señora valley(s). The Spaniards seem to have benefited by Indian intergroup hostility, for they were succored by other polities, one of which was Batuco and another was probably Corazones. In such a case we are left with the problem of Gallego's behavior toward Corazones. Perhaps the town changed its alliance (or perhaps Castañeda simply had his places confused!). The important thing is that the Spaniards had both allies and enemies, an indication that the statelets felt their own internal quarrels to be more important than unity against the Europeans.

The Ibarra expedition gives us most of our information about warfare in the Serrana. If Obregón is to be believed, each statelet considered itself to be surrounded by enemies. This did not in any way hinder the active trade, the movement of envoys, guides, and interpreters throughout the area and the formation of a widespread confederation against the Spaniards. Although he was met with friendship in the Oera region, Ibarra seems to have been generally badly received from the time he reached the Señora Valley. Although he won the battles, Ibarra clearly lost the war. Against the federation of the entire northern Serrana he felt it necessary to move on eastward. On returning, Ibarra attempted to avoid the Señora anti-Spanish alliance, and for the most part he succeeded, finally escaping--after weeks of terrible hardships--to the lower Yaqui Valley. That Oera was not quite as friendly as Obregón believed is suggested by the signal system that reached (surely with Oeran help) as far as Cinaro on the Fuerte River.

From the Obregón accounts (pp. 246-248), it is obvious that the Spaniards intruded themselves into a situation of chronic warfare, and in fighting the Ibarra forces the Indians were simply continuing normal activities. Part of the Oeran friendliness was clearly due to an attempt to get Spanish help against the people of Cinaro, and the willingness of Oera to supply guides and supplies as Ibarra moved into Señora also probably should be looked at in terms of Serrana diplomacy. One suspects that toward the end, the people of Oera decided (wisely enough) that Ibarra represented a greater threat than Cinaro and Señora.

Warfare in the Serrana area was carried on with considerable skill and sophistication. War parties in the hundreds or even in the thousands were known

(pp. 145, 157, 161, 168). The Indian warriors used bows and arrows, spears and darts of brazilwood, clubs, and shields (pp. 146, 148). There were fortress towns. Castañeda (Hammond and Rey 1940:232) mentions one on a prominence, a town called Valle de los Vellacos. Sahuaripa was another fortress. It was built on the crest of a ravine and had substantial walled buildings. One method of fighting was to hurl stones and shoot arrows from the walls of the fortress (Cuevas 1924:179-181). Hostilities lasted for a long enough time that there were special food preparations and provisions for warfare (p. 149). Eventually archaeological studies should allow us to say more about these fortress towns. A site in the Baserac area of the upper Yaqui drainage was visited by Bandelier in April 1884, and his description sounds something like that of Obregón for Sahuaripa (Lange and Riley 1970:277-278; Bandelier 1890-1892:Vol. 1, 59).

One special technique used in Serrana warfare was that of arrow poison from a shrublike tree. This poison was noted with awe and fear by virtually every Spanish party that entered the area in the sixteenth century. It is commented on by Cabeza de Vaca (1555:fol. xlvi), Jaramillo (Hammond and Rey 1940:297), Juan de Contreras and Juan de Paradinas (ICC), Castañeda (Hammond and Rey 1940:232, 273) in some detail, Juan Ruíz (PSM), and Obregón (Cuevas 1924:155-156) in great detail. In addition, many of the later writers on the Sonoran area discuss the poison tree (see, for example, Guiteras 1951:48; Lombardo 1702:fol. 7). The tree, which exuded a milky sap, was called mago in Opata and, according to the Rudo ensayo (Guiteras 1951:48), was also called "hierba de la flecha." It was used not only in warfare but also as a fish poison, the branches being broken and the bark crushed and put in still pools of water.

Beyond doubt this tree was one of the family Euphorbiaceae. Yerba de la Flecha, among the modern Tarahumar (Pennington 1963:108), is the term given to two of the Euphors, Sebastiana pringlei and Sapium biloculare, both currently used as piscicides. Among the Pima Bajo of Onavas, the name yerba de la flecha is given to Sebastiana appendiculatum and is also used to stupify fish (Pennington 1980:217). Today Sapium is found in the Serrana area, and Sebastiana at least on the edge of it (Shreve and Wiggins 1964:807, 809). There are, however, twenty-one genera of Euphorbiaceae in the Sonoran area and, given the fear and horror with which the Spaniards regarded the tree and its poison sap, one suspects that the Serrana poison came from a more virulent example of the family Euphorbiaceae than the ones utilized by the Tarahumar. In addition, as was indicated previously, the poison tree seemed more or less restricted to the Serrana area area area though its fame had spread from the Pueblos on the north to Indians of Sinaloa on the south.

Religion

The religion of the Serrana is known only from scattered remarks by the Spanish explorers, most of whom had very little interest in the Indian culture and who, in any event, generally regarded the religion with hostility. Two things do stand out, however. The Serrana people had a religion with a strong solar aspect; and animal hearts, especially deer hearts, were utilized in sacrifices (Cabeza de Vaca 1555:fol. xlvi; Cuevas 1924:146; Riley 1976a:20-21). There were special temples; for example, Castañeda, in referring to the Señora Valley, speaks of "temples in small houses, into which they drive numerous arrows, making them look like porcupines on the outside. They do this when war is about to break out" (Hammond and Rey 1940:250). Las Casas, also speaking of the Señora Valley, mentions "very tall stone and mud temples for idols and for the entombment of principal personages" (Riley 1976a:20). In one temple

> was a stone statue, filled with blood, and around its neck were many animal hearts. Near the statue there were also many dead, dessicated, disembowled human bodies leaning against the walls. They must have been the past lords of the valley, and that was their sepulchre (pp. 20-21).

The keeping of dessicated bodies of leaders is probably unique to the Serrana area, at least in the Greater Southwest. I have suggested elsewhere (1979) that it may have been an outgrowth of seated burials of the Casas Grandes Medio period (see also Di Peso et al. 1974:Vol. 8, 361). As late as 1624 Father Francisco Olindaño reported a shrine among the Aivinos of the Yaqui drainage. An "indio principal" of the group had been killed by lightning some years before. He was seated in his tomb, and the Indians brought offerings which included "cuentas blancas, de que se adornan, de caracolillos de la mar, mantas, plumas de colores y otras cosas que ellos estiman" (Pérez de Ribas 1944:tomo II, lib. VI, cap. X, p. 166).

One of the reasons that Ibarra's party had such success in warfare seems to have been that the Indians identified the discharge of Spanish culverins with thunderbolts and so regarded the Spaniards as "children of the sun" (Cuevas 1924:154, 171). We have already seen how politically important personages also had religious functions, especially in times of war (p. 174).

Other information on the religion comes from Las Casas (Riley 1976a:20). Only animal hearts were sacrificed, and these hearts were used more for sacrifice than for food. The ceremonial year revolved around two great ceremonies, one at the time of sowing and the other at harvest, but there were also other ceremonies at other times of the year. Las Casas also seems to suggest (though the context is not very clear) that the people of Señora were acquainted with the solar ceremonies carried out at Cibola (p. 20). There is some slight indication in the sources that four was a sacred or ceremonial number, and this certainly was true in later mission times (Johnson 1971:189). The number four, of course, is ceremonially important throughout much of the Greater Southwest. Both the sun and the moon continued to be important into later times (p. 189), and as late as the eighteenth century, as noted by Pfefferkorn (Treutlein 1949:224 ff.), descendants of the Serrana peoples continued to pay homage to the sun.

Considering the general sophistication of the Serrana area, by analogy with the Pueblo area—a region with which the Serrana Indians were in close contact—one would suspect that the Serrana groups had native priesthoods. If so, the nature and organization of such priesthoods cannot now be reconstructed except in the most general sort of way. The priests (if such they were) presumably were attached to the temples which, in turn, seem to have been located in most of the large towns. The religious leaders (whether we call them priests or not) directed the ceremonies and perhaps also the funerary rites of rulers or important men, whose bodies were collected at major temples. They also had some function in warfare, but the nature and extent is not known.

General Comments

Many of the culture patterns of the Serrana groups are poorly known. We have very little information on, let us say, the life cycle. The Serrana Indians practiced polygyny, and burial was probably by inhumation, though this latter point needs further archaeological testing. We get a picture of rich town-oriented cultures with relatively dense populations in the valleys and with a surplus of foodstuffs. Trade and warfare were very important in the life of the Serrana peoples. The "world view" encompassed the entire Southwest and beyond.

The Pueblo area was especially important to the life of the Serrana groups, not only in terms of the flood of trade goods that moved back and forth but also for military, political, and perhaps religious reasons that are not very clear today. So important, indeed, was the upper Southwest that the destruction of Pueblo culture toward the end of the sixteenth century must have been a factor, and perhaps an important one, in the collapse of the Serrana in the first part of the seventeenth century. Depopulation was surely another factor.

CHAPTER VII

THE DESERT PROVINCE

Of all the areas of the Greater Southwest--at least those occupied by agricultural peoples--the Desert province is least known. This is somewhat paradoxical, for the region of the Sonoran Desert (particularly the drainages of the middle Gila and Salt rivers) has a rich archaeology with a historical depth of many centuries. There is a sustained and continuing record in certain portions of the Gila Valley, particularly at Snaketown on the Gila River near Florence, Arizona. At Snaketown a sequence of Hohokam cultures began, probably in pre-Christian times (Vahki phase, Pioneer period), and lasted till A.D. 1100-1150 (late Sedentary, early Classic). The archaeological story for the Classic period can be traced in such large nearby sites as Casas Grandes and Los Muertos which were deserted by about A.D. 1450. The sixteenth century, archaeologically, is largely unknown; by the late seventeenth century large sites such as San Cayetano are clearly Piman.

In the region south of the Gila-Salt Basin the same situation is found. The Ceramic and Sedentary Sells phase in the Papagueria ends by perhaps A.D. 1450. There is some archaeological evidence that Sells materials merge into a Papago late prehistoric and early historic phase (Rosenthal et al. 1978:216) though a great deal of archaeology needs to be done on this particular time period and area (Masse 1980, 1981, 1982).

In the Trincheras area of the Altar-Magdalena drainage of western Sonora, riverine sites with associated terraced hills date perhaps to the fourteenth century and may be related to Hohokam (Johnson 1963:182-183; Stacy 1974:25; Di Peso 1979:161; Masse 1980, 1982). Again, securely identified sixteenth century archaeological sites are not available. However, by the seventeenth century the general area was occupied by Piman groups, especially the Hímeri who were first mentioned in 1630 and who at that time seemed to have occupied a number of northwest Sonoran valleys (Sauer 1934:52). Parenthetically, seventeenth century Hímeri seem to have been "enemies of the Opata" (p. 52).

The northern fringe of the Desert province, the shatterzone region of foothills north of the Gila-Salt rising to the highlands of central Arizona, seems to have been largely deserted by the sixteenth century (Spoerl 1979). The southern fringe of the region may have had a transient population of either Piman or Yavapai speakers; on balance, the case for the latter is probably stronger. On the eastern fringe of the Desert province some remnant groups of "late Mimbres" Indians (perhaps groups of the eastern Salado or Cliff phase) may have maintained themselves into the sixteenth century. The weight of present evidence, however, is that the region of southwestern New Mexico was deserted well before Spanish contact times (see LeBlanc 1976:4-6, 1977:1).

Natural Features

The general physiography of the Sonoran Desert has been discussed to some degree in Chapter VI. The region is basically one of contrasting desert and isolated mountain ranges. The mountains rise rather sharply from their gently sloping and often considerably eroded pediments. The mountains in the eastern part of this Basin and Range country often are of considerable height--Mount Graham in the Pinaleno Range of extreme southwestern Arizona reaches 3267 m, while Chiricahua Peak in the Chiricahua Range to the south and east is 2986 m. The eastern basins of the Sonoran Desert are from 600 to 1200 m, but both basins and interdigitated ranges in the western part of the area are lower, the basins sloping down to sea level north of the Gulf of California while the ranges rise from 300 to about 1000 m from the valley floors.

The Sonoran Desert is bordered on the north by a series of uplands which, in areas like east-central Arizona, rise abruptly to the high plateaus of the Mogollon, White, and Gila Mountains. Further west, along the northern boundary of the Gila-Salt, the rise tends to be more gradual to the high country along the Mogollon Rim, which divides the southern Arizona Desert country from the Colorado Plateaus (Merriam 1890:5).

Culturally, this area represents a major division between the desert-oriented cultures of the Hohokam (and later the Pima) and the mountain-oriented Mogollon-Anasazi. In the sixteenth century, however, essential desertion of the central Arizona area, except perhaps by semisedentary or nomadic Indians probably of Yuman speech, sharpened the distinction between the desert settlements and the Cibolan and Tusayan peoples to the north. In the sixteenth century this mountainous country was a despoblado, a wild and deserted region.

The climatic conditions in Sonora (see Chapter VI) also hold to a large degree in the northern and western sections of the Sonoran Desert. The area is for the most part included in Köppen's BWh (arid warm), with portions of the isolated ranges and the mountains and high country that flank the desert to the north and northeast in the BSh (semiarid or warm steppe). Higher regions of these mountains are in the Df (cold, moist winter) zone.

Rainfall in the Arizona portion of the Sonoran Desert is heavier in the east, reaching from 250 to 400 mm in the Salt River area above Roosevelt Lake, in the Gila-San Pedro drainage above Florence, and in the upper Santa Cruz. The average annual rainfall at Tucson is approximately 285 mm per year, while at Phoenix downriver it is a little less than 200 mm. At Gila Bend it drops to about 150 mm annually, and at Yuma on the Colorado River it is about 90 mm. To the south, rainfall totals rise a bit. At Altar, almost directly south of Phoenix, the annual rainfall is about 275 mm, while at Magdalena, nearly on a line south of Tucson, it is some 425 mm. In addition, the mountainous country south and east of Nogales, in which lie the headwaters of both the Magdalena-Altar and the Santa Cruz drainages, is relatively well watered, receiving 500 to 650 mm of rainfall annually. This area was, in fact, an important aquifer as were the upper and middle portions of the Salt and Gila rivers. Today, these underground sources of water are, in most areas, much depleted (Dunbier 1968:98-100).

As in much of the Serrana region, the Desert province receives its winter rainfall when the Pacific subtropical high pressure area moves far enough south that low pressure storms can move inland from the Pacific. The northern part of the Sonoran Desert is the main beneficiary of these winter rains; as one goes south the effect of this "Mediterranean" type anticyclone diminishes sharply. The summer rainfall, as in the Serrana area, comes from the Atlantic anticyclone, which reaches across Texas and the northern Sierra Madre to bring rain to the desert regions beyond. Winter rainfall occurs mainly from November into March, and the summer rains fall largely in the period July-September. Winter rains become more important as one goes from east to west and from south to north in the Desert province. At Tucson, winter rains provide the area with only 44% of the total rainfall budget; at Phoenix, they represent 56% of the total; and at Yuma they furnish 61%. In the southernmost part of the province the difference is even more dramatic. Winter rains at Altar account for only 27% of the annual total, and at Magdalena only about 8% (pp. 395-396). The watershed yield (taken in each case at the station of highest streamflow) of Desert province rivers, like those of the Serrana province, is rather low. It must be stressed that, especially for the Gila and Salt valleys, the yield has been drastically altered in the last century by water control systems. This is less true of the Altar-Magdalena systems where something akin to aboriginal

conditions likely exists today. In the Salt River Valley the yield is a little over 70 mm, but in the upper Gila it is only 15 mm. The annual watershed yield of the Altar River is even less, some 10 mm (p. 399).

The Desert province is an area of very hot summers and mild winters. The January mean temperature at Tucson is about 10°C, while the July mean is approximately 30°C. At Gila Bend, west of Phoenix, the figures are around 11.5°C and 34°C, respectively. Altar, in Sonora, has slightly higher temperatures in winter than does Gila Bend--some 13.3°C, but the July average is a little less (about 31°C). There are drastic variations from the norm as one would expect in a desert climate. At Tucson, a low temperature of -14.5°C has been reported, and summer temperatures of 45°C or more are known. Even at Altar, in the warm Altar-Magdalena Valley, a temperature as low as -7°C has been recorded. At Altar the highest known temperature is about 50°C. Humidity, of course, is very low throughout the Desert province; in June, before the summer rains, it may average no more than 30% at midday (pp. 32, 397-398).

Vegetation in the Desert province may vary somewhat with altitude and with latitude. Much of the lowland Sonoran area is a sandy desert soil that supports very little vegetation, and most of that is scrub monte such as the creosote bush (Larrea sp.) and bursage (Franseria sp., especially deltoidea, confertiflora, and dumosa). Other parts of the area, however, are covered not only with Larrea and Franseria but also with a succulent desert flora, including many cacti ranging from the sahuaro (Carnegiea gigantea) and organ-pipe (Cereus thurberi) through various of the agaves and opuntias to the small pincushion cactus (Mammillaria microcarpa). Grease wood (Sarcobatus) and other halophytic plants, palo verde (Cercidium), ocotillo (Fouquieria), mesquite (Prosopis), and salt bush (Atriplex) also appear. Throughout the Sonoran Desert, along the river drainages, are stands of cottonwood, willow, and various reedlike plants (cattails and arrowweed).

In the regions above 1000 m the desert gradually changes to a chaparral growth with scrub oak (Quercus turbinella), manzanitas (Arctostaphylos), and mountain mahogany (Cercocarpus). On the northern fringes of the Desert province, where the land rises to the mountains and plateau country of the Mogollon Rim, there is an evergreen forest with pinyon, evergreen oak, juniper, and, as one goes higher, ponderosa and southwestern white pines (Kearney and Peebles 1960:12-17).

The Desert province is one in which numbers of small mammals occur, including several species of mice, pack rats, kangaroo rats, various squirrels, and both the cottontail rabbit (Sylvilagus) and the hare, or jackrabbit (Lepus sp.). The area is home to both the white-tailed deer and mule deer, the bighorn sheep, and the desert antelope. Another artiodactyl, the javelina (Pecari tajacu), is known today in much of the area but may be (at least in any number) a recent migrant. Among the carnivores are found both the kit and grey fox, the raccoon, skunk, badger, black bear (Ursus americanus amblyceps), coyote, timber wolf, bobcat, and, in higher elevations, the mountain lion (Felis concolor) and jaguar (F. onca), the latter probably as an ambulatory visitor to wilder places such as the Huachucas. It has been suggested that the jaguar has followed the peccary northward, but it seems likely that in early times the jaguar was at least an occasional visitor to the Desert province. Bighorn sheep (Ovis canadensis) are reported from a number of regions in southern Arizona and likely were the sheep reported by Castañeda for that region (Hammond and Rey 1940:212).

Reptiles include a number of snakes (among them several species of rattlesnake), the poisonous Gila monster (Heloderma suspectum), and various small lizards. The Sonoran mud turtle (Kinosternon sonoriense) and the desert tortoise (Gopherus agassizi) are also found.

There are large numbers of birds, including various buzzards, falcons, hawks, owls, eagles, quails, doves, and members of the songbird group. The great California condor once lived in the mountains and deserts of the western part of this area and may exist in isolated parts today. Wild turkeys are found in the mountains that form the northern border of the Desert province, and in the Chiricahuas and Huachucas there are northern species of parrots (Hoffmeister and Goodpaster 1954:12-26, 41-43, 138-139; Grinnell 1914:120-121, 218; Miller and Alsberg 1956:23-25; Rosenthal et al. 1978:8-9).

The Desert province has a varied insect and arachnid life. The scorpion presents a certain threat, especially to infants and children, but the extremely poisonous varieties of scorpions found in west Mexico do not extend into this area. The variety of such pests as ticks, mosquitoes, cockroaches, and red bugs mentioned by Pfefferkorn for the northern Sonoran area (Treutlein 1949: 135-139) also infest the region of the Desert province.

Language

Evidence for specific language(s) spoken in the Desert province during the sixteenth century is most indirect; nevertheless it seems almost certain that Pima was the major tongue. We know, for example, that Marcos de Niza in 1539 had Piman-speaking Indians with him when he began to journey northward to Cibola and that Pima speakers had been with Cabeza de Vaca three years earlier, traveling with him from Sonora to present-day Sinaloa (Riley 1971:289). The word Pimaito, or Primahaitu, reported by Obregón and Cabeza de Vaca almost certainly refers to Pima.

One or more of the Piman dialects seems to have been spoken in the lower Colorado Valley, as reported both by Alarcón in 1540 and by Father Francisco de Escobar in 1605 (see Chapter VIII). In addition, Schroeder (1955-1956:275) suggests that the Ispa of Jaramillo in 1540 may perhaps have been the Jiaspi of the lower San Pedro River mentioned by Kino.

However this may be, there is no doubt that when the Kino group penetrated the upper Pimeria around A.D. 1700 the entire area of the central Gila-Salt was Pima speaking, or largely so. Schroeder's idea (pp. 277-281) that Indians met by Marcos de Niza and Coronado on the Salt River were Yavapai is reasonable enough. These Indians may have occupied the area of Chichilticale, but all the chroniclers agree that they were "barbarous" and generally on a lower socioeconomic level than the peoples to the south.

To sum up, there seems no reason to doubt that the Desert province was occupied in the main by Piman speakers in the sixteenth century. These people began to receive identifiable names in the seventeenth century. For example, the Hímeri of the northwest Sonoran area are mentioned as early as 1630 and are never lost sight of after that (Sauer 1934:52), and the Plato, or Soba, of the Altar region are known from the earlier seventeenth century (p. 53). By about 1650 the Mututicachi south of modern Nogales are identified (p. 52), and by the latter part of the seventeenth century names of groups in the present-day United States--particularly the Sobaipuri, the Pima Gileños, and the Papago--appear.

The real question concerns the relationship of these Pima Alto and the peoples of the Hohokam and Trincheras cultures, known only from archaeology. Haury (1976) assumes that there was a continuity from Hohokam to Pima, as does Ezell (1963). Fontana (1976:46) seems to question this belief, but I am not clear whether he believes that the Piman speakers were newcomers or were indigenous and had drastically changed their way of life. Masse (1981, 1982) also feels that there are serious questions about a Hohokam-Piman continuum. Di Peso (1956:562-565) has suggested that Piman speech for many centuries was used by the "ordinary" peoples of the Gila-Salt region but that the Hohokam were overlords who came and went. What the Hohokam spoke is not clear.

I must say in all candor that I find it diffi-cult to see the Piman-speaking peoples of southern Arizona as newcomers or even as the remnant "pea-sant" population of a Hohokam polity. As I have suggested in a recent paper (1980a), the Pima are much like the Hohokam if we except the latter part of the Classic period. This Hohokam late Classic, I believe, was profoundly influenced by Casas Grandes (Riley 1979; see also LeBlanc and Nelson 1976:77-78) and, for whatever reasons, failed to continue into the period after about A.D. 1400 when much of the Greater Southwest was undergoing a renaissance. Nevertheless, the Piman speakers do seem to have continued at a fairly high level of operation. They had irrigation agriculture, and although they had returned to something like the earlier dispersed dwellings, their populations may still have been fairly high (see discussion below).

Population

Since the peoples of the Desert province were visited only by members of the Marcos-Esteban party and the various other branches of the Coronado expe-dition (and perhaps by Cabeza de Vaca), we do not have the kinds of population estimates that we have for the Serrana to the south and especially for the Little Colorado, the Rio Grande, and the Pecos prov-inces to the north and east. For these latter there are more than counts of pueblos and estimates of numbers of houses, because the Spaniards returned in another two generations and after 1581 were never really out of contact with that part of the South-west. Even the Colorado River region, visited by Alarcón in 1540 and again by Oñate in 1605, has lists of groups and something about overall popula-tion. For the Desert province there are no securely identified towns and no estimates of populations; indeed, in many cases we have no idea exactly what portion of the Gila-Salt Valley was being visited. Only with the Spanish expansion, first into the Altar-Magdalena beginning around 1630 and then into the northern part of the Pimeria Alta beginning around 1690, do we get a picture of the peoples of the area. The Altar-Magdalena drainage is a part of the old Trincheras area, and in the seventeenth cen-tury it was still well settled. Sauer believes that the seven Hímeri missions of the Magdalena and its tributaries numbered "at least four thousand" (1935:30). He considers the figure for the upper Altar to be a minimum of 2000. Kino estimated 4000 souls (p. 31) in the lower Altar (the region of the

Soba, or Piato). There seems also to have been around 1500 Pima Alto in the desert somewhere south of the Altar, a group contacted by Kino and Father Gerónimo Minutili in 1706 (p. 31).

Sauer (p. 32) suggests that as of about 1700 there were perhaps 11,000 Upper Pima in the Altar-Magdalena (mainly Hímeri and Soba, or Piato) and perhaps 9000 Pima on the American side of the bor-der, the largest collection (about half the total) being in the middle Santa Cruz Valley. The Gila River proper, as of 1700, Sauer believes to have had only about 1000 inhabitants. Ezell (1961:17), how-ever, estimates that around 1700 the population of six villages of Gila River Pima (Pimas de Gila, or Pimas Gileños) was at least 3000. Sauer suggests that the Papago had a population of "perhaps" 10,000 as of this period (1935:32). Presumably, by "Papago" he means the upland or desert-dwelling peo-ples and does not include any of the riverine groups. This figure can be no more than a guess.

At any rate, in Sauer's round figures (p. 32), there were something on the order of 30,000 Upper Pima, including Papago, a total which agrees with the later estimate of Spicer (1962:119). The north-ern frontier, generally speaking, was the middle Gila River from about the San Pedro to below the Gila-Salt confluence. At least by 1700 the region of the Salt seems to have been partly or largely controlled by the Yavapai who inhabited stretches of the Mazatzal Mountains westwards and to the south-west extending across the Salt River to the Pinal Mountains (Ezell 1961:22-23). As of that date, Apaches were also beginning to menace the various Piman groups from their strongholds in the mountains north and east of Pimeria.

To the west, Piman-speaking peoples reached, at least on the Gila River, virtually to the confluence of the Gila with the Colorado (Burrus 1971:414-418). The major centers for the Upper Pima around 1700, however, were in the Altar-Magdalena, the San Pedro, the Santa Cruz, and in the desert to the north of the Magdalena and west of the Santa Cruz. In the pre-Kino years the mission of Cucurbe on the upper San Miguel River (founded in the mid-seventeenth century) was the furthermost thrust made by the Spaniards toward the Pimeria Alta; indeed, it marked the southern dilimitation of that area.

One would suspect, considering what happened in other parts of the Southwest, that population of the Pima Alto declined during the seventeenth century. I have already pointed out a similar decline in the Serrana area, and although the Spaniards had not actually penetrated to the northern portions of the Desert province, it seems most likely that their diseases had preceded them. Father Velarde in 1716 mentions the ravages of a disease generally in the

Upper Pima (Burrus 1971:671), and Manje mentions an epidemic in the Altar area in 1701 (pp. 495-497). One would expect Spanish diseases to run well ahead of the Spanish occupation, especially in this Piman region where contacts between peoples of similar speech, some under Spanish mission control, were longstanding.

In the Serrana this decline actually seems to have begun in the sixteenth century (see Chapter VI), and the same thing may have been true of the Upper Pima. If so, the Piman populations as of the time of Coronado may well have been considerably greater than the A.D. 1700 populations of the same area. As Dobyns, in a survey of New World population estimates, points out:

> Neither Sauer nor Ezell nor I could go back in time earlier than extant documentation in this [northern Pima] area, which lagged behind the spread of Old World disease agents which almost certainly reduced the aboriginal populace even before literate explorers arrived on the scene (1966:404).

Parenthetically, Haury (1976:356) has suggested (very tentatively) that in the Gila-Salt region during Classic Hohokam times there may have been 50,000 to 60,000 people.

The study of Dobyns (1963:164, 180-181) on the middle Santa Cruz Valley indicates a drop in population during the eighteenth century from an estimated 2400 Indians to about 100, a 24:1 depopulation in about a century. Dobyns considers this to be largely due to disease (p. 164). If disease was a major factor, it can scarcely have held off until Kino's arrival, for, as said above, contacts between the various Piman populations of the Arizonan and Sonoran areas existed even if the Spaniards did not penetrate to the Arizona rivers till around 1700. I can well believe that the population of the Pimeria Alta in the sixteenth century was greater than in 1700; how much greater is simply impossible to tell.

Subsistence

As far as is known, all the Upper Piman groups were agricultural in the sixteenth century, and this certainly was true of late seventeenth century and early eighteenth century Pimans, although the Papago had a somewhat more marginal agriculture than the river peoples. In the sixteenth century, however, one cannot speak of a Pima/Papago division, and probably the scanty reports that we have for the area

refer to riverine peoples (a possible exception being some of the information from Marcos de Niza).

Data for the Upper Pima in the sixteenth century, as far as documentary evidence is concerned, are mainly confined to a series of expeditions, the first of which was possibly the 1536 journey of Cabeza de Vaca. Both Sauer (1932:16) and Hallenbeck (1940:221-226) believe that the Vaca party entered Sonora after crossing southern New Mexico and southeastern Arizona. The arguments for this route are at least as strong as those for the more conventional routing of Vaca across the northern sierra. If Cabeza de Vaca indeed journeyed through southeast Arizona, then the northern Pima (perhaps those in the San Pedro Valley) were very likely the first of the peoples described by Vaca who had considerable material goods--deer, cotton mantas, maize, beans, and permanent settlements. This description of settled people is usually taken to be that of the Serrana groups, and of course in large part Vaca was describing the valleys of northern and central Sonora. However, Vaca (1555:fol. xlv) specifically states that he traveled through the rich populated area for over 100 leagues (more than 400 km). If Vaca actually did enter the Serrana from the north, not all of this 100 leagues could have been Serrana country, but a trip from the middle San Pedro to the middle Yaqui would be very close to this figure.

The Coronado documents, however, give us the major ethnohistorical picture of the northern Pima area; they can be augmented somewhat by comments in Tello and in Mota Padilla, taken from the Tovar papers, and in Las Casas, presumably taken from Marcos de Niza. Unfortunately, we are never exactly sure where any of the Coronado parties were when they crossed the Gila and Salt regions. The uncertainty lends an "iffy" character to any statement made about the Upper Pima. Archaeology would be useful and doubtless will be at some future date. At present the sixteenth century archaeology of the Pimeria Alta is somewhat limited. Doyel (1976:16) states that for the middle Gila River there are no known archaeological remains that date between 1450 and 1694 when the area was reached by Father Kino. Rosenthal et al. (1978:216) believe that there is some evidence of a prehistoric-to-historic continuum for the Papago in the Quijotoa Valley on the Papago Reservation west of Tucson. In the San Pedro drainage, Di Peso (1951:210-211, 239-241) seems to feel that the Babocomari site may bridge the gap between late prehistoric and historic times, but as both of his phases at Babocomari (Huachuca and Babocomari) contain the Salado polychromes, dating of this site will depend on the date of final production of these ceramic wares. In his later Sobaipuri report, Di Peso (1953:262) suggests that the Babocomari phase at Babocomari is post-1450, the earlier Huachuca being on the same time horizon as the Tucson phase at the Tres Alamos site, the Sells phase in the Papagueria, and the Civano phase in the Gila Valley (p. 261). From excavations at San Pablo de Quiburi (about 17 km northwest of Babocomari on the main San Pedro River) and San Salvador de Baicatcan (some 80 km further downriver), Di Peso (pp. 58-63), if I understand him correctly, suggests that puddled adobe compounds, some dating in this "hiatus" period, were derived from prehistoric compound structures of the area. Masse (1975, 1981), however, doubts that compound villages extended this late in time at Quiburi and among the Sobaipuri generally.

In excavations at San Cayetano del Tumacacori in the Santa Cruz Valley, Di Peso (1956:1-2) further develops his thinking on these matters, suggesting that the Babocomari village may actually have been the site of San Joaquín de Baosuca visited by Kino in 1697. The presently excavated San Cayetano--originally called the Paloparado ruin by Sauer and Brand (1931:76-78)--is considered by Di Peso to have been the Jesuit visita of San Cayetano, though Dobyns (1963:173) thinks that it may actually have been the old site of Calabazas.

As a result of these various excavations, Di Peso (1956:564-566) suggests for the Arizona portion of Pimeria Alta a "Classic Ootam" or "Ootam Reassertion" period (A.D. 1250-1300--A.D. 1690). During this time the Piman-speaking natives of the area lived in compound villages sometimes surrounded with a defensive wall, practiced extended inhumation as well as cremation burial, continued many of the old pottery forms but with some Mimbres influence (bean pots with lug rims), and introduced such new forms as the "duck" or "foot" effigy vessel. Large storage vessels were popular, and Gila polychrome continued to be made. The villagers used small irrigation ditches. Shell continued to be valued. In the area were also Great Houses whose builders practiced larger scale irrigation and whose buildings were multitiered structures of puddled adobe (pp. 265-267). It is not clear if the Great House builders were Ootam or overlords to the Ootam. Di Peso (p. 566) suggests that some of the Great House builders may have been in residence when Coronado went through the area in 1540.

Di Peso's reconstruction of the Classic Ootam has been criticized (see for example Reed 1958:316-317), and until the archaeological picture is clarified, I shall not try to describe sixteenth century Piman life from archaeological data. What Di Peso does point up is that an archaeological case can be made for heavy populations, at least in the San Pedro and Santa Cruz valleys during the sixteenth and early seventeenth centuries. It must be stressed, however, that some of the archaeologists currently working in the area consider the evidence rather weak (Masse, personal communication).

If we turn to the ethnohistorical sources and keep in mind the comments above on the Cabeza de Vaca journey, the first account from which we can reasonably expect information on the Desert province is that of Marcos de Niza in 1539. In Chapter III, I have already indicated my belief that Marcos reached the Altar-Magdalena region of western Sonora (see also Undreiner 1947; Riley 1975b, 1976b). I consider Vacapa to be a Piman town, perhaps of the Piata, or Soba, group. Marcos called Vacapa a "good sized settlement" and said that there was food in abundance since "this was all irrigated land" (Hammond and Rey 1940:65). Indians from the coast came to visit Marcos at Vacapa as did Indians who lived somewhere between Vacapa and Cibola and who were painted or tatooed (pintados) (p. 67). The Pintados Indians seem to have been willing to accompany Marcos, perhaps as guides. One wonders if they may not have been ancestors of the Papago, who, at least in historic times, painted and tatooed their bodies. Undreiner (1947:443) suggests that they were Sobaipuries. At any rate, from Vacapa, Marcos traveled northwestward where he probably intersected and moved up the valley of either the Santa Cruz or the San Pedro River (p. 451; see also Schroeder 1955-1956:267-268). On the San Pedro or Santa Cruz River and later on the Gila, Marcos found large settlements with irrigation; the people wore cotton and hides and had turquoise, "fine vases," an abundance of game animals (deer, rabbits, and quail), maize, and pinol (pinyon nuts? pinole?) (Hammond and Rey 1940:70). Eventually Marcos crossed another despoblado which seems to have been mainly the area between the Gila and Salt rivers. After four days he reached what both Undreiner (1947:460) and Schroeder (1955-1956:271-279) believe was the Salt River and the area of Chichilticale. Schroeder (p. 272) points out that the Spanish words used by Marcos change here in regard to the agricultural practices, and it seems likely that the natives of this area did not irrigate at all. Schroeder (pp. 281-282) suggests that the Indians of this area were Yavapai, and this certainly fits the late seventeenth century and eighteenth century distribution data.

In any case, Marcos described irrigation agriculture and large settlements all the way from Vacapa to what seems to be the area of the Gila River. The people had both agriculture and the produce of the hunt, and they made fine pottery. They either grew cotton or traded for it.

Marcos was probably on a shell trade route that ran from the northern Gulf of California through Vacapa (western Pima Alto), then along or near the Magdalena River through Hímeri country, and finally across the divide into the Gila drainage, perhaps to the region of the Sobaipuri Indians. Shells, turquoise, and hides passed along this route; in fact, large bison hide shields were brought to Vacapa by Indians of the coast who must have originally obtained them through this trade network (Hammond and Rey 1940:67).

The Marcos report makes it reasonably clear that there were considerable populations of trade-wealthy and sophisticated agricultural peoples stretching from the Altar-Magdalena through the south tributaries of the Gila River. Beyond the Gila there seems to have been a drop-off of culture. Irrigation was probably not practiced, and the general feeling is one of cruder culture. I am inclined to believe Schroeder's suggestion that even in 1540 this region was the Pima-Yavapai frontier (1955-1956:281, 1974:76-77).

The Díaz report of the winter 1539-1540 adds very little information on the Desert province. Most of the report is taken up with stories about Cibola, and Díaz' information on the latter place is basically correct--as, indeed, is Marcos' if a certain hyperbole is allowed. Both Marcos (Hammond and Rey 1940:70) and Díaz (pp. 159-160) talked with individuals who had been to, lived at, or were from Cibola, and this is a powerful indication that trade did indeed stream across the Mogollon Rim to the southern Arizonan and Sonoran valleys.

The remainder of the Coronado party gives little information on the Desert province. Melchior Díaz certainly crossed it in his trip to find Alarcón in the Colorado River, but the sparse and conflicting accounts of his expedition tell us nothing of the area.

When the two major parties of the Coronado expedition move from the Sonoran valleys of Corazones and Señora through the Gila-Salt region to Cibola, they give amazingly little information. Coronado himself has no comments on the trip from Corazones to Chichilticale except that he was constantly getting further from the seacoast, being fifteen days from the sea when he reached Chichilticale but only five days from the sea at Corazones. Coronado reached Corazones on May 26, 1540 (p. 164), and remained there several days. He seems to have arrived at Chichilticale on June 10 or June 11 (p. 166). Part of this journey was of course through the northern Serrana; even so, Coronado spent perhaps a week traversing the Pima Alto lands. Castañeda, discussing the northward journey of the main army, mentions a "province named Vacapan where there

were large quantities of prickly pears, of which the natives made large amounts of preserves" (p. 212). This was sometime in the late summer, and presumably the Spaniards were eating preserved fruits of one of the varieties of opuntia or possibly the dried fruit of the sahuaro. A day out from Chichilticale the Spaniards observed a flock of wild long-haired sheep. These sheep seem to have impressed Castañeda greatly, for he mentions them again later in his account, calling them "mountain goats with very large bodies and horns" (p. 251). Chichilticale is described in more detail. The people there lived in rancherias by hunting and collecting "without permanent settlements. Most of the region is uninhabited" (p. 252).

In the Relación del suceso, what seems to be the Gila-Salt area is described as having settlements of people with mat houses, some with low terraces. "The inhabitants all have maize, although not in great abundance, and in some places little of it; they also have melons and beans." The Relación, however, mixes in a discussion of Señora at this point, and it is really unclear to which area a given passage pertains (p. 284).

Jaramillo is much more informative. He talks of the army moving from Ispa (which was probably in the northernmost portion of the Serrana) across a four-day despoblado to an arroyo called Nexpa. Hammond and Rey (1940:297) identify Nexpa with the San Pedro River. "Arroyo," incidentally, is the word preferred by Jaramillo to designate the streams and valleys in this area. At Nexpa the Spanish party received "presents of little value, such as roasted maguey leaves and pitahayas" (p. 297). From the Nexpa arroyo the route led to the northeast, although Jaramillo seems uncertain about both directions and distances. In the Relación postrera de Cíbola, a general statement is made about the country from Culiacan to Cibola. In this region people built houses of reed mats, grew some maize, beans, and calabashes, and hunted deer, rabbits, and hares (p. 308). Since we do not know the specific area under discussion, it is difficult to make very much of this information.

On the return of Coronado in 1542, there is the same frustrating lack of data about the desert peoples of southern Arizona. Not till the Serrana is reached do we have meaningful information about the peoples of the area.

The Desert province was not visited again for a century and a half, though we do have some second-hand information from the Oñate expedition to the lower Colorado in 1604-1605. According to the Zárate Salmerón summary of this trip, written in 1626, the Pima-speaking Ozara

are settled along a large river, although
not as much water as that of Buena Esperanza [Colorado]. It is called Nombre de
Jesus [Gila] River; it runs between bare
mountains, and flows into the Buena Esperanza from southeast to northwest, twenty
leagues before reaching the sea. It was
learned that all the river is inhabited by
this nation, and that the people are
numerous. They drew on the ground twenty
rancherías or pueblos of this nation.
They make mantas of cotton; the dress and
hair are different from the rest; the hair
is long and they wear it braided, and then
covered with a cloth or deer skin (Bolton
1916:275).

Historically, of course, Piman men and women wore
their hair long, and the men braided and often covered these long tresses (Russell 1975:158-159).

Escobar, who chronicled this Oñate expedition,
calls the group at the Gila mouth Oseca, or Osera,
and also mentions the wearing of long hair. He
says:

The Nombre de Jesús River is inhabited by
one group who raised maize, beans, and
calabashes, like the people of Amacaua and
Bahaçecha [on the Colorado River], and
wove cotton blankets, some of which I saw
and which are coarse like those from the
province of New Mexico (Hammond and Rey
1953:1020).

If the Coronado group was uninformative in the
mid-sixteenth century and if Oñate's data at the
beginning of the seventeenth were a bit peripheral,
at least Kino at the end of the seventeenth century
gave considerable information. During the decade of
the 1690s, Father Eusebio Francisco Kino and Captain
Juan Mateo Manje explored large stretches of the San
Pedro and the middle course of the Gila and of the
Santa Cruz. They found extensive populations of
Piman-speaking peoples. Towns like Quiburi in the
San Pedro Valley had nearly 100 houses and 500
inhabitants. There was an abundance of maize,
beans, and cotton (Gossypium hopi?) in irrigated
fields (Burrus 1971:360-361). Near present-day Tucson on the Santa Cruz, Manje counted 800 Indians in
186 houses and noted irrigated lands with maize,
beans, cotton, calabashes, melons, and watermelons
(p. 348) These are but two of a number of examples
of the well-settled and prosperous middle Gila
region and of its north-draining tributaries.

Doelle (1976:16), following Winter, suggests
that the early Spanish visitors to the Gila did not
mention irrigation for the Pima and that it may have
been absent. In a later publication (1981), he
defends this position even more vigorously (however,
see Riley 1981b). Doelle also produces documentary
evidence that the overall population of the Gila
River in the late seventeenth century was quite low,
being only a little over 2000 people. He discounts
the explanation that disease had taken its toll,
pointing out that the same figures (from the Manje
journals) give a higher population in a much smaller
area for the Santa Cruz River. It may, of course,
be that some factor (or factors) as yet imperfectly
understood was inhibiting the settlement of the main
Gila River; for example, the area may have been
especially exposed at this period to enemy raids.
Still and all, depopulation must have been a crucial
factor for the entire area (see Dobyns 1966).

Winter (1973:69) makes the point that Kino and
Manje do not talk of irrigation on the Gila (presumably Winter means Gila River only). Ezell
(1961:37), however, seems to think that the Gila
Pima probably did have irrigation. See also the
comment of Haury (1976:150) on "echo" canals at
Snaketown.

Frankly, I find it very hard to believe that
Kino and Manje could have described such extensive
systems on the San Pedro and Santa Cruz rivers had
irrigation not been quite widespread and had it not
included canals on the Gila itself. The fault, I
think, lies in the nature of the Spanish documentation. Spanish writers for this period are notorious
for leaving out the obvious or, perhaps more confusing, mentioning it prominently in one place and
ignoring it in the next.

As to the kinds of food available, obviously
maize, beans, and squash formed the agricultural
basis of the diet in the sixteenth century. We do
not know what varieties of maize were used; of
course it was Zea mays of some kind(s). The beans
mentioned both in the sixteenth and in the late seventeenth centuries were, at least in part, the common bean (Phaseolus vulgaris) that had been grown in
the Gila-Salt area from early A.D. times (p. 118).
Haury (p. 118) reports one example of the tepary
bean (Phaseolus acutifolius) in a Sacaton phase
house at Snaketown and also notes its aboriginal
occurrence in the area south of Tucson. The tepary
has also been found archaeologically at the St.
Mary's site and at Punta de Agua in the Tucson
Basin, dating c. A.D. 850-1000 (Bohrer et al. 1969;
Miksicek 1979). Castetter and Underhill (1935:32)
point out that the tepary was reported as early as
1699, at which time it was considered native. In
later times it was grown throughout southern Arizona, as far west as the Cocopa, and as far south as
Sonora. The name itself, according to Castetter and

Underhill (p. 32), is a Spanish mispronunciation of a Papago phrase, † pawi (it is a bean). Taken all in all, it seems extremely likely that the tepary was grown in the Pimeria Alta in the sixteenth century.

The "calabazos" mentioned in both the sixteenth and the late seventeenth century accounts for the Pimeria Alta certainly include Cucurbita, and Castetter and Underhill suggest that both C. pepo and C. moschata were aboriginal. Some of the calabazos may also have been Lagenaria; at least this plant is probably known archaeologically in the area (Haury 1976:118). The melons and watermelons (sandias) mentioned in the Kino journey of 1697 perhaps were introduced by Kino earlier, as suggested by Castetter and Underhill (1935:36). However, as pointed out in Chapter VI, the Ibarra party in 1565 found melons in the Serrana area growing from seed that had been introduced by the Coronado party twenty years earlier. The melons, because of their similarity in planting and growth cycle to the cucurbits and because of their high amount of natural sugar and pleasing flavor, would probably spread very rapidly, especially in an area where trade networks had already been established. My guess is that the Upper Pima had melons and watermelons long before Kino and likely before the end of the sixteenth century. They probably were not growing in this area in 1540, although as Castañeda (Hammond and Rey 1940:251) points out, Spanish chickens had reached the Suya Valley in the upper part of the Serrana as early as 1540-1542.

It seems likely that the collected foods known from Kino's time on and discussed by Castetter and Bell (1942) and Castetter and Underhill (1935) were also used aboriginally. Castañeda (Hammond and Rey 1940:212) mentions preserved prickly pears that left the Spanish army drowsy with headaches and fever; these could have been made from the sahuaro, the pitahaya, or the prickly pear (Opuntia Engelmannii). In later times the Upper Pimans fermented a number of these fruits, either for ceremonial purposes or for pleasure. The fermented fruit in historic times was taken as a liquid, but the Spaniards may have been given fermented pulp, in which case their illness, perhaps, was nothing but a collective hangover.

The plants eaten in historic times by the Pima and Papago were available in the sixteenth century, but, except for Jaramillo's comments on roasted maguey leaves and pitahayas (p. 297) and Castañeda's prickly pear, they are not mentioned in the sixteenth century accounts. Masse (1975, 1981) has summarized the rather scanty information on (probably) seventeenth and eighteenth century Sobaipuri subsistence. It includes possibly flour corn of the

pueblo race, prickly pear, and Setaria in small quantities. Faunal remains include mule deer, cottontail, pronghorn, jackrabbit, and grey fox, plus domestic sheep, cow, and dog. However, from both the ethnological record of the nineteenth and twentieth century Pima-Papago and the archaeological record of Hohokam (Russell 1975; Gasser 1976), it is clear that a wide variety of wild plant foods was used in the area, and one can hardly doubt that such was true in the sixteenth and seventeenth centuries.

Summarizing the really scanty evidence from the sixteenth century, we can guess at large populations with irrigation and cultivation of maize, probably two kinds of beans, one or more kinds of squash, and cotton. Both hunting and gathering were important, and from the small amount of evidence it would seem that the same animals and plants were utilized as in later times. The comments on sheep by Castañeda suggest their importance in the native diet as does the speculation of Kino. Manje and Kino at Tusonimo on the Gila near modern Sacaton saw huge piles of wild sheep horns, indicating (to them) that such animals were a major food source (Burrus 1971:209). Fish were eaten in the area in prehistoric times (Haury 1976:115) as well as in the postconquest period (Castetter and Bell 1942:71). We have no data from the sixteenth century, but it seems likely enough that fish represented part of the diet, especially on the Gila.

Settlement Patterns

Dobyns (1963:180) makes the interesting point that in the late seventeenth and the eighteenth centuries (from Kino's time), settlements in the upper Pima area consisted of a few large villages with towns of 500 people or more and numerous small rancherias of 70 to 120 persons. The Kino-Manje party in 1697 mentioned one town of almost 200 houses in the Santa Cruz Valley. Houses in this period were usually of poles covered with mats and at least sometimes were arched (Burrus 1971:204). Other houses included adobe structures with beams and dirt-covered roofs (p. 199). Since the latter kind of structure was sometimes built especially for the Spanish party (p. 217), one wonders to what extent Spanish influence had spread ahead of missionization to the Sobaipuri area and the region of the Santa Cruz. Possibly, the "Great Houses" that Di Peso believed may have existed and have been occupied up to the time of the Spanish conquest of Pimeria Alta were the models. It seems unlikely that anything as elaborate as Casa Grande was in use in the late seventeenth century, for both Kino and

Manje were enormously impressed with that ruin (pp. 219-222). Although the context is not always clear, it seems reasonable that even the larger towns were, in a sense, rancheria settlements of dispersed houses, somewhat like those of the pre-Classic Hohokam or the modern Pima or Tepehuan.

If the population in 1540 exceeded that of 1690, one might expect even greater population clusters--that is to say, larger "towns." We simply have no good Spanish statements on this matter except for the Marcos accounts, and even here is a certain vagueness. Marcos describes Vacapa as a good-sized settlement with a great deal of irrigated land. It was forty leagues (about 170 km) from the sea. His Vacapa might be in the Altar-Pitiquín-Caborca region (except that Caborca is somewhat nearer the Gulf) which, at least in 1694, was an area of extensive irrigation. According to Manje, there were "muchas tierras de agricultura y acequias para su riego" in this area, and there seem to have been rather considerable numbers of Indians, 600 in the Caborca area alone (p. 293).

After three days' travel from Vacapa, Marcos came to a pueblo of unknown size but obviously important enough to be a center on the turquoise trade route. A day later Marcos reached another settlement (his Pintados guides continued with him through this part of the trip). Following this, for the next five days Marcos always found "settlements, good lodging, excellent reception, and many turquoises, hides of the cattle [bison], and the same information regarding the country" (Hammond and Rey 1940:69). Marcos was told that in two more days he would reach a despoblado which would take four days to cross. Before reaching it (within the next two days presumably), Marcos "came to a pueblo, in green irrigated land, where many people came to meet me, both men and women. They were clothed in cotton, some wearing skins of the cattle" (pp. 69-70). At this town there were many turquoises called cacona.

On entering the despoblado, Marcos found huts and plenty of food near an arroyo, and at night he was given lodging (perhaps at isolated rancherias) and food. This continued for the next four days which he spent in the despoblado, after which he came on another well-settled valley where people came to meet him with food, where much turquoise was worn, and where he saw many bison skins. Details of the settlement patterns, however, are missing.

The scattered information on Piman settlements from other members of the Coronado expedition has been given earlier in this chapter. Generally speaking, the area is not mentioned at all. One gets the impression that the Spaniards were simply not interested in a region that had a culture cruder certainly than the Serrana statelets. Only when they reached Chichilticale, the gateway to Cibola, do we get any sort of data, and they are mostly geographical. On the return from Cibola, the Spaniards were thinking forward to the hostile Serrana region and again ignored the desert peoples. There is, of course, the possibility that the Coronado group followed the route suggested by Di Peso et al. (1974:Vol. 4, 98). In such a case the entire expedition swung considerably to the east, crossing the present-day international border somewhere around Agua Prieta-Douglas, and marched between the Chiricahua and Pinaleno Mountains, eventually entering present-day New Mexico. The Spaniards then traversed the upper Animas drainage, recrossed the New Mexico-Arizona state line in the Duncan area, and went northward to Clifton. This portion of the route is the "Coronado Trail," U.S. Highway 666, except that Di Peso takes the army a bit farther east, following the drainage of the Blue River and finally crossing into New Mexico again. It avoids the Pima settlements of the middle Gila area, but it brings Coronado into very wild and rough country. If I were to postulate an eastern route, I would have the Coronado party swing through the edge of Mimbres country--eventually crossing the Gila somewhere around Cliff and roughly following the route of modern U.S. Highway 180 to the region of Luna--then either northward to Zuni or more likely northwestward into the Little Colorado drainage (see Figure 4, Proposed Coronado Route 2). On balance, however, it seems most likely that the reason Piman peoples are scantily mentioned by the Coronado party has to do with the nature of Spanish reporting discussed above.

Trade

If any one thing is clear about the Pimeria Alta in the sixteenth century, it is that there was a deep involvement in trade. As early as 1536 Cabeza de Vaca (see Chapter VI) indicated the movement of trade items between the Pueblo area and the Serrana area beyond, with turquoise and parrot and macaw feathers being especially important commodities. Again, most of our information during the period of initial Spanish contact comes from Marcos in 1539. It is necessary to stress once more that Marcos, from around the end of March to the end of April, 1539, was on a major trade route and during that period joined a second one. This part of his trip began at Vacapa somewhere in the Altar-Magdalena area, perhaps near the junction of the two rivers. Vacapa clearly was on the shell route. It had contacts with the Gulf of California, and Indians coming from the Gulf to visit Marcos had bison hide shields. Pintados Indians, whose territory formed an arc toward the east of Vacapa, came to see Marcos. They arrived some nine days after Marcos reached Vacapa and announced that they came because they had heard of the priest (Hammond and Rey 1940:67). With the Pintados (whether Papago or Sobaipuri) acting as guides and with two coastal Indians who wanted for some reason to travel with the party for seven or eight days (that is, up to the main northern settlements of the Pima), Marcos moved off north and east toward the settlements I have described earlier in this chapter. He soon met people who regularly went to Cibola for turquoises and hides (p. 68). Marcos was given a number of tanned and skillfully worked hides, and the natives stated that these goods had all come from Cibola (p. 69). If we assume that they were bison hides, this was almost certainly true. The further Marcos traveled, the more detailed stories he heard of Cibola, and the more riches in hides, turquoises, and cotton he saw. In this area Marcos was offered "many turquoises and skins of the cattle, very fine vases, and other things" (p. 70). One wonders if the "very fine vases, and other things" may not also have been trade wares coming along the Cibola route.

By this time Marcos had certainly intersected the major north-south route from the Serrana to Cibola and was no longer simply on the shell route that led to Vacapa and the coast (Riley 1976b:Map 1). Further north (perhaps in the Salt River Valley), Marcos mentions seeing 2000 extremely well-tanned hides of bison and much turquoise on strings. "The natives all say that it comes from the city of Cibola, of which place they have as much information as I have of the things I handle every day" (Hammond and Rey 1940:73). A little earlier, Marcos had made the same point somewhat more forcefully: "They knew as much here about Cibola as they know in New Spain about Mexico, or in Peru about Cuzco" (p. 71). Indeed, this seems to be the case, for Marcos describes with great accuracy the way houses were built, the way in which ladders were used to get to upper terraces, and other perfectly valid details.

If Marcos was, at this point, among the somewhat cruder rancherias of either the Yavapai or the more primitive Piman speakers, he also was among active traders. We know from the Coronado accounts that peoples from this area visited the Gulf of California "for fish, or for anything else that they need" (p. 165); and from Marcos we know that they went in the other direction as well. It may be that the actual mechanics of trade were in part in the hands of Pima and Yavapai groups. Nevertheless, as both the Marcos and Melchior Díaz stories indicate, there were people from Cibola who reached the Gila-Salt area. One very important point is that both Marcos and Díaz received good detailed information on Cibola--that of Díaz correct, that of Marcos correct if the stories that seem to relate to the Serrana are set aside. The confusion in Marcos' account comes from the fact that he intercepted the trade route about halfway between the Serrana towns and Cibola, did not visit the Serrana on this trip, and saw Cibola (if at all) only from a distance. Melchior Díaz, later in 1539, went through the Serrana area to Chichilticale and did not have such confusion.

That trade continued on past the sixteenth century is indicated by the Kino and Manje accounts. For example, in 1694 Manje notes that one of the Indians in the Gila River settlement of Coatoydag, or San Andrea, downriver from Casa Grande, was painted with a bright red paint--vermillion or a fine red ochre. When asked where he had obtained this material, the man said that it was traded "5 jornadas, al noroeste y río Colorado, que señaló lo traían" (Burrus 1971:344). A five-day journey toward the northwest would probably bring the Indians somewhere near the Jerome area, where Espejo and Oñate (a century or more before Kino) had discovered the rich mineral areas. Both the Espejo and Oñate parties noted both the local use and the extensive trade in powdered ores for painting purposes (Riley 1976b:37-38). Manje thought that the paint he discovered--the Indian youth had a ball of the material wrapped in buckskins which it stained--was a mercury ore, and this may well have been the case (Burrus 1971:345). There was other and rather intriguing evidence of trade. The Gila River Pima told the Kino party that "a tiempos, viene una gente blanca, al río Colorado, a caballo, con cueras, arcabuces y espadas, pero que no los disparan" (p. 345). Kino and Manje speculated that these individuals may have been apostate Hopi with Spanish arms from the period of the rebellion (1680-1692). There is no record of Spaniards from New Mexico trading with the Gila River Indians, nor were there Spaniards on the Gulf of California. The Indians also described a people who lived to the north and domesticated "caballos cervales" (deerlike horses) which both Burrus and Bolton suggest may have been a garbled reference to elk (Burrus 1971:213, n. 64). As Burrus (p. 213) points out, however, the passage is hopelessly confused.

That there was considerable contact between the Gila and Colorado River peoples in the 1690s is clear from the Kino-Manje accounts. In the 1699 expedition, Kino and Manje found a large town, with both Yuman and Piman inhabitants, very near the junction of the Gila with the Colorado. A local Pima Indian was recruited; he spoke fluent Yuman (p. 415). In this area Manje notes that the people used a great many white and black shells with beads resembling coral which were fashioned from a red shell (probably rock oyster traded from farther south on the Gulf). Some of the Indians had a pendant made of three or four shells of mother-of-pearl (conchos de nacar) in each ear (p. 415). A reasonable assumption would be that the mother-of-pearl was abalone from the California Pacific Coast, and in fact Kino identifies it as such (Burrus 1971:114-116).

There are other examples of Piman trade in the late seventeenth and the eighteenth centuries. I have suggested a trade route that linked the Gila-Salt Valley with the Jerome area and the Hopi country (1976b:41), and trade between this area and the Hopi is documented as late as 1750 (p. 22). It is likely that Piman Indians in the mid-sixteenth century were in trade contact with the lower Colorado peoples, for Alarcón found Piman speakers among the Yumans in 1540 (Riley 1971:302), including the one Yuman Indian that Alarcón met who had been to Cibola. At the time I wrote the 1971 paper cited above, I believed that Pima was a kind of lingua franca for at least the western part of the Greater Southwest (p. 302). A dozen years later, I see no reason to change that opinion. One obvious implication is that the Pima Alto in the sixteenth century served as important middlemen along four major trade routes. One stretched from the Gulf of California, running through Vacapa, and produced shell in exchange for dressed bison skins, manufactured skin objects, and turquoise. A second ran down the Gila River, the possible route of Melchior Díaz in 1540 (Riley 1976b:25), and brought shell and coral, including Pacific California Coast shell, in exchange for turquoise and worked hides. This route is certainly pre-Columbian. A recently studied large "Patayan" site (Lago Seco) in the Ajo area of southern Arizona seems to have contained a workshop for Gulf of California shell, presumably exported to the Hohokam of late Sedentary and early Classic times. Both Patayan and Hohokam ceramics are found at the site (Huckell 1979:133-138; Huckell and Huckell 1979:151-166). A third route ran up the Verde River to the Jerome area and probably involved the exchange of shell or other southern materials for pigments. The Verde route is perhaps centuries pre-Columbian (Gumerman and Spoerl 1980:148-149). A fourth major route was the camino real, running from the Serrana country to Cibola and bringing exotic southern materials (such as parrot and macaw feathers and birds) to trade for turquoise and other semiprecious stones (peridot especially), hides, and other things. These diverse trails seem to have met or crossed somewhere in the middle Gila Valley, and they must have been of enormous economic value to the Pima Alto.

Sociopolitical Organization

We have almost no data on the sociopolitical organization of the Pima Alto in the sixteenth century. Virtually our only source is Marcos de Niza, who speaks of the ruler of one of the pueblos, who with his two brothers were "very well dressed in cotton, adorned, and each wearing a turquoise necklace" (Hammond and Rey 1940:70). A little later this man is referred to as the chief of the pueblo. Later on, for the final leg of the journey to Cibola, Marcos chose "about thirty prominent men [one also a chief], all very well dressed, wearing turquoise necklaces, some with five and six loops" (p. 74) to accompany him to Cibola, along with people to carry provisions for the men and for Marcos (p. 75).

For the Pima a century and a half later, there is still some ambiguity as to the sociopolitical structure. Winter (1973:69), at least for the Gila River Pima, believes that each rancheria had its own leader or perhaps several people who exerted different aspects of leadership--a special war leader, for example. He sees no evidence for an extravillage, or tribal, leader. Dobyns (1974:322-324), however, makes a good case for an extravillage leader of the Kohatk group of Gila Pima as of Kino's time. I suspect that the Piman-speaking Indians of the Santa Cruz and the San Pedro might have had a more complex sociopolitical organization, but the sources are not very informative on this matter. In any event, if population is a causative factor in political complexity, the presumed larger populations of the sixteenth century might well have had more complex political organizations than did those of the late seventeenth century.

Warfare

There is no direct evidence of warfare in the Desert province for the sixteenth century. Marcos reports a considerable amount of warfare at Cibola and in the various "kingdoms" of the general region, as does Vázquez at the end of the sixteenth century, drawing probably from documents now lost (Vázquez de Espinosa 1948:183). In the account of Melchior Díaz, the people of Chichilticale were instructed by the Cibolans to kill the Spaniards, and if they were afraid to do so, "they should notify them and they would come and do it themselves" (Hammond and Rey

1940:160). The later accounts of the Coronado expedition simply are not informative on the matter of warfare, unless, indeed, some of the Upper Piman peoples played a part in the uprising at San Gerónimo de los Corazones. The most suggestive passage comes in Castañeda, who, speaking of Coronado's return to Mexico, says:

> Juan Gallego met the army on the second day out of Chichiticale . . . . The reinforcements [Gallego's forces] had endured considerable hardship to reach that place, having had daily skirmishes with the Indians of that region who were in revolt, as we have already told (p. 272).

One day out of Chichilticale would probably have put Coronado somewhere between the Salt and the Gila rivers if my earlier identification is correct. If Castañeda's meaning is that Gallego continued skirmishing up to the time he met Coronado, then some Pima Alto were involved.

By the late seventeenth century it is obvious that the Pima Alto were not peaceful, although the threat from the Apaches may have forced some basic changes in attitudes toward war in the intervening century and a half. At any rate, Kino and his party saw considerable evidence of warfare, not only in the Gila River frontier (Burrus 1971:340-343) but also along the San Pedro, where the Sobaipuri proudly displayed enemy Apache scalps (p. 336). There are many other indications that the Pima, as of around A.D. 1700, were involved in serious and frequent wars with the Apache.

Religion

Almost nothing is known of the religion of the Pima Alto in the mid-sixteenth century. The statement in the Relación postrera de Cíbola that "they do not offer sacrifices" (Hammond and Rey 1940:308) is not very informative, especially since we are not sure just who "they" involved. For religious activities of the later Pima Alto one can consult various eighteenth century Jesuit documents and later works such as Russell (1975).

General Comments

One might think that vocabulary items would give hints as to the situation in the Pimeria Alta in the mid-sixteenth century. In fact, they help very little. Jaramillo talks of the settlement of Ispa, where an irrigation-using people lived on the upper reaches of the Señora River. According to Jaramillo:

> From here we continued in general along the said arroyo, crossing its meanderings, to another Indian settlement called Ispa. It must be one day's journey from the confines of the last one. These people are of the same customs as the preceding ones. One goes from here in four days over a despoblado to another arroyo, which we understood was called Nexpa. Some poor Indians came out to meet the general, bringing presents of little value, such as roasted maguey leaves and pitahayas. We continued down this arroyo for two days; leaving the arroyo we went to the right in two days' travel to the foot of the cordillera, where we learned that it was called Chichilti-calli (Hammond and Rey 1940:297).

Schroeder (1955-1956:275) believes that Ispa might possibly be the Jiaspi of Kino (see Burrus 1971:202). If Ispa is indeed to be equated with Nuestra Señora del Rosario de Jiaspi and if Schroeder is correct that Jaramillo was confusing the Señora and Suya valleys, it might put the last San Gerónimo (the Suya Valley one) on the San Pedro River (see Schroeder 1955-1956:275-276). In such a case the Indians who revolted and killed Diego de Alcaráz (Hammond and Rey 1940:269) and perhaps the ones who attacked Coronado during the return journey probably were Upper Pima. Of course it is quite possible that Castañeda's statement, "at some places there were outbreaks by the Indians, and some horses wounded and killed" (p. 273), refers in part to the Pimeria Alta. But from other sources (see, for example, the various testimonies in the ICC) and from statements of the Ibarra party concerning the whereabouts of San Gerónimo (Cuevas 1924:152-153), it is quite clear that the Suya Valley itself was deep in Serrana country. On the other hand, the Nexpa Valley, which according to Jaramillo (Hammond and Rey 1940:297) was reached after the Spaniards crossed a four-day despoblado, may well have been the San Pedro. As far as I know, the word Nexpa has never been identified as Piman, but the Spanish rendition is doubtless very corrupt.

The place name Vacapa used by Marcos de Niza (p. 66), and the "province named Vacapan" of Castañeda (p. 212) are not the same place; the first is likely in the Altar-Magdalena drainage and the latter somewhere in the Gila drainage, probably south of the

Gila River. The word Vacapa(n) does have a very Piman sound.

The place name Chichilticale is a bit more complex. It is first mentioned by name in one of the reports of the 1539 Díaz expeditions (ICC: Zaldívar testimony) and verified by Castañeda (Hammond and Rey 1940:205). The main Coronado party refers to it several times. Coronado himself mentions reaching Chichilticale (pp. 212, 251-252, 272) and gives the first indication that it was so called because it contained a large brown or red house, probably used as a fortress. Jaramillo (p. 297) mentions Chichilticale as the beginning of mountainous country. Tello describes Chichilticale as "una casa que estaba en él embarrada de tierra colorado ó almagre, y aquí se hallaron pinos con piñas de piñones muy buenos" (1891:334).

The important problem concerns the origin of the name Chichilticale. Schroeder (1955-1956:293) has pointed out that, in the 1555 Molina dictionary of Mexican words, Chichiltic-calli (the same spelling variant as that used by Jaramillo—see Winship 1896:585) is given as "red house." The Castañeda narrative seems to have been written, or at least completed, in the early 1560s, and Schroeder (1955-1956:293-294) raises the possibility that Castañeda simply borrowed the definition from Molina. There is a possibility that Tello, who also gives the meaning "red house," got his information from the lost Tovar papers. In the eighteenth century, Mota Padilla (Day 1940b:93), who also was supposed to have available the Tovar documents, gives the "red house" definition. Of course both Tello and Mota Padilla could have taken the definition from Molina or from Castañeda, or Mota Padilla from Tello. In any case, Schroeder makes the important point that a Nahuatl derivation for Chichilticale is not certain. There are alternatives, including the Apache Tli-chi-kowa (red house) or Chi-chil-kain (Oak People clan) or the Yavapai Chi-chi-itch-kwali (mother plants) (Schroeder 1955-1956:295). Bolton (1964:106) suggests the Yaqui words Chichilte and calle (red house). To the best of my knowledge, no one has suggested that the name Chichilticale is Piman, but it might well be some variation of the Piman word for house or wall--kih, or kihki (see Saxton and Saxton 1969:24; Pennington 1979:20).

Another word, this time not a place name, given in what seems to be the midst of Upper Piman territory, is cacona, which Marcos (Hammond and Rey 1940:70) said was a local name for turquoise. Possibly it relates to the Pima-Papago word chehdagi, or chehedag, "to be green or blue" (Saxton and Saxton 1969:71). Certainly one should not make very much of this; for one thing, it seems likely that Marcos did not have a very good ear for sounds. For example, his Spanish seems to have been rather poor even after years in the New World (Chavez 1968:11).

CHAPTER VIII

COLORADO PROVINCE

The region of the lower Colorado River was certainly the least firmly attached polity of the Greater Southwest in the sixteenth century. The Indians of the area lacked many of the sophisticated traits that can be demonstrated to exist in the Serrana and Pueblo areas and that seem extremely likely to have been part of the Desert province. Colorado River peoples were agricultural, but their agriculture seems not to have been a central activity in the economic scene, and, in all probability, irrigation, with the exception of a very primitive type, was missing. Although populations were dense, the town life, so well documented for the Serrana and the various Pueblo areas, was probably absent, even though the extended rancheria settlements along the valleys and channels of the Colorado may not have been so very different from the "towns" of Pimeria Alta as described by Marcos and other members of the Coronado group. Political organization was probably not developed much beyond a village headman, although the evidence is not always clear.

I am justified in including the Colorado River people with the Greater Southwest, however, because, as I said in Chapter II, the "world view" of the Indians of that area did indeed encompass the Greater Southwest. Relationships, at least in trade, were very important and long standing. General knowledge of the lower Colorado on the part of other southwestern Indians is surely part of the reason for the Spaniards' continuing interest in the area and especially why Juan de Oñate was drawn into an expensive expedition to the region in 1604-1605. One might, of course, make the same argument for the peoples who lived on the eastern fringe of the Greater Southwest: the Querechos, Teyas, Jumanos, and other largely unidentified groups whose trade with the eastern Pueblos was intense and mutually important. In this case, however, one is dealing with shifting and often hostile nomadic tribes whose main livelihood came from the bison and other Plains animals. Their relations with the Greater Southwest were symbiotic but marginal, as were the relations of internally marginal peoples such as the Cruzados, Pintados, and Querechos. On the other hand, the Colorado peoples were peripheral but not marginal. Although I am not using the static culture area concept of an older generation of anthropologists, it seems clear enough that if I were talking about culture areas, the southern river Yuman peoples would fit with the Greater Southwest. This surely is in large part due to the fact that they were controllers and middlemen on one of the important trade routes—that to the California Pacific Coast (see Brand 1973:100)—and that they pumped varieties of shell (Haliotis especially, but also Pecten, Conus, and some of the olives) to various parts of the Greater Southwest. It is possible that the scatter of Haliotis cracherodii and H. fulgens found in the Medio period at Casas Grandes (Di Peso et al. 1974:Vol. 6, 550) came via the lower Colorado. Haliotis rufescens is found in some quantity at Site 616 on Mariana Mesa, some 70 km south of Zuni. The site was deserted about A.D. 1300 (McGimsey 1980:42, 165-166). It is extremely likely that the relatively large number of both worked and unworked Haliotis shell found at Pecos by Kidder (1932:193-194; see also Riley 1978a:59) came via the Colorado River middleman route. This will be discussed in greater detail below.

Archaeologically, the Colorado province is the least well known of any of the major subareas of the Greater Southwest, with the sole exception of the Serrana. Archaeological work in the region has been summarized in Chapter IV. Briefly, a sequence of agricultural peoples who have been called Yuman (Gladwin and Gladwin 1930, 1934; Rogers 1945), Patayan (Hargrave 1938; Colton 1945), and more recently Hakataya (Schroeder 1957, 1979c) lived in the lower Colorado Valley for a number of centuries before Spanish contact. The groups in this area made a painted brown, gray, or buff ware, sometimes with simple painted designs. The tepary bean, maize, and squash were grown in the river floodplain (Lipe 1978:381), but there was no ditch irrigation. Schroeder (1960) has suggested considerable Hohokam influence, especially in the buff wares and decorated ceramics. The vessel forms of some late Classic red wares are quite similar to those of the Yumans (Haury 1945; Masse 1975). Another indication of Hohokam contacts comes from the excavation at Lago Seco, a Patayan site some 30 km northwest of Ajo, Arizona. There a shell bracelet industry utilized Glycymeris as well as other Gulf of California shell. According to Huckell and Huckell (1979:165-166), Lago Seco may have served as a manufacturing center for the Hohokam in the period around A.D. 1000-1050.

A tantalizing possibility of further Hohokam influences during the late Classic comes with the scattered mentions of large houses of thick-walled adobe, reported as early as the De Anza expedition of 1775 and as late as 1903. These have been discussed in Chapter IV. In modern times no such structures have been found, but their existence cannot be ruled out completely.

The peninsular situation of Baja California was

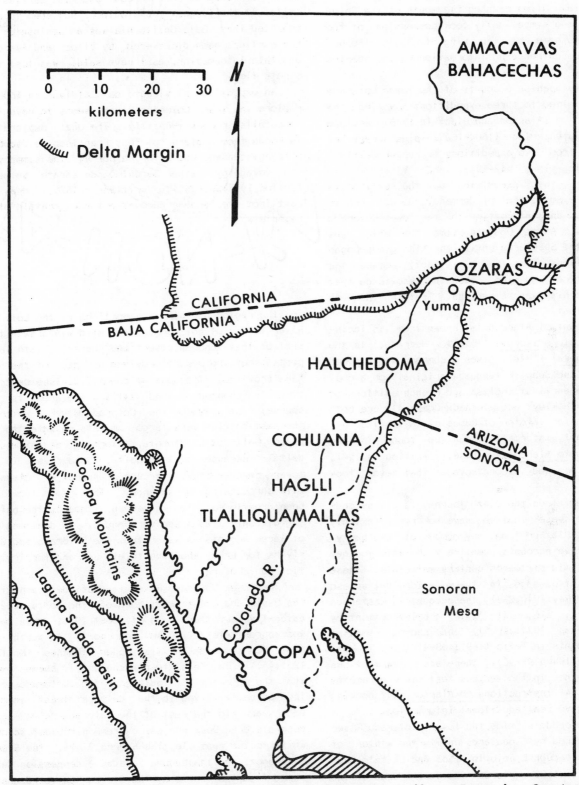

Figure 9. Approximate Location of Delta Tribes Seen by Onate
in A.D. 1605.

discovered in 1539 by Captain Francisco de Ulloa, a sea captain sent by Cortés to explore the upper Gulf of California. Ulloa reached the mouth of the Colorado River and symbolically took possession of the area in the name of the king of Spain (Forbes 1965:84). He gathered no information on the peoples of the area.

The early Spanish accounts of the lower Colorado River are limited to three expeditions--two from the Coronado period (Alarcón and Díaz in 1540) and one from the Oñate period (1604-1605)--plus scraps of information from two expeditions to upper California--Cabrillo in 1542-1543 and Vizcaino in 1602-1603. Other expeditions up the California coast, for example that of Cermeño, do not seem to have produced any information on the lower Colorado River area. After Oñate's time the region was ignored by the Spaniards until the Kino group began its explorations after 1690; in fact, between the Coronado period and Kino, even the knowledge that Baja California was a peninsula rather than an island was lost.

The account of Alarcón is known from its inclusion in Ramusio's Viaggi (1556). Herrera, in the Historia general (1944), gives a summary which seems to be from the Spanish language original or a copy of it. The earliest English and French editions of this voyage (Hakluyt and Ternaux-Compans) are both from the Italian version of Ramusio. A small amount of additional information can be found in the Instructions to Alarcón. These, written in 1541, were for a planned second voyage that never took place.

The material on the Díaz journey is all second-hand in the sense that we have no report extant, either from Díaz or from any member of his party. There are five accounts dealing with this journey that utilize mid-sixteenth century materials. These are the brief passages in the Relación del suceso (Hammond and Rey 1940:278), the account in Castañeda (pp. 210-212, 216, 231-232), a brief comment by Obregón (Cuevas 1924:24-25), and short, somewhat variant accounts in Tello (1891:408-410) and in Mota Padilla (Day 1940b:94-96). There are a few mentions of Díaz' journey in the various testimonio documents and in the 1541 Instructions to Alarcón, but nothing that would give real additional information.

After Coronado's time the lower Colorado River was not reached by Spaniards until the winter of 1604-1605 (although Espejo in 1583 and Oñate's Captain Farfán in 1598 explored the Jerome area of the upper Verde River--see Riley 1976b:36-38). The expedition of 1604-1605 started from Hopi and may have crossed from the Verde drainage to that of the Bill Williams River, following the latter to the Colorado. The Oñate party pushed on to near the mouth of the Colorado (which river they called the Buena Esperanza as the Alarcón and Díaz parties had called it the Tizón). Oñate does not seem to have realized that Baja California was a peninsula, as had earlier been discovered by Ulloa and Alarcón, and this information, as I have said, was lost till Kino's time.

An expedition by Vicente de Zaldívar in 1606 to explore the lower Colorado River seems to have left no details (Forbes 1965:111). The Oñate exploration is known from a diary of Fray Francisco de Escobar, a Franciscan who was with the party. The summary of the voyage by Father Gerónimo de Zárate Salmerón (Bolton 1916:268-280), written in 1626, draws in part from the Escobar account but does contain other material.

Natural Features

The region of the lower portions of the Colorado River is one of hot summers and mild winters. It is part of the Sonoran Desert and shares, with large portions of the Desert province and part of the Serrana province, its general conditions (see descriptions in Chapters VI and VII). The area is, of course, dominated by the Colorado River, which in the past carried very large amounts of water to the upper Gulf of California, forming an extensive delta. Because of this delta, the river in its lower reaches flows through a number of channels with surrounding marshlands. The river flow has been greatly modified in modern times by the building of control dams upriver and by the draining off of large amounts of water from the Colorado and Gila rivers for urban and industrial use and for irrigation agriculture.

The lower Colorado River is basically a part of the Basin and Range area; however, the delta area is naturally very flat. As of about 1930, this delta was approximately 150 km from north to south and some 50 km wide in its upper reaches (Kniffen 1931:43). In the sixteenth century it seems likely that the majority of Indians of the Colorado province actually lived in the delta at least part of each year. To the east of the Colorado Delta is the desolate Gran Desierto of extreme northwest Sonora, while to the west lie the Sierra Pinta, the Sierra de Juarez, and the Laguna Salada, a depression separated from the delta by the Sierra de los Cocopas. The Colorado Delta is bounded on the north and west by the Imperial Valley and the Salton depression (p. 43).

Upriver to the east is the Santa Clara Mesa, and north of that are the Gila Mountains, with elevations of almost 1000 m. Above the Gila-Colorado confluence there is a series of low ranges on either side of the Colorado (the Chocolate Mountains are an example). Near Yuma and Pilot's Knob, a bit downstream from the Gila mouth, the Colorado narrows as the hills press in. At that point such nineteenth century explorers as Pattie (1827) and Major Heintzelman (1851) reported the width of the river as 200 to 300 m. Heintzelman also noted that the river was considerably wider below Pilot's Knob, varying from almost 1 km to about 2 km in width. The channel at that time was nowhere "less than four feet," and at one point Heintzelman recorded a tidal rise of at least 3 m, flowing with great velocity (Sykes 1937:15-19). In fact, a tidal bore reaches up the Colorado, and tides may cause the river to rise by 3 m or more, depending on the current. In very low water the tides may reach 150 km upstream (Kniffen 1932:177).

The Lower Colorado province--as far as the actual settlements of Indians were concerned--is low, dry, and very hot and is part of Köppen's BWh (warm desert). At modern Yuma, Arizona, in the northern portion of the province, the altitude is only about 45 m, and parts of the lower delta are considerably below that. At the recording station at Yuma, the January mean temperature is about 13°C, and the July mean is nearly 33°C. The coldest temperature ever recorded at Yuma was -5.5°C and the hottest about 50.5°C. The annual rainfall at Yuma is about 90 mm, of which some 60% falls in the winter and 40% in the summer months (Dunbier 1968:396-398). In this area figures on watershed productivity are not meaningful since the Yuman Indians utilized only a tiny fraction of the Colorado watershed. The amount of water discharged by the Colorado varied drastically in the past. In June of 1903, flooding brought the river level at Yuma to 8.5 m. The following year the amount of water discharged fell to 6% of the previous year's high (Sykes 1937:52-53). In 1909, the flood peak brought twice as much water as the flood of 1903 (pp. 52-54, 58). According to Grinell (1914:58), annual river flow may vary from around 100 m^3 to 3000 m^3 per second, with lowest water at midwinter and high water usually ranging from May 15 to July 1, but with smaller fluctuations at other times of the year. Even at periods of low water the Colorado originally carried a large sediment load so that waters were opaque at all seasons (pp. 57-58). In fact, the sediment load in the Colorado is greater than that of any other major river in the world, with a ratio (silt:water) of 1:277 (Kniffen 1932:165). Parenthetically, the average annual flow of the Colorado at Yuma is twenty billion m^3, or about one-fourth that of the Nile, a river to which the Colorado is often compared (p. 163).

Although the various Indian groups in the delta and near-delta areas of the Colorado utilized the resources of nearby mesas and mountains, the overall orientation was to the river itself. Kniffen (1931:51) has estimated that there were about 120,000 ha of arable land in the lower Colorado in 1605, and presumably the figure in the previous century would have been roughly the same. By arable land he meant that land that was annually inundated by the Colorado and so was available for primitive agriculture. Kniffen (p. 51) excluded lands that were saline and too swampy for cultivation. He makes the point that the Colorado Delta lacks a parallel in the New World but is reminiscent of the lower Nile Valley and, to a degree, of the lower Tigris-Euphrates (p. 43). In both cases--especially in the case of the Nile--a massive river system drains across deserts into the sea, its delta and lower course an oasis in an otherwise barren land. The line of demarcation between desert and delta in the lower Colorado (as in the Nile) is abrupt, with the dense mesophytic vegetation of the valley floor terminating and being replaced with desert xerophytic plants (pp. 43-44).

The thick vegetation growth in the lowlands that are within reach of seasonal water includes thickets of tule and arrowweed, with willow, cottonwood, and other trees. Where there is less available water, large areas are thickly overgrown with mesquite. Actually, there is considerable differentiation and sorting of vegetation. Cottonwood, which prefers a continual but not overly abundant supply of water, lines the banks of the channels, and willow, which needs even more water, clings to the wetter and lower areas near the river. The rushes and tules grow in areas of permanent surface water and are found in the quieter portions of channels and in lagoon or swampy areas. Mesquite cannot live in standing water for any length of time, although it does need water available to its roots, so it tends to grow back from the areas of flooding (Kniffen 1932:174).

As one moves away from the watered areas onto the mesas, vegetation changes to the cacti, especially various of the opuntias. There are also ocotillo and especially the creosote bush (Larrea sp.) the latter plant tends to dominate this portion of the desert. In the sandy washes are desert willow, palo verde, and the smoke tree (Dalea spinosa). On the slopes are palo fierro and visnaga, with the maguey higher in the sierras, especially in the Sierra de Juarez. In the higher valleys of the Juarez and Cocopa ranges are also Washingtonia palms (Kniffen 1931:43-44, 1932:155). Pinyon and juniper grow in uplands of the Juarez Mountains, and in the

San Pedro Martir Range south of the delta (Kelly 1977:22).

Animal life in the lower Colorado area, like plant life, involves forms common to the Sonoran Desert and those adapted to riverine life on the stream or its immediate environs. Desert-adapted animals include a number of small mammals: mice, rats, packrats, skunks, badgers, gophers, raccoons, squirrels, both cottontail rabbits and hares, kit foxes and grey foxes, coyotes, and bobcats. Among the larger animals, the desert bighorn (Ovis canadensis nelsoni) was once common near the river, and deer and antelope seem to have been quite prevalent at one time, as was the beaver. There is a vast variety of birds, including songbirds, warblers, meadowlarks, orioles, sparrows, linnets, goldfinches, mockingbirds, and bluebirds. The desert roadrunner is found throughout the area from the desert to the water's edge. A number of riparian birds (falcons, hawks, ospreys, and owls) are also common, and, as would be expected, so are wading birds such as the green heron, the American egret, the night heron, the blue heron, the ibis, and the crane. A variety of ducks winter in the area, the most numerous being the green-winged teal (Nettion carolinense). An important bird in the Indian economy was the desert quail (Lophortyx gambeli), though this species tends to be scarce in the delta proper (Grinnell 1914:113-296; Forde 1931:91).

There are several kinds of reptiles in the area, including the rattlesnake. As might be expected, populating the large river is also a considerable piscifauna, including carp, catfish, suckers, and the "Colorado salmon" (Ptychocheilus lucius). These often live in the quieter backwaters, where the settling of the sediment clarifies the water. Fish in the main stream tend to be somewhat sparse (Grinnell 1914:62). In later times, at any rate, fish was the leading animal food on the lower Colorado (Castetter and Bell 1951:218). For groups in the lower delta especially, clamming and collection of oysters and mussels were known in historic times (p. 223), though they do not seem to have been overly important, at least not in the nineteenth century. However, the extensive shellmounds noted by Kniffen (1931:47-48) suggest heavier utilization in earlier times, perhaps including the sixteenth century.

In any discussion of the Colorado River area it should be noted that, at least for the delta, the configurations of the river in the sixteenth century are uncertain. The lower channel at that time presumably was somewhat to the east of Hardy's River, as it is today. A survey by J.C. Ives was made in 1858, and the Sykes (1937:38) exploration of 1891 showed that even in that short period of thirty-three years the main channel had been displaced

eastward, in places as much as 10 km or more. In the sixteenth century the channel may have been more westerly. The Salton Sea (in a basin that extends northwestward from the delta and includes the Imperial Valley), of course, is of recent origin. The area north of the delta--that is, from above the Gila River mouth--has a much more circumscribed valley, being flanked on the east and west by the Chocolate Mountains and on the east by the Trigo and Dome Rock ranges.

Language

There can be no real doubt that in the sixteenth century most of the people in the lower Colorado River area spoke Yuman languages. A number of the tribes that occupied the lower river can be identified by names which were still in use in later historic times or, in some cases, even today. This can best be presented in tabular form beginning with the groups farthest south (see Figure 10).

The few words that are given in the Alarcón and Oñate documents have been generally identified as Yuman. Kroeber, for example, points out that the legendary woman, Ciñaca Cohota, simply means "woman chief" which is, indeed, the translation given by Escobar (Hammond and Rey 1953: 1026; Kroeber 1925:803). In addition, as Kroeber indicates, the cultural situation of the lower Colorado peoples in Alarcón's time remained rather static for the next several centuries:

> Alarcón's data . . . specify the Quicama (Halyikwamai), Coana (Kohuana), and Cumana (Kamia?), and allude to many elements of the culture of later centuries: maize, beans, squashes or gourds, pottery, clubs, dress, coiffure, transvestitites, cremation, intertribal warfare, attitude toward strangers, relations with the mountain tribes; as well as characteristic temperamental traits--enthusiasm, resistance to fatigue, stubbornness under provocation, an ebullient emotionality (p. 803).

That a Piman dialect was spoken around the mouth of the Gila River in Oñate's time is indicated beyond any reasonable doubt. This was the Oseca, or Ocara, nation of Escobar (Hammond and Rey 1953:1020). Escobar, who probably had never seen a Pima Indian, identified the Oseca as Tepehuan, who are, of course, linguistically related to the Pima. Escobar (p. 1020) seems to imply that the whole Gila

Alarcón (1540)	Oñate (1605)	Modern Name
Unnamed group near mouth of Colorado	Cocapa (on lower river)	Cocopa
Group whose leader was called "interpreter" (Naguachato)		
Group on opposite (west) side of river		
Unnamed group		
Quicoma where people could understand Alarcon's interpreter	Agalle and Agalec-qua-maya (Tlalliquamallas)	Maricopa(?) Halyikwamai (?)
Coana or Coama	Coguana	Cohuana
	Alebdoma	Halchedoma
Cumana (around or north of Pilot's Knob area)	Ozara (Osera, Oseca)	Pimans Kamia (?)
	Bahacecha	Mohave sub-group (?) Yuma proper (?)
	Amacava or Amauaca	Mòhave (?)

Figure 10. Position of Lower Colorado People in Early Historic Times.

area was inhabited by this one people, and it may be that his term Oseca was meant not only for the settlements near the river mouth but for all the Gila River Pima. This certainly was indicated by Zárate Salmerón (Bolton 1916:275), who (writing some twenty years after Oñate) drew from Escobar and from other sources to describe this expedition. Zárate Salmerón called the group Ozara and stated that they occupied the whole Gila Valley. The name Oseca-O-cara has not been identified to my knowledge, though Forde (1931:98-99) brings up the slim possibility that it is the "Opa" group of the Anza expedition of the 1770s. Just conceivably, the word Oseca (Ocara, Ozara) might be some corruption of o-otam or o-od-ham, the Pimas' name for themselves.

Apropos of Piman speakers on the Colorado, I pointed out some years ago that Alarcón's interpreter was most likely a Piman-speaking Indian (Riley 1973:302). Not only were there individuals who could converse with the interpreter, but in the land of the Quicomas, a group that is normally identified with the more recent Halyikwamais (Kroeber 1925:803; Forbes 1965:96), Alarcón found a settlement where most of the inhabitants seem to have spoken a language known to the interpreter. This settlement might, in fact, have been a Piman outrider in Yuman territory, or perhaps it was made up of individuals of mixed Piman and Yuman ancestry, like towns on the lower Gila discovered by Kino (Burrus 1971:415). It might even have been a Yuman town involved in the Gila River trade.

Population

The impression given by the Alarcón and Díaz parties, and sixty years later by Oñate, is of large numbers of people in the lower Colorado area. Alarcón barely got beyond the junction of the Gila and Colorado, and this is likely true of the Díaz expedition as well. In the delta portion of the river, Alarcón's first contact with the Indians--probably Cocopas near the mouth of the Colorado--brought out 150 armed men (Hammond and Rey 1940:127). Two leagues upstream (about 8 km), Alarcón came upon 1000 armed men plus many women and children (p. 129). Population continued to be dense as Alarcón moved on upriver. At one point he met a chief who told him that there were twenty-three language groups near the river plus others "not far away" (p. 138). As he continued upriver, Alarcón saw other multitudes (pp. 142-147) who lived on both sides of the river (that is to say, the main channel of the Colorado). While it is not possible to arrive at anything like an exact figure for population from

Alarcón's comments, there were obviously some tens of thousands of natives in the lower Colorado area.

The accounts of the Díaz expedition are very difficult to use, because they differ somewhat as to where the party actually was at any given time. Nevertheless, Díaz and his men saw large armed groups (Hammond and Rey 1940:211-212). Escobar, in 1604-1605, gives a count of both rancherias and of people. On the east bank of the river alone, he estimates 30,000 people, and on the west bank he says, "We were told that they were numerous" (Hammond and Rey 1953:1022). The people beyond the junction of the Gila and the Colorado (that is, from the Alebdoma south to the Cocapa) numbered 20,000, and from the rancheria count there were perhaps 2000 to 3000 Piman-speaking Osecas. Escobar would seem to have estimated 6000 to 7000 Indians for the upriver Amauaca and Bahacecha. Parenthetically, Zárate Salmerón states that there were "more than twenty thousand persons on that [east] side of the river alone" (Bolton 1916:277).

The population of the lower Colorado continued to be relatively high throughout the Spanish period. In 1776, Garcés (Kelly 1977:6) listed some 19,000 Yuman-speaking Indians, including the Maricopa and Yuma on the Gila River. As late as 1826, Lieutenant Hardy noted some 5000 to 6000 Indians gathered near the confluence of the Colorado and Hardy's River (1829:355).

Subsistence

The sixteenth century Yuman groups were agricultural, but both hunting and gathering were important. From the Alarcón accounts it is clear that maize and some sort of squash were cultivated, as well as "some grain like millet" (Hammond and Rey 1940:139). The latter was perhaps Amaranthus sp. or Chenopodium sp., both of which are known archaeologically from Snaketown as collected wild plants (Castetter and Bell 1942:33). In more recent times the Cocopa harvested pigweed (Amaranthus palmeri) in considerable quantities and considered it an important food source (Kelly 1977:36). According to Forde (1931:113-114), the Yuma proper actually planted and harvested several of the wild grasses, at least in the nineteenth and early twentieth centuries. One of these was probably Sacaton grass (Sporobolus airoides). Gifford (1931:24) states that the historic Kamia utilized the seeds of both Anemopsis californica and the grass Cyperus erythrorhizos. Utilization of numbers of quelites, or greens, is indicated by the later accounts. It is extremely likely that such foods were common in the sixteenth century, but we have no direct evidence of them. A detailed discussion of usage of wild plant and animal foods by modern Yuman-speaking Indians can be found in Castetter and Bell (1951:179-223).

Pigweed normally ripened in October as did maize, so Alarcón, who was given maize ears as well as cakes made from maize, may have been drawing on the previous year's supply. There is, however, an early planting in January among modern Yuman-speaking Indians, especially in the delta region, though this often fails for lack of water in the crucial growing period. In any case, enough storage of foodstuffs, whether from year to year or from season to season within a year, is indicated so that the Indians in the area were able to supply the Alarcón party. Identification of the sixteenth century maize has never to my knowledge been made from archaeological specimens, but Castetter and Bell (p. 101) point out that modern maize grown by lower Colorado Indians, like that grown by Pima and Papago, is the same type grown earlier by the Hohokam (varieties of the Pima-Papago race).

Alarcón received beans as well as maize and squash (Hammond and Rey 1940:144), though whether these were the common kidney bean or the tepary is unclear. Castetter and Bell (1951:107) seem certain that the tepary (Phaseolus acutifolius) was aboriginal in the area but that the kidney bean (P. vulgaris), though native to the Southwest, was introduced to the lower Colorado groups in post-sixteenth century times (p. 108). The squash is probably Cucurbita moschata. Rogers (p. 109) has reported pottery "as early as Yuman I" that seems to imitate pumpkins.

Alarcón does appear to make a distinction between a pumpkin that is eaten cooked and "small gourds" (Hammond and Rey 1940:136, 139). Castetter and Bell (1951:115) feel that the use of this specific terminology may indicate Lagenaria siceraria, either cultivated or obtained in trade. Unfortunately, all editions of Alarcón are derived from the Ramusio Italian translation, and all references to squash and/or gourds use the word zucche. Rogers (p. 115) points out that pottery copies of double-lobed gourds are known as early as his Yuman II.

Alarcón was also given mesquite bread (Hammond and Rey 1940:128). This could have been made from either mesquite (Prosopis juliflora) or screwbean (Prosopis odorata), both of which were extensively used in later times (Castetter and Bell 1951:181). Mesquite ripens in June in the lower Colorado and the screwbean in August, so that Alarcón's late summer trip probably would have been in a time of plentitude for either plant. In addition to the mesquite bread, Alarcón was presented with "some rabbits and yucca" (Hammond and Rey 1940:142). He

describes Indians who carried a bag "a span long" on the left arm filled "with some seed from which they make a kind of beverage" (p. 130). In another region Alarcón mentions the cooking of "fine fish which are found in the river" (p. 139), and in a number of places there are accounts of the use and hunting of deer (see, for example, p. 149). The Spaniards also observed the growing of a little cotton, and Castetter and Bell (1951:118) suggest that it may have been Gossypium hopi.

The Díaz accounts add very little on Yuman subsistence. Castañeda does mention that the Indians ate "corn bread as large as the big loaves of Castile, baked by the heat of ashes" (Hammond and Rey 1940:210). Melchior Díaz, incidentally, had taken sheep with him for food (p. 231). The Spanish party had at least one dog, called by Castañeda "a greyhound belonging to a soldier" (p. 231), by Mota Padilla (Day 1940b:95) a "little dog," and by Tello (1891:410) a "bad little dog," whose chasing the sheep led indirectly to Díaz' death. Mota Padilla (Day 1940b:95) also mentions that Indians of the area lived on maize and fish from the sea, but this statement may refer to the Indians to the south, along the Gulf of California. One of the serious problems with using Díaz as a source is that the accounts do not agree on his route. For example, Tello states that the Díaz party came to the shores of the sea where they found a friendly group of Indians who were of great size and who lived mostly on fish even though they had bread. Their land was some three or four days from the mouth of the Colorado (Tello 1891:409). Castañeda simply says that Díaz traveled between north and west for some 150 leagues (Hammond and Rey 1940:210). They then came to a province of giants who lived in huts of straw, a hundred people or more sleeping in one hut. I have suggested (Riley 1976b:24-25) that Díaz traveled by way of the Gila River to the Colorado. Until we get more documentation or until archaeological evidence can be brought to bear on the subject (neither particularly likely), we must all use the Díaz information with considerable caution.

In the Oñate expedition of 1604-1605, heavy settlements were encountered from about the mouth of the Bill Williams River southward. In the somewhat narrow river bottoms, among the Amauaca, or Amacava, nation (who may have been a subgroup of the Mohave), Escobar reported maize, beans, and calabashes, much use of the mesquite "which is plentiful throughout the valley," and many grass seeds (Hammond and Rey 1953:1017). Escobar believed that the Amauaca had no great surplus of maize in spite of the "many extensive cornfields," because they "were not adequate for the great number of people living there" (p. 1017). This seems to have been the same situation as for the Bahacecha group who lived just to the south and who were perhaps also subdivisions of the Mohave. Zárate Salmerón, however, comments that more than forty Indians loaded "with maize, beans, and gourds" to give to the Spaniards arrived from the Amacava (Bolton 1916:271).

As they went on downriver, past the Piman-speaking Oseca to the Alebdoma and other delta Yuman groups, the Oñate party again noted the growing of maize, beans, and calabashes and the gathering of "much mesquite" (Hammond and Rey 1953:1021). Everywhere they were given "maize, beans and calabashes," but, in Escobar's words, "not much in quantity, nor according to the large number of people, nor to our needs, until we returned to the province of Moqui, and we were forced to eat seven or eight horses before we arrived there when we came back" (p. 1023). This is an interesting statement, for Oñate had only thirty soldiers, though of course there may have been a number of servants and slaves (p. 1013). It was also winter; Oñate presumably was drawing from the stored harvest of the Yumans; and he had a large area of despoblado to pass through between the lower Colorado River and Hopi country. Even so, it would seem that either the Yumans were not overly eager to give up their food or they did not have spare supplies. Castetter and Bell (1951:66) have pointed out that in spite of the great natural riches of the lower river area, food supplies often did become short, especially in the late spring and early summer.

Escobar, incidentally, mentions that the Oseca wove cotton mantas (Hammond and Rey 1953:1021) and leaves the impression that this was true of the other groups further south. He mentions ditch irrigation for the delta area generally, but from the descriptions it was a very primitive form of runoff irrigation: "We saw many cornfields, but they were not irrigated. There were some branches which extended out from the river and carried water all the year round, and from which, in case of lack of rain, some ditches could be made" (p. 1021).

At some point in the sixteenth or the seventeenth century, Spanish melons spread to the Yuman area where they became extremely popular, as they did in other parts of the Southwest. On October 6, 1700, Kino, traveling in the area of the Gila-Colorado confluence, recorded that the Yuman-speaking Indians of that area had "fields of maize, beans, calabashes, and watermelons, the beans and maize were not yet ripe" (Bolton 1948:249). Less than a half century later in 1746, Sedelmayr visited the lower Colorado region and mentioned both watermelons and melons (Ives 1939:108). Lack of mention of Spanish melons in the Oñate accounts makes me suspect that these cultigens had not reached the lower

Colorado Indians by Oñate's time, though arguing from negative evidence is somewhat risky.

Settlement Patterns

All the early sources describe large populations and collections of individuals that reached—in some cases—thousands. However, neither settlement plans nor house types are very well described. Alarcón (Hammond and Rey 1940:129) mentions an "arbor." In some settlements, houses were close together, for Alarcón comments that the Indians had erected a large cross he gave them "amid their houses that all might see it" (p. 136). The Yuman Indian descriptions of Cibolan towns, however, seem to indicate something strange and exotic. Escobar refers to the settlements of his time as rancherias and the dwellings as huts. Some of the settlements were large; the most extensive one among the Alebdoma had 160 huts (Hammond and Rey 1953:1021).

As far as they go, these sixteenth and seventeenth century ethnographic accounts fit the archaeological picture. Winter houses in the protohistoric Yuma period were circular domed huts with dirt-covered walls. In summer, houses had brush walls with open ramadas for camping (Rogers 1945:187). Parenthetically, the more modern Yuman Indian houses tend to be square or rectangular (Gifford 1931:18-19; Forde 1931:120-121; Kelly 1977:46).

The one mention in Alarcón of details of house structure was of a group (perhaps Cocopa) who lived along the river in summer and at the foot of a mountain (Sierra de Cocopa?) in winter. Their houses "were built of logs covered with mud on the outside. I learned that they built a big round room where they lived all together, men and women" (Hammond and Rey 1940:138). The Relación del suceso, drawing from Alarcón and Díaz, says that "the houses in which they live are shacks and resemble pigsties, being almost underground. The roofs are of straw and made without any skill" (p. 287).

All in all, what Alarcón and the Oñate group seem to be describing is the kind of dispersed settlement that late seventeenth and eighteenth century explorers found and which are indicated in the more recent ethnographic accounts. One suspects that the arbors mentioned by Alarcón were summer houses, and Oñate's "huts" may have included the more enclosed winter houses. Again the comments of Kroeber (1925:803) as to the cultural conservatism and continuity of the Yumans from the sixteenth century to modern times seem to be valid here. In terms of this conservatism, even in the nineteenth century the Yuman groups lived in scattered rancheria settlements with houses as much as 100 m apart (see for example Gifford 1931:18).

Trade

The bonds that united the Colorado province peoples with the rest of the Greater Southwest were, of course, forged by trade. Lower Colorado Indians had access to the various shells, including coral in the Gulf of California, and, in addition, they controlled the trade routes for Pacific Coast shell, especially the much-valued abalone (Haliotis sp.). That the lower Colorado River peoples were involved in this trade in the sixteenth century is certain; indeed, as I pointed out at the beginning of this chapter, important trade goods such as species of Haliotis, Pecten, Olivella, and various other shells had been working their way into the Greater Southwest for centuries before the Spaniards arrived. Summaries of the shell trade situation are given by Brand (1973), Tower (1945), and Jernigan (1978), but there is also an extensive archaeological literature on Pacific Coast shell in various subareas of the Southwest (Fewkes 1896; Kidder 1932; Morris 1919; Haury 1976; Di Peso 1974; Di Peso et al. 1974, to mention only a few). A fragment of abalone appears on the floor of a Vahki phase house at Snaketown, and Haliotis is found at Snaketown from early Pioneer times into the Classic (Haury 1976: 68, 307-308). The vigor of the trade in abalone shell in later pre-Spanish times is well documented at such sites as Pecos (Kidder 1932:193-194), among others. Hohokam materials, including red-on-buff pottery, are known from the Pacific Coast of California as well as Cibola Black-on-white and sixteenth or seventeenth century Hopi pottery (Haury 1976:307; Ruby and Blackburn 1964:209-210); it is very likely that this material passed through lower Colorado Indian lands. I am here, however, mainly interested in the relationships of the Colorado province peoples with the rest of the Greater Southwest.

The documentary evidence for the middleman position of the Colorado groups in the sixteenth century, and especially for their ties to the major southwestern centers further east, is quite clear. The information from Alarcón will be discussed below. In 1542, two years after Alarcón, Juan Rodríguez Cabrillo explored a portion of the California coast. As his two small ships beat their way northward from the home port of Navidad (northwest of present-day Manzanillo), he received extremely interesting and significant information concerning Spanish parties farther to the east. In late August

of 1542, somewhere around modern San Quintín, Cabrillo first heard of Spaniards to the east--men who wore beards and had dogs, crossbows, and swords. These Spaniards were supposed to be five days away, and there were also many Indians with much maize and many parrots (Bolton 1916:19). Cabrillo's informants, perhaps Nakipa Indians, were obviously in touch with more eastern groups (Kiliwa? Cocopa?) and were reporting something they had actually heard or seen. The Spanish group to which they referred might have been that of Alarcón, though it is a bit surprising that his ships were not mentioned. More likely they were talking about the Díaz party, though they could have been discussing the main Coronado group, either giving information on the northward trip or on the retreat to Mexico (very up-to-date information indeed if the latter is the case).

On September 30, somewhere in the area of San Diego Bay, Cabrillo received considerable information from Indians in the region. This area, in the eighteenth century, was occupied by Diegueño groups who were Yuman-speaking and who had a tradition of contacts with the lower Colorado peoples. Whatever their linguistic identification, the Indians of Cabrillo's day told the Spaniards:

> In the interior men like us were travelling about, bearded, clothed, and armed like those of the ships. They made signs that they carried crossbows and swords; and they made gestures with the right arm as if they were throwing lances, and ran around as if they were on horseback. They made signs that they were killing many native Indians, and that for this reason they were afraid (p. 23).

This report certainly was not of Alarcón, whose relationship with the Indians was peaceful with much mutual trust. It might have been a story of Coronado's activities from Cibola or Coofer or perhaps of the fighting done by Alcaráz and other Spaniards in the Corazones area. The strongest possibility, however, is that the Indians were describing Díaz and his party, who seem to have crossed the Colorado and explored portions of the California side.

In the San Clemente and Santa Monica areas, Cabrillo continued to hear news of Spaniards to the east:

> They said that in the interior there were many pueblos, and much maize three days' journey from there. They call maize Oep. They also said that there were many cows; these they call Cae. They also told us of

people bearded and clothed (p. 26).

Although Bolton (p. 26, n. 6) suggests that the "cows" were actually elk, it might be remembered that from the time of Cabeza de Vaca and Coronado this was the common Spanish word for bison. At that point the Spaniards were in an area that Farmer (1935:154-157) considers to be the western terminus of a crucially important prehistoric trade route. This route ran from the coast, with the Diegueño, Kamia, Yuma, and Mohave acting as middlemen to bring olives and other shells from the Pacific Ocean to the lower Colorado and eastward. In addition, if later ethnographic accounts can be projected back to the sixteenth century, the Mohave, at least, actually traded directly with the coastal Indians (p. 157).

I do not want to belabor this point, but it is important that two years after Spanish contact in the interior, a great deal was known of them at a number of points on the California coast, stretching over some hundreds of kilometers. I cannot help believing that the mention of parrots and of bison (if in fact they were bison), animals which provided raw materials for important trade items in the Greater Southwest, had some significance.

That the Caifornia connection with the Southwest was still operative a half century after Cabrillo is indicated by the report of Father Antonio de la Ascensión on the Vizcaino expedition of 1602-1603. In the area around San Diego Bay, Ascensión reports:

The Indians paint themselves white, and black, and dark London blue. This color comes from certain very heavy blue stones, which they grind very fine, and dissolving the powder in water, make a stain, with which they daub the face and make on it lines which glisten like silver ribbons. These stones seem to be of rich silver ore, and the Indians told us by signs that from similar stones a people living inland, of form and figure like our Spaniards, bearded, and wearing collars and breeches, and other fine garments like ours, secured silver in abundance, and that they had a name for it in their own language (Bolton 1916:117).

Bolton (p. 117, n. 2) suggests that this may have been a reference to members of the Oñate expedition which had entered New Mexico a few years before. In any case, it indicates a continuing knowledge of events to the east on the part of coastal California Indians.

The first direct contact with the Colorado River

people by Spaniards came with the Alarcón expedition of 1540. In August of that year Hernando de Alarcón (or, more correctly, Alarçón) entered and made two trips up the Colorado River to about the mouth of the Gila. As he voyaged upriver, he found a number of Indians who could converse with his interpreter, most likely a Piman speaker (as indicated above). The Indians seemed eager to trade with Alarcón throughout the journey, giving him shell and beads, "well tanned skins," maize, and maize cakes (p. 130-131). Alarcón, in turn, gave beads, pieces of cloth, seeds (including wheat and other grain), Spanish hens and cocks, sweet preserves, and "trifles." He probably also gave beans--at least Alarcón carried beans with him (pp. 128, 131, 150, 152). While still in the Colorado Delta country, Alarcón was pointed out "a village located on a mountain" (Sierra de Cocopa or Sierra de Juarez?) whose large number of inhabitants traded deerskins for maize with the lower Colorado people and who lived in big stone houses. Alarcón was shown a woman with a long deerskin skirt who came from that area. From further conversation it would seem that this mountain group spent summers planting on the river and winters at the permanent town (Hammond and Rey 1940:138). The passage is somewhat confused, however (see below under Sociopolitical Organization).

That there were Indian traders is also indicated by the instructions given Alarcón by Mendoza in 1541, when the Spaniards were planning a return voyage to the Colorado River. Alarcón was instructed to question traders to find out about the surrounding areas (pp. 120-121).

While on his journeys, Alarcón gathered a considerable amount of somewhat garbled information about Cibola, including details of events surrounding Esteban's death the year before (pp. 141, 145, 148). The lower Colorado people visited Cibola on occasion and had a good general knowledge of its direction and distance (p. 147). On his trip Alarcón saw warriors with hide shields which, from the descriptions given him, were rather clearly of bison skin (p. 146). Parrot feathers were obviously important to the Indians, for one head man made a special trip to bring some to Alarcón (p. 151). At one point, perhaps among the Cocopa, Alarcón interviewed a man who had been to Cibola and who described it with fair accuracy (tall stone houses of three and four stories with "windows"). He also indicated that the Cibolans wore "many blue stones which were dug from some hard rock" (p. 141). This is very likely a reference to turquoise, but Alarcón does not mention if any of the material reached the Colorado groups. In the Coano (Kohuana) area Alarcón's interpreter overheard Indians saying that at Cibola there were "bearded men like us who said they were Christians" (p. 146). This was around the sixth of September, and Coronado had been in Cibola for almost exactly two months. Among the Coano at any rate the anti-Christian feeling was running high, and the natives felt that Alarcón and his men should be killed (p. 146). The Indians demanded to know if Alarcón was a Christian "as the others are, or a son of the sun" (pp. 146-147). A curious bit of dialogue followed:

> The old man came to me and said: "You asked me if there were in the country of Cíbola other men like yourselves. At that time I pretended I was amazed and replied that it was not possible. These people assure me that it is true and that two men had been there, had seen them, and said that they carried firearms and swords as you do." I asked him if those people had seen them with their own eyes. He said no, but that some of their companions had seen them (p. 147).

What comes out of the Alarcón account is that lower Colorado River people were in rather close contact with Indians of the upper Southwest. There is no specific indication that the Indians who had been recently to Cibola were traders, but this is the most likely interpretation.

Unlike the rich information of the Alarcón account, the confused and conflicting accounts of Díaz' journey to the lower Colorado River give relatively little information about trade and very little dependable information of any sort. As indicated above, the very route of Díaz is in considerable question. In any case, he seems to have crossed into present-day California, apparently the first Spaniard to have done so (Alarcón visited the western side of the Colorado only in its lower, Baja California reaches). As already mentioned, in 1542 Cabrillo probably picked up information about Díaz' depredations while visiting the San Diego area.

The Oñate expedition to the lower Colorado River in 1604-1605 gives the next look at the trade situation. Among the Bahacecha group, who may be equated with the southern Mohave, or perhaps the Yuma proper, a chieftain

> told us, and after him many others at this river, we having shown him a coral, that they procured this substance not far from here, toward the south, and that the Indians dug it from the sand at low tide. The governor found some corals among the Indians of this river, and even more in the

province of Zuñi on our way back. This is because the Indians who live in the direction of the coral coast trade more with the people of this province than with the people at the river of Buena Esperanza (Hammond and Rey 1953:1018).

The Buena Esperanza is the Colorado River. What Father Escobar, who wrote this passage, seems to be saying is that more corals pass on to the Southwest than remain among the lower river peoples.

The Zárate account of this Oñate journey has a curious statement on the trading of coral. Of the Piman-speaking Ozara of the Gila-Colorado confluence area, Zárate says:

> Having arrived among the Ozaras Indians, as they had already inquired of the other nations, and all had said that this nation is very extensive and runs along the coast, and that these are the ones who get from the sea the coral which they call quacame, they made inquiry and found a few. They said that since they were a long distance from the coast they did not have many; but further up the Buena Esperanza River, among Indians of this same nation, a few more were found, and in the province of Zuñi still more were found and bartered for. They said the Indians of the valleys of Señora brought them there to sell; and that they are no more than seven days' journey from there, and that they get them out of the sea, and are not far from there; and that this nation extends to that place (Bolton 1916:278-279).

This somewhat garbled account seems to link the Zuni, the lower Colorado people, the Pimans, and the Serrana groups in a trade network. In the Colorado Delta, Zárate mentions that the Indians had many "white pearl-shells and other shells, very large and shining, which they make into squares," presumably for trade (p. 275). It is conceivable that "quacame" has some relationship to the Piman word kakais, with its implication of wealth (Saxton and Saxton 1969:23).

Confused and distorted stories of what seems to be the Pacific Coast of California as well as the lower Colorado were found in Oñate's time throughout the Southwest from the Cruzados (Yavapai?) in the west to the Tewa on the Rio Grande. Escobar, for example, told of Indians who came

from the west, bearing numerous shells

like those that we now brought from there. Some soldiers told me that when we were at the Buena Esperanza River they had heard about these savage Indians and that they lived between the Buena Esperanza River and the sea (Hammond and Rey 1953:1028).

One of the more interesting bits of information received by Oñate from the Bahacecha was that of "metal" and its location on an island five days' journey to the west, an island that was reached by "canoes or pirogues, whose form and shape they drew on the ground" (p. 1018). The "metal" was soft, and vessels made from it were scooped out rather than hammered. The Spaniards thought that it might be tin or perhaps silver (pp. 1018-1019); in any case it seems to have been common, and both metates and cooking bowls were made from it. Forbes (1965:109) suggests that the "metal" was actually steatite from Santa Catalina Island and that the shell made into squares described by Zárate was abalone.

Assuming that the lower Colorado people were trading in Santa Catalina steatite, it is unclear how much of this was reexported to the Southwest proper. Steatite appears--at least one worked example--at Snaketown as early as the Pioneer period (Haury 1976:298); Kidder at Pecos notes a realistically carved bivalve of "gray soapstone" (1932:92), though the time period is unknown. Steatite is certainly traded in the Southwest, but it is also true that local sources of steatite are known in various parts of the area, and often the provenience of given artifacts is not known. It would be most interesting if the California coast did, in fact, supply Santa Catalina steatite to the Southwest generally, as it may have done to the lower Colorado area. Sophisticated chemical or proton-neutron activation analyses in the future will provide a great deal more information on this matter.

Sociopolitical Organization

From the accounts of the Coronado and Oñate periods I suspect that the social and political uses, like those of other parts of culture, have changed very little in the Colorado area from the sixteenth century to recent times (see also Kroeber 1925:803). The actual data from the early accounts leave many gaps, but what comes across clearly is that small groups, each probably speaking its own dialect, occupied segments of the river and, at least in some cases, had winter habitations back from the river area along the slopes of the mountain ranges. Each group had its own recognized bit of

territory (Hammond and Rey 1940:138), and one headman indicated to Alarcón that there were twenty-three language groups along the river, plus others back from the Colorado (p. 138). At one point Alarcón was told that "every house chose its own chieftain" (p. 139). Elsewhere, however, Alarcón seems to have dealt with men who could control hundreds of individuals; Oñate's chief Otata also seems to have been a person of some consequence, as was the chief Curraca, "which in their language means Lord" (Bolton 1916:271), of the Amacavas, or Amauacas. The term Curraca is honorific, meaning "Old Man" (Kroeber 1925:802), just as the Cohota of the Bahacechas (Bolton 1916:273) seems to be identical with the kohota, or "entertainment chief," of the nineteenth century Mohave (Kroeber 1925:802). As Kroeber remarks, "the languages of the Colorado have changed as little in three centuries as the speech of the Chumash that Cabrillo recorded" (p. 803).

There are certain indications of greeting or peace ceremonials. For example, when Alarcón (probably somewhere among the Cocopa) met groups of armed Indians, they put down their weapons in a pile and each came to receive trade goods. Before this happened, a man "bearing a staff, in which certain shells were set . . . entered the water to give it to me" (Hammond and Rey 1940:127). This particular encounter did not end well. Alarcón asked for food (his interpreter could not make himself understood so that signs were necessary), and the Indians requested that he fire a harquebus. This action created something of a panic except in two old men who stood their ground and scolded the group for its timidity. As the Indians began to collect their weapons, Alarcón attempted to placate the most vocal of the old men, offering him a "silken cord of several colors, but he, with great rage, bit his lower lip hard and hit me on the chest with his elbow, and began to talk to his people with greater fury" (p. 128). Alarcón thereupon reentered his boat and began to sail upriver. The Indians tried to lure him ashore by offering ears of maize, but Alarcón decided to stay well out in the river (p. 129). It is difficult to know exactly what went on at this particular meeting. The old man who hit Alarcón was perhaps a shaman and may have feared witchcraft after the episode of the cord.

Continuing upriver, Alarcón saw large numbers of individuals, as many as 1000 at one place. He picked up small amounts of information on settlement patterns. In Quicoma, for example, he was told that the Indians came to the river area only in summer to gather the harvest.

Alarcón was somewhat ethnographically minded; he questioned various of the Indians on aspects of culture. According to his information, the Indians married only one wife, and marriages were arranged, with the groom's father bringing presents (pp. 138-139). Actually, this information may be a bit misleading, for it comes in response to a question about whether women were held in common. The Indians told Alarcón that women were guarded before marriage and that adultery after marriage was a serious offense. Marriage between brother and sister and between close relatives was forbidden. Postmarital residence seems to have been neolocal, but the information here is rather vague (p. 139).

The major cause of illness and death, according to Alarcón's informants, was a disease which caused vomiting of blood through the mouth (tuberculosis?). Healing was done by professionals:

> They have their medicine men who heal them with words and by blowing on the sick. The dress of these people is the same as of the others before. They carry their reed tubes to perfume themselves in the same manner as the people of New Spain use tobacco (p. 139).

Although the context does not make it clear, I am tempted to believe that the "reed tubes" actually refer to healing ceremonies; this would, at any rate, fit the later historic picture. The dead were cremated, as they were throughout historic times, and widows were constrained from remarrying for half a year to a year (p. 139).

Alarcón noted considerable details on transvestites and also saw "prostitutes." Considering the casual attitude toward sex in later times, I suspect that this information on prostitutes lost something in the translation. Nevertheless, Alarcón's data, as far as it goes, would be generally applicable in the nineteenth century, before modernization destroyed the bases of Yuman culture.

Material Culture

Alarcón (pp. 139, 142) lists a number of material items that are known from archaeology or from later ethnographic accounts. These include pots, grinding stones, bags of rattan fiber, staffs, and, of course, various weapons (see Warfare, below). There is no mention of boats by Alarcón, but when Díaz reached the Colorado River shortly after Alarcón departed, the Díaz party crossed the river either on rafts (p. 211) or in large baskets made watertight with tar--"pasaron á cada español en uno como escriño ó cesto grande que los indios tienen aderezados con un betún que no lo gasta ni pasa el

agua" (Tello 1891:410). In more modern times, Yuman Indians used rafts made of cottonwood logs and bundles of tule. They also used large pottery vessels to ferry children and goods, a swimmer pushing the pot in front of him (Forde 1931:127).

Alarcón gives considerable information about costume, and, again, it fits quite well with later ethnographic accounts:

> They have their noses pierced, and from them hung some pendants, while others wore shells. They have their ears pierced with many holes in which they place beads and shells. All of them, both small and large, wear a multi-colored sash about the waist; tied in the middle is a round bundle of feathers which hangs in the back like a tail. Likewise, around the muscles of their arms, they wear a narrow band wound around so many times that it extends the width of a hand. They wear some small blades of deer bones, tied around one arm, with which they wipe their sweat. From the other hang some reed canes. They wear also a sort of bag a span long, tied to their left arm, using it as an arm band for the bow, filled with some seed from which they make a kind of beverage. Their bodies are branded by fire. Their hair is cut in front, and in the back it hangs to the waist. The women go about naked. They wear a large bunch of feathers, painted and glued, tied in front and behind. They wear their hair like the men. There were among these Indians three or four men dressed like women (Hammond and Rey 1940:129-130).

Chiefs had more fancy garments. One among the Quicama, who had "five or six thousand men" surrounding him, is described by Alarcón:

> He wore a garment closed in front and back and open on the sides, fastened with buttons worked in chequered black and white. It was made of the fiber of rattan, very fine and well made. When he came to the edge of the water, his attendants took him in their arms and placed him in my boat (p. 151).

Sixty years later Oñate also notes garments (or lack of same). Among the Amauaca and Bahacecha, according to Escobar:

> The custom in regard to dress is not

to wear any, but to go naked from the sole of the foot to the head, which is the general practice among all the people who live along this river. Only the women cover merely their privy parts with two bunches of grass or fibre, which at least cover them, but they do not try to cover any other portion of the body. They all wore their hair loose, reaching only to the shoulders. The nature of the land permits them to go about in this scanty attire (Hammond and Rey 1953:1017).

Warfare

Throughout historical times, the Yuman tribes were known for their warlike attributes, which curiously were combined with friendliness and hospitality, especially an open and generous approach to strangers. These conflicting cultural attitudes are documented by Alarcón. While going up- and down-river, Alarcón was flooded with gifts. Doubtless some were considered exchange for the many gifts that the Spaniards handed out, but the generous offers of food, especially, seem to be a matter of hospitality and good will. On the other hand, Alarcón was threatened a number of times, and armed men in large numbers were commonly seen along his route. The Indians described "big wars over trifles. Whenever they had no cause for war they would get together and some one of them would say: 'Let us go wage war at a certain place,' and immediately they would set out with their weapons" (Hammond and Rey 1940:135).

A little after he heard this statement, Alarcón found that his local interpreter (who also seemed to have been a chief of some sort) would not go beyond a certain point, for "the people we should meet on our way now were his enemies" (p. 139). Alarcón heard of war waged with people from across the mountain and of evil people upriver (pp. 135, 142). The latter group (apparently the Coano) had sentries "watching at the border of their country" (p. 142). Still further up river, in Cumana country, an "enchanter" attempted to block Alarcón's voyage up the Colorado by placing reeds across the stream. The Indians in this area were standoffish, and the Cumana chief refused to meet with Alarcón (p. 154).

The Díaz party seems to have met a great deal of hostility on the part of the lower Colorado Indians, but this, at least in part, was due to Díaz' brutal behavior (pp. 212-213). The Oñate party noted little or nothing in the way of fighting, except to say that their guides feared to go very far and that

Indians on the opposite (west) bank of the river were hostile.

The weapons described by early Spanish explorers, especially by Alarcón, sound very much like the inventories taken by modern ethnologists. Both Alarcón and Díaz mention bows and arrows (pp. 127, 129, 141, 142, 212). Alarcón also mentions shields, some most probably of bison hide (p. 146). A distinction is made between maces and clubs—the Indians had both types of weapons (p. 141). Quivers were tied to the left arm of the warriors (p. 130), and the bow and arrow seems a specially favored weapon. In one place, Alarcón notes 250 men armed with this weapon; in another, 1000 (pp. 127, 129). War parties also carried banners "like the Indians of New Spain" (p. 127). At another place, Alarcón (p. 129) describes the bows and arrows as being of hard wood and two or three types of maces made of fire-hardened wood (p. 129).

Religion

Alarcón everywhere found evidence of sun worship. To some degree this may have been influenced by his assertion that he was "son of the sun," but the descriptions also suggest an aboriginal interest in, and ceremonies to, the sun. For example, at various points in his journey up the Colorado, Alarcón noted that offerings, especially of food, were made by tossing bits into the air (pp. 135-136). They also "took maize and other grains in their mouths and sprinkled me with them, saying that that was the way they offered sacrifice to the sun" (p. 144).

One curious mention is made in Alarcón of hearts of men killed in battle: "They carved out the hearts of some and ate them, others they burned" (p. 135). The burning of hearts as sacrifice, of course, is reminiscent of the Serrana, but the terseness of Alarcón's statement makes it dangerous to read too much into it. That the lower Colorado Indians had some knowledge of western New Spain was indicated by an informant who stated that "the old men say that very far from their country there were other bearded men like ourselves" (p. 134). Another informant told Alarcón that he had heard of a large river where there were alligators so big that their skins were made into shields (p. 143-144).

The most intriguing information on religion concerned the old woman from a mountain who had metal like that of some bells shown the Indians by Alarcón (p. 143). This perhaps was the same old woman who lived in a hut "at a certain lake" and who was given many blankets, feathers, and maize by people in the area. She seemed to live somewhere between the lower Colorado and Cibola, perhaps upriver; her name was Guatuzaca (p. 145).

In the Escobar account of the Oñate expedition, the stories of the supernatural woman became mixed with stories of fabled peoples who seem to come more from European medieval travelers' tales than from the Indians (Hammond and Rey 1953:1025-1026). One persistent theme, however, is that of an island where lived a woman giant. Her name was Ciñaca Cahota, which "signifies 'principal woman' or 'chieftainess.'" She lived with a sister on the island, and most of the men on this island were bald-headed (p. 1026). Zárate adds a bit more information (Bolton 1916:274-276). The island was called Ziñogaba, and this was also the name of the people who inhabited it. These people had boats seventy feet long and twenty feet wide with sails. On that island were many pearl shells. One instrument used was a stick "from which are pendant many pieces of that metal of which they make dishes from which they eat; and, making a great noise, they dance in pairs to the sound" (p. 274).

The Oñate party got this information from the Bahacecha, probably the Mohave, who, at least in later times, had a tradition of direct contact with the Pacific Ocean south of the San Gabriel Mountains. Zárate (or his source), at any rate, was convinced that the Indians had seen the boats (p. 274). As the Oñate party traveled further down the Colorado River, they continued to hear stories of the island of Ziñogaba. Pearls there were as large and thick as rosary beads. The mistress of the island

was a giantess, and . . . she was called Ciñacacohola, which means chieftainess or mistress. They pictured her as the height of a man-and-a-half of those of the coast, and like them very corpulent, very broad, and with big feet; and that she was old, and that she had a sister, also a giant-ess, and that there was no man of her kind, and that she did not mingle with anyone of the island. The mystery of her reigning on that island could not be solved, whether it was by inheritance, or tyranny by force of arms. And they said that all on the island were bald, having no hair on the head (p. 276).

The Indians of the California coast did, of course, have boats. One in the Santa Catalina area described by Vizcaino in 1602 was "so well constructed and built that since Noah's Ark a finer and lighter vessel with timbers better made has not been

seen" (pp. 87-88). Still and all, the accounts given by Oñate's men might be confused descriptions of Spanish ships which by 1605 were occasionally seen along the California coast.

Kroeber makes an interesting comment on the Ziñogaba story:

The mythical island Ziñogaba in the sea sounds as if it might be named from "woman," thenya'aka in Mohave, and ava, "house." Its chieftainess, Ciñaca cohota, is certainly "woman-kohota." "Acilla," the ocean, is Mohave hatho'ilya. Other modern dialects have "s" where Mohave speaks "th." It is clear that the languages of the Colorado have changed as little in three centuries as the speech of the Chumash that Cabrillo recorded (1925:803).

I would hazard a guess that the island of Ziñogaba was not mythical but, instead, a confused account of Santa Catalina. Kohota, incidentally, is the modern name given by the Mohave to the festival chief. This officer, at least in later historic times the same as the kwoxot of the Yuman peoples downriver from the Mohave, had powerful religious and sociopolitical functions. It seems likely that some of Alarcón's chiefs and "old men" with authority either had the position of kwoxot or of kwanami (war chief).

General Comments

This account of the lower Colorado River people obviously leaves a great many informational gaps. It might be well to stress once more that from the Alarcón and Oñate accounts, and from minor information contributed by the Díaz party, it seems clear enough that the major elements of Yuman culture as they were reported from the eighteenth and nineteenth centuries were also present in the sixteenth. It is also clear that, all in all, the Yuman peoples, in both the sixteenth century and in later times, were and are basically southwestern in culture (see, for example, Kroeber 1928). As indicated above, a major factor in producing this inclusion in the southwestern way of life was the favored position of the lower Colorado peoples as middlemen in both the Gulf of California and Pacific Ocean trade. As Brand (1973:92-101), among others, has demonstrated, this trade goes well back into pre-Spanish times.

By the time the Spaniards arrived in the 1530s

and early 1540s, the lower Colorado Indians had long-standing contacts and were close enough to the heartland of the Southwest to be affected by the vagaries of political and social change further east. The avid interest of Alarcón's Yuman informants in Cibola was no accident.

CHAPTER IX

LITTLE COLORADO PROVINCE

In this and the following two chapters, I deal with the northern part of the Greater Southwest. This is, to a large degree, the old Anasazi area, although leavened and modified by intrusions of Mogollon peoples, especially in the Little Colorado area and parts of the Rio Grande Basin. This Pueblo region, as it is usually called because of the distinctive architecture and town patterns, has received more attention than any other part of the Greater Southwest, not only from archaeologists but also from ethnohistorians, historians, and ethnologists. It began to attract scholarly attention as early as the 1870s and 1880s, and from the beginning there was a concept of combined diachronic and synchronic studies--the prehistory interpreted and elucidated by investigation of the historic and contemporary peoples. In addition, turbulence on the Spanish frontier, especially in the seventeenth century, gave rise to a very large amount of documentation which throws light on Spanish politics of Church and State and culture in a remote border area. It is unfortunate that the Spaniards were so interested in their own internal quarrels and rivalries that relatively little information on the newly conquered and missionized native peoples is contained in the various documents. Nevertheless, there is enough to indicate that Indian life was being modified by the pressures of Church and State, but modified rather slowly, and most drastically in certain limited directions--for example, in the adoption of Spanish agricultural techniques and plants and animals.

The Spanish world was, of course, not alone in the ruthless application of missionization. The Puritans in New England, in this same seventeenth century, were harsher, more single-minded, and more immediately successful, coupling missionization with brutal military operations that destroyed not only Indian culture but the very Indians themselves (Jennings 1971).

In the eighteenth century, after the trauma of the Pueblo Revolt, the overt pressures to change Pueblo culture--pressures that in part caused that revolt--seem to have slackened. It was, generally, a more tolerant century. Religion, even in the backward and traditionalist-minded Spanish Empire, was not quite the burning issue it had been in the past. Even though Spain itself, not to mention New Spain or its remote and rude outpost of New Mexico, hardly provided a favorable climate for Voltaire, the French Encyclopaedists, or works of the Scottish

Enlightenment--and though the Inquisition continued until the early nineteenth century--still, the eighteenth century saw a certain shift in attitude in the Spanish world. On the northern frontiers of New Spain it took the form of redefinition. In the seventeenth century, the Franciscan Fathers and the civil government, operating from Santo Domingo and Santa Fe, would have dealt out floggings and even harsher punishments for Pueblo Indians trying to practice native weather control and fertility ceremonies. In the eighteenth century these same ceremonies were increasingly held to be "harmless superstitions." It is fairly clear that to practice Pueblo Indian religion in the eighteenth century was safer than in the evangelical and missionizing seventeenth century. In addition, the eighteenth century saw the western edge of San Felipe de Nuevo Mexico--that is, the region of the Little Colorado River--become largely independent. In the Tusayan-Hopi area the Spaniards never really reestablished control after the 1680 Pueblo Indian revolt, and even in Zuni that control was minimal.

I must say at the outset that the three chapters of the Pueblo world delineating the provinces of the Little Colorado, the Rio Grande, and the Pecos have a certain arbitrariness. To some degree these provinces are geographic conveniences; the three names represent three major river drainages. However, the two components of the Little Colorado province do, in fact, hold together quite well. It can be demonstrated archaeologically and ethnologically that Cibola-Zuni and Tusayan-Hopi were culturally close together from pre-Spanish times to the present day, though they differed, and still differ, in language. Together, they formed the nuclear group of western pueblos in the sixteenth century, as they do in the twentieth. The Rio Grande, however, involved a number of varied pueblos, of which the Keresan, historically, seem to form a kind of bridge between the western and eastern pueblos. Again, there are two major language groups: Keresan and Tanoan. My reasons for lumping this very large area (and, in fact, it is unclear how large it was--that is, how far up and down the Rio Grande and its tributaries the settlements extended) are mostly because of the generalized and often unlocalized nature of the information. I suspect that a good case could be made for several Rio Grande provinces if information was available (see Chapter X). Of course, the same statement could be made for the Serrana province.

Since I have taken the position of a "lumper," one might argue that the Pecos province should also be subsumed under Rio Grande. It is true that Pecos spoke a Tanoan language; Pecos was Towa-speaking, and its closest relationships, linguistically, were to the pueblos on the Jemez Plateau. The nearby

Tanos towns of the Galisteo Basin spoke a slight variant of Tewa, another Tanoan language. Here, however, the position of Pecos as the Pueblo power of the east and the eastern center for trade to the Plains gave the town a very special position both in the eyes of the Spaniards and of other Pueblo Indians, a position that practically demands special treatment. One might say with fair accuracy that Pecos was a province in the political sense, belligerent and bold in contact with the Plains peoples and forever dabbling in the affairs of the greater Pueblo world at its back. It was the conduit par excellence through which the goods of the Plains world poured into Pueblo land and beyond, and it took great advantage of its position. Even in the sixteenth century Pecos may have been challenged by Picuris and perhaps by the Salinas pueblos, but little is known about this aspect of the politics of trade. In the eighteenth century the people of Taos, linguistic kinsmen of Picuris, undercut Pecos and took over the trade routes, although by this time Spanish influences had much muddied the waters. In any case, sixteenth century Pecos was the great eastern hub of the Pueblo world, and nearby Tanos (just across Glorieta Pass in the Rio Grande drainage) seems to have been greatly influenced by Pecos. It is necessary to make statements like this with some diffidence, however, for we actually know very little of the Tanos pueblos in the sixteenth century. I shall discuss the Pecos situation in detail in Chapter XI below.

The Little Colorado province had a somewhat different post-Spanish history than the previous areas I have discussed (as in fact did the Rio Grande and Pecos), and archaeological investigations have been oriented differently. The Spanish period started very early (in 1539), and from that initial contact there was no real break with the mesoamerican-Spanish world. Spaniards actually visited the area in considerable numbers in the period 1539-1542, and when the Coronado party retreated from the Pueblo world in 1542, it left behind a number of mesoamerican Indian allies, many of them (probably most of them) at Cibola-Zuni. These Indians bridged the gap between the Coronado expedition and those Spanish entradas of the early 1580s, a number of Mesoamericans being still alive at the latter date, including, it would seem, both Tarascan and Nahuatl speakers. Indeed, at least one descendant of the original mesoamerican settlers still lived at Zuni in Oñate's day, and surely there were more. A Pecos Indian was kidnapped by Espejo in 1583, and one conceivably brought by the Coronado expedition returned with Oñate in 1598 (Riley 1974:32-33). Oñate also found Indians left by the Castaño expedition (1590-1591) who could speak Nahuatl and one or more

Pueblo Indian languages, though as far as is known, none in the Little Colorado area.

Not only was there direct contact, but the Indians had indirect connections through the trade routes that ran northward from Sonora and, after about 1560, from Spanish settlements in Chihuahua and Coahuila. In addition to the legal and semi-legal entradas, there were outlaw expeditions to the Southwest. There are some records of one, that of Leyva and Humaña in 1593 or 1594.

Because of the nature of Spanish contact and the lack of any real break in continuity, it is somewhat difficult to decide at which point in time to end the account of Little Colorado and other Puebloan peoples. Yet this continuity is in many ways more apparent than real. In the sixteenth century the richest accounts come from the earliest expeditions--those associated with Coronado. The next most valuable source is from the 1580s. The Oñate expedition, in spite of the massive documentation available, gives relatively little information on Indian culture, though of course there are important data on population, group distribution, etc.

This situation continues in the seventeenth century, especially for the Little Colorado region. The writings of men like Benavides and Perea in the early part of the century contain rich though somewhat equivocal demographic information. Generally, however, the archival and other sources for this century concern the relationships of Spaniards to Spaniards, the Indian being simply a human element in the landscape. Such information as we do glean comes for the most part indirectly or casually. Indeed, much the same situation is true for the eighteenth century. It is not until the ethnological and archaeological studies of the latter part of the nineteenth century that we again get the cultural information on Pueblo Indians found in the Coronado documents and to a lesser extent in those of Chamuscado and Espejo. By Oñate's time there were already some changes in Pueblo Indian life, and with the coming of Oñate, forced drastic acculturation began in earnest. As said above, it seemed to have been quite selective, and in certain areas that the Spaniards considered vital (religion, for example) it failed in large part. When modern ethnological accounts of Zuni and Hopi (and other Pueblo groups) are compared with what is known of the sixteenth century, certain changes seem, at least on the surface, fairly clear. The Spanish system of secular governance was superimposed on the religiously oriented structure, and certain ideas, bits of iconography, and ritual forms originating in Catholicism can be easily identified. Still and all, we do not know to what extent the Pueblo Indians had a group of secular political officials in pre-Spanish times, and we are not certain of the depth or even of the nature of the changes in religion due to Spanish contact. It is quite possible that Pueblo officers with Spanish names today are simply the descendants of a secular group already in existence, though it is even more likely that these modern officials personify secular functions of pre-Hispanic religious officers. Quite possibly the Christian and post-Spanish mesoamerican elements in Pueblo Indian religion (incorporation of saints and the Moctezuma cult, for example) are nothing more than a working out of the long-standing tendency of Pueblo religion to incorporate mesoamerican elements, a tendency that led to a heavy mesoamericanization of Pueblo religion centuries before Coronado (Di Peso 1968b; Kelley 1971; Kelley and Kelley 1975).

Because of the sharp drop-off in intensity of cultural information, my analysis of the Little Colorado and the other Pueblo areas will depend most heavily on that pristine contact by Coronado in the period 1539-1542. This will be augmented by the information gleaned in the 1580s (and for the eastern group of pueblos, the early 1590s), by materials from the Oñate expedition, and to a minor degree from other major early seventeenth century documents (Montoya, Benavides, Perea, Zárate Salmerón). As with other provinces, then, major reliance will be on sixteenth century materials.

Archaeology and Early History

The archaeology of the Little Colorado region is fairly well known. A review of earlier Anasazi cultures is not particularly germane to my purpose, except to say that at such sites as Village of the Great Kivas near present-day Zuni (Roberts 1932:129, 164-169) there seems to have been an original Chaco-oriented settlement to which later groups of "Mogollonized" Indians came, bringing traits that foreshadow Cibola-Zuni (p. 169; see also Riley 1975b:145-147). There were numbers of sites in the upper Little Colorado drainage south and west of the Zuni area, some, such as Kiatuthlanna, dating from Basketmaker times (Roberts 1931). At Mariana Mesa some 70 km south of Zuni, McGimsey (1980:11) found sites that date back to the mid-ninth century A.D. Work by Martin, Rinaldo, and their associates has given considerable information on a series of sites in the Holbrook - St. Johns - Springerville areas. Though they begin earlier, settlements cluster around the twelfth to mid-fifteenth centuries. To some degree they are clearly ancestral to Cibola-Zuni, and it seems likely that Tusayan-Hopi also

drew from them. The Little Colorado sites have both Anasazi and Mogollon influences. There were also Sinagua influences (Schroeder 1977:62-63; Martin et al. 1967; Martin et al. 1962, 1964; Martin and Rinaldo 1950, 1960a).

As I indicated above, the Zuni-Hopi area and, to some degree, Acoma and certain Rio Grande pueblos form a western Pueblo area, which is clearly a mixture of Anasazi and Mogollon (plus conceivably Hohokam) elements. There are a number of marker traits in this tradition; they include the square kiva, brownware pottery (often with a red or white slip) or polychrome ware, extended burials, specific color-direction association, towns with multiple plazas, and the three-quarter grooved ax (Martin and Rinaldo 1960b; Dutton 1963b; Johnson 1965; Lipe 1978:377; Reed 1950:128-131; Riley 1963; Rouse 1962:38-41).

Before the thirteenth century the Tusayan were basically Anasazi, but after that time, and especially during the fourteenth and fifteenth centuries, Tusayan became increasingly western Pueblo (Reed 1950:130-131). By the time of first Spanish contact, both Tusayan and Cibola had shrunk to small areas, but ones that kept in close contact with each other. Evidence of this contact was found at Hawikuh in a series of excavations by Hodge and his associates in the period 1917-1923, an archaeological project that is of the utmost importance in any interpretation of Cibola-Zuni. Other work on the contact period sites includes the excavation in 1923 at Kechipawan and recent research by members of the Zuni Archaeological Enterprise, whose work includes survey at the historic Cibolan town of Kyakima (see Ferguson et al. 1977). The most useful work on late prehistoric and early historic Tusayan results from the extensive Peabody excavations at Awatovi which have been published in part in the Peabody series (see below).

The early Spanish accounts of the Little Colorado province come in three parts. In the period 1539-1542, the area, especially Cibola, was the initial region of the upper Southwest contacted by the Spaniards, first by the Marcos-Esteban parties, then by the main Coronado group. After Coronado's retreat, the area was left without direct Spanish contact (though, as mentioned above, Hispanicized Indians from central and west Mexico continued to live there) until the Chamuscado expedition reached Zuni sometime in late 1581 or very early 1582 and gained some information about--though they did not visit--Hopi. In 1583, the Espejo expedition did reach both Zuni and Hopi and made a side exploring trip into what is almost certainly the Jerome area to look for mines (Bartlett 1942).

The Castaño de Sosa expedition of 1590-1591 did

not reach the Little Colorado province, but when Oñate finally settled New Mexico beginning in 1598, he quickly contacted both Zuni and Hopi. Acts of "Obedience and Vassalage" were promulgated at Zuni on November 9, 1598, and at Hopi on November 15 of the same year (Hammond and Rey 1953:357-362). Incidentally, as early as Chamuscado's time, variations on the modern name for Zuni were beginning to appear and Tusayan was being replaced by Mohose or some variant (see below for fuller discussion).

The western Pueblo area, though visited a number of times by the Spaniards, was not brought into the Spanish orbit by missionization until about thirty years after the initial conquest by Oñate. In the year 1629 a mission was founded at Hawikuh by Fray Francisco de Porras and Fray Roque Figueredo, and in the same year a mission at Awatovi was founded by Fray Francisco de Porras. A second Hopi mission (with an attached convent) at Oraibi began the following year under the direction of Fray Bartolomé Romero (see Scholes 1949; Scholes and Bloom 1944-1945).

Spanish control over the Hopi-Zuni area was never firm during the seventeenth century. In 1632 Fray Francisco de Letrato was killed at Hawikuh, and his associate, Fray Martín de Arvida, was killed by Zuni companions en route to Sonora. The following year Fray Porras died at Awatovi and was reported to have been poisoned (Montgomery et al. 1949:12-13). The revolt at Zuni disrupted the mission there, and it was not reestablished until the 1640s. At the time of the Pueblo Revolt in 1680 there were mission stations in the Zuni town of Halona (the missionary at Hawikuh having been murdered by Apaches in 1670) and at the Hopi sites of Oraibi, Shongopovi, and Awatovi. Zuni and Hopi both cooperated with the insurgents, as did most of the Pueblo Indians, and all the priests in the west were killed. Although the Spaniards managed to reopen their mission at Halona (which gradually became modern Zuni), it declined throughout the eighteenth century and eventually was deserted for a time. The Hopi never allowed missionaries to return; the one town, Awatovi, that invited them back was sacked by the Hopi themselves (see Hanson 1980). In the words of J.O. Brew:

> The struggle, lost by the Christian God in Tusayan in 1680, stayed lost. The Kachinas won then and the Kachinas hold the field today. From that time on, Spaniards appeared on the Hopi mesas only as unwelcome visitors; except at Awatovi. And Awatovi did not live long to enjoy the reunion (Montgomery et al. 1949:18).

Of all the Pueblo provinces, that of the Little Colorado is the most peripheral in terms of Spanish contact. Like the rest of the Pueblo area it absorbed Spanish thrusts in the sixteenth century, but unlike the Rio Grande and Pecos areas it managed to hold the Spaniards at arm's length during the seventeenth century and essentially withdrew from Spanish control in the eighteenth. The result is that the western group of pueblos, even today, remains somewhat less acculturated to European ways. The curious thing, however, is that this differential acculturation is not more sharp and clear cut. All in all, the culture of the Pueblo Indians, generally, was a tough and flexible fabric, giving wherever and whenever necessary but scarcely tearing, much less shredding. It accepted alien patterns into the weave as had been the case for many centuries, but incorporated them into a truly Pueblo pattern. For a people who had absorbed the essence of Mexican gods and ideas, Christianity and Anglo-Spanish ways, generally, presented difficult but not unsolvable problems.

Natural Features

Settlements in the Little Colorado province were situated on tributaries of the Little Colorado River. One group was on the Zuni River in the upper valley. Another series of towns was near intermittent streams or washes that flow from Black Mesa across the Painted Desert to the middle course of the Little Colorado. In the Cameron area, the Little Colorado enters a deep canyon through which it flows in a generally northwesterly direction until it enters the main Colorado River somewhat downstream from Marble Gorge and at the eastern edge of the Grand Canyon proper. The topography of the Little Colorado and Colorado rivers is important in understanding how contacts were channeled from the Cibola-Tusayan region to the west and southwest. The major aboriginal trail crossed the Little Colorado somewhere in the modern Winslow region. It continued into the middle Verde Valley around Jerome and eventually reached (via the Santa Maria and Bill Williams River drainages) to the lower part of the Colorado River. Another trail, perhaps following the line of modern Interstate 40, reached the Colorado River above the confluence with the Bill Williams River; it seems to have been connected with a northerly route from Tusayan north of the San Francisco Mountains and in part along the south rim of the Grand Canyon.

From the Cibolan towns to Tusayan, the major road seems to have run north and west along the southern edge of Black Mesa and probably partly followed the line of modern Arizona State Highway 264. I am less sure of the roads southward from Cibola; one of them may have crossed the mountains somewhere in the Fort Apache area, while another might have run south into the Quemado and Reserve regions, perhaps following the San Francisco River for a time but eventually crossing the Gila somewhere in the vicinity of the modern town of Cliff. Alternatively, the route may have swung west from Luna into the Blue River drainage to the San Francisco and the Gila somewhere near Clifton (see Trade, below, for further discussion; also Di Peso et al. 1974:Vol. 4, 101; Bolton 1964:108-110; Chapter VII, above).

Like the rest of the Greater Southwest, the Little Colorado province is shaped culturally by its particular environment. Unlike the warm deserts to the south and west, this is an area of great seasonal climatic contrasts. The region is generally rather high, being for the most part contained in the Colorado Plateaus. In point of fact, I am concerned with only a small section of this much larger area--the upper drainage of the Little Colorado and its tributary the Zuni (Cibola) and the region along the southern flanks of Black Mesa (Tusayan). The Cibola area is set in a broad valley of the Zuni River which rises in the highlands near the continental divide, draining westward from the western slopes of the Zuni Mountains and the area around Ramah. At Black Rock, about 8 km east of present-day Zuni (old Cibolan Halona), the river descends to the broad Zuni Basin which extends off to the southwest and through which the Zuni River flows, skirting the plateau country to the south. The river picks its way southwestward through the dissected edges of this plateau and eventually reaches the Little Colorado River some 100 km from Black Rock. The Zuni Basin itself is about 1850 to 1975 m in altitude. The modern town of Zuni, which actually straddles the Zuni River, is about 1960 m. Within the basin are several remnants of the plateau that skirts the basin to the south. These are the twin buttes, Kwilliyallanna, and the Zuni sacred mountain, Dowa Yalanne. The tops of these mesas are about the same altitude as the plateau, something on the order of 2000 to 2150 m. The highest point on Dowa Yalanne is 2170 m; the flat surface of the sacred mountain is generally around 2160 m, more or less approximating the mesa country south of the basin.

The Zuni River has a drainage basin of nearly 15,500 km^2 and an extremely variable annual watershed yield. Its flow is intermittent, in part because of the draining away of water for irrigation purposes; it is not clear if the flow in the sixteenth century was perennial. However, in historic times the Zuni River has tended to flow throughout the year in the upper basin, fed by large springs in the Ramah and Pescado areas where water gushes from under breaks in the lava beds and from Nutria Creek, which in its upper course is a permanent stream. A series of intermittent streams adds seasonal water from both the broken plateau country to the north and the plateau that borders the basin on the south (Spier 1917:216-217). Beyond the Cibola settlement area, in the lower Zuni Basin, the river sinks into the ground and is normally found only in pools (p. 217).

Rainfall at Zuni is about 310 mm annually. Like the rest of the Little Colorado region, the heaviest fall comes in the period of late summer, and the driest part of the year is the spring (April-June). Beyond Zuni in the Ramah area, at an altitude of about 2130 m, the rainfall is marginally heavier (340 mm annually), but the pattern of fall is about the same as elsewhere in the Little Colorado system (Vogt and Albert 1966:41-43; Crampton 1977:8-9). Dry farming at Zuni is possible because of the concentration of rainfall in the crucial summer months. In the mid-nineteenth century it seems to have been the preferred way of farming (Whipple 1856:Vol. 1, 67). The spring is very dry, and persistent windstorms tend to turn the surface soil into dust. The growing season in the Zuni Basin is rather short. Frosts are encountered as late as the end of May and as early as mid-September (Roberts 1932:27).

In the Tusayan area all the south-draining streams are intermittent and cannot properly be called rivers. An eastern delimitation of the area might be the Puerco of the West (also intermittent in its lower course). This river has its headwaters in New Mexico; it drains the area around Gallup, then runs in a southwestern direction to meet the Little Colorado around Holbrook. North and west of the Puerco is the Painted Desert region, and further north is the southern escarpment of Black Mesa, with a series of small tonguelike mesas that contain the Hopi towns. Old Tusayan was in the same area, but some of the towns were built on lower ground. In historic times the Hopi moved to the mesa tops for defense against the Spaniards and the Navajo. In more recent times, some towns or parts of towns have again spread from the mesa tops to the flat areas below.

The area of the upper and middle Little Colorado falls within Köppen's BSb (semiarid continental), with the exception of the very upper drainage, which is on the edge of the Dfb (humid microthermal)--Zuni, by the way, falls in this latter zone. In terms of rainfall patterns, the region is characterized by relatively low annual rainfall except in the higher elevations. At St. Johns, for example, at an altitude of 1746 m on the upper Little Colorado near its confluence with the Zuni, there is an annual precipitation of around 290 mm, almost half of which falls in the months of July, August, and September; only about one-tenth of the total falls in the spring months of April, May, and June. January temperatures average about -1°C, and the July temperature about 23°C. The frost season normally begins in early October. There is a considerable diurnal range of temperatures throughout this region. Extremely hot days (above 38°C) are not common and occur only about every other year. On the other hand, the lowest reading ever recorded at St. Johns is about -30°C. Such readings are uncommon, but readings below -15°C may occur at least once a year.

At Oraibi, on Third Mesa, at a slightly greater altitude (1807 m), the average annual rainfall is a little less (some 195 mm). Here the three high months are August-October, with approximately 75 mm rainfall, about 39% of the annual yield. Again the three driest months are in the spring and early summer (April-June), with a total of 30 mm of rainfall, some 15% of the total. Actually, with the exception of the very dry months of May and June, whose combined total is only about 11 mm, rainfall does not vary greatly from month to month. August, with its total of 31 mm, is an exception, but like the Little Colorado in general, there is considerable variation in the kind of precipitation. Winter rain (and snow) usually falls slowly, with lasting effects, while summer rainfall tends to be sudden, violent, and brief.

The average July temperature at Oraibi is 23.7°C, and the January average is about -1°C. Summer temperatures may be as high as 40°C, while a record temperature one January day in 1963 saw a low of -28°C. The growing season at Oraibi, incidentally, is normally from mid-May to late September, with considerable variation from year to year (Bradfield 1971:6).

At Keams Canyon, on the eastern edge of Hopi country at a somewhat higher elevation (1894 m) than Oraibi, there is also a slightly higher precipitation (257 mm), but the monthly variation and type of rainfall are much the same. The highest daily temperature recorded at Keams Canyon, as at Oraibi, is about 40°C, and the lowest recorded is approximately -30°C.

The entire Little Colorado province is part of a rainfall system that sees a slight winter precipitation coming from Pacific cyclonic storms. Only when they move farther south than usual is there significant moisture. The larger amounts of summer rain are normally from moist Gulf Coast air which pushes into the region, though occasionally a Pacific Coast

storm will break across the mountain barriers in late summer and fall, sometimes bringing heavy rains. Whether or not winter precipitation falls as snow depends somewhat on altitude and somewhat on local conditions. Only one-third of the precipitation falls as winter snow at Keams Canyon, about one-half at St. Johns, and virtually all the 67 mm of cold season precipitation at Jeddito. The latter station is at 2040 m and is situated some 8 or 9 km southwest of Keams Canyon, just east of Jeddito Wash (Sellers and Hill 1974:272, 282, 426; Vogt and Albert 1966:41-43).

The drainage basin of the Little Colorado as a whole-- measured from Grand Falls, the first measuring point downstream from the Hopi towns (thus including all of Cibola-Tusayan)--is a bit under 55,000 km^2. It also has an extremely variable watershed yield, averaging perhaps 5 mm over the entire watershed. I have not been able to find figures for the Hopi washes.

The flora and fauna are essentially that of the desert. Only in oasis spots and along the watercourses of the more-or-less permanent streams, in the heights of the Zuni Mountains that border the area on the east, and on the Mogollon Rim that delimits it on the south are there areas of mesophytic vegetation.

In the Zuni area itself, the river floor is generally free of forest land and is covered with sagebrush and grama; however, stands of both cottonwood and hackberry are found. In the higher elevations, along the upper slopes that lead to the plateau, there is juniper (Juniperus monosperma, J. osteosperma, J. Deppeana), pinyon, and scattered stands of yucca. The Zuni region has several oaks: Gambel, Arizona white, and Emory. There is sagebrush in the plateau area as well fourwing saltbrush (Atriplex canescens) and Indian paintbrush. Various cacti are found, including cholla, prickly pear (Opuntia), and the fishhook cactus (Mammillaria). In the bottomlands are cottonwood, juniper, oak, willow, rabbit brush, sagebrush, and fourwing saltbush, as well as cholla. Blue grama (Bouteloua gracilis) and other grama species grow both in the higher country and in the river bottoms. Other widespread grasses include squirreltail, deer grass, and sacaton grass. In the higher reaches of the Zuni Mountains are stands of the larger conifers. To the east of Zuni some 50 or 60 km lies the malpais, an area of lava extrusions that forms its own microenvironment for flora and, to a lesser degree, fauna.

The Tusayan-Hopi region lies between the high and dry plateau of Black Mesa and the deserty lower reaches of the Little Colorado River. Again, this area is characterized by cottonwood and hackberry in the lowlands and along streams and washes. There are the monosperm and Utah species of juniper and the Gambel oak, species which also extend into the uplands north of the Little Colorado. On Black Mesa are localized stands of ponderosa pine and Douglas fir (Gumerman 1970:10). Also widespread in the Hopi region and extending from the valleys up the slopes of the plateaus are fourwing saltbush, sagebrush, both cholla and prickly pear, Mormon tea, and blue and side oats grama. Squirreltail tends to be found in the uplands, and common cattail in the river bottoms, where it can become something of a pest, clogging marshy areas.

There are a considerable number of flowering plants that occur in parts of the area: sand verbena and verbena, sunflower, Indian paintbrush, mariposa, and lupine (Havens et al. 1973:50-55, 59-65; Benson 1969:29-106; McDougall 1973; Tidestrom and Kittell 1941; Kearney and Peebles 1960).

The animal life is fairly typical of much of the Southwest. In the Black Mesa area to the north and along the Painted Desert to the south of Tusayan-Hopi, animal life is relatively scarce, though this probably relates to overgrazing in historic times. Recent archaeological investigation at Black Mesa indicates that around the twelfth century A.D. there was a considerable variety of lagomorphs (both cottontails and jackrabbits), chipmunks, ground squirrels (Spermophilus) of several species, prairie dogs, gophers, mice, and rats, as well as coyotes, raccoons, weasels, and bobcats. Among the artiodactyls were mule and white-tailed deer and mountain sheep. There are today large numbers of lizards and rattlesnakes in the same general area; these, because of their fragile bones, are not common in excavations (Douglas 1972:225-238; Ward 1972:213).

From the site of Awatovi, occupied in the sixteenth and seventeenth centuries, studies of animal remains reveal a reasonably wide range of mammals, including the wolf, coyote, fox, mountain lion, bobcat, and weasel or skunk. Artiodactyls at Awatovi include both deer and pronghorn antelope as well as bighorn sheep. There are large numbers of rodents, including, among the lagomorphs, both rabbits and jackrabbits. Other rodents found are the porcupine, beaver, prairie dog, mouse, and gopher (Lawrence 1951:3-4). Bison bones were originally reported (p. 37), but more recent analysis sugggests that the "bison" may in fact be an ox (Bos taurus). The question remains unresolved (Olsen 1978:10). The Hopi area is on the extreme western edge of the range of Bison bison bison (Plains bison) and too far south for the variety athabascae, the woodlands bison (Olsen 1960:2). There are a large number of birds in the Hopi region: various songbirds, water birds, and falconid forms, including the ceremonially important eagle (see Bradfield 1974). In fact,

both Hopi and Zuni put a great deal of ceremonial importance on birds, not only eagles and hawks but parrots and macaws, as well as less exotic forms.

Animal life in the Zuni area is generally similar to that of neighboring Hopi. Like plants, animals in this area are to a great extent adapted to environments controlled by altitude with its concomitant variation in rainfall and temperature.

The Little Colorado province is not noted for fish. Neither the historic Zuni nor the Hopi were fish eaters; indeed, the Zuni tabooed fish as a food, perhaps relating to the fish ancestor stories in the Zuni origin legends (Parsons 1939:210-211). Fish, of course, by reason of the environment, could not be utilized much by the Hopi with their dry or intermittent streams. The chronicler Castañeda, who visited the area of Cibola in 1540, mentions "barbels like those of Spain" (Hammond and Rey 1940:208) in a river which commentators have taken to be the Little Colorado somewhere near its confluence with the Zuni. Castañeda may have been mistakenly thinking of one of the European Cyprinids (perhaps Cyprinus carpio); the Cyprinoids of course would not have been in the Little Colorado or Zuni rivers in 1540 (Goode 1903:413). He could also have meant some species of catfish (many of which are heavily barbelled). Strout (1971:36) tentatively identifies Castañeda's "barbel" as a species of Ictalurus (perhaps lupus or furcatus). However, Koster (1957:74) definitely states that I. lupus has been planted in western New Mexico and that "catfish are not native" west of the Continental Divide (p. 74). Conceivably, the barbel could have been a Colorado River chub, although the description does not fit very well. In any case, fish do not seem to have been very important in the Little Colorado drainage, in part certainly because of the uncertain stream conditions. There may well be an ecological reason for the indifference to, or avoidance of, fish by the Zuni and Hopi.

The Little Colorado province is one in which large numbers of desert-adapted reptiles, mainly of the lizard and skink variety, are found. There are also numerous snakes, including the western rattlesnake (Crotalus viridis, with various subspecies). Snakes, particularly the rattlesnake, have been important in later historic times in the ceremonial life of the Little Colorado people and the more eastern Puebloan groups. Toads and frogs, especially the western spadefoot, Scaphiopus hammondii (as well as certain species of Bufo, Hyla, Pseudacris, and Rama), are found throughout the area (Stebbins 1954:142-143, 144, 147, 150, 509, 511). It is worth noting that web-footed creatures are important in the ceremonial life and mythologies of the area, at least in later times. There is a rich insect and arachnid life; in marshy areas and along rivers, mosquitos, gnats, and a variety of flies are plentiful. With such a wealth of insects, bats, as might be expected, are found throughout the area.

Language

There seems no doubt that the Cibolans in the sixteenth century spoke Zuni and the people of Tusayan spoke Hopi as they do today. Peoples who used Tiwa, Tewa, or Tano dialects seem to have moved into the Hopi area as the result of the Pueblo Revolt and Spanish reconquest and date for the most part around A.D. 1700. Only the First Mesa town of Hano, or "Tewa Village," a Tano-speaking settlement, remains today from this postconquest migration period. Zuni is a language and language stock, connected by some linguists to a macro-Penutian phylum but considered an isolated language and language family by others. Tusayan-Hopi spoke and still speak a Shoshonean language, related to the Ute, Paiute and Comanche. All these tongues are part of a large language family called Uto-Aztecan, which includes a variety of languages mostly to the south, the best known probably being Nahuatl or Aztec but also including Opata, Tarahumar, the Cahitan groups, and Piman. Many present-day linguists relate this language family, in turn, to a larger family called Azteco-Tanoan and bring the bulk of the eastern Puebloans (Tiwa, Tewa, Towa, Tano, Piro, Tompiro) under the same generic umbrella. A few consider this to be part of the hypothetical macro-Penutian group of languages. Regardless of classification, Zuni and Hopi laguages are very far apart indeed, and any relationship between them must be searched out in the dim recesses of a distant past.

Population

A number of projections of prehistoric populations in the Little Colorado province have been made, often from a relatively small, or overly subjective, data base. One thing seems to be reasonably clear. The upper portion of the Little Colorado drainage was largely depopulated in the period before A.D. 1400 or perhaps A.D. 1450, and very likely a part of the population went to historic Cibola. The Tusayan area had some considerable population fluctuation during the late prehistoric period. By the beginning of the fifteenth century, population was concentrated in the Jeddito area and in the region to the north and west (Adams 1981).

Ellis (1974:256) gives the Hopi population as of A.D. 1400 at about 7400.

In 1540 the first Spanish contact with both Cibola and Tusayan produced documentary evidence for population. Although the Spanish documents speak of the "seven cities of Cibola" (see for example Coronado's letter to Mendoza dated August 3, 1540--Hammond and Rey 1940:170), there may, in fact, have been only six permanently occupied towns. It is true that Coronado, in the Mendoza letter, mentions the occupied town of Hawikuh as having 500 hearths, another somewhat larger, another of the same size, and four smaller (pp. 170-171). The Relación postrera also speaks of seven pueblos at Cibola although the commentary delineates only six: "The largest one must have 200 houses; two others have 200, and the rest sixty, fifty, and thirty houses" (p. 309). Relación del suceso speaks of pueblos that "consist of three hundred, two hundred, and one hundred and fifty houses each," though this writer also seems to be referring to "the seven pueblos" (p. 285).

Jaramillo has a somewhat different story:

> There are in this province of Cíbola five small pueblos, including this one. They all have terraces and are built of stone and mud, as I have stated . . . . These pueblos are one league and more apart, forming a circuit of about six leagues (pp. 298-299).

The most detailed demographic information from the Coronado period comes, as one would expect, from Castañeda. According to him, there were seven pueblos of Cibola, the first of which had 200 warriors but "some of which are by far larger and stronger pueblos than Cíbola [Hawikuh]" (p. 208). Elsewhere Castañeda states that the largest town in all of Pueblo country contained between only 800 and 1000 inhabitants (p. 246), and it is by no means clear that this was in the Cibola area. In another passage, Castañeda lists seven pueblos for the province of Cibola and a total of sixty-six, which all together had about 20,000 men (p. 258). Actually, Castañeda's list contains sixty-one rather than sixty-six pueblos, and it is not entirely clear what he meant by "men" (hombres). Bandelier (Bandelier and Hewett 1937:192) considers the word men, here, to mean "people" and believes that Cibola and Tusayan combined had "an aggregate population of 'three or four thousand' men, that is people" (p. 193, from the statement of Castañeda in Hammond and Rey 1940:253). Of course, there is no compelling reason to believe that Castañeda meant "people" when he said "men," since elsewhere he makes a clear enough

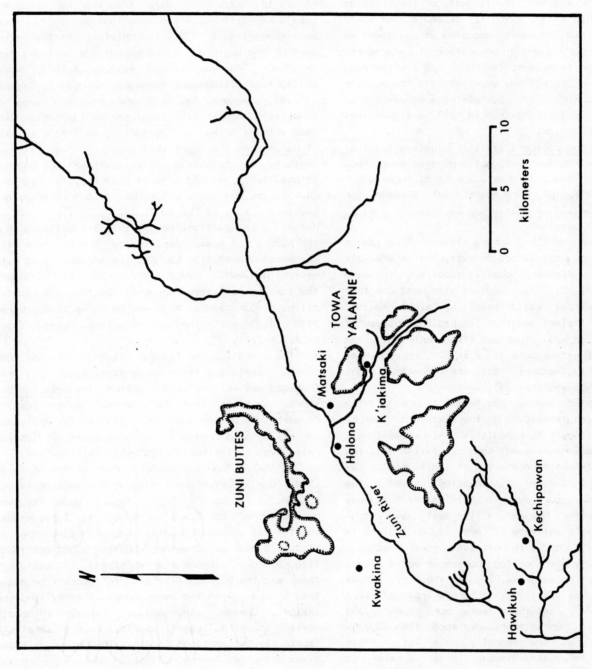

Figure 11. Zuni Towns at the Time of Coronado.

distinction.

In any case, Bandelier's figure is too low. If the first pueblo of Cibola had 200 warriors (see also Mota Padilla's statement--Day 1940b:93), this town alone must have had three to five times that many inhabitants, and according to Castañeda and Coronado, it was not the largest of the Cibolan pueblos. Smith et al. (1966:12) estimate that Hawikuh may have had 500 rooms occupied at any one time during this period and a population of around 660 people. Their formula--three rooms and four persons to a family--I suspect may underestimate the population. Hodge (1937:115) postulates a population of around 1750 souls for Hawikuh in 1540, a figure that probably is too high.

The Relación postrera lists in Cibola a total of 740 houses, which might suggest a population of 1000 or more. Coronado, moreover, speaks of three Cibolan towns of 500 or more hearths (at Granada, or Hawikuh, some 200 of these were enclosed in a wall, with the rest outside).

Writing around 1550, Gómara states: "The famous seven cities of Fray Marcos de Niza, that are within a space of six leagues, contain about four thousand men" (1922:Vol. 2, 233). Gómara also mentions that "Sibola" [Hawikuh] was defended by "eight hundred men who were inside" and that it had 200 houses "of earth and rough wood, four and five stories high and with doors like trapdoors of a ship. They climbed to them with log ladders that were removed at night and in times of war" (p. 233.).

As indicated above, population figures in the Cibolan-Tusayan area during the sixteenth century are very difficult to calculate. It seems likely that there may have been some population decline during the sixteenth century, at least at Cibola-Zuni, in part due to the disruption caused by the Spaniards and in part due to the diseases that they and their central Mexican allies must have introduced. Luxán's estimate of over 12,000 Indians in the Hopi area "armed with bows and arrows, and many Chichimecos, who are called Corechos" would give a population of perhaps 40,000 in the early 1580s (Hammond and Rey 1966:189). Espejo (pp. 225-226) states that at Zuni there were more than 20,000 Indians and at Mohose there were more than 50,000. Espejo's figures are generally much inflated--at least, that is usually assumed to be the case--but his numbers do suggest that the Hopi country was more heavily populated than Zuni, something also suggested by Suceso and to some degree by Jaramillo forty years earlier (Hammond and Rey 1940:286, 299). The famous Benavides population figures, collected some forty-five years after Espejo, give a population of 10,000 for Zuni and about the same for Hopi (Benavides 1954:30, 32).

The Coronado expedition gives few names for the Cibolan towns. The term Cibola was clearly used for the whole group and also for the first town, which the Spaniards renamed Granada and which is now known as Hawikuh. Castañeda (Hammond and Rey 1940:251) mentions a town named Mazaque, and Marcos calls one Ahacus (p. 72). The data from the Chamuscado and Espejo expeditions, and from that of Oñate, have been summarized in Riley (1975b:143). In the latter part of the century, every expedition mentions Maca (Mazaque), Aguico (Allico, Aquico, Acinco, Aquicobi), Alona (Alonagua, Aconagua, Holonagu), Caquema (Aquima, Quaquema, Aquiman), and Coaquina (Quaquina, Quequina). These five towns can be identified with modern towns or ruins: Matsaki, some 3 to 4 km east of Halona on the northwest side of Towa Yalanne; Hawikuh, approximately 16 km southwest of Halona; Halona itself, at the site of modern Zuni; Kyakima, or K'iakima, on the south slope of Towa Yalanne; and Kwakina, some 10 km west and slightly south of Halona. In addition, Hodge (1937:61) believes that the pueblo of Acano reported by Pedrosa from the Chamuscado expedition was Kechipawan, some 3 to 4 km east of Hawikuh. Hodge (pp. 57-58, 61) considers the six towns listed above to be the six Cibolan cities of Coronado's time and believes that a seventh did not then exist (see also Spier 1917:271-272).

The situation for Tusayan is also somewhat confused. Castañeda lists seven pueblos for that area (Hammond and Rey 1940:214, 259). The Relación del suceso mentions that Tusayan had seven pueblos "somewhat larger than those of Cíbola" (p. 286), and Jaramillo also mentions seven pueblos at Tusayan "with even better houses [than Cibola]" (p. 299).

Following the exploratory trips of the fall of 1540, one led by Pedro de Tovar and another (which reached as far as the Grand Canyon) under the command of García López de Cárdenas, the Tusayan-Hopi country was unmolested until Espejo reached Hopi in 1583. A year or so before, Gallegos had mentioned five pueblos, though the Spaniards did not visit them, and the Pedrosa list also indicates five pueblos. Luxán gives the names Aguato (Awatovi), Gaspe (Walpi), Comupaui (Shongopovi), Majanani (Mishongnovi), and the largest pueblo, Olalla (Oraibi); Espejo himself mentions Aguato. The Obregón account gives the names Aguato, Oalpes, Moxanamy, Xomupa, and Oloxao (Cuevas 1924:294-295), somewhat out of the order as reported by Luxán.

On November 15, 1598, Juan de Oñate accepted the Act of Obedience and Vassalage from the Indians of Mohoqui. According to this document: "Panauma, Hoynigua, Xuynuxa, Patigua, and Aguatuba, [were] chiefs of the pueblos of this province named Oraybi, Xumupami, Cuaurabi, and Esperiez" (Hammond and Rey

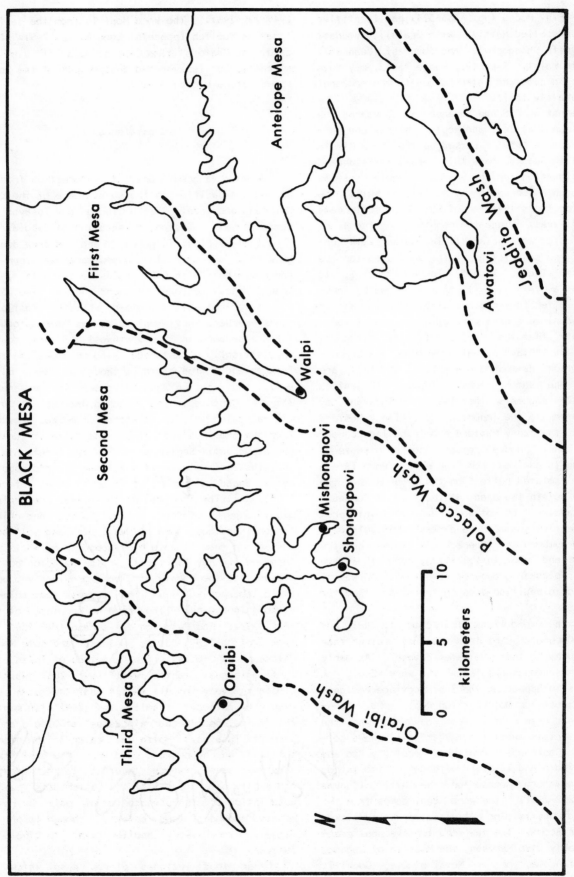

BLACK MESA

Antelope Mesa

First Mesa

Second Mesa

Third Mesa

Walpi

Mishongnovi
Shongopovi

Oraibi

Awatovi

Jeddito Wash

Polacca Wash

Oraibi Wash

N

0   5   10
kilometers

Figure 12. Tusayan-Hopi in the Sixteenth Century.

1953:360). F.W. Hodge (pp. 363-374) has identified Oraybi (also spelled Naibi) with Oraibi, Xumupami (Xumupavi) with Shongopovi, and Cuaurabi (Cuanrabí) perhaps with Walpi. Esperiez, Hodge feels, may have been a chief's name and interchanged in the document with Aguatuba (Awatovi).

An interesting change in emphasis concerns the "province" names at Zuni and Hopi. Esteban and Marcos de Niza, in 1539, picked up the term Cibola while still in Sonora, and this became the standard Spanish designation for the area as a whole. It is clearly enough a corruption of Ashiwi, or Shiwi, the Zuni name for themselves, or of Shiwona, their name for the Zuni area. Since the people along the Sonoran trade routes were primarily in contact with Zuni this is not too surprising. The word used for the Hopi, Tusayan (Tuçan, Tuçano, Tucano, Tuzan), is something of a mystery. It was introduced by Coronado's men after they reached Cibola-Zuni, and is probably a Zuni word or a corruption of a Hopi word. It is likely that the "valley of Asay" given by Bustamante and "Osay" by Gallegos from the Chamuscado expedition (Hammond and Rey 1966:131, 137) are basically the same terms. Hodge (Benavides 1945:296-297) suggests that the word Tusayan may possibly refer to the important Hopi Tansy Mustard Clan (Asa), the Tansy Mustard people having connections with Zuni. Hodge rejects another etymology, that Tusayan is derived from the Navajo word Tasaun "country of isolated buttes" on the grounds that the Navajo were not in the area at the time of Coronado and Chamuscado. I am not so sure. If I interpret Luxán correctly (Hammond and Rey 1966:201-202), there were numbers of "Querechos" in the country between Zuni and Hopi in 1582-1583, and these are most likely Apachean groups of some kind. However, the Coronado expedition does not mention them for that area.

All of the expeditions that came to Zuni and Hopi after Coronado came from the east rather than from the south, so that the names change. As early as the Chamuscado expedition, the word Zuni, or Suni, begins to appear as the Zuni province designation, and Mohose, or Mojose, for Hopi. Only Obregón, who had been on the West Coast and knew the Coronado materials well (he may actually have soldiered with Castañeda) continues regularly to use the terms Cibola and Tusayan although he too introduces the new term Mohose for the latter (Cuevas 1924:263, 292-293). The word Zuni comes from the Keresan word Sunyitsi, or Su'nyitsa, probably picked up at Zia or Acoma. The new word for the Hopi pueblos is probably also Keresan, the Mosicha of Laguna, the Mo-ts of Acoma, or the Motsi of Zia, Cochiti, and San Felipe. A less likely derivation is some variation on the Zuni word Ahumkwe (Benavides

1945:295-296). The word Hopi is from the self designation Hopituh (peaceful people) (p. 295). In any case, by Oñate's time Cibola was still used occasionally, but Tusayan had dropped out of the Spanish nomenclature vocabulary.

Subsistence

We have a great deal of information from the Coronado expedition on the subsistence of the Little Colorado province. Both Cibola and Tusayan were agricultural. Castañeda, speaking of Cibola, says: "The Indians plant in holes, and the corn does not grow tall, but each stalk bears three and four large and heavy ears with 800 grains each, a thing never seen in these regions" (Hammond and Rey 1940:252).

It is not entirely clear what the last phrase means—perhaps that Zuni maize was more productive than elsewhere in the Southwest (a very doubtful proposition). Castañeda also mentions maize at Tusayan and cotton cloth, though he says, mistakenly, that cotton was not grown in the area (p. 215). Coronado, who reached Hawikuh on July 7 (Julian calendar), found stores of maize, presumably from the previous year since the maize at Zuni does not ripen until September. In the nineteenth century the Zuni stored at least one year's supply of maize ahead in event of crop failure (Stevenson 1904:353). The Traslado de las nuevas, referring to Cibola, speaks of "much maize, beans, and chickens larger than those here of New Spain, and salt better and whiter than I have ever seen in my whole life" (Hammond and Rey 1940:181). The Relación postrera states that the people of Cibola grew "maize, beans, and calabashes . . . . They possess some chickens, although not many. They have no knowledge of fish" (p. 309). The Relación del suceso (p. 286) also speaks of "maize, beans, melons, and some Mexican chickens" at Cibola. The "province of Tuzán, thirty-five leagues to the west" (p. 286) was like Cibola in every respect except that the Tuzan people also grew cotton. Jaramillo (p. 299) also mentions the "maize, beans, and calabashes" at Cibola and the same at Tusayan. Maize was eaten in the form of tortillas which Coronado said were the best "that I have ever seen anywhere, and this is what everybody ordinarily eats" (p. 172). Castañeda's (p. 255) description of the preparation of maize by use of metate and mano (see below), though taken from Tiguex, very likely applied also to Cibola and Tusayan.

Other food included pinyon nuts which were stored from one year to the next (p. 253) both at Cibola and Tusayan. At the latter area they seem a prized food since the Indians gave them to pacify the Spanish party under Tovar, along with dressed hides, maize meal, turkeys, and turquoises (p. 215).

Animals were also eaten, according to Coronado: deer, hare, rabbits, perhaps wild goats, bears, and wild boar (at least Coronado deduced this from seeing the skins of these animals) (pp. 172-173). Just what Coronado's "wild boar" represented in the animal world is not clear. It is very doubtful that it was a peccary, which seems to have been a latecomer in the Southwest (though the evidence is equivocal). I suppose that it is barely possible that Spanish pigs (Sus scrofa) could have gone feral and reached the Southwest by 1540. Two generations later the Espejo party talks of communal rabbit hunts (Hammond and Rey 1966:187).

Accounts of the two exploring parties in the 1580s add something to the subsistence picture of the Little Colorado. They make it clear that inhabitants of Zuni did not grow cotton (at best, only a little) but traded with the Mohose people for raw cotton (pp. 184-185). At Mohose, specifically a short distance from Awatovi, the Spaniards of Espejo's party were given "tortillas, tamales, roasted green-corn ears [in April?], corn and other things" (p. 189). At Awatovi

> about one thousand Indians came, laden with corn, ears of green corn, pinole, tamales, and firewood. They offered all these as a gift, together with six hundred pieces of cotton cloth, small and large, white and figured, so that it was a marvelous sight to behold (p. 190).

At Gaspe the Espejo party was met by a party of Indians, and according to Luxán:

> More than one thousand souls came, laden with very fine earthen jars, containing water, and with rabbits, cooked venison, tortillas, atole, (corn-flour gruel), beans, cooked calabashes, and quantities of corn and pinole, so that, although our friends were many and we insisted our hosts should not bring so much, heaps of food were left over. Then they presented us with six hundred pieces of figured and white cloth and small pieces of their garments (p. 191).

Espejo's men also remarked on irrigation projects, though not at Hopi where Luxán's attention was caught by the fact that "the natives cultivate sandy places without difficulty because they carefully guard the moisture from the snow" (p. 191; for

modern Hopi parallel practices see Hack 1942; Bradfield 1971).

At Zuni, however, Luxán speaks of an irrigation system with two canals (Hammond and Rey 1966:186), and at Acoma he remarks: "We found many irrigated cornfields with canals and dams, built as if by Spaniards. We stopped by the said river [probably the San Jose]" (p. 182).

In the excavations at Hawikuh, considerable amounts of food or food by-products were found with the burials. These included maize or corn cobs, squash, and beans, often found carbonized with cremations. One burial contained two kinds of beans. Pinyon nuts were also found (in seven cremations and nine inhumations), usually with other food. Three inhumations in association with Matsaki polychrome pottery (mid-1400s--late 1600s) have sunflower seeds and several kinds of wild seeds, unfortunately none of them very clearly identified. Only one European food was identified (from seeds) in Hodge's notes, and that was the watermelon. Much of the animal food was not from graves but from trash heaps. Animals include cottontail and jackrabbit, white-tailed and mule deer, turkey, grouse (?), prairie dog, and pocket gopher. There were also a few traces of bison, pronghorn, bear, and a number of other animals, several of which were probably not used for food (Smith et al. 1966:227-232).

Excavations in the Hopi area have not been so informative, but somewhat the same range of animals and plants has been found at sites like Awatovi in late prehistoric and early historic times (Smith 1952; Lawrence 1951; Kent 1957). A few animals can be added to the inventory: bighorn sheep, beaver, and porcupine, for example (Lawrence 1951:4).

The use of cotton in pre-Spanish and early historic times has been documented by Kent (1957). The cotton grown was the specialized Gossypium hopi, with its short growing season of eighty-four to one hundred days (p. 465). Kent feels that relatively little, if any, cotton was grown at Zuni in the mid-sixteenth century (p. 469), though as Spier points out (1924:64) it was grown in the mid-nineteenth century. At that time, cotton was planted in July and was hand-watered for three days in a row at three-day intervals until it ripened, which occurred in late September or early October.

In the sixteenth century, Hopi seems to have been the big cotton supplier for the Southwest and perhaps beyond. According to Kent: "From all accounts Hopiland was supplying Zuni and the Rio Grande towns with woven cloth and also some cotton fiber, a practice which has continued until the present time" (1957:469).

A considerable amount of information is known about the manufacture of cotton materials. In historic times ginning was done by beating with twigs fastened at the butt ends to make a switch with several prongs. Such twig bundles have been found in archaeological contexts in the northern Arizona region (in a Pueblo III site near Kayenta), and there seems no reason to doubt that the sixteenth century Hopi used the same implements (pp. 470-471). In the nineteenth century Hopi cotton was carded by combing with the fingers, the commercial comb being introduced around 1852 (p. 470). Shaft-and-whorl spinning was known throughout the aboriginal Southwest. This is the spinning technique used in later times both at Zuni (Spier 1924:66) and at Hopi (Kent 1957:474). From the position of the yarn and whorl on a spindle shaft found at Canyon Creek, a site between the Salt River and the Mogollon Rim which dates in the fourteenth century A.D., historic and contemporary spinning seem to follow the aboriginal pattern (pp. 474-475).

According to Kent (p. 476), nearly all the loom-woven cotton in the aboriginal Southwest was one-ply Z-spun; that is, the fibers were twisted up-right, down-left, regardless of how the thread was held (as opposed to S-spun which produces a mirror image of Z-spun). Heavier thread (two strands or more) is normally used for embroidery, sewing, selvages, or braids, and seldom for loom weaving. This heavier thread usually takes the form of S-spun, probably as a strengthening measure, since it reverses the original direction of spinning of the component single threads. The Hawikuh material examined by Kent (p. 663) seems to have been Z-spun. In the Hawikuh materials uncovered by Hodge (Smith et al. 1966:248-252), large amounts of cotton textiles were noted, though the details of weaving, etc., are not very clear. At Awatovi there clearly were textiles since kiva floors have loom anchor holes and the murals show textile decorations (Kent 1957:660). Again, details are lacking.

For further discussion of cotton, see under Trade and under Costume below.

Settlement Patterns

The towns of Cibola, Tusayan, and the rest of the Pueblo area seem to have fascinated both the Spaniards and Indians from outside the area. As early as 1536, Cabeza de Vaca was told (while in Sonora) of people who lived in the "towns of many people and very large houses" (Cabeza de Vaca 1555:fol. xlv). Marcos (Hammond and Rey 1940:79) described Hawikuh as a town of houses of stone with terraces and flat roofs. This was supposedly from personal observation, but when still back in Sonora

(or perhaps extreme southern Arizona), Marcos had information of towns with houses four stories high, with terraces going up and up and reached by ladders (pp. 66, 71)--in fact, generally a good description of a pueblo.

Melchior Díaz, in 1539, from somewhere in the Sonoran or southern Arizona area, got a reasonably accurate description of the pueblos:

> Their houses are built of stone and mud, rudely constructed, in this manner: There is a long wall, and at both ends of this wall some rooms twenty feet square are partitioned off, according to what they say. These rooms are roofed with rough timbers. Most of the houses are entered from the terraces, with ladders to the streets. The houses are three and four stories high. They say that there are few which are two stories high. Each story is more than one estado and one-half high, except the lower one, which must be only a little more than one estado. Ten or twelve adjoining houses are served by one ladder. The inhabitants use the lower stories for service and live in the upper ones. On the ground floor they have some slanted loop-holes as in the fortresses in Spain (p. 158).

I quote this at some length since it was given by a man who, at that time, was never less than several hundred kilometers from the nearest pueblo settlements.

An on-the-spot description of the Cibolan towns, perhaps specifically of Hawikuh, was made in 1540 by Coronado:

> There are very good homes and good rooms with corridors, and some quite good rooms underground and paved, which are built for winter, and which are something like estufas. Most of the ladders which they have for their houses are movable and portable and are taken up and placed wherever desired. They are made of two pieces of wood, with rungs like ours (p. 70).

Surprisingly, only one kiva from this period was found by Hodge in the Hawikuh excavations. This structure was rectangular, measuring about 4.25 by 6.4 m, with an inside height of something over 2.0 m. The floor was paved with squared slabs of sandstone, and the roof supported by eight main beams. There was a hatchway in the roof to serve as an entrance to the kiva. Across the south side of the room was a broad bench. The ventilating shaft ran under the bench and connected to a vertical shaft in the south wall. There was a firepit at the ventilator opening protected by a stone deflector. Walls were heavily plastered but not painted. Smith et al. (1966:42-43) suggest that this kiva was built shortly before the arrival of the Spaniards (presumably they mean Oñate rather than Coronado since they remark that the kiva was filled in and deserted soon after). It is interesting to note that this particular kiva was not semisubterranean but part of the house group. It is very likely that more than one kiva existed at Hawikuh in the sixteenth century.

On the other hand, a number of kivas have been studied in Hopi country: at Sikyatki, Kawaika-a (on Antelope Mesa), and especially at Awatovi, a few kilometers to the southwest on the southern extension of Antelope Mesa. All the Hopi kivas are rectangular in plan and vary in length from a maximum of 7.9 m to a minimum of 4 m, and in width from 4.8 m to 2.7 m. They are almost always entered by a hatchway in the roof. The broad bench is usually on the west or south side of the room, and the ventilator shaft enters under the bench. Kivas at Hopi might be encased in the house complex, and they may or may not be semisubterranean. A number of them contain complex religious paintings on the walls.

Most of the sixteenth century pueblos were built of stone and mud mortar, though occasionally mud brick was used. Castañeda (Hammond and Rey 1940:254) describes the making of mud brick in the Rio Grande area, and Smith (1952:9) notes it archaeologically at Awatovi in pre-Spanish contexts.

Trade

I have suggested elsewhere (Riley 1975b, 1976b, 1978a) that Cibola-Zuni was the western terminus of the complex of trade routes running in various directions. It is important, therefore, to consider the evidence for that trade. I have mentioned the fact that descriptions of Cibolans--their houses and towns, and their way of life--appear at least as far south as the Sonoran area and as far west as the lower Colorado River (see Chapters VI and VIII). It is also clear from the Coronado accounts that a trading expedition from Pecos arrived at Hawikuh not long after the Spaniards took up residence (Hammond and Rey 1940:217). This party brought dressed skins, shields, and headpieces to trade. Skins reaching Cibola not only came from the High Plains, but "they prepare and paint them where they kill the cattle" (p. 173). Dressed bison skin in quantity was noted by Marcos the year before, traded from Cibola south. He also received bison skin shields from coastal Sonoran Indians (surely traded to them from the north and east), so one suspects that the Pecos party was simply carrying the usual trade goods to be redistributed from Cibola (pp. 67, 69). Marcos (pp. 67-73) also mentions floods of turquoise coming from Cibola. This, too, must have been retraded, since it very likely came from the Cerrillos mines in the Rio Grande Valley. Three years before Marcos, Cabeza de Vaca (1555:fol. xlv) had described turquoises, as well as "emeralds," coming from what must have been Cibola, and Melchior Díaz, in 1539, also mentions receiving some sort of gem stones from Cibola (Hammond and Rey 1940:159). Parenthetically, Díaz knew of the cotton-producing Tusayan which he called Totonteac, although he does not actually say that cotton was being shipped to the Sonoran area. Díaz does mention, however, that the Cibolans received their cotton from Totonteac. At least some of the cotton was unworked, for Díaz makes a point of saying that "men [in Cibola] weave the cloth or spin the cotton" (p. 159). He also gives a garbled account of some sort of woolly animal that is sheared to make "colored wigs which they wear, like the one I am sending your Lordship" (p. 158). It would seem, thus, that these "wigs" were also traded; again, one wonders what were the "headpieces" offered by the Pecos people to Coronado. They may have been some sort of decorative headgear made of bison hide and/or hair.

Alarcón, on the lower Colorado River in 1540, gathered a great deal of more-or-less current information on Cibola, and there is some suggestion that the Colorado peoples traded for turquoise--at least they were interested in it (p. 141). Certainly, sixty years later Zuni was on the coral route from the lower Colorado (Bolton 1916:279), and considering the extraordinary distribution of California shell in the Southwest, especially in Pecos and on the Rio Grande, one can hardly doubt that Cibola-Zuni was on the shell route as well. Indeed, Escobar (Hammond and Rey 1953:1028) indicates as much.

Turquoise, probably from the Cerrillos mines, also reached the Hopi area; at least Castañeda mentions that the Tovar party received turquoise as "gifts," after cotton cloth, dressed hides, flour, pinyon nuts, maize, and turkeys had already been given (Hammond and Rey 1940:215). Following Tovar's return to the base camp at Cibola, Coronado sent García López de Cárdenas to do further exploring. Cárdenas stopped at the Tusayan pueblos, where he obtained food and guides, and pushed on westward in search of Alarcón and the lower Colorado River. Their route is not entirely clear, but they probably crossed the Little Colorado at some point between present-day Grand Falls and Cameron, continuing on northwestward until they reached the Grand Canyon. They followed the canyon for an additional four days (Castañeda says "up," but surely he means downriver) at which time the Hopi guides warned that they were entering a waterless area. The important thing about this rather aimless journey is that the guides knew the country and even had a technique for leaving water at strategic places. At a guess, the Spaniards reached somewhere around the edge of the Coconino Plateau, and they seem to have been on a trade route used by the Hopi. If so, the Hopi route must have swung sharply southward to reach the Bill Williams River. The major route, however, must have run south of the San Francisco Mountains, and it is this trail that Oñate's party took in 1604-1605, most likely guided by either Hopi or Zuni Indians. By that time two Spanish parties (Espejo in 1583 and Farfán in 1598), both launching their expeditions from Hopi country, had pushed southwestward to the Jerome area. What is important here is that, although Cibola-Zuni seems to have been the key western redistribution center for the Pueblo area, trade coming from the west, especially from the lower Colorado region and from the middle Verde Valley, seems in part to have been funneled through the Hopi pueblos. However, in order to go to Hopi from the east, and to a large degree from the south, it was necessary to go through Zuni. Certainly, no Spanish party in the sixteenth or early seventeenth century ever had any idea of doing otherwise. The Hopi, then, may have been responsible for some of the trade in pigments that is mentioned in a number of accounts (Hammond and Rey 1953:412; 1966:194-197; Cuevas 1924:295-296). The mines were well known at Zuni, and it was considered necessary to reach them through Hopi country (Hammond and Rey 1966:184). When Espejo, with his contingent of Hopi guides, reached the Jerome region, the Spaniards received a welcome that sounds more like a well-worn ritual than a spontaneous greeting. The party was brought ore samples and guided to the mines (p. 197). Somewhat the same thing befell Marcos Farfán de los Godos, Oñate's captain. He was offered powdered ores of different colors, as well as food (Hammond and Rey 1953:409-412). The natives of the area mined for the colored ores; one shaft was 6 m deep, with a large dump. Ores from the mine were brown, black, yellow, green, and an intense blue (p. 412). Questioned about the rivers that the Spaniards had crossed, the natives explained that they joined, flowing through an abra, or opening, and then became

wide and large, and that on both banks there were numerous settlements of people who planted extensive fields of maize,

beans, and calabashes in a very level country of fine climate, and, because of the snow which they pointed out to him on the sierra and which they were leaving behind, they said that it never snowed at the sierra of the mines or at the settlements by the river, as it was a temperate land, almost hot. They said that the information about this river and settlements extended as far as the sea, which they pointed out was salty. They indicated this by dissolving some salt in water (pp. 412-413).

These Indians had pearl shells which they obtained from the sea. The Spaniards estimated that this sea was some eighty to ninety leagues away, that is, approximately 325 to 375 km. Clearly the Indians were talking about the lower Colorado River and peoples, and likely this account was one of the motivating factors that led Oñate to make his journey to the lower Colorado six years later. The statements on drainage patterns are a little confused, unless by this time Farfán was in the Santa Maria drainage. More likely something was lost in translation from the original Pai (?) language, unless, indeed, the Indians realized that the Verde, the Little Colorado, and the Santa Maria-Bill Williams all eventually joined.

One reason the Hopi were interested in pigments was that they were major suppliers (if I read the evidence correctly), both of raw cotton and manufactured cotton goods, to the New Mexican portions of the Southwest. As far as we know, all this trade went by way of Cibola-Zuni. In the sixteenth century there were no settled areas—at least not Pueblo areas—other than Zuni between Hopi and the Keresan towns west of the Rio Grande. A major trail from Zuni ran south of the Zuni Mountains, via El Morro along the edge of the malpais (or perhaps through a narrow part of it), roughly following the route of New Mexico State Highway 53 to near the McCarty area and to Acoma (see Figure 1). This is the route taken by the Spaniards in 1540, and they seem to have had relatively little trouble even though burdened with wagons and thousands of stock. Even then, the trail was well worn!

We lack much firsthand evidence on the various kinds of cotton cloth traded by the Hopi, though from Kent's survey it is clear that the late prehistoric peoples of the area had considerable sophistication in cloth weaving. Cloth was decorated both by painting and with woven designs. The Spaniards indicated that this was true, specifically, of sixteenth century Mohose. Luxán stated that the Hopi villagers at Walpi gave the small party "600 pieces of figured and white cloth" (Hammond and Rey 1966:191). At Awatovi the party received "six hundred pieces of cotton cloth, small and large, white and figured" (p. 190). In the Shongopovi and Mishongnovi (Second Mesa) area, the party received 600 pieces of cotton cloth, and at Oraibi "over eight hundred pieces of cotton cloth, large and small, as well as a quantity of spun and raw cotton which, with some other mantas, we gave to our allies" (p. 193).

Espejo himself had a somewhat more inflated story:

> The natives gathered together from various parts of the province more than four thousand cotton blankets, colored or white, hand towels with tassels at the ends, and many other things, including some of the blue and green ores sought by them for coloring their blankets (pp. 226-227).

Other items that both Zuni and Hopi may have traded were "garnets" and "emeralds;" at any rate both Coronado (Hammond and Rey 1940:171) and Oñate (Hammond and Rey 1953:1028-1029) mention them. The garnets and emeraldlike stones Coronado found at Cibola probably came from the Hopi country. The "garnets" may well have been garnet, but the "emeralds," according to the geologist Stuart Northrop, were "almost certainly peridots" (1959:382). When Chamuscado journeyed through Zuni in 1581-1582, he was told of mines in the Hopi country (Hammond and Rey 1966:108), though this may have been a garbled reference to the Jerome mines that were reached through Hopi country. In addition, Oñate, in the Hopi area, found a mine that produced both red and green varieties of stone. Apropos of Northrop's identifications, I suspect that the "emeralds," probably traded from Cibola and obtained by Cabeza de Vaca at Corazones, may also have been peridots. The glassy stones sent by Díaz in Sonora, which came from Cibola (Hammond and Rey 1940:159), were probably the same kind of material.

Although Cibola-Zuni was basically a transshipment center for trade goods coming from various directions, there was at least one important local product. As early as 1539, while still far to the south, Díaz had news of the Cibolan salt lake (p. 159). The Coronado party (p. 181) had high praise for Cibolan salt, and Oñate makes a special point of mentioning the salt lake (Hammond and Rey 1953:327). We have no definitive proof that salt was being traded from Cibola-Zuni, but we know that it was much desired and traded for in the Sonoran area (Cuevas 1924:146-147), especially at Oera, where the inhabitants imported "mantas, salt, feathers, and

provisions, especially salt which they do not possess" (p. 146). These things were obtained by trading slaves (and presumably other commodities; the context is not entirely clear).

To sum up, it would seem that Cibola was the major trade center for routes going east, south, and northwest. The Tusayan towns (or perhaps one or a portion of them) dominated the trade route from the upper Southwest to the Verde area and to the lower Colorado River. Tusayan supplied Cibola, and through Cibola the rest of the upper Southwest and the Gila-Salt and Sonoran area, with Verde area pigments and, at least the upper Southwest, with Gulf of California and California Pacific Coast shell (Riley 1976b:36-38; Tower 1945:Map, 37-46). What percentage of the shell entering the upper Southwest actually came through Hopi to Zuni is not clear, but Haliotis fulgens and Olivella biplicata were both found in the Winslow, lower Chevelon Creek, and Chaves Pass area dating perhaps to the fourteenth or early fifteenth century (Fewkes 1896:359-360, 366). From the same area, Fewkes discovered a turquoise mosaic in a frog design with a jasper center inlaid on a Gulf of California Glycymeris maculatus shell (p. 363). Haliotis, widespread throughout the Southwest, extends over a number of centuries and a very wide area, being found in places as far apart in space and time as Ridge Ruin in the twelfth century (McGregor 1943), Aztec in the thirteenth (Morris 1919:92-95), and Pecos perhaps as late as the sixteenth or even seventeenth century (Kidder 1932:181-194; Riley 1978a:59). Ridge Ruin (near Flagstaff, Arizona) is especially interesting for establishing the antiquity of the trade routes. In the "Magician's" burial, dating in the early twelfth century A.D., McGregor found not only Haliotis but also Turritella, Cardium, Dentalium, Glycymeris, and Conus. There were objects of lignite and elaborate mosaics of turquoise, shell, and red argillite set in lac. In addition, there were turquoise, obsidian, jasper, and many minerals, which were often in powder form for paint (kaolin, yellow ochre, hematite, malachite, iron pyrites, cinnabar, and azurite). Pots found there indicated a connection with various nearby regions including the Tusayan area (McGregor 1943:278-280, 283-284, 290-292, 295-297). According to the author (pp. 290, 292, 297), the turquoise probably came from Cerrillos, the malachite and azurite from the Verde Valley, argillite from the Prescott area, lignite from Black Mesa, kaolin from the Painted Desert, and the lac from the Phoenix area. Lac is produced by insects who live on either Larrea mexicana or Coursetia glandulosa, neither of which grows near Ridge Ruin.

The important thing about Ridge Ruin is that it is very near the major route that in the sixteenth century ran from Tusayan to the lower Colorado River. The materials in this Ridge Ruin burial include some of the finest turquoise mosaics ever found in the Southwest and, in a room above the burial, skeletons of two macaws (p. 298). This wealth of grave deposits led Reyman (1978:256-257) to suggest that the Magician was in fact a pochteca trader, perhaps centered on one of the Hopi towns. In any case, Hopi Indians working with McGregor were able to identify some of the objects and project from them certain ceremonies the Magician may have utilized, though individuals from different Hopi towns gave drastically different interpretations (McGregor 1943:295). As Reyman (1978:257) points out, these "identifications" by no means preclude the possibility that the burial was of a pochteca member.

Fewkes' archaeological work in the Tusayan area produced not only Pacific Coast shell but also Glycymeris, Strombus galeatus, and Melongena patula, as well as specimens of Cardium painted with black lines and clay models of Glycymeris (Fewkes 1896:360-366). Most or all of this shell came from the Gulf of California and could have reached Tusayan either by the Cibolan route or by the western one. Tower (1945:26) also mentions, from the Peabody Awatovi collections, clay imitations of Glycymeris, Olivella, and Conus.

Collections of shell at the Cibola-Zuni site of Halona, perhaps dating to the historic period (at least not much earlier) include Pacific Coast shell (Olivella biplicata and Venericardia nodulosa) and Gulf of California shell (Aletes, Conus princeps, Olivella dama, and Glycymeris maculatus) (pp. 20-21).

Tusayan-Hopi, in return for blankets and other cotton goods and transshipped shell and pigments, received turquoise, worked bison hides, fibrolite (probably in the form of finished axes, according to Montgomery 1963:46, 48), and perhaps salt.

Relatively little pottery seems to have been traded to Tusayan, if the excavations at Awatovi are any indication (Smith 1971:575, 612). A certain amount of pottery does seem to have come from Cibola, however, ranging from the fourteenth century Heshotauthla wares to seventeenth century Hawikuh polychrome. Tusayan, however, was an exporter of pottery, especially the beautiful yellow pottery. Such wares as Jeddito Black-on-yellow are distributed over practically the whole Pueblo area in Pueblo IV times (Colton and Hargrave 1937:151); indeed, they go well beyond, for early historic Jeddito pottery is found in south coastal California (Ruby and Blackburn 1964:209-210). Smith (1971:612) does feel that the trade in Tusayan ceramics had slackened somewhat by the sixteenth century, though

it certainly had not stopped. Cibola not only imported Tusayan wares but sometimes copied them; for example, Matsaki polychrome is a cruder copy of the exquisite Sikyatki polychrome (Smith et al. 1966:329; Hodge 1924a:14-15). Smith points out that the imbalance produced by pottery shipped out of the Tusayan region demanded some sort of trade balance: "It may have been turquoise from Cerillos, shells from the Gulf of Mexico, and maybe even cotton" (1971:612). If my own scenario is correct, eastbound Tusayan pottery would have been funneled, at least in major part, through Cibola--a situation that would explain the general influence of Tusayan ceramics, stylistically, on Cibola. Instead of Smith's suggestion about cotton coming into Tusayan (the area, as noted above, was probably a major exporter of cotton goods), I would postulate bison skins, parrot and macaw feathers, and probably the birds themselves. The importance of these birds is clearly enough indicated in the Jeddito area kiva murals.

For Cibola-Zuni I have surveyed the exchange situation in previous publications (Riley 1975b, 1976b). Let me simply say here (and the list is certainly incomplete) that Cibola received dressed bison and deerskins, turquoise, and fibrolite from the east; cotton and cotton products, shell and coral, mineral pigments, semiprecious stones, and pottery from Tusayan; and parrot feathers and birds, shell, metal objects, pottery, and perhaps such perishable goods as peyote from the south. Turquoise, semiprecious jewels, bison skins, probably cotton cloth, and salt went south into Sonora; turquoise, skins, parrots and macaws and/or feathers, and worked fibrolite went to Tusayan and beyond to the lower Colorado; and parrots, cloth, shells, coral, pottery, blue pigment (carried by Zuni Indians "to sell to the settlements of New Mexico" --see Bolton 1916:269), probably salt, and perhaps semiprecious stones went to the eastern Pueblos and beyond. Slaves were important in Sonora; some experts, including Di Peso (1968b:52), feel that the upper Southwest may have been a supplier of slaves, in which case they would most likely have been routed through Cibola. There is no hard evidence for this, however, though the Coronado chroniclers do suggest that some of Marcos' followers may have been enslaved at Cibola, and they mention slaves for the Pecos area (see also Schroeder 1972:49). There is an intriguing note in the Luxán journal of the Espejo expedition, however, that may have a bearing on the subject. After returning from Hopi country, a slave girl escaped from the Spaniards and fled to a group of "Curecho" Indians near Acoma. According to Luxán:

It was agreed that they should return to us one of the Curechos women given us at Mojose (belonging to one of the companions, Francisco Barreto, although she had fled from us the morning of the skirmish); and that we should give them a girl we had taken from them (Hammond and Rey 1966:201).

The exchange was arranged for the following day:

As they sent the Indian woman belonging to Francisco Barreto to her land, they took one of their relatives and sent her over, wearing her feather crest so that we should not recognize her, with the intention of recovering their own girl and giving us nothing but a discharge of arrows. This was planned with the help of the interpreter, who was another Indian woman (belonging to Alonso de Miranda) and who was trying to escape (p. 201).

Several things stand out in this account. The Curechos were in numbers in the Acoma area and, as we have already seen, there were Curechos, or Querechos, in Hopi country. The identity of these groups is not certainly known, but from their treatment of the captive girl who escaped the Spaniards, it would seem that the Acoma area Curechos were in contact with those at Hopi and perhaps related in some way. Surely they were Apachean-speaking (see also Wilcox 1981), and my own guess is that they were Navajo. If so, it represents the first historic documentation of what was to be commonplace in later centuries--Navajo-Hopi hostilities. I doubt if the Hopi had any well-defined mechanisms for exploiting slaves--likely only women and children were taken captive and perhaps were incorporated in the victor's group as were captives elsewhere in the Southwest. The Hopi clearly did not consider the captive women as fully integrated Hopi, however, for one thing noted from Coronado's time on was the solicitude and protective attitudes of western Pueblo peoples toward their women. The point here is if captives were given or traded to the Spaniards, why not to the Sonorans? Again, it is necessary to stress that we have no firm evidence, either documentary or archaeological, one way or the other.

Sociopolitical Organization

The political organization of both Cibola and Tusayan is summarized by Castañeda: "The province [of Tusayan] is governed like Cíbola, by an assembly of the oldest men. They have their chosen governor and captains" (Hammond and Rey 1940:215). Later, talking about Cibola but stressing that Tusayan had the same "dress, ceremonies, and customs" as Cibola, Castañeda says:

A man has only one wife. There are estufas in the pueblos, in which they gather to take counsel, and which are located in the patios or plazas. They have no rulers as in New Spain, but are governed by the counsel of their oldest men (p. 253).

Coronado, in the Mendoza letter, makes the point that Cibola is the name of the province, each town having its separate name (p. 170). Later in the letter Coronado mentions that no single pueblo seems to have been dominant or to have contained a "principal house by which any superiority over others could be shown" (p. 174). Coronado visited the largest Cibolan town and asked to see the leader. "Later, an old man, who said he was their lord " (p. 174) came and told Coronado that he and the rest of the chiefs would meet with the Spaniards in three days' time. Elsewhere, in the testimonio, Coronado talks of sending for "some of the Chieftains" (p. 324) at Cibola.

Forty years later, Luxán, at Mohose, found that each of the Hopi pueblos was ruled by "three or four caciques and the cacique has as little power as the ordinary Indian; hence they are all equal" (Hammond and Rey 1966:193-194). Espejo also makes a distinction between the "caciques," of which there were several at each town, and the other people, but he is otherwise not very informative (pp. 226-227).

The sources agree that monogamy was the prevailing practice throughout Pueblo country (Hammond and Rey 1940:255, 1966:187; Cuevas 1924:267). Castañeda says that when someone wants to marry, he or she must have the permission of the rulers:

The man must spin and weave a blanket and place it before the woman. She covers herself with it and becomes his wife. The houses are for the women, the estufas for the men. If a man repudiates his wife he must come to the estufa (Hammond and Rey 1940:255).

It is not entirely clear if this statement is supposed to apply to all the Pueblos or just to the Rio Grande groups. It certainly sounds more western Pueblo, but Castañeda was speaking in the context of the eastern Pueblos.

Warfare

The Coronado party became very well acquainted with patterns of Pueblo warfare, both at Cibola-Tusayan and in the Rio Grande Valley. In the latter place, a major engagement, one involving a siege of eight weeks or more, took place. Coronado's introduction to Cibola came with hostilities at Hawikuh. The Cibolan Indians knew something of tactics; they arranged to occupy and hold a strongpoint, probably one of the narrow defiles in the broken country south and west of Cibola. When driven off, they "sounded a little trumpet as a sign of retreat" (p. 167). On the plain outside Hawikuh, the Indians massed a large number of men, mostly bowmen it would seem. A cavalry charge scattered the Indian forces, but many of them withdrew into the town which, like most or all pueblos at this time, had a fortress aspect, with few openings on the ground floor. The Indians threw stones from above, knocking Coronado down, and rained arrows down on the Spanish forces (pp. 169-170, 208). Coronado, in later testimony, states that "three hundred Indians with bows, arrows, and shields" (p. 323) were involved in the fighting outside of Hawikuh. After Coronado had penetrated the entry (by a passageway which opened from the lower tier of rooms), he and other soldiers had to fight their way through the narrow alleys, the Indians continuing to hurl boulders from above. Mota Padilla (Day 1940b:93) says that more than twenty Cibolans were killed in the initial attack in front of the town.

In discussing the weapons at Cibola, Coronado lists shields, mallets (probably some sort of war club), and bows and arrows, including arrows with bone points. Coronado was much taken with these bone points, "the like of which have never been seen" (Hammond and Rey 1940:177). At the excavations at Hawikuh there were found one point of bone and one unfinished and two finished points of antler. The antler implements might have been used for another purpose, but the bone one is clearly a point. It is small (35 mm long), notched, and serrated (Hodge 1920:119, Fig. 33). We do not know if the war clubs were of the macana or flint-edged type, but such were reported by several members of the Coronado party for Tiguex (see ICC and RSC) and by both Luxán and Espejo two generations later for the Piro Indians of the middle Rio Grande Valley.

From the little available evidence, the Tusayan Indians utilized much the same kind of weaponry as the Cibolans. According to Castañeda, when Tovar first contacted the Tusayan somewhere in the Awatovi area, the Indians

formed their ranks and set out after them, well armed with arrows, shields, and wooden maces. They came in wing formation without confusion. There was opportunity for the interpreters to talk to them and to make the requisition for peace upon them, since they were an intelligent people; but withal, they drew lines, requesting that our men should not cross these lines toward their pueblos, but that they should be orderly (Hammond and Rey 1940:214).

The Spaniards attacked on horseback and drove the Indians back. In fact, as Castañeda points out while speaking of the Pueblos in general, horses were feared by Southwestern Indians, even more than artillery (p. 282).

Since the major Spanish fighting in the sixteenth century took place in or near the Rio Grande Valley, a more detailed discussion of warfare will be given in Chapter X. It should be stressed that for Cibola-Tusayan there was a great dependence on the bow and arrow and, to some extent, the war club. The Indians could improvise, throwing stones from the rooftops (perhaps metates or even boulders gathered specifically for that purpose). They fought in good order, using, at Tusayan, a wing formation (in other words, grouping their forces into a right and left section). The Southwest Indians, at least in the Rio Grande area and probably at Hawikuh, employed the principle of enfilading fire from redoubts.

Religion

From the sixteenth century there are only bits and pieces of information about Pueblo religion, but what we do have does not indicate any drastic changes from what was found in the nineteenth century. Castañeda, observing Cibola in the late fall of 1540 but drawing on a number of other accounts for Cibola and Tusayan, remarks that there were estufas (the common Spanish designation for the kiva, or ceremonial room) in the patios and plazas. Speaking specifically of Cibola-Zuni, Castañeda says:

They have their priests, whom they call papas, who preach to them. These priests are the old men, who mount the high terrace of the pueblo in the morning as the sun rises, and from there, like town criers, preach to the people, who all listen in silence, seated along the corridors. The priests tell the people how they should live. I believe they give them some commandments to observe, because there is no drunkenness, sodomy, or human sacrifice among them, nor do they eat human flesh, or steal. They work in common in the pueblo, and the estufas are for all, but it is considered sacrilegious for the women to enter them to sleep. As an emblem of peace, they make the sign of the cross. These people burn their dead, casting with them into the fire the tools the deceased used in their occupations (Hammond and Rey 1940:253).

A few comments about this passage are in order. The term "papa" is one of the few Pueblo words preserved in the Coronado documents, in fact the only one from Zuni, except for a few place names. It means "elder brother" and has a strong religious and symbolic meaning as well as a consanguineous one (Hodge 1937:44). Indeed, the Indians may have been identifying the Elder Brother Bow Priest, and the word became extended by the Spanish into a wider usage. The town crier, in all probability, either interpreted the wishes of the religious hierarchy or perhaps was a member of some secular organization charged with keeping order in the pueblo. We have no way of knowing if the complex modern situation at Zuni with its six esoteric cults existed in the sixteenth century or if, in fact, modern Zuni represents a kind of cult amalgam of individual cults originally associated with separate towns, as Parsons (1939:876) thought might be the case.

That the Cibolans did not have drunkenness seems likely since the Pueblo Indians lacked alcoholic beverages. Human sacrifice is hinted at in the mythology (see, for example, Parsons 1939:218-223 ff.) but did not exist at conquest or later times, nor probably did cannibalism (though for an alternative view of the latter see Turner and Morris 1970:328). In the nineteenth century transvestism was well known among the Zuni; whether or not it was associated with homosexual relationships is not entirely clear. Likely, the Spaniards, who at no time during the sixteenth century after Coronado's stay observed the Zuni in depth, simply missed it. After all, Matilda Coxe Stevenson (1904) was a long-time friend of a prominent transvestite and was unaware for years that her friend was not a woman. Castañeda's statement on the kivas is probably more-or-less correct. In the nineteenth and twentieth centuries, the Zuni kivas were and are used primarily for kachina ceremonies, and only boys are initiated into the kachina society--each boy joining

one of the six kiva memberships, the kiva of his godfather and ceremonial father (Parsons 1939:878). The question of the use of the cross is not so clear. Parsons (p. 1073), while pointing out that the cross as a star symbol is very old among the Pueblos, stresses that making the sign of the cross is post-Spanish in origin.

Perhaps the most interesting part of this passage is Castañeda's reference to cremation. In the Hodge excavation at Hawikuh, 996 burials were reported, and, of these, 317 (31.8%) were cremations, most of the remainder being of the extended inhumation type (Smith et al. 1966:193, 195-196). As I have pointed out elsewhere (Riley 1975b:151), this is not only an indication of trade contacts with southern Arizona but of other, more intimate, relationships as well. Most of the datable cremations come from the period around A.D. 1475 to the early seventeenth century (Smith et al. 1966:188-192). For nearby Kechipawan, where sixty-six cremations were found, Bushnell's analysis also suggests dates mainly in the latter part of the fifteenth century or later. One of the cremations at Kechipawan was associated with Gila polychrome (Bushnell 1954:662); whether imported or a local copy is unknown. In any case, Smith et al. (1966:102) believe that cremation was introduced into the area somewhere between A.D. 1400 and 1450. These dates fit very well with the opening of the trade routes that went through Sonora and the Gila-Salt area to Cibola.

There are a number of other references to the religion of the Cibolan area. Coronado, for example, mentions "some quite good rooms underground and paved, which are built for winter, and which are something like estufas" (Hammond and Rey 1940:170). Suceso adds a bit, saying that at Cibola there were winter estufas in the middle of the patios and summer estufas outside the pueblo (p. 285). Conceivably, the Relación may be talking about a winter-summer moiety system somewhat like that used in the Rio Grande pueblos, but traces of moieties in historic Zuni are very obscure (Parsons 1939:62), and likely something entirely different is being referred to here. The Relación del suceso goes on to state:

They hold their rituals and sacrifices before some idols, but what they worship most is water, to which they offer painted sticks, plumes, and powders of yellow flowers, this usually at the springs. They also offer some turquoises which they have, although they are of little worth (Hammond and Rey 1940:286).

The Pueblo attitude toward water is well known; at Zuni, in a sense, all water is sacred. The "idols" were probably kachina figures or perhaps cult fetishes such as the hunt god figures described by Cushing (1883; see also Hodge 1920). Another possibility is that they were actually masks or masked dancers. The description of prayer sticks and plumes, of course, would apply with equal force today. The "powders" are likely corn pollen; powders are also mentioned in the Alvarado and Padilla account for Tigua (Hammond and Rey 1940:184).

Jaramillo also mentions "estufas" at Zuni (p. 299). Parenthetically, I should point out that a common assumption is that the Spaniards used the term estufa because the kiva actually looked like the round Spanish stove or oven. However, when the term was first used by Coronado in the August 1540 letter to Viceroy Mendoza, the Spaniards had seen only the western Pueblo kivas, which are square or rectangular, built into the room blocks or on the patios near them, and, from the outside, not noticeably different from ordinary rooms. It may be that the warmth aspect rather than the shape was the reason for the peculiar Spanish terminology. In any case, estufa in sixteenth century Spain could also mean a sweat bath or warming room, and this seems to be the sense used by Gómara (1922:Vol. 2, 233) when commenting on the estufas of Cibola.

One interesting aspect of Cibolan religion concerned snakes. Both the Gallegos account of the Chamuscado-Rodríguez expedition and the Luxán narrative of the Espejo expedition mention ceremonies with live snakes; the Gallegos account is very detailed. In addition, Obregón reports a snake dance from information given by Gallegos (Cuevas 1924:265-266). Luxán's account is localized to the Rio Grande area, but the stories of Gallegos and Obregón apparently were meant to include the entire Pueblo region. I shall deal with these statements when discussing the Rio Grande pueblos.

Snake handling, specifically at Zuni, was reported by one of the early custodios of the Franciscan missions of New Mexico, Fray Esteban de Perea. Fray Perea, visiting Zuni in 1629, saw there

> some enclosures of wood, and in them many rattlesnakes that, vibrating their tongues, giving hisses and leaps, are menacing as the fierce bulls in the arena. And (our men) desiring to know the object of having these serpents imprisoned, they told them that with their venom they poisoned their arrows, wherewith the wounds their opponents received were irremediable (Hodge 1924b:119).

Hodge (pp. 111-119) at Hawikuh found three small structures which he, at any rate, was convinced were snake pens, though they may have been macaw cages, especially since a bowl painted with likenesses of macaws was found placed in one of them (p. 117). In any case, it seems likely that Perea missed the point of the penned snakes. He may well have been purposefully misinformed by the Indians who, naturally enough, were reluctant to discuss their religious practices with the friars. A religious concern with snakes appears in modern times both in the western and eastern pueblos, the most famous example being the theatrical "snake dance" held in the Hopi pueblos in late summer.

Costume

We know a considerable amount about the costume of Pueblo Indians, especially from Castañeda. Speaking of Cibola-Zuni, he says:

> The natives here are intelligent people. They cover the privy and immodest parts of their bodies with clothes resembling table napkins, with fringes and a tassel at each corner, tying them around the hips. They wear cloaks made with feathers and rabbit skins, and cotton blankets. The women wear blankets wrapped tightly around their bodies, and fastened or tied over the left shoulder, drawing the right arm over them. They also wear well-fashioned cloaks of dressed skins, and gather their hair over their ears in two wheels that look like coif puffs (Hammond and Rey 1940:252).

Coronado was also interested in costume. According to him, the Cibolans--or most of them--went "entirely naked except for the covering of their privy parts" (p. 171). It might be well to point out in this regard that the observation just quoted was made in late summer and that Coronado had as yet not seen a Pueblo winter. Coronado does go on to say that the Cibolans had painted blankets and many skins of hare, deer, and rabbit (pp. 171-172). The chief at Hawikuh owned a "portion of a blanket made of many pieces" (p. 174); the Cibolans gave presents of "little ragged blankets" and also painted two cloths for Coronado, one with pictures of animals and the other of birds and fish (p. 175). Coronado sent the viceroy

> twelve small blankets, such as the people of this country ordinarily wear, and a

garment which seems to me to be very well made. I kept it because it seemed to me to be of very good workmanship and because I do not think that any one else has ever seen in these Indies any work done with a needle, unless it was done since the Spaniards settled here [!] (p. 176).

He also sent a bison skin, two earrings of turquoise, and fifteen Indian combs (pp. 176-177). The latter were probably of wood inlaid with turquoise; at any rate, such combs were found by Hodge at Hawikuh (Smith et al. 1966:260).

Turquoise, shell, bone, and seed beads were probably worn quite commonly, if the evidence of burials and cremations, many of them in association with the sixteenth century Matsaki polychrome pottery, is any indication (pp. 360-363). Other Hawikuh burials produced shell and stone pendants; stone and shell tinklers; bracelets; turquoise pendants; a bone, seed, and shell necklace (this latter, however, found in conjunction with glass beads of European manufacture); and hundreds of bone pins, virtually all made from the metacarpal and metatarsal bones of jackrabbits (pp. 258-259, 260-263; Hodge 1920:118). One large mosaic of turquoise and jet, set into a large bivalve, represented one of the two finds of turquoise at Hawikuh that are earlier than mid- to late-fifteenth century. It was in association with a Kwakina polychrome bowl, which dates approximately A.D. 1325-1400 (Smith et al. 1966:261, 311).

In the burials from the sixteenth century (or probably sixteenth and early seventeenth centuries) at Hawikuh, Hodge found cotton kilts, blankets, fragments of skin garments, and various stringlike fibers. In one grave was a "grass-like woven girdle" (p. 248-252). Parenthetically, spindle whorls seem to have been rather common at Hawikuh, although only one was recorded in a burial. One whorl of turtle shell (Chrysemys) was noted, but spindle whorls were commonly made of potsherds and occasionally of stone. Various other artifacts associated with cloth manufacture, for example bone and wooden weaving tools, were found in burials (pp. 146-147; Hodge 1920:144-145).

Coronado, while at Hawikuh in 1540, made a few more observations on women's costume which tend to reinforce the evidence of archaeology:

I am unable to give your Lordship any certain information about the dress of the women, because the Indians keep them guarded so carefully that I have not seen any, except two old ones. These had on two long skirts reaching down to their feet and open in front, and a girdle, and

they are tied together with some cotton strings. I asked the Indians to give me one of these which they wore to send to you, since they were not willing to show me the women. They brought me two blankets, which are these that I am sending, almost painted over [embroidered?]. They wear earrings, like the women of Spain, which hang somewhat over their shoulders (Hammond and Rey 1940:177).

The expeditions of the 1580s add a small amount of information about Zuni-Mohose costume. According to Luxán, writing of Zuni: "For even though they wear the same sort of dress as the others, the cloth is of agave fiber, since they gather little cotton because the land is cold. The women wear their hair done up in large puffs" (Hammond and Rey 1966:184). A few passages later, Luxán adds:

The Indians spin cotton and weave cloth. They say, however, that they obtain part of the cotton in trade from the province of Mohose . . . which is a temperate land. The clothing which the men and women wear is made of agave fiber, so well carded that it resembles coarse linen (p. 185).

In Mohose or Hopi, Luxán had the following to say: "The men cover their privy parts with a piece of cloth similar to a hand towel, figured and with tassels. When they feel cold they wear cotton blankets. The women are always well dressed and have their hair done up in puffs" (p. 192).

The agave mentioned for the Zuni is almost certainly yucca, which according to Kent (1957:478) was normally two-ply S-spun Z-twisted. It makes a cloth somewhat like coarse linen which, indeed, is how Espejo (Hammond and Rey 1966:226) described it for Zuni, as did Luxán in the passage quoted above. Apocynum (dogbane) was also used, spun and woven, probably in the same way. Species of Apocynum are found throughout the area.

I have discussed costume in considerable detail because it sheds light on the needs of the area and the reasons why the Hopi cotton had such a considerable trade value. Much of the Pueblo area had and still has cold winters, as the Spaniards found to their dismay, and clothing is vital to the well-being of the inhabitants. Both the wealth of skins coming in from the Plains and the cotton from Hopi were welcomed throughout the upper Southwest and beyond. It might be noted that the squash blossom hairstyle for women so clearly described in the Spanish accounts was, until recently, common in both the Zuni and Hopi regions.

Aesthetic Patterns

In terms of art forms and techniques, both the people of Cibola and Tusayan have a clear continuum from the sixteenth century (and earlier) to the present day. The brilliant Hopi ceramics that were so popular in the period from the A.D. 1300s throughout the early historic period continue. Indeed, Hopi ceramics and basketry reproduce design elements not only of the sixteenth century pottery but of the Jeddito murals, though of course much of this is a deliberate reintroduction dating from fairly recent times. The mural paintings, parenthetically, give evidence of masked figures in the fifteenth and sixteenth centuries, and some of the mural figures can be tentatively identified with masked god figures of the present day (Smith 1952:306-312). Schaafsma and Schaafsma (1974:538, 544) believe that masked kachina dancers reached the western Pueblos from the Jornada area of southeast New Mexico in the fourteenth century and acted as cultural integrators in a time of environmental stress. Certainly the kachinas became very popular, especially in the west.

Although the Zuni pottery of the nineteenth and twentieth centuries is perhaps not as artistically pleasing as that of Hopi, it is a competent ware and a valid art form. It does not particularly resemble the old Cibolan wares, and the Zuni renaissance in pottery was well under way by A.D. 1800. It mostly resembles the historic Hopi wares and probably was influenced by them. Apropos of that, we should remember that Cibola-Zuni from pre-Spanish times had some tendency to copy Tusayan-Hopi as far as pottery making was concerned. For further comments on historic ceramics see Mera (1939:19-21 ff.).

General Comments

As far as the accounts go, there is very little that would distinguish the sixteenth century Cibola-Tusayan people from nineteenth century Zuni or Hopi, except of course for the Spanish or Anglo-Saxon traits that have filtered in over the centuries. Many of the resemblances between sixteenth century western Pueblos and Zuni and/or Hopi in the nineteenth or even twentieth century are quite specific. They include building techniques, town layout and usually the very names of towns, use of the squash blossom hairdo by women, a woman's costume that leaves one shoulder bare, cotton weaving by men, use of corn pollen, prayer sticks, veneration of water, the form and internal arrangements of kivas, and a ritual interest in snakes. A domestic example of continuity is in the technique of grinding maize. Castañeda (Hammond and Rey 1940:255) described a grinding room which, though it was in the context of a discussion of Tiguex, may have been intended to have a wider application (as indeed it does). Castañeda tells of a separate grinding room with three stones set in mortar. Three women ground, one crushing the maize, the second grinding it finer, and the third finer still. All this was done to the music of a flageolet and singing. The use of three mortar units set together predates the Spanish occupation of the Southwest by centuries in various parts of the region. For Hawikuh only seven mealing bins were found in the Hodge excavations, and the dating on them is not entirely clear. Hodge, however, believed that the bins were dismantled when houses were deserted or filled in, so that originally there were many more than actually found (Smith et al. 1966:34). In any case, the three milling stones set in a box where three women could grind simultaneously was common in both nineteenth century Zuni and nineteenth century Hopi.

Another rather homey touch that brings the sixteenth century Indians closer to us is the habit, described by Coronado, of women carrying jars of water on their heads from the spring (at Hawikuh) and up ladders without touching the jars (Hammond and Rey 1940:177). Each woman wore a roll on her head to help cradle the water jar (p. 177). Headrings are known archaeologically at least as early as P-III times, and, of course, the practice of carrying water on the head, balancing with a headring, continues today.

Some resemblances are more general: the suggestion of a council of elders who performed religious and secular duties, the basic autonomy of separate towns and general egalitarianism, patterns of warfare, use of trading parties, communal rabbit hunts, art motifs, masked dancers in a variety of ceremonials, and many others. One suspects that a modern Zuni Indian would have much in common with his Halona counterpart living in 1540. It is doubtful if a modern Spaniard would have much to say to Coronado.

CHAPTER X

RIO GRANDE PROVINCE

Because of complications touched on in Chapter IX, data from the Rio Grande province will be sampled rather than treated in detail. The province is so large and it involved such a variety of peoples (covering several dialects of two separate language groups) that statements about the area can be made only in terms of generalities. In addition, the ongoing archaeological work in the area, growing in large part out of active conservation archaeology projects, is changing, year to year, our knowledge of the early historic alignments of the area. To do justice to the Rio Grande peoples would take a volume in itself.

In Chapter IX, I spoke of perhaps three separate provinces or subprovinces within the area. Actually, if one utilizes the term province to imply a strong sense of ethnic unity ("us" versus "them"), as I suggested in Chapter II, there might well be at least nine, breaking along linguistic lines. To the south was the series of Piro towns, strung along the middle course of the Rio Grande from roughly San Marcial to somewhere south of present-day Isleta. East of them, and best reached from northern Piro territory, were the kindred but separate Salinas (Maguas, Tompiro) people along the eastern slopes of the Manzano Mountains. To the north, from around Isleta to beyond modern Bernalillo, was Coronado's old province of Tiguex, or Tigues, (mostly Tiwa-speaking but perhaps with some Tano), the center of the early Spanish interests in the Rio Grande. On the river further north were the eastern Keresan group (Coronado's Quirix, Espejo's Quiris); and beyond that, reaching into the Chama Basin, were the Tewa pueblos. On the Jemez River to the west, Keresan-speaking Zia (and perhaps two or three satellite towns) were separate to some degree; it is not clear to what extent Coronado considered Zia as a part of Quirix, but the explorers of the 1580s seemed to have made a distinction. The western Keresans were represented by the isolated and bellicose settlement of Acoma in the San Jose drainage west of the Rio Grande. At least by the last half of the century Acoma was involved in a complex trade-raid relationship with the Querechos (Navajo? Apache?) who lived in the area. Farther up the Jemez were the Towa towns, clustering in the general vicinity of modern Jemez. Far up the Rio Grande were the isolated northern Tiwa towns of Picuris and Taos.

In writing this volume I originally placed the Tano groups of the Galisteo area with Pecos, though I never felt very secure in doing so. There is no doubt that Tanos speakers interacted with groups farther west, and the ceramic-producing pueblo of Tonque north and east of Bernalillo may have been composed, at least in part, of Tano speakers in the sixteenth century (Warren 1969:37).

An argument can be made for placing Tanos with Pecos. The Tano area was in sharp decline in the first part of the sixteenth century and, by the second half of the century, if not before, seemed to have fallen somewhat into the Pecos orbit. However, details of the Galisteo region are, to say the least, anything but crystal clear, and in Coronado's time the Tanos towns may have been interacting most strongly with Tiguex. One thing does seem to be of interest. Though the Galisteo area settlements were primary exploiters of the Cerrillos turquoise and ore mines, the major trade benefits seem to have gone to Tiguex to the west and Pecos to the east. Late in the sixteenth century, after the Spanish had upset and changed the power formula in the central Rio Grande, nearby Keresan towns became involved in the turquoise trade according to their own traditions (Bandelier 1890-1892:Vol. 2, 92-93; White 1935:27-28, 1942:33). In this publication I shall tentatively treat the Tanos pueblos as a part of the Rio Grande oikomene.

Since my major thrust is to examine the unity and interaction of the Greater Southwest and the mechanisms whereby this interaction was maintained, I shall concentrate here on the central part of the area. In 1540 it looks very much as if Tiguex was the major focus of the Rio Grande province, situated (with Acoma) on the main trade routes that led from Pecos to Cibola. Coronado's brutal exploitative activities had a devastating effect on Tiguex. It is reasonable to believe that the greater attention paid to the Keresan groups, the Tewa, and even the Tano by the explorers of the 1580s and 1590s is a reflection of the fact that Tiguex, though still considered important, had not recovered from Coronado. Probably, it lost the premier trade position as middleman on the trade routes. Certainly, Tiguex' military abilities were much depressed by the latter part of the century, and the Tiguex people usually fled to the hills at the coming of the Spaniards. Resentment of the Spaniards must have been intense. When two friars from the Chamuscado party chose to stay behind in Tiguex, they were promptly killed at Puaray. A year or so later Espejo's tiny party seemed to have no difficulty sacking Puaray and killing a number of its inhabitants. Tiguex in the 1580s obviously was an area in some kind of culture shock. The area never regained any sort of central position; Castaño scarcely visited it, Oñate established his political headquarters to the north among the Tewas, and the Franciscan headquarters was placed in the Rio Grande Keresan area. Nearly a century later many of the southern Tiwa (the remnants of old Tiguex), with a strange docility, followed the Spaniards southward in the aftermath of the Pueblo Revolt.

We have more information on the Rio Grande province in the sixteenth and early seventeenth centuries than on any other part of the Southwest. The Coronado expedition spent parts of three years in the central Rio Grande Valley, and all later expeditions followed the Rio Grande northward to explore New Mexico, except for that of Castaño de Sosa, which approached along the Pecos Valley. When Oñate finally settled New Mexico, his capital was at San Juan near the junction of the Chama and the Rio Grande (soon to be moved to Santa Fe, some 45 km to the southeast). The mission headquarters for Franciscan friars was at the Keresan pueblo of Santo Domingo.

The Rio Grande was even more central to Spanish New Mexico in the eighteenth century. The west was given up entirely except on paper (Hopi), or held as a very marginal operation (Zuni). In the east both Pecos and the Tanos towns withered for lack of protection and from loss of trade, and the Tompiro pueblos were deserted entirely, their place gradually taken by scattered Hispanic ranches. In both the seventeenth and eighteenth centuries much of what went on along the frontier was undocumented. For example, on the Pecos River near modern Santa Rosa, Albert E. Ward has discovered a vigorous commercial (?) settlement--perhaps a mixture of Pueblo, Hispanic, and marginal Plains peoples--that flourished in the eighteenth century. The outpost seems to have been trading bread or parched maize to Plains Indians; at least some ninety-eight ovens were found at the site (Ward, personal communication).

Natural Features

The Rio Grande province lies partly in the Southern Rockies and partly in the eastward extension of the Basin and Range. The Southern Rockies extend to the Sangre de Cristo Mountains east of the Rio Grande. To the west is the San Juan Range, separated by the valley of the Chama River from the Sierra de los Valles and the Jemez Mountains. South of this region is a series of isolated, north- and south-trending ranges with detrital-filled basins at their floors. Historically, it might be said that the northern Tiwa, the Tewa, and the Towa Indians lived in the shadows of the Rockies, while most of the eastern Keresan, the western Keresan, Tano, the

southern Tiwa, Piro, and Tompiro inhabited the Basin and Range country. Since most or all the pueblos were actually along watercourses, the physical diversity from north to south was not so great. Climatic patterns remained much the same; however, due to the general southward tilt of the land, there was considerable difference in altitude with its concomitant differences in rainfall and temperature.

The Rio Grande province lies in the Köppen climatic zones BSk and BWk, with the mountain areas in Dfb. The province has sections with the highest rainfall totals in the Southwest; in the Jemez and Sangre de Cristo Mountains readings may reach 1000 mm annually. This region is generally elevated. Two peaks in the Sangre de Cristo Mountains, Wheeler and Truchas, rise to an altitude of 4011 and 3970 m, respectively. Even in the isolated ranges in the southern part of the area, individual peaks may reach 3000 m or more. Santa Fe, which lies on the flanks of the Sangre de Cristos at an altitude of nearly 2200 m, has some 360 mm annual precipitation; Galisteo, a few kilometers to the south and somewhat lower, has 312 mm; Albuquerque, in the old Tiguex area at about 1560 m, has 200 mm; San Marcial, on the southern fringe of the Rio Grande province at an altitude of around 1375 m, has less than 125 mm of precipitation annually. The growing season also sharply reflects this difference in altitude. At San Marcial the frost-free average is something on the order of 180 days per year, as it is in Albuquerque and throughout much of the Tiguex area. In Santa Fe the frost-free season is only around 120 days per year, and at Taos it is only 100 days per year. In general, in New Mexico there is a temperature gradient of some $0.8^{\circ}C$ to $1.3^{\circ}C$ for every degree of latitude. For every 300 m of altitude (1000 ft) there is a gradient of about $2.7^{\circ}C$.

Most of the precipitation in the Rio Grande province comes from high-intensity, short-duration storms moving in from the Gulf of Mexico during the summer months (June-September). Snow falls throughout the province; the mountains collect snow in winter and provide a major source for the streams of the region. Above about 2000 m, snow makes up half or more of the the entire annual precipitation budget. For a more detailed discussion of the general climatic situation of the upper Southwest, see Chapter IX.

River flow of the Rio Grande and its major upper basin tributaries is now greatly altered by dams, irrigation projects, and regional water planning. Figures from around the turn of the century, however, give a somewhat more accurate picture of the aboriginal situation, though even at that early date, river control measures were fairly well advanced. At San Marcial the discharge of the Rio

Grande, averaged over the period 1896-1913, was a little more than 125,000 ha/m annually, but the flow of the river varied dramatically year to year and month to month. This leads to an average distribution of about 15 mm per km^2 of water over the 70,000 km^2 drainage area of the Rio Grande north of the southernmost Piro settlement. Again, averages, as in all desert areas, must be used with caution.

Vegetation in the Rio Grande province, of course, varies a great deal with altitude and to some degree with latitude. In the Basin and Range region that forms the southern part of the province, there is the semidesert vegetation found throughout much of the Southwest. It includes various of the desert grasses, creosote bush (Larrea), mesquite and screwbean (Prosopis), and soapweed. In somewhat higher elevations there are the more valuable grazing gramas, as well as sagebrush and snakeweed. Various of the cacti and several varieties of yucca are found in New Mexico and climb the sides of the mountains to considerable elevations. In the valleys and washes are salt grass, and the desert willow and cottonwood. A scrub forest of pinyon and juniper is found throughout much of the province, often interspersed with stretches of semidesert or dry grasslands. In the upper elevations there is oak and some of the larger conifers, including ponderosa pine. Above about 2400 m are Douglas fir, Colorado spruce, yellow pine, bristlecone pine, white pine, and aspen.

Wildflowers in the Rio Grande province include columbine, lupine, and, in the higher elevations, sedges, gentian, and larkspur. Some plants, at least in historic times, were valued by Pueblo Indians for their curing power--for example, Jimsonweed (Datura Stramonium), Mormon tea (Ephedra sp.), and Yerba Mansa (Anemopsis sp.) (Tidestrom and Kittell 1941:1-10, 128, 154, 705, 744-746; Work Projects Administration 1945:13-15, 26-27; Robbins et al. 1916).

Fauna of the lower portions of the province does not differ significantly from that of the Little Colorado province. In the Coronado accounts the most distinctive animal was probably the bison, which ranged especially in the eastern and southern part of the province. The really large herds of bison were found further east, however, in the valleys of the Pecos, Canadian, and upper Red rivers. Both cottontails and jackrabbits abound in the lower elevations, as do the mule deer, various squirrels, and the badger, skunk, and coyote. The mountain lion (Felis concolor) was common enough to be mentioned in the Coronado documents and was important in the religious systems of the later Pueblo Indi-

ans. Wolves, elk, and mountain sheep (although the present mountain sheep are Canadian imports) are found in the high areas, as is the black bear.

Birds include the wild turkey, the grouse, and a number of migratory game birds, such as ducks and teals. In the very high elevations are found the nutcracker and grosbeak. The area has a variety of turtles, including the yellow mud turtle and the painted turtle, and a great number of lizards, including several whiptails (Cnemidophorus sp.) and skinks (Eumeces sp.). Most of the snakes are harmless; exceptions are the western rattlesnake (Crotalus viridis) and the western diamondback rattlesnake (C. atrox). There is a large collection of frogs and toads. The Rio Grande area has the usual component of insects and arachnids, one dangerous type being the black widow spider. Another common spider is the tarantula; scorpions appear but are not a menace in this region.

Fish include blue sucker (which no longer appears in the upper Rio Grande), trout, catfish, and chubs, among others. Although the Rio Grande Indians were not indifferent or hostile to fish as a food, it was, in all probability, not very important in the economy (Work Projects Administration 1945:15-20, 33; Stebbins 1954:144-145, 193, 327, 509-510; Caywood 1966:36; Lange 1968:202; Koster 1957; Henderson and Harrington 1914).

Language

I have already summarized the languages of the Rio Grande pueblos. There seems no reason whatsoever to believe that any great linguistic shifts have taken place from Coronado's time till the present, excepting that, as victims of the shrinking population, the dialects of Piro and Tompiro have disappeared and Tano survives only in the Hopi country. Possible linguistic affiliation of the Tanoans was discussed in Chapter IX. Many linguists consider them to be part of an Aztec-Tanoan phylum which also embraces Shoshonean (including Hopi), Aztec (Nahuatl), and, as some believe, Kiowa. Keresan, like Zuni, is an isolate, but attempts have been made to link it to a widespread Hokan-Siouan phylum. Various people have speculated as to the direction of origin of these various languages before they reached the Rio Grande area, but as stated above, in earliest historic times the languages were in about the same places as today.

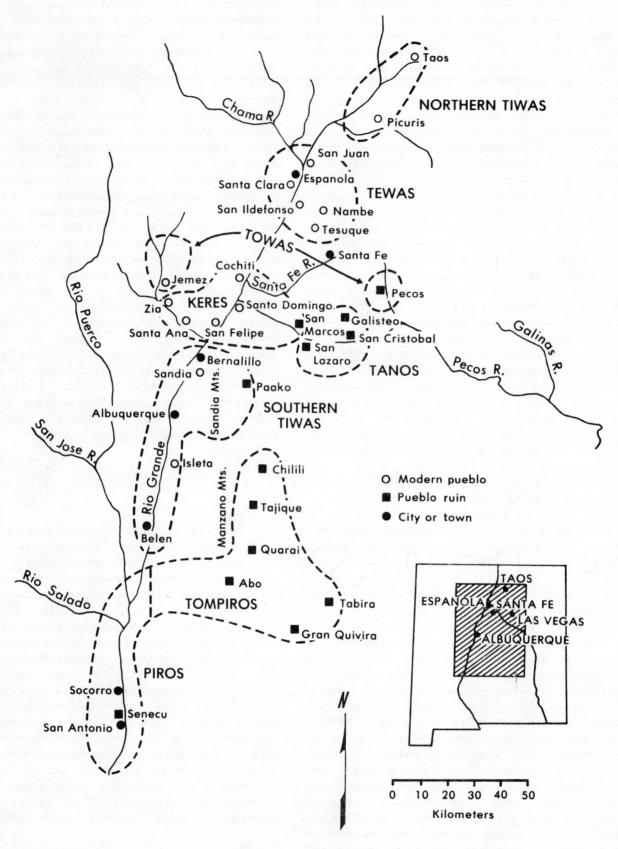

Figure 13. New Mexico Pueblo Linguistic Groups.

Archaeology

Unlike the near absence of archaeology in the Serrana and high uncertainty in the Desert and Colorado provinces, at least for the sixteenth and seventeenth centuries, archaeology in the Rio Grande province is relatively rich. There have been a large number of historic sites excavated, partially excavated, tested, or collected. They include Bandelier's Puaray and Kuaua among the Tiwa; various Salinas sites; Kuapa, Tashkatze, Pueblo del Encierra, Rainbow House, and Tyuonyi in the Keresan area; Te'euinge, Cuyamungué, Pesedeuinge, Poshuouinge, and Puye in the Tewa region; Unshagi and Giusewa in the Jemez country; various Tano sites; and many more. For further information see Schroeder (1979d).

In the account that follows I shall not try an exhaustive survey of the archaeological sources but instead will sample data from the various areas. The major focus will be on Tiguex for the Coronado period, and general statements will probably be true for Tiguex whether they are or are not for the region as a whole. Later accounts have less cultural information but generally better identify the specific area under discussion.

Population and Pueblos

Castañeda has a list of southwestern pueblos which, if the Little Colorado and Pecos group are subtracted, gives his count of the Rio Grande groups. Other pueblo counts and identifications were made by two members of the Chamuscado party and by Luxán and Espejo of the Espejo party. In addition, pueblos are noted by Oñate in a series of documents, pueblos which have been conveniently listed by Hodge (Hammond and Rey 1953:363-374). Another source is the Enrico Martínez map of 1602, done in Mexico City at the request of the viceroy. There are, of course, later population counts-- for example, that of Benavides, first published in 1630 but drawn from data that were collected in the mid-1620s. Figure 14 below gives the count of pueblos by these various sixteenth century and early seventeenth century authors.

I should stress that the number of Indian towns given in Figure 14 does not pretend to be accurate. The numbers are approximations; in many cases definite identification of pueblos is not made, and it is not always clear if given settlements were occupied, temporarily deserted, or in ruins at the time they were visited. Also, the same pueblo may be counted twice.

Names of the pueblos are very difficult to identify with modern groups, at least until the time of Oñate. For the Rio Grande area Acoma (Acuco, Acus, etc.) is always clearly indicated in the Coronado documents, and this pueblo is mentioned as early as 1539. The pueblo of Zia (under the name Chia) is also identified by Coronado's party, as are Jemez (Hemes), Tiwa (Tiguex), and Keres (Quirix). The Tewa pueblo of Yuque-Yunque in the Chama area is mentioned, but, generally speaking, Coronado's men do not seem to have had much contact with the Tewa. The Spaniards occupied a Tiguex pueblo they called Alcanfor, or Coofor; had control of a nearby one called Alameda; and destroyed one called Arenal, or Circo, and another called Moho, Moñi, or El Cerco. A pueblo, perhaps Picuris, referred to by the Spaniards as Acha, is mentioned. Taos, called by the Spaniards Braba, or Valladolid, was visited by Hernando de Alvarado and Father Juan Padilla in September or October of 1540. It is extremely difficult to retrace the route of the Alvarado-Padillo party, but I am tempted to believe that it may have gone first to Pecos and then swung around the east side of the Sangre de Cristo Mountains (Hammond and Rey 1940:182-183, 219). Later, in the summer of 1541, Francisco de Barrionuevo was sent on a food-collecting expedition to the Jemez towns and up the Rio Grande as far as Taos. His exact route is not known. Castañeda's description of the trip is rather puzzling:

> [Maestro de Campo Tristán de Arellano] sent Captain Francisco de Barrionuevo with some men up the river toward the north. He found two provinces, one of which was called Hemes, containing seven pueblos, and the other Yuque-Yunque. The pueblos of Hemes came out peacefully and furnished provisions. Those of Yuque-Yunque abandoned two very beautiful pueblos which were on opposite sides of the river, while the army was establishing camp, and went to the sierra where they had four very strong pueblos which could not be reached by the horses because of the craggy land. In these two pueblos were found abundant provisions and beautiful glazed pottery of many decorations and shapes. Our men also found many ollas filled with a select shiny metal with which the Indians glazed their pottery . . . .
>
> Twenty leagues farther up the river there was a large and powerful river--I mean pueblo--called Braba, and which our men named Valladolid. The river flowed

(Indian Group)	Castañeda (1540-42)	Gallegos-Pedrosa (1581-82)	Luxán (1583)	Espejo (1583)	Obregón (1583)	Castaño (1590-91)	Oñate (1598-99)	Martinez map. (1602)	Benavides (1630)
Piro	8	11	10	10	?	?	more than ten	10	14?
Tompiro	7?	5	several	11	11	?	?	?	14-15
Southern Tiwa	12	8	13-16	16	16	14	12	11	15-16
Keresan	9	13	7	?	11	6-8	10	7	8
Tewa	6	10	?	?	?	11	13	6	8
Towa	10	13	?	?	?	?	10	4	2
Tano	3	3-4	2 or more	5?	3-4	3	3	4-5	5
Northern Tiwa	2?	?	?	?	?	1?	2	2	2

(Cuevas 1924 : 298-304; Benavides 1954: 14-30; Hammond and Rey 1966: frontispiece map, 102-22, 206, 228; Hammond and Rey 1953: 363-74; Schroeder and Matson 1965: 109-76).

There are uncertainties in all of these figures, even in ones that do not have question marks. In many cases definite identifications of pueblos are not made; it is not always clear if given settlements were occupied, temporarily deserted, or in ruin; and the same pueblo may be counted twice. Treat the figures as approximations only.

Figure 14. Number of Pueblos in the Rio Grande Province as Reported by Various Sixteenth and Seventeenth Century Writers.

through the center of it, and the river was spanned by wooden bridges built with very large and heavy square pine timbers. At this pueblo there were seen the largest and finest estufas that had been found in all that land. They had twelve pillars, each one two arms' length around and two estados high. This pueblo had been visited by Hernando de Alvarado when he discovered Cicuye (p. 244).

It is hard to know what to make of this account. Could it be that Barrionuevo reached the Jemez towns via the Chama, crossing the divide into the Jemez River drainage from the north or northwest? Alternatively, he could have gone up the Jemez River, following it into the highlands around Valle Grande and then working his way off the escarpment, perhaps on the north side, reaching the Chama Valley. In either case, he went into very rugged country. The two pueblos mentioned were most likely the Yuque-Yunque of Oñate's time and, across from it, the forerunner of modern San Juan. Their inhabitants' mistrust of the invaders probably related to Spanish actions at Tiguex earlier that same year. In any case, as I said above, the Spaniards had minimal contact with the Tewa.

Although Gallegos and Pedrosa of the Chamuscado expedition listed large numbers of pueblos, unfortunately the Spaniards mostly gave European or Nahuatl names to the towns they found. Acoma is an exception; the native name was well fixed (Acoma is from Keresan Ako, "white rock," plus ma, "people," Pearce 1965:2). Puarai, Puaray, or Puala is perhaps another exception; at least the name sounds Tanoan. The location of Puaray is still something of a mystery; in the 1930s the site of Puaray as identified by Adolph F. Bandelier was extensively excavated (Tichy 1939). This site is a few kilometers south of Kuaua, both being on the west side of the Rio Grande. The excavated site of Bandelier's Puaray falls into the period of the sixteenth century clearly enough, but otherwise it does not seem to be the historic Puaray. For one thing, Villagrá (1933:142) in the Oñate party reported wall paintings depicting the deaths of friars left behind by Chamuscado. Such wall paintings were not found in the excavations.

Bliss (1948:218-219) believes that the Puaray of Bandelier was in fact the pueblo named Culiacan by Pedrosa and Gallegos (Hammond and Rey 1966:104, 117). The real Puaray was across the river and somewhat downstream (Bliss 1948). Kuaua may have been the site of La Palma given by Gallegos as upstream from Culiacan (Hammond and Rey 1966:104; Bliss 1948:219). For additional discussions of the

locations of various Tiguex towns including Puaray see Hackett (1915); Mecham (1926); Vivian (1932); Schroeder and Matson (1965); Snow (1975); and Riley (1981a).

Luxán, a year or so after Gallegos, gives a series of names for the Tiguex pueblos:

Since only eight of us able to fight were left, not counting the sick or wounded, we determined to go back by way of the Tiguas, our enemies. These are the thirteen pueblos where the friars were killed, namely: Poguana, Comise, Achine, Guagua, Gagose, Simassa, Suyte, Nocoche, Hacala, Tiara, Taycios, Casa, and Puala, which is the place where the friars were killed. Diego Pérez de Luxán acted as guide and in two and one-half days brought the camp to the Río del Norte close to the insurgent pueblo of Puaguana. Here we caught three Indians and a few warriors at some huts on the day we arrived, and through them we talked of peace with the Tiguas. In order to reassure them we freed the prisoners. The next day, the twentieth of June, we passed near Puala, where we rested the following day (Hammond and Rey 1966:203).

It is difficult to reconstruct the actual placement of pueblos from this list, though some of the names are perhaps Tanoan. Obviously Poguana, or Puaguana, was near Puala (Puaray). The Spaniards marched at least part of the twentieth of June and rested on the twenty-first. On the twenty-second of June they seemed to have reached Puala, having first passed two nearby pueblos where the people were not overly friendly. The Spaniards, on reaching Puala, siezed the four corners and with a small party captured a number of Indians:

We put them in an estufa. And as the pueblo was large and the majority had hidden themselves there, we set fire to the big pueblo of Puala, where we thought some were burned to death because of the cries they uttered. We at once took out the prisoners, two at a time, and lined them up against some cottonwoods close to the pueblo of Puala, where they were garroted and shot many times until they were dead. Sixteen were executed, not counting those who burned to death (p. 204).

This suggests that Puaray was near the Rio Grande or at least near a stream lined with cottonwood. The attack on Puaray was in revenge of the murders of the Friars Agustín Rodríguez and Francisco López from the Chamuscado expedition. Luxán's account also links Puaray with the Coronado expedition. While at Hawikuh, Luxán learned some interesting things about the Tiguex:

We learned from the interpreters that two of Coronado's captains were in this pueblo for two years, that from here they went to discover some provinces, and that when Coronado was at Puala de los Mártires (where the friars had been killed) he came to the above-mentioned pueblo of Acoma, made war on the inhabitants, and they surrendered. In Acoma, he was informed that the inhabitants of Puala, who are Tiguas, and those of the surrounding district, had killed ten of the horses left there by Coronado for the people in the garrison. When Coronado heard of the incident, he set out for Puala, whose people are Tiguas, and besieged them near a pueblo encircled by mountains. He pressed them so hard that those who did not die at the hands of the Spaniards--Coronado's people, whom the natives called Castillos--died of hunger and thirst. (Chamuscado and his men were not ignorant of this. They knew it all, but refrained from telling about it in order that others might come to settle the land). Finally the people of Puala surrendered and threw themselves on Coronado's mercy, and he took as many, both men and women, in his service as were necessary, and returned to this pueblo [Hawikuh]. From here he set out for the valley of Samora, which must be one hundred leagues distant from this province (pp. 185-186).

This astounding story has generally been ignored by commentators on the sixteenth century contacts of the Spaniards with Pueblo Indians, whose interest in Puaray traditionally concerns the relationships of sixteenth century Puaray with the seventeenth century town of that name. Here, however, Puaray is tied to one of two towns destroyed by Coronado. The location of Puaray, very probably in the flat country east of the Rio Grande and fairly near the river (see Snow 1975:477), sounds as if it were the town of Arenal, which was burned by Coronado in the winter of 1540-1541 and many of whose inhabitants were slaughtered. The description of Luxán, however, makes it reasonably clear that he is talking about Moho, or El Cerco, a second Tiguex pueblo besieged

by Coronado for about two months, the people finally being forced to give up the highly fortified town because of lack of water. However, the highly successful defense of Mojo against the full weight of the Spanish army, which with Indian allies included perhaps 1200 men, indicated that it was in a very defensible place. Actually, the Coronado accounts say as much; and Luxán's statement, "pueblo surrounded by mountains," may also indicate it, though it may mean only that there were high mountains in the general area.

Two explanations come to mind. One is that the inhabitants of Puaray withdrew to another pueblo, perhaps in the rough country west of the Rio Grande, since the accounts make it clear that they were near the river. Castaño in 1590-1591 suggests that some or most of the Tiguex in the valleys "had gone to the mountains and to other pueblos" out of fear (Schroeder and Matson 1965:168); Castañeda, speaking of the Tewa, also mentions that the people of Yuque-Yunque had a nearby stronghold in the mountains (Hammond and Rey 1940:244). It is more likely, however, that Luxán (or his Indian informant) was confusing the two accounts. In such a case, Puaray was Arenal, and Luxán mixed up the Coronado attack on Arenal with the later fighting at Moho (see Riley 1981a:210).

Luxán also identified the Keresan pueblos as Catiete (La Tiete), Gigue, Tipolti, Cochita, and Sieharan. Catiete (Oñate's Castixes) is probably the modern San Felipe whose native name is Katishtya. Gigue is likely Oñate's Gipuy and was one of the earlier sites of Santo Domingo. Tipolti (Oñate's Tamy, or Tamaya) is believed by Hammond and Rey (1966:204 n. 121) to be Santa Ana. Cochita is probably Cochiti (or perhaps San Felipe), while Sieharan may be Zia (p. 204 nn. 119, 120, 122).

In the Espejo account there is a province called Ubates which had five pueblos. Reed (1943:262) suggests that these were Tewa pueblos and that Espejo really did not visit them as the account implies but simply knew them from hearsay. This is possible; but the greater likelihood, it seems to me, is the one suggested by Hodge (Benavides 1945:266), following Bandelier, that Ubates is simply a corruption of the name Puya-tye, the Keresan designation for the Tano.

Whereas Coronado concentrated on Tiwa country, and the Chamuscado and Espejo expeditions had unpleasant relations with the Tiwa but seem to have been well received by the Keresans, Castaño de Sosa in the period 1590-1591 approached the Rio Grande from another direction. He first explored Tewa country, then marched south to the Keres, and, rather casually, visited the Tiwa. Castaño seems to have reached most of the Tewa pueblos, though it is sometimes hard to identify them exactly. He certainly penetrated upriver as far as the San Juan-Yuque-Yunque area before turning south. Schroeder and Matson (1965:126-128) believe that Castaño also contacted the northern Tiwa town of Picuris on a quick two-day trip.

With the Oñate entrada some seven years after Castaño, the Pueblo area entered essentially unbroken contact with Spaniards. There are still pueblos that are not identified or whose identity is debated (Puaray, for example), but New Mexico entered a fully historical phase starting in 1598.

Population

Population figures from the sixteenth and early seventeenth century documents vary a great deal; generally, it might be said that the figures for the earliest Spanish entradas are too low, while those of the later accounts are too high. If we adopt the model of Dobyns (1966:414), we would expect the pernicious effect of Spanish-introduced disease and other kinds of debilitating pressures to have been felt by the time of Espejo and Oñate. I strongly suspect that this was, indeed, the case and that population figures as reported are badly skewed,
----
Population Estimates for the Rio Grande Province.

Castañeda (1540-1542)   Perhaps 45,000 (depending on whether Castañeda's use of the word "hombres" meant "males," "adult men," or "people." If the latter, the figures would be much lower.)

Pedrosa (1581-1582)   15,000 (this figure is an extrapolation from the house count and must be taken with great reserve.)

Espejo (1582-1583)   Perhaps 130,000

Velasco (1609)   Over 20,000 (30,000 for the entire Pueblo area.)

Benavides (1630)   Perhaps 54,000
----
probably for internal Spanish political reasons.

It seems unlikely that one can take the Espejo figures seriously. Trying to extrapolate from the number of houses listed by Gallegos and by Pedrosa is very difficult since we do not know exactly what

a "house" consisted of. Schroeder (1972:42), if I interpret him correctly, believes there may have been about 50,000 Indians in the entire Pueblo area in the late sixteenth century.

Based on these various indications, I will suggest here that in the 1540s the Rio Grande area had some 40,000 to 50,000 inhabitants; by the 1580s this had dropped drastically, perhaps cut in half. The Benavides figure from the 1620s of about 50,000 is probably exaggerated for purposes of church politics. If the Dobyns model is employed, one would expect an even lower figure than that of 1582-1583. The numbers of Pueblo Indians continued to decline during the seventeenth and eighteenth centuries. In the seventeenth century both the Piro and Tompiro areas were largely or wholly deserted, and many of the towns of Tiguex and Quirix also fell into ruins. By the time of the Domínguez inventory of 1776 there were in the Rio Grande province only about 6000 Pueblo Indians, and Spanish-speaking settlers from New Spain were beginning to fill in the vacant areas, especially along the river valleys. This is a trend that continues to the present day, with Anglo-Americans adding to and partly replacing the Hispanic population influx after the first quarter of the nineteenth century. Modest growth of certain present-day pueblos is generally an indication of their utilization of modern production and distribution techniques and ties their demographic patterns to that of the larger regional society.

Subsistence

At the time of the first Spanish entrada the Pueblo Indians were all agricultural, and had been for centuries. The first Spaniards to arrive in the Rio Grande area, Alvarado and Padilla, were struck by the abundant maize, beans, and chickens (Hammond and Rey 1940:182). Reaching the Rio Grande somewhere in the Tiguex area, the explorers found that

the Nuestra Señora [Rio Grande] river flows through a broad valley planted with fields of maize. There are some cottonwood groves. There are twelve pueblos. The houses are of mud, two stories high. The people seem good, more given to farming than to war. They have provisions of maize, beans, melons, and chickens in great abundance. They dress in cotton, cattle skins, and coats made with the feathers from the chickens (p. 183).

Castañeda describes the agricultural practices

in this way:

> The men spin and weave; the women take care of the children and prepare the food. The land is so fertile that they need to cultivate only once a year, just for planting, for the snow falls and covers the fields, and the maize grows under the snow. In one year they harvest enough for seven years. There are numerous cranes, geese, crows, and thrushes which feed on the planted fields. With all this, when, in the following year, they proceed to plant again, they find the fields covered with maize, which they had not been able to gather fully.

> There were in these provinces large numbers of native hens and cocks with gills. These, if not dressed or cut open, could be kept for sixty days after death without giving any smell. . . . All their bread is made with flour, mixed with hot water, in the shape of wafers. They gather large quantities of herbs, which they dry and keep for their cooking throughout the year. There are no edible fruits in this land, except pine nuts (pp. 255-256).

This is one of the few mentions of quelites in the diet of the Pueblo Indians; for an indication of the later utilization of wild plants in the area, see Robbins et al. (1916). The point about snow covering the maize may refer to the fact that snows may come after the April/May plantings or perhaps before the October harvest. Although Castañeda does not refer specifically to irrigation (it is mentioned later in the century; see, for example, Hammond and Rey 1966:282), there seems little doubt that at least small-sized irrigation ditches were in use, as they were in other parts of the upper Southwest. Incidentally, the Tiguex and Quirix provinces are on the northern limits of cotton growing and marginally in the zone of dry farming (precipitation averages only from 250 to 300 mm, but two-thirds of it falls in the period April-September, in other words, during the growing season). For further comments on Cochiti at the very northern limits of the old Tiguex-Quirix area, see Lange (1959:3-6, 77-190) and comments below. At Cochiti the coldest month (January) averages 0°C, while the hottest (July) has an average of 21°C.

There are numerous other mentions of the subsistence of the Rio Grande pueblos in the Coronado, Chamuscado, Espejo, Castaño, and Oñate expedition accounts. A sample only will be given here.

According to Luxán, traveling in the desolation of Tiguex in 1582-1583:

> During this time we inspected some pueblos. All were deserted, but contained large quantities of corn, beans, green and sun-dried calabashes, and other vegetables; also dew-lapped cocks and hens, and a lot of pottery. We provisioned ourselves well with these things (Hammond and Rey 1966:178).

Gallegos, describing the central Rio Grande area, talked of the use of head pads for carrying water and the grinding and cooking of maize tortillas by women and mentioned large supplies (among the Tiguex) of "corn tortillas, corn-flour gruel, calabashes, and beans." He also noted in some detail the use of cotton for garments (pp. 84, 85-86). Espejo, when among the Quirix, noted that the Spanish party received cotton blankets, many turkeys, and some corn and at Zia cotton blankets and "ample supplies of corn, turkeys, and bread made of corn flour" (p. 223). Castaño, among the Keresans, stated that the people brought "corn, flour, beans, and turkeys in abundance" (p. 286). This generous contribution came in midwinter and represented stored supplies. With the specter of Tiguex always with them, the Rio Grande Indians tended to be generous in the latter part of the sixteenth century.

The picture in the sixteenth century is of Indian groups that had considerable stores of the basic foodstuffs (corn, beans, and squash) and enough cotton materials to give the Spaniards cotton garments. Doubtlessly the central Rio Grande Indians remembered the frantic attempts of the underdressed Coronado expedition to obtain clothing from unwilling villagers, especially those of Tiguex, and the terrible retribution visited on those towns that refused cooperation. The peoples of the Rio Grande grew their own cotton, according to the Coronado reports (Hammond and Rey 1940:255). Cotton was grown at Cochiti, the northernmost Keresan pueblo, as recently as about 1900, and in the eighteenth century cotton growing seems to have been relatively common among the Keresans (Lange 1959:95). Parenthetically, tobacco (Nicotiana sp.), so popular in the Rio Grande in historic times, may not have been domesticated aboriginally; at least there is no conclusive evidence of it (see Castetter 1943:320-321). There are, of course, wild tobaccos, and Lange (1959:97, 149-150) points out that other wild plants, including Arctostaphylos pungens (pointleaf manzanita), Eupatorium sp. (thoroughwort), and Rhus cismontana (sumac), are smoked today at Cochiti, sometimes mixed together or mixed with tobacco. It should be remembered in regard to the use of tobacco that pipes have their greatest aboriginal distribution in the upper Rio Grande, and especially at Pecos.

Settlement Patterns

The Rio Grande pueblos were, generally speaking, similar to those of the Little Colorado province. Perhaps the most interesting variation from the more common Anasazi-Pueblo pattern of house and village building was the use of coursed adobe and even of adobe brick. This is mentioned as early as Castañeda:

All these pueblos have, in general, the same ceremonies and customs, although some have practices among them not observed elsewhere. They are governed by the counsel of their elders. They build their pueblo houses in common. The women mix the plaster and erect the walls; the men bring the timbers and set them in place. They have no lime, but they mix a mortar made with charcoal ash and dirt, which is almost as good as if it were made with lime. For although the houses are four stories high, their walls are built only half a yard thick. The people gather large amounts of brush and reeds, set fire to it, and when it is between charcoal and ash, they throw in a large amount of water and dirt and mix it, then make round balls with it, which they use as stones when dry. They set them with this same mixture, so that it becomes like a mortar (Hammond and Rey 1940:254).

Castaño, in the Tewa country in early 1591, spoke of one pueblo being of adobes with houses "very well made, two and three stories high, and well whitewashed, all having wood ovens" (Schroeder and Matson 1965:118). Schroeder (p. 120) identifies this pueblo as San Ildefonso and suggests that the adobe may have been coursed adobe, as this type of construction is well known, both in prehistoric and early historic times, along the Rio Grande. He suggests the possibility that the "ovens" (the name variously given as "arnifas," "harnifas," and "artrifas") may have been introduced by Coronado's men (p. 118), but since the Tewa pueblos had little contact with Coronado, this seems to me unlikely.

Kivas are well known archaeologically and are mentioned in a number of the early historic sources.

According to Castañeda:

These [unmarried] young men live in the estufas, which are located in the patios of the pueblo. They are built underground, either square or round, with pine columns. Some have been seen having twelve pillars, four to the cell, two fathoms thick; the common ones had three or four columns. The floors are paved with large smooth slabs like the baths in Europe. In the interior there is a fireplace like the binnacle of a boat where they burn a handful of brush with which they keep up the heat. They can remain inside the estufa as in a bath. The top is even with the ground. We saw some so large that they could be used for a game of ball (Hammond and Rey 1940:254-255).

Trade

The Rio Grande province was situated between the major centers of Cibola on the west and Pecos on the east, and a great deal of trade involved redistributing materials that came from either one or the other of these sources. Trade goods are noted in a large number of sites. They include bison products from the Plains area, a variety of worked stone material, flattened mouthpiece pipes (especially in sites along or east of the upper Rio Grande), which Wendorf et al. (1953:98) suggested may have originally diffused from the Mississippi Valley, and ceramic material from the Pecos area. At Rainbow House, a fifteenth century pueblo in the Frijoles-Bandelier area, Caywood (1966:36) noted a piece of fresh-water mollusk (Quadrula sp.), perhaps from the Red River area. Rainbow House also traded for fibrolite axes, likely received from Pecos (pp. 25-26). Coming in from the west were Hopi and Zuni glazes and glaze-polychrome wares. In fact, Rio Grande glazes, so much a marker of protohistoric and early historic times, originated in the Little Colorado area. In addition, there was a variety of shell, including Conus, Oliva, Olivella, Glycymeris (as far north as Taos), and Pacific Coast abalone. There is archaeological evidence of parrots and macaws and some suggestion that cotton materials may have been traded from Hopi country.

The Rio Grande province did contain a tremendous resource in the Cerrillos turquoise mines, lying in the heart of the area between Pecos-Tanos and the Keresan-Tewa areas. Considerable amounts of turquoise are found in late prehistoric and early historic sites in the Rio Grande province. Much of this probably came from the Cerrillos mines, though there is no really clear indication as to when the Cerrillos actually began its production of turquoise. Northrop (1973:11), following Sigleo (1970:75), suggests that the main exploitation of the Cerrillos mines came after around A.D. 1300. Warren (1974:13), however, indicates that mining in the Cerrillos area began by A.D. 900. In fact, if one considers that Cerrillos turquoise spread to the Chalchihuites region of central Zacatecas by c. A.D. 500-600, it is obvious that exploitation of the mines goes back at least to the early Christian centuries.

Interestingly, Warren (p. 3) notes that not only turquoise but also lead, copper, and iron ore were mined, presumably for pigment, including the lead-based glaze used in many prehistoric and early historic ceramics. For comments on the protohistoric archaeological indications of trade, see, among many other sources, Alexander and Reiter (1935:35, 53, 54, 60); Wendorf et al. (1953:26, 30, 57, 65, 87); Toulouse (1949:20); Lambert (1954:175-179); Reiter (1938:148, 157-158, 160, 162); Tower (1945:20); Kent (1957:469); Jones (1936:51-53); Dutton (1963b:116-117, 119, 175); Toulouse and Stephenson (1960:23, 32, 39-40); Tichy (1939:157-158, 160-161); and Lange et al. (1968:125).

The documentary evidence for trade contacts is very considerable and spans the entire sixteenth century. Large parts of the information have been summarized in previous publications. See for example Riley (1976b) for general trade, Schroeder (1968) for trade in birds and feathers, and Brand (1973) and Tower (1945) for trade in shells.

As indicated by Alvarado and Padilla (Hammond and Rey 1940:182-183), the Tiguex area of the Rio Grande province and Acoma were on the major route east and west. Between Cibola and Acoma the route diverged, one road running into the Jemez Valley. The trade route stretched eastward from Tiguex into the upper Galisteo region and across Glorieta Pass to Pecos and the High Plains beyond. The Indians at Tiguex knew about the Plains Indians and described their houses. There is a fair amount of evidence from later historic times that Rio Grande Indians made long trading trips. In fact, the first historical record of such a trip comes from 1540, when Coronado's party at Hawikuh met the trading party from Pecos led by "Bigotes" and "Cacique" which also included Indians from the province of Tiguex (Melchior Pérez' testimony, ICC). Frisbie (1975:126-127) has collected a number of mentions of Rio Grande Pueblo Indians making long trade pilgrimages--Zia Indians to the Pacific Coast until about

1875 and Cochiti to the West Coast. One suspects that these may have been held with the cooperation (and perhaps as part) of the Zuni trade parties that went to the Pacific Coast regularly (see Bloom 1936:94). Adolph F. Bandelier (Lange and Riley 1966:99-100), in 1880, actually helped the Santo Domingo Indians organize a trading party to the Plains, probably one of the very last of its kind (see also Ford 1972). The Relación del suceso points out the lack of markets in Tiguex, and it seems likely that the market on the Aztec model was absent in the Southwest north of the Serrana country. Market or not, the Spaniards received many goods at Acoma: cotton blankets, bison and deer skins, turquoises, turkeys, and other food. What was given in exchange is not indicated (Hammond and Rey 1940:288).

As described in the Coronado testimony (pp. 329-331), the Spaniards attempted to obtain their desperately needed food and clothing at Tiguex and in the nearby Quirix by trade. They were particularly interested in cotton blankets, feather blankets, maize, turkeys, and skins.

When the Spaniards returned to the Southwest in 1581-1583, Tiguex no longer figured so importantly in their activities. Many examples of trade were noted. In the Rio Grande area, Gallegos mentions copper, white and red coral, a bar of iron, and turquoise; some of these items by inference seem to have come from upriver (Hammond and Rey 1966:76-77, 81). The Brief and True Account mentions Spaniards receiving tanned buffalo robes (p. 142). Luxán has a number of indications of trade, especially with the Keresan. At Cachiti (San Felipe or Cochiti) the Spaniards exchanged iron and small bells for maize, tortillas, turkeys, pinole, and "very fine buffalo hides" (p. 179). At Acoma the Spaniards received bison hides and blankets as well as foodstuffs (p. 182). Espejo (p. 222), probably among the Tiguex, makes the interesting statement that his party found "metal" in the houses of the Indians. At a guess, this metal was in the form of ores and was to be pulverized to make paint or glaze. What the metals were is unclear. Lead is the most likely candidate, though Espejo mentions seeing evidence of antimony along the way, and he seemed certain that there was also silver.

Castaño entered the Pueblo area from the south and east and made his first contact with Pecos and then the Tanos pueblos. He moved from the Galisteo area to the Tewa and probably upper Tiwa portions of the upper Rio Grande Valley. Castaño then turned southward and contacted the Keresan groups, making still another foray into the Tanos region. He explored the southern Tiwa towns but almost as an afterthought. Castaño found much evidence of trade in the upper Rio Grande region and mentions bison hide robes, "rich stones," and, of course, turquoise for the area (p. 285).

By Oñate's time I suspect that the trade network into the Rio Grande Valley was considerably disrupted, but, certainly, it was still in existence. The Cibolan towns continued to feed materials eastward, and Pecos represented the eastern door for Plains goods that were sent on to the west. At this date it is hard to distinguish a primary center within the Rio Grande Valley itself. Possibly it was in the Chama region; at least this region was first chosen by Oñate for his headquarters area. Oñate's choice, however, may have been for other reasons, possibly because of the availability of agricultural land.

Acoma seems to have been important in the trade picture throughout the sixteenth century and to have maintained its cultural vigor up to the time of its destruction by Oñate in the winter of 1598-1599 (see Villagrá 1933). However, Acoma seems never to have been a retransport and redistribution center in the sense that Hawikuh, Pecos, and probably one or more of the Tiguex towns were. It was, rather, in all probability, a safe stopover point, perched on its seemingly impregnable rock, in an increasingly hostile area. We have no very good evidence from the Coronado period that the region between the pueblos was occupied, but from the time of Espejo it is clear that Querecho Indians controlled parts of the area from the Little Colorado to the Rio Grande. Possibly they arrived after Coronado—even being drawn into the area by the unsettled conditions that followed his invasion of the Southwest. Alternatively, they may have been in the area in 1540. The size of the Coronado force (well over 1000 fighting men) probably would have discouraged these nomadic wanderers from attacking the Spaniards, but it does seem strange that they would not have wished to trade.

In any event, Tiguex seems to have been the trading center of the Rio Grande province in the first part of the sixteenth century. During the latter part of the century it looks very much as if the entire Rio Grande province was attempting to reestablish equilibrium following Coronado and the devastation wrought by his invasion of the Southwest.

Sociopolitical Organization

Nothing in the sociopolitical picture of the pueblos in the sixteenth century is at variance with that of the nineteenth if the accretions of Spanish traits are subtracted. It is clear from Castañeda (Hammond and Rey 1940:224) that the individual towns, at least in Tiguex, were basically autonomous. In the Rio Grande province, government was by "the counsel of their elders" (see also the comments of Padilla, p. 183). Young people wishing to marry had to have the permission of these elders (p. 255), and a man spun and wove a blanket, placing it before the woman to propose marriage (p. 255). Women controlled the houses and if a man "repudiates his wife he must come to the estufa" (p. 255). In fact, the habit of boys giving girls their marriage costume was still known in the twentieth century (Parsons 1939:Vol. 1, 41).

A description of a marriage ceremony generalized for the Rio Grande area is given by Gallegos (Hammond and Rey 1966:101-102). According to Gallegos, the festivities lasted for three days. The father- and mother-in-law present the young couple with a house three to four stories high, of eight to ten rooms [!]. The couple sits on a bench with a bridesmaid on one side and a groomsman on the other. An old man in handsome woven clothing presides. The groom covers his bride with blankets, and she covers him "in such a way that they clothe one another" (p. 102). After a speech by the old man, the bride has a grinding stone (metate), an olla, a flat earthenware pan (comal), and drinking vessels placed in front of her and a grinding stone or mano put in her hand, all entirely new. In front of the groom are placed a Turkish bow, spear, war club, and shield. He is also given a cacaxtle (a kind of small box or crate for transporting birds or produce) and a mecapal (a fiber band used to strap objects for carrying on the shoulders). He also has a hoe placed in his hand to indicate that he is to till the soil and is given lands in which to plant corn.

Following the ceremony there is a dance, after which the couple is escorted to their new home. A feast, consisting of turkey, bison meat, tamales, tortillas, and other things, continues throughout the day. Gallegos was struck by the orderliness and organization of the ceremony. There is nothing in this ceremony that is strinkingly non-Puebloan, though certain central Mexican elements seem to have been incorporated in the telling.

Warfare

The Spaniards, by their very presence, introduced a series of war situations to the Pueblos. However, warlike activity was a part of Pueblo life before the arrival of the Spaniards, as is indicated by the defensive nature of a number of towns, Acoma especially, and the numbers of weapons noted in the early accounts. Acoma usually seemed willing to fight any stranger; for example, it offered battle to Alvarado in the late summer of 1540 (Hammond and Rey 1940:218). The Pueblo Indians fought with bows and arrows and defended their pueblos with missiles, including rocks and even pottery, flung from the rooftops (p. 222; ICC, Juan Troyano account).

In the Coronado inquiry documents Escobar mentions that one of the reasons for the Pecos party's journey to see Coronado was that those Indians wanted Spanish "aid against other pueblos, their neighbors with whom they were at war" (ICC). Such neighbors were presumably not the Tiguex, who had a contingent traveling with the Pecos people. It is also rather difficult to believe the later testimony of Coronado (who, in any case, was trying to deny or shift guilt for the catastrophe in Tiguex country):

> Bigotes and Cacique . . . told him that they and those of their pueblo [Pecos] were enemies of those of Tiguex, and that they were short of land, of which there was an abundance in the province of Tiguex, and they asked him to give them a pueblo there in order that they might settle it with their people, and that they would come and help him in the war (Hammond and Rey 1940:328).

I feel quite certain that Bigotes and Cacique of Pecos never told Coronado any such thing, although as we shall see in Chapter XI, Pecos, like Acoma, did have quite a reputation for warfare.

Descriptions of the Spanish capture of Arenal and their successful siege of Mojo, or El Cerco, is found in Castañeda, in the various trial hearings, in Tello (drawing from the Tovar papers), and in various other accounts. At Arenal, the Spaniards attacked, and the Tiguex retreated to the upper stories of the pueblo and rained arrows and missiles down on the enemy. The Spaniards retaliated by setting the pueblo on fire, driving out many of the Indians, who were then captured and murdered under a sign of truce.

El Cerco, or Mojo, another Tiguex town but one that was on a height back from a river (presumably the Rio Grande), seeing the fate of the Arenal natives, refused to surrender. From the descriptions it seems that the town could be successfully attacked only from the front, the other sides being atop precipitous slopes. The resulting siege was an interesting one from a military viewpoint. The Spaniards tried a standard ruse: they threw a cavalry force against the front part of the pueblo; then, as a hail of arrows met them, the Spaniards

feigned flight, drawing a number of Indian warriors after them and trapping them on the flat areas that stretched in front of the pueblo. The Spaniards then tried to batter down the front wall of the pueblo, but inside the wall found a palisade of logs set in the ground and interwoven with branches. The Spaniards attempted to use a homemade battering ram against this palisade, but a fierce enfilading arrow fire drove them back. Ladders were tried, but again the Indian firepower and clever use of rocks forced the Spaniards to pull back. In fact, the arrow fire from a series of towers with portholes that protected the wall was so heavy that the Spaniards retreated with a number of dead and many wounded. It would seem that the Spanish forces were never able to get near enough to the walls to use the fire technique that had been successful at Arenal. The siege lasted for some fifty days and ended only when the Indians became desperate from thirst. Finally the natives attempted to fight their way out of the town, and many of them reached and crossed the Rio Grande. Others were captured and killed or enslaved.

As we have seen above, the pueblo called Puaray (or Puala) by the Chamuscado and Espejo expeditions may have been Coronado's Arenal, and its inhabitants were clearly hostile to the Spaniards. In 1582, when Chamuscado's party returned from New Mexico, they left the friars Francisco López and Agustín Rodríguez behind in Puaray, and the two were killed shortly after the Spanish party departed. The following year (1583) Espejo's group sacked Puaray, set fire to the pueblo, and killed a number of Indians by burning, garroting, and shooting. There was no further overt trouble with the disorganized and discouraged Tiguex group of pueblos, at least not on any large scale, until the Pueblo Revolt, and even then a considerable part of Tiguex remained "loyal" to the Spaniards.

Weapons of the Indians included the macana by at least 1580. Both Espejo and Luxán mention that particular weapon for the Piro in 1582. According to Espejo:

> The weapons used by the natives are bows and arrows, flint-edged wooden clubs (macanas), and shields (chimales). Their arrows are made of fire-hardened shafts with sharp-edged flint tips which can easily pierce leather armor. The shields are made of buffalo hide, oval in shape; the battle clubs—half a yard long and very heavy at one end—are used as defensive weapons by persons inside their own houses. We did not hear that these Indians were at war with any other province.

They respect each other's boundaries (Hammond and Rey 1966:221).

Luxán speaks of "flint-edged clubs and hide-wrapped stone bludgeons about half a yard long. They have few and poor Turkish bows and poorer arrows" (p. 173).

There are also mentions of macanas at the battle of El Cerco--for example, see Mota Padilla's account of "flint sabers or clubs that they use" (Day 1940b:100) and RSC, where the term macana is used several times. Of course it is possible that the true Mexican macana was either introduced or vastly popularized by Coronado's Mexican soldiers.

Religion

The religion of the Rio Grande province, as reported in the sixteenth century accounts and as reconstructed from archaeology, again does not differ from that of the nineteenth and twentieth centuries, as far as the evidence goes. Indeed, such similarities led Bertha Dutton (1963a) to ask modern Pueblo religious leaders to interpret the pre- and immediately posthistoric Kuaua murals.

Of course, considerable influence from Spanish Catholicism has infiltrated the Pueblos, giving both a series of parallel religious festivals and ceremonies and, more subtly, modifying the native religion itself. This influence can usually be sorted out without too much difficulty.

A rather detailed account of religious practices for the general Rio Grande area is given by Gallegos (Hammond and Rey 1966:99-100). This commentator says that the ceremonial dances, for which he uses the Nahuatl name (mitote), are performed when there is a need for rain. They begin in December and continue for four months at intervals of about every two weeks. The ceremonies begin in the morning and continue through the night, being held around a special altar and only men taking part. The major focus of the ceremony is a dance and ritual lashing of a dance leader with flexible willow whips. Snakes are used in the ceremonies, which include the carrying of rattlesnakes through the crowd while the dances are going on. The lashed individual also dances with the snakes, and then they are carried away in the mouths of helpers. After the snake portion of the dance, two Indians dressed as coyotes go among the dancers, howling and cavorting. The "coyotes" were probably koshare dancers. Curiously, there is no mention of masks.

An interesting custom in one tiny part of the Rio Grande province needs to be discussed here. In the excavations at Pueblo Pardo, cremations of a number of adult individuals were found in seven of the rooms. The investigators (Toulouse and Stephenson 1960:34) believe that the cremations in three rooms were associated with upper floors (the burials penetrated to between the later and earlier floor surfaces of the rooms), and cremations in the other four rooms extended below the earlier floor surface and were rather tentatively assigned to the lower floor occupation. Dating is not very secure, but associated with one "upper floor" cremation was a Glaze D bowl, while with a "lower floor" cremation was a Glaze C bowl (p. 35). Such ceramic associations suggest dates of late fifteenth to sixteenth century. At Gran Quivira (Humanas), Hayes et al. (1981:12, 173-176) discovered cremations which they date to the mid-sixteenth century and later.

One wonders if there might not have been some sort of colony, perhaps a trading group from Cibola, at Pueblo Pardo and at nearby Gran Quivira during late pre-Spanish and/or protohistoric times. Except for the cremations themselves, there is no particular evidence for such a group unless one considers a tiny scatter of Zuni glazed and Heshotauthla polychrome to constitute evidence. On the other hand, the Gran Quivira region is easily enough reached from Zuni by a branch-off (perhaps down the valley of the San Jose) from the major road that ran to Acoma and Tiguex (Hammond and Rey 1940:220). Indeed, Coronado may have taken this route in 1540, though from Castaneda's description it is possible that Coronado swung southward into the Augustine Plain. In such a case, he could either have followed the line of modern U.S. Highway 60 or detoured north of the Gallina Mountains, thus reaching the Rio Grande via the Salado River. In either case he would have arrived at the Rio Grande in the Piro area, at a point near the main trail to Tompiro country. Since he had, in Castaneda's words, "experienced guides" (p. 220), it seems clear that Cibolans or visitors to Cibola knew the route well, whichever it was.

Aesthetic Patterns

The Spaniards were impressed with the pottery; in the words of Castañeda, they found ceramics "glazed with alcohol, and jugs of such elaborate designs and shapes that it was surprising" (p. 256). By the word "alcohol," Castañeda, incidentally, meant antimony or lead, for the glaze ware was based on lead. The blankets of the Indians are also praised by sixteenth century Spaniards. For other examples of aesthetics see Hammond and Rey

Life Cycle

The sixteenth century sources generally describe customs that would not be too unusual in the nineteenth century. Perhaps the most aberrant statement comes from Castañeda:

> From one of our Indians who had been a captive among these [Rio Grande] people for a year, I learned some details of their customs. In particular I asked him why the young women went about naked in that province when it was so cold; he answered that the maidens had to go about that way until they took a husband and that as soon as they had relations with a man they covered themselves (Hammond and Rey 1940:256).

The "nakedness" of young women has not lasted into later historic times, but as recently as the late eighteenth century the Spaniards were having problems with it. According to Domínguez in 1776, speaking of Taos puéblo:

> The little boys and girls, [go] absolutely in puribus until they are twelve to fourteen years old. In this regard Father Claramonte [mission priest at Taos since 1770] forced them to half cover themselves by whipping them, and as a reward for this good work, he was accused of imprudence with minors (Adams and Chavez 1956:259).

Although I have skimmed the voluminous evidence for the Rio Grande peoples, it seems quite clear that Tiguex and probably Acoma had very important roles in the earlier part of the century—not because of their military power (although Acoma was generally considered impregnable) but because they lay across the east-west trade routes from Cibola to Pecos. Their control over these routes was somewhat blunted, however (at least on the west), by the fact that an alternate trail, branching off well west of Acoma, ran to Zia and the Jemez country. As I suggested above, there may well have been a direct Cibolan contact with the Piro-Tompiro which at least avoided Tiguex and perhaps Acoma as well.

To the east, we have less information; but contact between the Salinas (Tompiro) area and Pecos is well documented archaeologically in terms of trade goods.

Question of the control of the all-important Cerrillos mines looms very large for this time period. From analysis that has been done to date (see Warren 1969:36-42, 1974:14, 24-25; Snow 1973:47), it would seem that the Tanos groups, the Tiguex peoples, and Pecos were all users of Cerrillos. The mixed-language (?) pueblo of Tonque seems to have been especially active in the mines until the mid- to late sixteenth century. It is quite possible that no group actually "owned" the various Cerrillos area mines but all shared in them. However, according to Bandelier, as late as the latter part of the nineteenth century, Tanos who had fled to Santo Domingo (after the Pueblo Revolt) still claimed mining rights in the Cerrillos area (Bandelier 1890-1892:Vol. 2, 93-94; White 1935:17, 27).

CHAPTER XI

THE PECOS PROVINCE

The lone pueblo of Pecos was to some degree a world apart in the sixteenth century. The single most important outrider of the Pueblo world to the east, it was the conduit through which trade with the Plains area and beyond was funneled to the Southwest and beyond. Although the single-town Pecos province was the smallest in population and area of any of the provinces, it was by no means insignificant. In the words of A. V. Kidder:

At the time of the coming of the Spaniards it contained, without much doubt, more human beings than any other permanent community in what is now the territory of the United States (1924:4).

Whether this statement was true of the entire United States, it was very likely true of the Pueblo area. Unlike the crowded, land-hungry situation in the Rio Grande province, Pecos controlled more than adequate territory. From historical hints one can guess that the Pecos utilized the valley of the Pecos River at least as far south as modern Santa Rosa and eastward and northward into the valleys of the Rio de la Vaca, the Gallinas, and the Tecolote.

One of the reasons for the importance of Pecos was its location. The town is situated on a low mesa overlooking a broad valley, only a few kilometers from where the Pecos River devolves from the narrow canyon of its headwaters. Pecos pueblo is located at that part of the river most convenient to Glorieta Pass, the gateway to the Rio Grande. Indeed, Glorieta Pass has been a major route east and west between the valleys of the Pecos and the Rio Grande for many centuries, and it remains so today. The pass and its approaches stretch for some 50 km around the south side of the Sangre de Cristo Range from Cañoncito west of Glorieta to Starvation Peak on the east (Johnson 1969:E 2). Westward from Pecos by way of Glorieta Pass the sixteenth century traveler could reach Tanos, the Tiguex country, or the Salinas region simply by skirting the western escarpment of Glorieta Mesa to Galisteo and beyond. To reach Tegua territory an ancient route threads the foothills of the Sangre de Cristo Mountains, northwestward to the Santa Fe River and the Tesuque area.

The Spaniards first saw Pecos in the fall of 1540. In Chapter X, I suggested that the first Spanish party to reach the pueblo of Taos might have done so by a route from Pecos around the east side of the Sangre de Cristo Mountains. If so, the Spaniards probably followed what was later to be the Santa Fe Trail, but then swung westward along, perhaps, either the Coyote or the Pueblo rivers to the Taos or the Taos-Picuris area.

Language

Although there have been more or less ingenious arguments that the Pecos people spoke some other tongue (see Chapter IV above), the overwhelming evidence is that Pecos was, at the time of the early Spaniards, a Towa-speaking pueblo, sharing this language with the Jemez people of the middle and upper Jemez Valley. When Pecos was finally deserted around 1840, the survivors went to Jemez to join kinsmen there (Lange and Riley 1966:78).

There are a number of indications that the Pecos were bi- or multilingual as, indeed, were many other Pueblo Indians. This would be expected in a town that depended on trade for its livelihood and one which was a focal point for Plains Indians to meet, trade, and even reside for extended periods of time.

The name for Pecos is somewhat in dispute. The Spaniards, when they were first introduced to a Pecos trade party--one mixed with Tiguex Indians--in the late summer of 1540, referred to the Pecos people and their town as Cicuyé. Later, they continued to use some variant of that name (Ciquique, Sinque, Cicuique, Ciciuc) until the time of Oñate (1598) or possibly until that of Castaño (1590-1591), when the term Pecos was used (Kessell 1979:48, 78, 519).

Hodge (1907-1910:Vol. 2, 221; see also Hodge, in Benavides 1945:271) believed that Cicuyé was the Tiguex name for Pecos. Use of a Tiguex name would be logical since the Spaniards of the Coronado expedition approached the pueblo by way of the Tiguex country and were much influenced by the Tiguex. Still and all, I have often wondered why Coronado did not use a Pecos or Cibolan name since he met the Pecos Indians at a Zuni town and since he had Zuni interpreters. In fact, Schroeder (1979b:437) has suggested that the Pecos name for themselves was k̯akora, "place down where the stone is on top," and tshiquite (tziquite), the latter term being corrupted by the Spaniards into Cicuyé, or Cicuique.

The term Pecos is probably a Towa name, although it may have been introduced to the Spaniards in a Keresan form, poyokona, perhaps from the Towa pakyoola, "place where there is water" (Pearce 1965:118). For additional discussion of the origin of such names as Cicuyé and Pecos see Schroeder (1979b:436-437) and Kessell (1979:48, 78).

It is worth pointing out that, as with the early Spanish names for Zuni and Hopi, the direction of entry into the Southwest by the early Spanish expedition had a great deal to do with the attaching of particular Europeanized names to various Indian towns and provinces.

Natural Features

In considerable part, the discussion in Chapter X will also apply here. Pecos itself, on a low, elongated mesa, nestles against the southern edge of the Sangre de Cristo Mountains at an elevation of approximately 2100 m. The crest of Glorieta Pass is some 2250 m. East and south, the Pecos River picks its way through Basin and Range topography before breaking into the flat country west of the Llano Estacado. For centuries the river valley was a highway, both for Indians and for early Spaniards. To the east and north a series of valleys afforded easy access to the vegas, or grasslands, that stretch out from the eastern flanks of the Sangre de Cristo Range.

In other words, as discussed above, Pecos was superbly positioned to exploit the trade possibilities in a number of directions. At the same time, the town was in an area of river bottomland, with rich stone and timber resources nearby. Certain materials which were very much in demand for trade--for example, fibrolite--could be obtained within a few kilometers, and the Cerrillos mines with their richness in turquoise and various lead, antimony, and mercury ores were only 50 km away. A major preoccupation at Pecos, to which both the documentary sources and the archaeological ones attest, was trade (see Riley 1978a).

Although the area around Pecos is in the first sizeable stretch of valley following the emergence of the Pecos River from its mountain gorge in the southern part of the Sangre de Cristos, the larger region available to the Pecos people included mostly Basin and Range country to the south and east. The river itself drains the area south of Truchas Peak with a series of short streams flowing either southeastward or soutwestward to the main river, which in its headwaters runs almost directly south. Tributaries in the extreme upper Pecos Valley include the Valdez-Mora coming in from the east and the Jacks, Panchuela, and Holy Ghost creeks draining from the north and west. Even today this area is very heavily timbered, and it was certainly so in the sixteenth century. At a point not far from the town of Pecos, the river begins to swing south and east, paralleling the sharp, wooded escarpment of Glorieta

Mesa. The river drops very rapidly in elevation. It is about 2100 m near Pecos pueblo, but little more than 1800 m at the San Miguel ford only 25 km to the south and east. Another 15 to 20 km farther east and south, beyond the Villanueva area, the river turns northeastward, then southeastward, and, in a series of wide curves, picks its way through the cliffs around El Cerrito. Beyond this point the Pecos flows in broken but relatively open country. It is joined by the Tecolote about 75 km from Pecos pueblo and by an important south-draining tributary, the Gallinas River, some 100 km from the pueblo. The Pecos River, in total length, is about 960 km; I am, of course, concerned only with the upper 20% or so of its drainage.

If we consider the area of the Pecos River and its tributaries to about Santa Rosa as representing the effective utilization area of the Pecos people--but remember that any such statement as this is arbitrary in view of the scanty information for the sixteenth century--we are dealing with a watershed area of approximately 7200 km^2. The annual runoff of the Pecos and its upper tributaries is exceedingly variable. In 1906, for example, it was over 16,100 ha/m, and in 1912-1913 the runoff was approximately half that much, nearly 8200 ha/m.

The upper drainage of the Pecos has about 20 mm average distribution of water over the entire 7200 km^2 watershed. This again is exceedingly variable. For example, in early fall 1904, an enormous flood devastated the entire upper Pecos Valley with up to 175 mm of rain falling over the entire upper Pecos watershed in one to two days.

The flora and fauna of the Pecos River area does not significantly differ from that of the Rio Grande watershed immediately to the west. The region of the pueblo is very heavily wooded with forests that include oak and ponderosa pine. As one goes into the higher elevations (2400 m or more) there are bristlecone and western white pine, Douglas fir, and aspen. In the region of the Pecos Valley there is a considerable scatter of juniper, pinyon, sage, and the numerous cacti and yucca. Beyond the broken country of the Tecolote Range to the east and Glorieta Mesa to the south, several of the short grasses appear in the increasingly vegalike country. This is the area where Basin and Range merges into the High Plains. The various animals described in Chapter X also appear in the Pecos province. However, Pecos is at the edge of the great bison range, and bison was an important fact of life for the Pecos Indians.

The Pecos province lies mainly in the Köppen climatic area BSh or BSk with the uplands of the Sangre de Cristos in the Df zone. BS, or semiarid, climates are those characteristic of the Basin and

Range and the western edge of the High Plains, while the Df climates are ones of considerable cold with several months of snow cover and relatively humid winters. There is a dramatic variation in frost-free days; at the pueblo itself around 120 days per year are frost-free, about the same as in Santa Fe. Above Pecos, in the very upper Pecos drainage in the sierra, it is 100 days or less. As one goes east and south the opposite is true; at Santa Rosa there are about 180 frost-free days per year. Rainfall also drops off as one goes from northwest to southeast. Pecos in its valley has some 475 mm of rainfall per year, while Santa Rosa (at an altitude of about 1400 m) at the southeastern end of the Pecos range has nearly 360 mm annually. The rainfall pattern of the upper Pecos Valley is not significantly different from that of the upper Rio Grande Valley. The major amounts of rainfall come during the months of June-September with low rainfall in the midwinter months, though the percentage of winter rainfall goes up with altitude (Wernstedt 1972:476-479).

Archaeology

In the sixteenth century there was only the pueblo of Pecos in the upper Pecos River area, but earlier settlements in the region are well known. As late as the thirteenth century there were settlements in the Pecos Valley near Santa Rosa (Jelinek 1967:159-164). In addition, there were sites in the Rowe area and elsewhere in the upper Pecos Valley, as far south as Anton Chico and as far east as Tecolote near Las Vegas (Kidder 1932:2, 1958:2-4, 43). In the last two or three centuries before the Spaniards arrived, however, the area saw a steady consolidation, with the population eventually being grouped into a few large towns in the extreme upper Pecos Valley, and then in Pecos itself. One large site, Forked Lightning Ruin, was on the Arroyo del Pueblo approximately 1 km south of Pecos pueblo (see Figure 15). By about A.D. 1300, however, the Forked Lightning people had shifted their residence to the Pecos Mesa. By A.D. 1400 or perhaps a little later, the populations of other towns--including Loma Lothrop, across the Arroyo del Pueblo from Pecos, and Arrowhead, also on the Arroyo del Pueblo but further northwest (near Glorieta)--had also joined Pecos. By the time of the Spaniards, Pecos dominated the area and may have shared the upper Pecos Valley only with nomadic hunters and traders who periodically moved into the valley from the edge of the Great Plains (Kessell 1979:11-12). There are traditions recorded by Hewett (1904:433-435) from Pecos survivors at Jemez that the Pecos area had originally been settled not only from Jemez but also from the northern Rio Grande and from the Manzano region to the south. If these stories are true, such a situation might account for the variation in physical type noted at Pecos especially in late prehistoric times (Schroeder 1979b:430). Also, as discussed below, there is some possibility of at least one satellite town that continued to be occupied into the sixteenth century.

I gave a thumbnail sketch of archaeology at Pecos in Chapter IV. To expand a bit on that account, I can say that Pecos, deserted by its Indian inhabitants from about A.D. 1840, was first seriously investigated by Adolph F. Bandelier in the fall of 1880. As a result of a few days' exploration (Lange and Riley 1966:74-83), Bandelier produced a short monograph the following year (1881). After Bandelier's work, very little was done at Pecos for a number of years (but see Hewett 1904). In 1910, A.V. Kidder and K.M. Chapman made a pottery collection from the ruins, and in 1914 Chapman and J.P. Adams of the School of American Research, Santa Fe, conducted a survey of the ruins and built a (reconstructed) model of the post-Spanish pueblo. In 1915, the fieldwork of the Phillips Academy began under the direction of Kidder and continued intermittently through the summer of 1929 for a total of ten field seasons (Kidder 1958:xi), studying not only Pecos but other sites in the area. The large collection of field data was published in a series of volumes (Kidder 1924, 1931, 1932; Kidder and Shepard 1936; Hooton 1930; and a number of other shorter reports). Years later, Kidder (1958) published additional notes on Pecos and other earlier ruins.

In 1938, Edwin Ferdon began an excavation of the south pueblo, the historic portion of Pecos, with the intent to do reconstruction. This work was carried on, beginning in January 1939 and ending in September 1940, by William B. Witkind. In 1956 Stanley A. Stubbs, Bruce T. Ellis, and Alfred F. Dittert, Jr., (1957:67-92) of the Museum of New Mexico excavated parts of the Spanish mission church. Their project was stimulated by the translation and publication in 1956 of the Domínguez document by Eleanor B. Adams and Fr. Angelico Chavez. Meanwhile, work at Arrowhead Ruin near Glorieta was undertaken between 1933 and 1941 by W.C. Holden, and in 1948 by W.M. Pearce, both of Texas Technological College (Holden 1955:102; Kidder 1958:49).

Pecos was made into a national monument in 1965, and the National Park Service took over the excavations under the direction of Jean M. Pinkley. In 1967, Mrs. Pinkley discovered footings of a much larger mission church than had been hitherto suspected. Pinkley continued to work until the end of

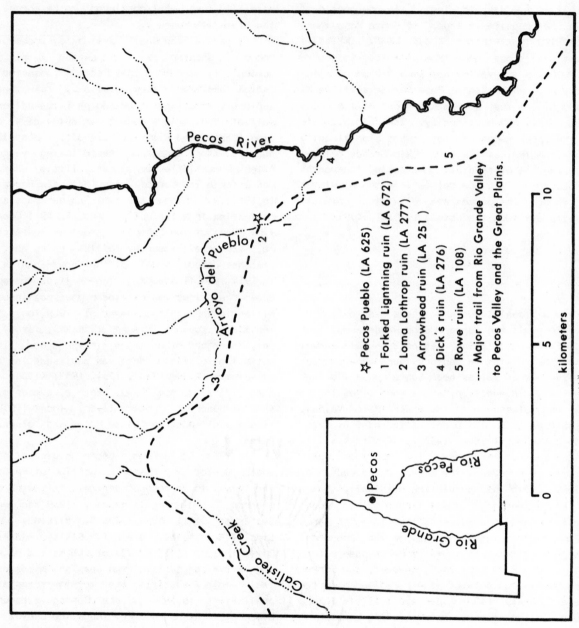

Figure 15. Pecos Pueblo in the Sixteenth Century with Nearby Ruins.

Pecos River

Arroyo del Pueblo

Galisteo Creek

☆ Pecos Pueblo (LA 625)
1 Forked Lightning ruin (LA 672)
2 Loma Lothrop ruin (LA 277)
3 Arrowhead ruin (LA 251)
4 Dick's ruin (LA 276)
5 Rowe ruin (LA 108)
--- Major trail from Rio Grande Valley
to Pecos Valley and the Great Plains.

kilometers

0   5   10

Rio Grande
Rio Pecos
● Pecos

1968. After her death in February 1969, Roland S. Richert and Alden C. Hayes were given the task of completing the work and producing a report on the superimposed mission churches of Pecos (Hayes 1974:ix-xiv). Work, mainly in stabilization, continued at Pecos throughout the 1970s.

Population

The fluctuations in population at Pecos have been tabulated by Kessell (1979:Appendix 1, 489-492). Beginning with Kidder's archaeological estimates ("little less than 2000 for the period 1500-1600"--p. 489), Kessell summarized the leading documentary sources for the period 1540-1849. Briefly, it can be said that no document indicates a population significantly under 2000 for the sixteenth century. This state of affairs continues into the seventeenth century. In the 1620s two independent estimates, those of Fr. Andrés Juárez and of Fr. Alonso de Benavides, put the population at about 2000. Then the population of Pecos began to fall. By the end of the seventeenth century it was probably well under 1000; by A.D. 1750, under 500; and by A.D. 1800, under 150 Pecos Indians (pp. 489-491). Kessell phrases it another way: "In human terms, where three Pecos had lived in 1622, only two lived in 1641, and only one in 1694" (p. 170). Here he is comparing the Juárez figures of 1622, the "Report on the Missions" of 1641, and the Fr. Diego de Zeinos count of 1694. Even if we utilize somewhat more optimistic documents, the loss of population during the trying seventeenth century must have been very great.

Subsistence

The Pecos people, like the rest of the Pueblo world, depended heavily on agriculture. However, at Pecos, with the forested uplands of the Sangre de Cristos near at hand to the north and the Buffalo Plains nearby to the south and east, hunting provided an attractive alternative. In the excavations carried out by Kidder, bones of the mule deer were very abundant, and lagomorphs, antelope, mountain sheep, and elk were also found. Bison bones were everywhere in great numbers, although, interestingly, skulls were absent and pelves rare. Kidder (1932:196) suggests that the bison were killed at some distance from Pecos and the meat cut up for transportation to the pueblo. This method of operation certainly fits the descriptions of the Coronado party in their discussions of bison butchering camps of the Teyas and Querecho Indians. According to Castañeda (Hammond and Rey 1940:261-262), these Indians brought their produce, especially bison skins but probably also meat, to Pecos to sell. Two generations after Coronado, Chamuscado describes large-scale trading of meat and meat products in the area, and Montoya and Zaldívar do the same a generation later (Riley 1976b:35-36; also see below for additional discussion).

It is reasonable to assume that the Pecos Indians used the same bison-hunting techniques as the Plains groups. Mid-seventeenth century documents suggest that the Pecos people journeyed to the Plains at least to trade (Kessell 1979:194-196). In the eighteenth century there is ample documentation for Pecos hunting parties on the Plains (pp. 322, 379, 396 ff.). The information about bison given by the Pecos party that first met Coronado at Hawikuh was presumably learned firsthand, and one of the Indians had the picture of a bison painted on his body (Hammond and Rey 1940:217).

In terms of other wild animals utilized, Castañeda specifically mentions "excellent trout and otters. Big bears and fine falcons multiply in this region" (p. 258). Otter and bear bones have been found in the refuse areas in the Pecos excavations, as have those of various hawks (the latter probably used for their feathers). It is interesting, however, that no fish bones were found by Kidder (1932:195-196) at the Pecos site, and Kidder (p. 196) believes that the Pecos Indians did not eat fish. It was certainly not a matter of availability, for not only does Castañeda stress the abundance of fish, but others do as well. Zaldívar, during his 1598 trip to the Buffalo Plains, somewhere in the upper Pecos drainage, caught 500 bagres (perhaps Ameiurus melas) with a single hook in a single night "and many more on the following day" (Hammond and Rey 1953:398). Parsons (1939:1000), commenting on Kidder's failure to discover any fish bones archaeologically, suggests that the Pecos Indians may have had a practice similar to the Pima who threw fish bones into the river so that they might again become fish.

In the excavations at Pecos, Kidder found considerable evidence of maize in the form of cobs, stalks, and husks of twelve-rowed corn. In addition, squash skins, charred beans, yucca fruit, pinyon nuts, and sunflower seeds were found at the pueblo (Kidder 1932:302-303). Unfortunately, the context is not always clear, but all the cultivated and wild food plants mentioned above seem to belong to either pre- or proto-Spanish horizons. Kidder suggests that the sunflower seeds were from cultivated plants (p. 303). The question of sunflower cultivation in the pre-Spanish Southwest is anything but clear. Historically, the plant (Helianthus annuus var. macrocarpus) was cultivated among the Pueblos (Heiser 1951:436-437), and it has been suggested that the wild sunflower originated in the Southwest, though there seems to be no particular evidence for this (Yarnell 1978:289). Nor is there clear archaeological evidence for the domesticated sunflower in the aboriginal Southwest (p. 291), although Yarnell does point out the historical and ethnological references to the cultigen. Of course, Kidder's statement might be taken as evidence of a sort, but I have been unable to find any further identification of this particular cache of seeds as to cultivated or wild variety or, for that matter, any attempt to fit it more securely into the Pecos chronology. Obviously, more archaeological work is needed to resolve this problem. The Pecos Indians may well have utilized the wild potato (Solanum Jamesii or S. Fendleri). These grow in the area and were eaten by other southwestern Indians (Correll 1962:276, 277, 383).

Coronado collected provisions at Pecos for his large army sometime around the first of May 1541. According to Castañeda, the people of Pecos "were friendly and furnished provisions" (Hammond and Rey 1940:234), by implication, willingly. When one considers that these supplies must have been stored from years past as a hedge against bad harvests and remembers that the outrages committed by the Spaniards in the winter and early spring of 1541 were in part against Pecos, it is probably safe to question the "willingness" of the Indians to give up their foodstocks. In addition, if Pecos was forced to supply the major part of the food for Coronado's army of 1300 men and hundreds of livestock, it is clear that the grain supply would have been seriously depleted. And yet there is some reason to believe that the Tiguex and Quirix groups of pueblos had already been squeezed dry, so Pecos may indeed have been forced to be a major supplier. Apropos of all this, we must remember that what Di Peso calls the "Chief Bigotes plot" (1974:808-815) was well underway, and Pecos planned the great Coronado force to lose itself in the Plains. Perhaps no sacrifice seemed too hard to bring this about.

As early as Chamuscado's time (1581-1582) there is evidence of trade of both maize and blankets for bison and deer skins and meat (Hammond and Rey 1966:87). Chamuscado was probably in the Galisteo area when he made those observations, but it seems safe to assume that nearby Pecos was in the same exchange network. It does suggest that maize was plentiful enough to trade, at least in some of the eastern pueblos. On the other hand, Espejo, a year or two later, was refused maize both in the Galisteo

area and at Pecos (the Indians claiming shortage because of lack of rain). Espejo's party went through the area in early July 1583, and the Indians, indeed, may have been worrying about the developing crops. A show of force did produce food at Pecos--according to Obregón (Cuevas 1924:300) enough to last the entire trip back to Nueva Vizcaya--and two Indians were kidnapped to take Espejo's party to find the bison. Espejo also had his eye on the future, and he was exceedingly impressed by Pecos, considering it, according to Obregón, "the best and largest of all the towns discovered by Francisco Vázquez Coronado" (p. 299). He dreamed of returning to New Mexico, and Pecos certainly loomed large in his plans. One of the kidnapped Indians was taken to Mexico, where, under the name Pedro Oroz, he taught Towa to several Mexican Indians. Curiously, one of these latter men was eventually to reach Pecos but not to the benefit of Espejo (Chavez 1972:17-18). In any case, the taking of guides from Pecos to find the bison herds indicates that the Spanish leader had a pretty good notion that the Pecos were well acquainted with the uses of bison hunting.

A number of sources indicate that Pecos was well supplied with food. The Relación postrera speaks of "abundant maize, beans, calabashes, and some chickens" (Hammond and Rey 1940:310). From the very large number of turkey bones in the ruins, Kidder (1932:196) believes that the turkey formed part of the diet at Pecos.

The most detailed account of subsistence and of daily life at Pecos in the sixteenth century comes from Castaño de Sosa who visited the pueblo in the winter of 1590-1591:

> This pueblo had five plazas. It was also provided with such an abundant supply of corn that everyone marveled. There were those who maintained that the total must amount to more than thirty thousand fanegas, since each house had two or three rooms full of it, all of excellent quality. Moreover, there was a good supply of beans. Both corn and beans were of many colors; it seemed that some of the corn was two or three years old. In the houses, the natives also store quantities of herbs, chili, and calabashes, and many implements for working their cornfields (Hammond and Rey 1966:278).

Parenthetically, a fanega, or "bushel," is a dry volume measure of some fifty to fifty-five liters. The "herbs" likely were quelites or potherbs. The "chili" was probably the wild chili, Capsicum

annuum, although it is possible that Mexican domesticated chili peppers had been introduced to the
Southwest by 1590. Referring to the Espejo party of
1582-1583, Obregón remarks:

> In all these provinces and pueblos
> there is not a single kind of fruit, there
> is only Castile flax which the land pro-
> duced without cultivation. There is no
> chili, though the natives were given seed
> [presumably by Espejo's party] in order to
> plant it (Cuevas 1924:304).

From the Coronado testimony, it is clear that
the Spaniards obtained both skins and cotton blankets from Pecos (Hammond and Rey 1940:325). The
Relación del suceso states that the Pecos people did
not grow cotton, but it also says that turkeys were
not raised at Pecos (p. 289). The latter statement
is certainly incorrect as shown by the archaeological evidence. Obregón, drawing from the Espejo
party, mentions the use of cotton for clothing at
Pecos (Cuevas 1924:300), and Castaño received
"shirts, cloaks, and pieces of sackcloth" there
(Hammond and Rey 1966:289). It seems at least possible that some cotton (Gossypium hopi) was grown at
Pecos, although the pueblo is environmentally near
the outer limits of successful cotton growing. At
any rate, cotton was probably spun at Pecos, for
numbers of perforated pottery and bone disks that
seem to be spindle whorls have been found there in
addition to eyed bone needles, some of the latter
definitely pre-Spanish. In addition, a few pieces
of cotton cloth and a curious cotton-piled fabric
were found in the excavations (Kidder 1932:152,
222-225, 236, 301-302). Kent (1957:469, 649-650)
believes that the Hopi in the sixteenth century were
suppliers of both raw cotton and woven cloth to the
rest of the Pueblo world.

It is not clear from either the sixteenth century sources or the evidence of archaeology whether
Pecos practiced ditch agriculture. The area has
sufficient rainfall for dry farming, especially
since much of the rainfall comes in the summer
months. Irrigation or not, as Kidder (1958:314)
points out, farm produce was very likely a major
export item at Pecos, especially to the Plains, and
the Castaño accounts make it clear that great quantities of foodstuffs were stored at the pueblo.

Settlement Patterns

The pueblo of Pecos rests on a low sandstone
mesilla, extending roughly north to south with the
sharper relief on the northern side. The mesilla is
about 400 m long and is approximately 125 m at its
widest point. In the sixteenth century the major
structure at Pecos was what Kidder called the "North
Building," or in later publications the "Quadrangle," a massive stone pueblo enclosing courtyards
and situated near the northern end of the mesilla.
This structure covered more than one hectare. A
second group of rooms, somewhat to the south, was
constructed in the seventeenth century, as was the
mission church, whose ruins are still prominent
today at the extreme south end of the mesilla.

In the sixteenth century a low wall, so
described by Castañeda (Hammond and Rey 1940:257),
actually about one meter high (Kidder 1958:113),
skirted the edge of the mesilla. This could have
had no important defense function. The defensible
part of Pecos was the Quadrangle itself. Built in
the fifteenth century in what looks to be a unified
plan, this massive pueblo stood three to four floors
high. Ground floor walls were blank, and second and
third floor galleries of corridors were reached by
ladders (pp. 64-69, 113-114). Unlike certain of the
Rio Grande pueblos, the Pecos people never used
adobe. From the beginning, the pueblo was built of
coursed sandstone, some of which was obtained from
the northwest slope of the mesilla (p. 55).

The descriptions of the sixteenth century Spanish explorers fit very well with the archaeological
data on Pecos. First, that of Castañeda:

> Cicuye is a pueblo containing about 500
> warriors. It is feared throughout that
> land. It is square, perched on a rock in
> the center of a vast patio or plaza, with
> its estufas. The houses are all alike,
> four stories high. One can walk on the
> roofs over the whole pueblo, there being
> no streets to prevent this. The second
> terrace is all surrounded with lanes which
> enable one to circle the whole pueblo.
> These lanes are like balconies which pro-
> ject out, and under which one may find
> shelter. The houses have no doors on the
> ground floor. The inhabitants use movable
> ladders to climb to the corridors, which
> are on the inner side of the pueblos.
> They enter them that way, as the doors of
> the houses open into the corridors on this
> terrace. The corridors are used as
> streets. The houses facing the open coun-
> try are back to back with those on the
> patio, and in time of war they are entered
> through the interior ones. The pueblo is
> surrounded by a low stone wall. Inside
> there is a water spring, which can be

diverted from them (Hammond and Rey
1940:256-257).

A half century later a member of the Gaspar Castaño de Sosa party also described Pecos:

> The most interesting things seen were six-
> teen underground estufas, very large and
> very well whitewashed, built for protec-
> tion against the bitter cold. The natives
> light no fires inside them; instead, they
> bring in from the outside many braziers
> banked with ashes, in a manner so ingeni-
> ous that I find no words to describe it.
>
> These estufas are entered through small
> trap doors, large enough for only one per-
> son at a time, and the natives go down
> into them by means of ladders set up for
> that purpose.
>
> The houses in this pueblo are built
> like military barracks, back to back, with
> doors opening out all around; and they are
> four or five stories high. There are no
> doors opening into the streets on the
> ground floors; the houses are entered from
> above by means of portable hand ladders
> and trap doors. Each floor of every house
> has three or four rooms, so that each
> house, as a whole, counting from top to
> bottom, has fifteen or sixteen rooms, very
> neat and well whitewashed (Hammond and Rey
> 1966:277).

What the Castaño document describes are double
back-to-back apartments of which there were a great
many, each containing a number of rooms (Kidder
1958:122).

There is no information from the sixteenth century documents nor (as far as I know) from archaeology on field houses and other isolated structures in
the Pecos area. These were noted by early Spanish
chroniclers for other pueblos, however (Moore
1979:21-23), and they are common in later pueblos.
Since the Pecos people must have had a considerable
walk to reach fields that were on or near the Pecos
River, it seems likely that some kind of temporary
or small-scale shelters were constructed. There is,
in addition, the somewhat ambiguous statement of
Castañeda:

> There are seven other pueblos by the side
> of this road in the direction of the snowy
> sierra. One of them had been partly
> destroyed by the aforesaid people
> [Teyas?], who live under the jurisdiction
> of Cicuye (Hammond and Rey 1940:258).

The "snowy sierra" is surely the Sangre de Cristo
Range. Whether Castaneda is talking about summer
villages that serviced Pecos or whether he meant the
Tanos area is anything but clear. Conceivably, he
might be referring to Ton-ch-un, which, according to
the Pecos informants of Hewett (1904:433-435), was
the last nearby pueblo to amalgamate with Pecos (see
also Schroeder 1979b:435).

Trade

Both the documentary and archaeological evidence
make it very clear that Pecos pueblo used its position on the edge of the High Plains to enhance
trade. The very first contact that the Spaniards
had with this pueblo (in the summer of 1540)
involved a trading party of Pecos and probably some
Tiguex Indians. The party was led by a tall, robust
young Pecos man whom the Spaniards named "Bigotes"
(Whiskers). With the group was an interpreter
(Riley 1975b:139-140). The trading party, whether
it had heard of the Spaniards' arrival or was simply
carrying out a standard trade mission to Cibola, had
"dressed skins, shields, and headpieces" (Hammond
and Rey 1940:217). It is already clear from Marcos'
account the previous year that bison hide shields
were traded as far as the Gulf of California and
that large numbers of bison (and probably also deer)
skins were shipped south and west from Cibola (pp.
67-69). Díaz, in his report to Viceroy Mendoza
dated March 20, 1540, also mentions that the Cibolans utilized bison shields and bison hide robes (p.
158), though bison herds were not found in the province of Cibola (p. 159). The Indians of Cibola
"keep in their houses some woolly animals resembling
large Castilian hounds. These they shear, and with
the hair they make colored wigs, which they wear,
like the one I am sending your Lordship" (p. 158).
If the dog-shearing part of the story is discounted
(it was not mentioned when the Spaniards actually
arrived at Cibola), the headpieces of the Bigotes
party come to mind. Díaz was in northern Sonora
when he received the Cibolan materials, and his
specimens presumably came down the trade route. As
I suggested in Chapter IX, the "wigs" were likely
retraded by Cibolans from an eventual Pecos source.
I suspect that they may have been constructed of
bison hair. Certainly, a good case can be made for
the suggestion of Kidder that Pecos Indians were
"more or less monopolistic middlemen" (1958:313) for
the sixteenth century western movement of bison
skins, caps, and rawhide shields.

Trade at Pecos can be documented in the

archaeological record. Kidder has recorded extensive amounts of shell, especially Olivella dama from the Gulf of California (about 2000 specimens). From the same area came species of Glycymeris (about 100 examples), Turritella tigrina, Oliva angulata, and Conus princeps (from 10 to 40 examples of each). From the California coast came Haliotis cracherodii (abalone), some 75 specimens. The Gulf of Mexico supplied 200 examples of Alectrion vibex as well as Oliva sayana, Strombus gigas (which Kidder believed came from the Florida Keys), and a number of other varieties of shell (Kidder 1932:183-184).

There was also a considerable amount of freshwater shell, some probably local, like Unio, which was used for beads and pendants (p. 183). More interesting from a viewpoint of trade were three whole specimens and some fifty worked pieces of Lampsilis purpurata which likely came from east Texas, and which were used for beads and pendants (p. 183). One curious find was a bead (?) of the land shell, Cerion incanum, a form that comes from southern Florida. Unfortunately, the provenience of this particular artifact is uncertain. It was found in one of the rooms, but Kidder's notes do not make it clear if it was from post-Columbian fill or from the earlier deposits underneath the floor (p. 184). The 1000 or more pieces of wastage show that at least part of the shell was worked into finished shape at Pecos, and the size and good condition of some of the discards indicate that Pecos was very well supplied with shell, even Pacific Coast abalone (p. 194).

Some of the Pecos shell seems to have been retraded eastward into the Plains (although we cannot demonstrate that any given piece of shell actually came from Pecos). The position of the pueblo and its known trade with the Plains at the beginning of the historic period, however, made Pecos the logical port of entry and exit for trade eastward.

That such trade between the Plains and the Pueblo area existed is beyond question, even if one leaves out the historic accounts. Turquoise appears archaeologically in the big bend of the Red River in what is probably late pre-Spanish times, as does Chupadero Black-on-white pottery (Krieger 1946:207-208; Housewright 1946:10; Riley 1978a:62). In east-central Oklahoma, especially in or near the drainage of the Canadian, a number of southwestern (or southwestern-derived) items are found: pinyon nuts, Olivella shells, turquoise, petrified wood, agate, and obsidian. Farther east, in the Arkansas drainage of Oklahoma, Olivella shells appear, and at the Spiro site along the Arkansas River in extreme eastern Oklahoma there have been discovered a number of pieces of turquoise identified by neutron activation studies to be from the Cerrillos mines in New Mexico. All the sites listed above date to late pre-Spanish or early historic times (Sharrock 1959a:40, 1959b:50; Lawton 1968:30, 66, 74; Lopez 1973:75-77; Wiegand, personal communication; Riley 1978a:62). Trade, in this case specifically from Pecos, can be demonstrated as late as A.D. 1650-1700 into the Canadian drainage of western Oklahoma by finds of turquoise and Glaze V pottery, the latter very likely made at Pecos (Hofman 1978:64, 100, 105).

What these two distributions--one along the Red River, the other in or near the Canadian River drainage--represent are two major trade routes running eastward, probably from Pecos. Even more clear-cut is a third route that roughly followed the line of modern U.S. Highway 54 northeastward into the great bend of the Arkansas River in central Kansas. Here is a cluster of sites, mostly dating in the sixteenth century. They contain turquoise beads, Olivella beads which resemble those manufactured at Pecos, glazed ware either from Pecos or from the Galisteo area, Chupadero Black-on-white, Biscuit B ware, Alibates flint, jasper, obsidian, quartzite, a Puebloan (probably Pecos) type incised pottery pipe, and steatite ridged and grooved arrow straighteners that are reminiscent of those from Pecos. Scraps of sixteenth century Spanish chain mail have also been found (Wedel 1959:245, 289, 290-292, 296, 308, 310, 319-320, 332, 505, 576, 585; Riley 1978a:63-64).

Since the area of central Kansas was visited by Coronado in 1541, by Padilla in 1542, by Humaña and Leyva around 1594, by Zaldívar in 1598, and by Oñate in 1601, there is considerable firsthand knowledge of the region and people. It seems likely that all the above-named Spanish parties originated at or went through Pecos; in fact, the Spaniards in the sixteenth century seem to have assumed as a matter of course that Pecos was the gateway to the east. I certainly have no inclination to doubt my earlier evaluation (1978a:54) that Pecos was the most important redistribution center for trade going to the Plains and beyond. It is worth mentioning that southwestern influence actually penetrated well east of the Plains during this proto-historic period. The find of turquoise beads and a turquoise pendant in a Mississippian burial in northern Mississippi (Peabody 1904:50-51) is a case in point, as is the discovery of turquoise, Alibates flint, and perhaps Pueblo pottery (the latter may be intrusive), plus a form of pipe indicative of western Kansas in an Oneota site from central Missouri (R.T. Bray, personal communication).

There is Spanish documentary evidence that ties the east Texas area to the Pueblo world, though not specifically to Pecos. Moscoso, the leader of the

De Soto party after the latter man's death, was in the area of the Neches or the Trinity River in the summer of 1542. There he met with Indians identified by Swanton (1942:37) as Hasinai. According to the Gentleman of Elvas, the Spaniards

> found some turquoises, and shawls of cotton, which the Indians gave them to understand, by signs, were brought from the direction of the sunset; so that they who should take that course must approach the country of Christians (Lewis 1907:246-247).

Swanton says:

> This was in 1542, and it is evident that the European settlers in Mexico could have had nothing to do with them. There were two articles of trade for which the Caddo were noted, salt and bow wood, the latter from the Osage orange or bois d'arc. Of course, there were plenty of salines west of the Caddo country, so we should not expct to find them exporting salt in that direction, but it was otherwise with bow wood (1942:37).

Bois d'arc, used in later times for bows by Pueblo Indians, was traded from the east and considered superior to any wood that grows in the Southwest (Robbins et al. 1916:68).

It should be pointed out that, at least by the latter part of the sixteenth century, other pueblos were also involved in the Plains trade. In 1581 Gallegos mentions that local Pueblo Indians, presumably from a pueblo that the Chamuscado party called Malpartida and which probably was one of the Tanos towns (perhaps San Marcos), received ores from "Indians in the region of the buffalo" (Hammond and Rey 1966:87). These were probably used for body painting, for in the next sentence Gallegos mentions that the local Indians painted their bodies. The bison-hunting people also traded with the local Indians:

> They were enemies of our informants, but nevertheless came to the pueblos of the latter in order to trade such articles as deerskins and buffalo hides for making footwear, and a large amount of meat, in exchange for corn and blankets; and that in this way, by communicating with one another, each nation had come to understand the other's language (p. 87).

At some point the Chamuscado group visited the Buffalo Plains, but we simply do not know the route. It might have been over Glorieta Pass to Pecos and beyond, or the Spaniards may have followed the southwest flank of Glorieta Mesa, perhaps reaching the Pecos somewhere around Anton Chico or even farther south and east.

It would be useful if we knew whether the Chamuscado party ever actually visited Pecos. Hammond and Rey (p. 59) believe that the town of Nueva Tlaxcala (so named by both Gallegos and Pedrosa), the largest pueblo in the region and one so important that it was assigned to the King rather than to an individual encomendero, can be identified with Pecos. Reed (1943:260), on the other hand, considers the pueblo of Piedrahita, also on both the Gallegos and Pedrosa lists, to have been Pecos. According to Reed, if Pecos was ignored in the Chamuscado documents,

> the Chamuscado-Rodríguez expedition was unique in not visiting or mentioning it. They could, undoubtedly, have gone southeast from San Cristóbal, down Canyon Blanco, to reach the Pecos River and the plains; but they would surely have heard of the great pueblo of Cicuyé (p. 260).

It may well be that the Chamuscado party was thinking more about Pecos than about the Tanos pueblos when describing trade with the Plains Indians. This would fit with the observations of Castañeda about the Teya and Querecho trade with Pecos (Hammond and Rey 1940:258, 261).

Still and all, pueblos other than Pecos were in the trade picture. In September 1598, Vicente Zaldívar, somewhere in the upper Canadian drainage, perhaps north of modern Tucumcari, notes that a number of "Vaquero Indians"

> who were returning from trading with the Picuríes and Taos, populous pueblos of New Mexico, had just passed that way. The Vaqueros sold meat, skins, fat, tallow, and salt in exchange for cotton blankets, pottery, maize, and some green turquoises which they use (Hammond and Rey 1953:400).

In the Valverde investigation of 1602 (investigating the Oñate expedition of 1601 to the Plains) the "Vaqueros" are identified as Apache who "follow the buffalo and kill them for their fat and tallow, which they sell and trade to the pueblo Indians for corn, blankets, and tobacco (piciente)" (p. 864).

Even though other pueblos were involved in the Plains trade, it seems clear that as late as the

mid-seventeenth century Pecos was the main entry
port for trade to the Plains (see Kessell
1979:156-157; Gunnerson 1974:88-89; Scholes 1935a,
1935b, 1936-1937, 1937). Some specific borrowings
at Pecos have been pointed out by Krieger
(1946:207-208, 221-237), who sees influence from
late prehistoric and early historic Caddoan peoples
of east Texas on Pecos ceramics, especially in the
Glaze III-V periods. These influences include such
things as shouldered and carinated bowls and
exterior decoration by scoring or brushing.

Pecos pueblo also had a large representation of
various kinds of tools mainly used for dressing and
preparing hides. These include snub-nosed scrapers,
two- and four-edge chipped knives, and bone end
scrapers. Such artifacts have an eastern distribution and are rare in pueblo sites to the west, even
in the nearby Galisteo Basin (Kidder 1958:313-314).
Beginning as early as Glaze I times (early fifteenth
century) but with the main concentration in later
Glaze IV and V (say, from the late sixteenth century
to the Pueblo Revolt period), large numbers of these
were made of Alibates flint, suggesting to Kidder
(1932:44) the intensification of contacts with
tribes to the east, at least those of the Texas Panhandle. Chipped tools occur in all levels at Pecos;
what seemed to be happening was that the Indians,
using Plains techniques and tool types, processed
bison for trade westward from early historic times
on. By the time of the first continuous Spanish
contact, the Pecos Indians had picked up a taste for
the handsome banded Alibates flint, which came from
deposits near the upper Canadian River north of
present-day Amarillo, and they continued to import
it even during the depressed seventeenth century.

Parenthetically, this material is sometimes
referred to as "Alibates dolomite" in the archaeological literature. The dolomite, however, is actually the matrix from which deposits of the tough
Alibates flint can be extracted. The dolomite
itself was used in house construction and for
metates, but it was not traded widely as far as I
know.

There were large numbers of pipes, usually constructed of clay although occasionally made of a
local green schist (p. 83). A few are elbow pipes,
and there was a great variety of decorations. Some
of the pipes were modeled in highly unusual forms
including zoomorphic shapes (pp. 156-182). In Glaze
III and IV times, essentially the proto-Spanish
period at Pecos, there appear aberrant forms of
pipes used in a mortuary context. Pecos is far
richer in pipes than any other Pueblo site, although
pipes are also found in the upper Rio Grande Valley.
Both Kidder (p. 170) and Wendorf (1953:65) have suggested that at least the elbow pipes indicate

influence from the Plains or some area to the east
of the Pueblo region.

Of the materials traded eastward, much was
transshipped from points farther west. I have compared Pecos, the major redistribution center for
trade going to the Plains, with Hawikuh, the primary
center for trade to the Sonoran statelets (Riley
1978a:64). For example, it is clear from the early
accounts that turquoise was a major reshipment item
from both Pecos and Hawikuh. It is interesting that
very little turquoise has been found archaeologically in either place (certainly nothing like the
tens of thousands of pieces found at Chaco Canyon).
Kidder speculates on this:

> That so little turquoise was recovered
> during the excavations at Pecos is due to
> the fact that it was very seldom buried
> with the dead, and that it did not often
> form part of ceremonial caches; while a
> substance so precious could, of course,
> not be expected commonly to find its way
> into the rubbish heaps. The Pecos, how-
> ever, were evidently very well supplied
> with turquoise, as Castañeda, writing of
> the Coronado expedition of 1540-1542, men-
> tions specifically its abundance at the
> pueblo, nor is this surprising, for the
> great Cer[r]illos deposits were distant
> only forty or fifty miles and the Pecos
> were, as we know, inveterate traders.
> What ultimately became of the great
> amounts which must once have been owned is
> a mystery; perhaps in the period of
> decline . . . the Pecos were forced to
> dispose of much of their turquoise
> (1932:103).

Two other factors may have been involved, both
suggested in my discussion of the paucity of turquoise at Hawikuh as well as at Pecos (Riley
1975b:148-149). One is that turquoise was so important to the trading mechanisms at both places that
it passed very rapidly through the areas with no
great stocks built up. The other reason is that
both towns were under Spanish domination, each with
a mission church, for many decades. This very
likely disrupted all the trade patterns, not only
that of turquoise. The latter commodity, however,
precious to Spaniard as well as to Pueblo Indian,
might well have been diverted to Spanish control.

According to the early accounts, cotton goods
were an important trade item. Since Pecos raised
little or no cotton, it must have come from else-
where--the Rio Grande Valley or, more likely, the
Hopi country. The latter area seems to have

supplied a great deal of the raw cotton and finished cloth to the Pueblo world and beyond in the sixteenth century (Jones 1936:51-53; Kent 1957:469, 649; Riley 1976b:43). Pailes (1980:36) has pointed out that the Sonora Valley area may have been an exporter of cotton. Conceivably, some of this cotton could have reached Pecos via Cibola.

One kind of raw material that occurs near Pecos and that was processed in the pueblo for trade is fibrolite, in the form of axes. Fibrolite, a schistose rock, extremely hard with microscopic grain and ranging in color from pink to bluish black, is found at Pecos throughout all the Glaze periods. Because of its hardness and high polish, fibrolite was popular throughout the Pueblo area, appearing as far west as Cibola and the Tusayan area. The most likely source is the Truchas Peaks region of the upper Pecos River Valley (Montgomery 1963:46-48), although an alternate source near Lubbock, Texas, has been postulated (Witte 1947:78-79). The finds of large numbers of axes at Pecos suggest that the fibrolite was shaped there and traded in finished form.

In all likelihood, Pecos received its turquoise from the Cerrillos mines, though the mechanisms of production and distribution are not known. My own guess is that the Pecos Indians mined turquoise in their own right, at least in the sixteenth century. During that period Pecos does seem to have had some moral or physical control over the Tanos groups who lived nearest to the mines.

Some macaw bones (Ara macao) have been found at Pecos (Kidder 1932:196), very likely brought up the trade routes from Sonora and shipped to Pecos via Cibola. Other items reminiscent of Cibola are the bone flageolets and whistles, numbers of which are found in the Pecos ruins (pp. 249-253). Most of the flageolets are made from the ulnae of golden eagles, although one is from the ulna of a whooping crane (p. 249). Probably most or all of them were locally manufactured.

That there were strong connections with the western pueblos is indicated by the trade ceramics. There are considerable numbers of sherds (some 165 from the various levels) of the extremely popular Hopi pottery that was traded over much of the Pueblo Indian world. At Pecos it is in stratigraphic contexts from around A.D. 1400 up to Spanish times. Hopi pottery includes Jeddito Black-on-yellow and Sikyatki polychrome (Kidder and Shepard 1936:367-370). Kidder (1958:320) feels that this pottery was either manufactured at Hopi or, possibly, retraded from Pottery Mound west of the Rio Grande, a site that contains large amounts of Hopi pottery. Pottery Mound, however, was deserted by approximately A.D. 1450, and, on balance, I believe

that the Hopi pottery was made in the Tusayan area. In addition to the Jeddito wares, there is Zuni area pottery, beginning with the pre-Spanish Saint John's polychrome and Heshotauthla polychrome but also including seventeenth and eighteenth century Zuni wares.

Pottery traded from the Rio Grande Basin included Sankawi Black-on-cream and Potsuwi'i incised, both probably dating from the sixteenth or early seventeenth century (Kidder and Shepard 1936:369-372). There is also one sherd of Casas Grandes polychrome, found at Loma Lothrop (p. 366), Zia and Acoma polychromes, both perhaps eighteenth century in date (pp. 377-380), and one sherd, probably central Mexican but otherwise of unknown provenience. Its position in the Pecos sequence seems to be unclear (p. 382). One sherd of High Plains pottery, Panhandle paddled, probably in association with Glaze V wares, dating from the seventeenth century, has been found (pp. 380-381).

I have, of course, taken only selected examples of trade or probable trade with Pecos as the hub, or middleman. All of the early Spanish parties were impressed with Pecos as the center through which Plains materials, especially products relating to the bison, came to the Greater Southwest. From the various accounts and from the evidence of archaeology, it would seem that this was a major operation, with large consignments of skin products streaming westward from Pecos every year. The town also utilized its control of the fibrolite sources to ship the valued axes westward. Pecos may also have sent turquoise to the western redistribution centers, although there is no firm evidence of that. By the end of the sixteenth century, Alibates flint was a popular trade item coming into Pecos, but little of it seems to have been transshipped to the west.

Eastward into the Plains, the Pecos people traded maize, receiving meat as well as bison hides. They also traded tobacco, shell, turquoise, and, to some degree, pottery into the Plains. I might say here that I disagree with Kidder that the "turquoise seems not to have been favored eastward of the Pueblo range" (1958:314). Both the archaeological and documentary evidence indicate otherwise.

From the west the Pecos Indians received the macaws and probably parrots that were so needed in ceremonies and ceremonial costumes. They also received cotton and cotton products probably from the Hopi-Tusayan area, though Sonora should not be ruled out. Shell from the Pacific Coast and from the Gulf of California reached Pecos in considerable quantities.

To me it seems likely that most of this material came through the Cibolan towns and was transshipped there. We have no historical evidence of a significant trade route from the eastern Pueblo area that bypassed Cibola on its way to Hopi-Tusayan or to Sonora. Tower (1945:Map 1) has suggested a route from Pecos down the Pecos River to the Rio Grande and the Gulf of Mexico. Such a route seems probable if one considers the amount of Gulf of Mexico shell found at Pecos. Apropos of that, it might be well to remember that the Vaca party, while traveling perhaps along the southern edge of the Edwards Plateau, received cotton blankets and a copper rattle which came from the north (Hedrick and Riley 1974:54, 83, 138).

Tower (1945:Map 1) also suggests a trade route that angled from Pecos across the Tiguex area, then southwestward through the Mimbres region to Casas Grandes. If such a route existed, it most likely was not in use in the sixteenth century.

Sociopolitical Organization

All too little is known about the political organization at Pecos in the sixteenth century, even less than about other eastern pueblos. The Spaniards, in the summer of 1540, met a political official from Pecos whom they called Bigotes. Exactly who this young leader of a trading party was is unclear. I have suggested that he may have been a "war chief or a society chief or possibly some other officer, who traditionally was a special leader of the trading party" (1978a:55). Kessell says that he was "evidently a war captain," and likely "a trader, well traveled, experienced, and somewhat affected by his dealing with foreigners" (1979:7). A second officer whom the Spaniards met at Pecos was called by them Cacique, meaning simply "head man." This elderly individual in all probability was an important member of the religious hierarchy. There were also "old men," presumably religious leaders in the power structure (Hammond and Rey 1940:271). In point of fact, however, the early Spaniards were not really very informative. According to Castañeda: "The inhabitants [of Cicuye] are of the same type and have the same customs as those in the other pueblos" (p. 257).

In the case of Pecos, comparisons with contemporary or nineteenth century pueblos would likely be very misleading. The Pecos shared a language with the people of Jemez, and in the period 1838-1840 the last remnants of Pecos Indians migrated to Jemez. It seems unlikely, however, that the Pecos Indians were organized very much like those of Jemez. As early as 1776 Father Domínguez makes the point that Pecos corresponded to Jemez in language but in no other respect (Adams and Chavez 1956:181). A list of Pecos clans given by the last Pecos survivors living at Jemez to Hewett (1904:431) and Hodge (1896:Plate VII) produced the following: Ant, Antelope, Badger, Bear, Buffalo, Calabash (Squash), Cloud, Corn, Coyote, Crow, Deer, Eagle, Earth, Fire, Mountain Lion, Oak, Pine, Sand Elk, Sun, Turkey (Wild Turkey), and Turquoise. To what extent these clans were operating in sixteenth century Pecos is unclear, and their relationships to the large numbers of kivas found at Pecos at that period is unknown.

Kidder makes the point that the Pecos (like Taos and Picuris), being on the frontier, may have had some "Plains traits" (1958:314). It does seem that the sixteenth century Pecos Indians were perhaps more warlike and assertive than most other Pueblos (see Warfare below).

The Coronado party found slaves at Pecos, all of them Plains Indians—The Turk, Isopete, and perhaps Xabe. What the word slave meant to the Pecos people is anyone's guess, but very likely not what it meant to the Spaniards.

Aside from the general observation that the Pecos Indians likely had some sort of "eastern Pueblo" sociopolitical and religious organization (see Religion below), with its basic egalitarianism and indirect social control, there is very little that one can add to the statements given above.

Warfare

There seems little doubt that the Pecos Indians had a reputation in the Pueblo world for being especially warlike. Castañeda, who comments that Pecos had 500 warriors, describes them this way: "The people of this town pride themselves because no one has been able to subjugate them, while they dominate the pueblos they wish" (Hammond and Rey 1940:257).

The first meeting of the Pecos with the Spaniards was cordial. After the trading party led by Bigotes had contacted Coronado in Cibola, a party under Alvarado marched to the eastern edge of Pueblo country. After visiting Tiguex, five days farther on

> Alvarado reached Cicuye, a very strong pueblo four stories high. The people came out to meet him and their captain [Bigotes] with demonstrations of joy and took him into the pueblo with drums and flageolets, similar to fifes, of which they had many. They presented the Spaniards with quantities of clothing and turquoises, which are found in abundance in

that region (p. 219).

The honeymoon with Pecos did not last. Bigotes and Cacique were taken captive, and the Pecos Indians watched with misgivings the Spanish devastation of Tiguex in the winter of 1540-1541. When Coronado left on the search for Quivira, the Pecos contributed food and Indians from the Plains, especially the slave, Turk. This cooperation was clearly not due to any desire to rekindle friendship with the Coronado group. According to Castañeda:

> They asked the Turk . . . why he had lied to them and guided them so perversely. He replied that his country was in that region, that the people of Cicuye had asked him to take the Spaniards out there and lead them astray on the plains. Thus, through lack of provisions, their horses would die and they themselves would become so feeble that, upon their return, the people of Cicuye could kill them easily and so obtain revenge for what the Spaniards had done to them (p. 241).

While Coronado was on the trip to Quivira, the main Spanish party returned to Tiguex. Eventually, Tristán de Arellano, who had been left in command of the main army, decided to go in search of Coronado. Arellano reached Pecos with forty men and was attacked there. After some days of inconclusive fighting, he received word that Coronado was on his way. Securing Glorieta Pass for the general, Arellano met Coronado in the Pecos area, and the combined parties returned to Tiguex (p. 245). Obregón (Cuevas 1924:299) claims that Coronado besieged Pecos for forty days but was forced to retire, leaving the Pecos people victorious. This story sounds like a confused account of the El Cerco battle, perhaps mixed in with events at Pecos a few months later!

The Pecos Indians seem to have done a great deal of fighting, certainly in large part because of their exposed position on the eastern frontier of Pueblo land. Around 1525 there was an attack, according to Castañeda (Hammond and Rey 1940:258), by large numbers of Teyas Indians who ravaged the Tanos pueblos. In 1540 these Galisteo peoples still had not recovered from the attack (p. 257). The Teyas then besieged Pecos but were unable to take it. By Coronado's time, what must have been a more typical trade relationship between the Teyas and the Pecos had been resumed, and the Teyas often spent the winter camped outside the great compound at Pecos.

Certain writers (see, for example, Schroeder

1979b:436; Gunnerson 1974:7, 16) have stressed the statement in the Coronado testimony that Bigotes and Cacique from Pecos had tried to make an alliance with the Spaniards whereby Pecos would be given a Tiguex pueblo and some of the Tiguex land (see Hammond and Rey 1940:328). I must say that this story sounds completely apocryphal to me.

The techniques and methods of fighting at Pecos did not differ significantly from those of other pueblos. The bow and arrow was used extensively, and stones were thrown from the terraces. Castaño (Hammond and Rey 1966:272) also mentions slings. The bison hide shield surely was employed at Pecos since the Pecos Indians seem to have had something of a trade monopoly on the shields. Macanas are mentioned by the Coronado chroniclers for the Rio Grande area, and they were also noted by the Espejo party in the 1580s. It seems likely that this particular weapon--a club embedded with flint or obsidian chips--was used at Pecos.

The greatest defensive weapon of the Pecos was their tightly built stone pueblo, with its blank walls on the lower floors. Coronado (especially after the months-long siege of El Cerco, or Mojo, a similarly built pueblo) chose not to invest the men and time in reducing Pecos in spite of the obviously hostile intentions of that town. Luxán claims that the six men of the Espejo expedition entered the town and forced the inhabitants to give supplies of food (p. 206), but it is impossible to believe that such a small party posed any real threat to Pecos. Castaño de Sosa, with a much larger party and with cannon, in late December 1590 and early January 1591, attacked Pecos and managed to break into the inner courtyards, but he never reduced all the houseblocks. After a stand-off situation of two or three days, Castaño withdrew his guards from around the pueblo, and the two parties disengaged, more or less peaceably.

Religion

The same general statement must be made about religion as about sociopolitical organization--that we have very little data for the sixteenth century. Kidder has adequately expressed the frustration in trying to completely understand sixteenth century Pecos: "Unfortunately, we have no first-hand account of what the Pecos were actually like. As a matter of fact, we really know very little beyond the most obvious externals, of the still extant eastern Pueblos" (1958:316).

In 1590-1591, Castaño reported sixteen kivas all underground (Hammond and Rey 1966:277). Kidder excavated seventeen round kivas plus four square above-ground structures which he called "guardhouse kivas" (Kidder 1958:144). There were, in fact, larger numbers of kivas, "a good many more," according to Kidder (p. 144). The guardhouse kivas are late, all very likely dating after A.D. 1600, and two of them perhaps after 1680 (p. 219). None of the kivas excavated by Kidder had mural decorations (p. 250).

One suspects that some of the kivas may have been clan kivas. It is possible that others served as society or moiety structures, but as we know almost nothing about the socioreligious organization in sixteenth century Pecos, this is highly conjectural. There were in the nineteenth century persistent stories of a serpent cult at Pecos that had some sort of kiva association (see Kidder 1958:227-229; Bandelier 1890-1892:Vol. 1, 305-307; Lange and Riley 1966:78; Curtis 1926:20) and also a sacred and undying fire (Kidder 1958:229-231; Lange and Riley 1966:78).

Most burials at Pecos were found in the trash heaps, and normally they were flexed. In fact, out of a total of almost 2000 inhumations, Kidder found only four extended adult burials from the pre-Spanish period. Even those from the period of Spanish occupation were usually not extended. There was no evidence of cremation at Pecos (Kidder 1958:279-305). Kidder has an interesting insight on the sociopolitical and religious organization of the Pecos Indians as seen through burial customs:

> Nothing more clearly illustrates the classlessness of the Pecos than the uniform simplicity of their graves. Not one of the nearly two thousand we opened was outstanding in construction or, as will be seen, in wealth of offerings (p. 289).

Costume

Castaño gives details of costume, and he also is interested in clothing but limits himself mainly to the observations that the Pecos are like the other Pueblos in this regard. The only thing that Castañeda repeats is the fact that at Pecos, as at Tiguex, unmarried maidens go naked: "For they say that if they do anything wrong it will soon be noticed and so they will not do it. They need not feel ashamed, either, that they go about as they were born" (Hammond and Rey 1940:257).

Castaño gives considerable detail on costume:

As for their clothing, we noticed that most of the men, if not all, wore cotton blankets and over these a buffalo skin, since this was the cold season; some covered their privy parts with small pieces of cloth, very elegant and elaborately decorated. The women wore a blanket tied over the shoulder and left open on one side, with a sash the width of a span wrapped around the waist. Over this blanket they wear another, nicely decorated and very fancy, or a kind of robe made of turkey feathers, as well as many other novel adornments, all of which is quite remarkable for barbarians (Hammond and Rey 1966:278).

Castaño does not mention the naked maidens, but then, as he says, it was the cold season.

General Comments

Castaño (p. 278) describes the glazed pottery at Pecos and praises its pottery making. He also provides a description of trough grinding:

Each floor of every house has three or four rooms, so that each house, as a whole, counting from top to bottom, has fifteen or sixteen rooms, very neat and well whitewashed. Every house is equipped with facilities for grinding corn, including three or four grinding stones mounted in small troughs and provided with pestles; all is whitewashed. The method of grinding is novel, the flour being passed from one grinder to another, as these Indians do not make tortilla dough, although from this flour they do make many kinds of bread, corn-flour gruel, and tamales (p. 277).

In general the descriptions of sixteenth century Spaniards do not show a Pecos significantly different from the Rio Grande province pueblos. Where Pecos does differ--for example, in the tightly defensive house structures, the reputation for warfare, and the strong interest in trade--this difference can, to some degree at least, be explained by Pecos's position on the fringe of the Plains at the very edge of Pueblo land.

CHAPTER XII

CONCLUSIONS AND FUTURE DIRECTIONS

The purpose of this study is simple. I wish to make sense out of the sixteenth century Southwest and to understand the human activities of that period in the larger setting of the mesoamerican Great Tradition. As discussed in Chapter I, I have been extremely cautious in interpreting the data and have resisted, insofar as possible, the introduction of nineteenth and twentieth century ethnographical data to explain sixteenth century situations. Heaven knows, the often casual and always biased documentation of the Spaniards provides enough distortion, not to mention the sometimes inadequate methodologies of the older archaeology and the occasional tunnel-vision of the newer.

The fact is that we know a great deal less about the sixteenth century Southwest than is generally supposed. We have a fair, but by no means overwhelming, understanding of the sixteenth century environment. The general outline of the various sociocultural subsystems (or at least some of them) is reasonably clear, but the details are usually vague. Consider, for example, religion in the Pueblo provinces, the region for which we have the most knowledge in depth. If we examine the evidence on sixteenth century kivas, we can say with a certain confidence that these had more or less the same functions as they did in the thirteenth century or the nineteenth century. We are much less sure of the relationship of given types of kiva structures to clans, moieties, societies, or other sodalities. The socio-religious system of the pueblos is fairly clear in that it had the same egalitarian but religion-dominated base in the sixteenth century as it has in more recent times. However, when it comes to specificities of structure and function of sixteenth century Pueblo society, the hard evidence is mostly not there. With the non-Pueblo provinces we are on even more shaky grounds.

In certain activities that are important to this paper, especially those relating to trade, intergroup relationships, and widespread movement of information and ideas, we are in somewhat better shape. We have both the direct evidence of archaeology and the specific statements of sixteenth century observers that allow us to highlight certain kinds of knowledge. Even so, it is necessary to avoid the temptation of what might seem to be straightforward ethnographic analogy. One might, for example, interpret the Bigotes expedition to Cibola in the summer of 1540 in terms of the Santo Domingo expedition to the Plains in the fall of 1880. There are clear enough similarities. Both expeditions were for the purpose of trade, they were of somewhat the same size, both included individuals from other pueblos, and both had some internal organization. Unfortunately, we know all too little about the differences.

If I have resisted ethnographic analogy, I also have been very hesitant to utilize the sociocultural reconstructions which involve systems or processual archaeology (see Longacre 1970; Hill 1970). I have no doubt that the processual approach will prove valuable if used carefully enough. Take, for example, the tentative suggestion of Martin et al. (1967:160-164) that Broken K Pueblo, a town in the Old Cibolan area, deserted by A.D. 1300, had uxorilocal residence patterns. This is the kind of information, if and when it checks out, that will eventually be useful in more detailed studies of the sixteenth century Greater Southwest.

There are, however, obvious (and not so obvious) pitfalls in utilizing models drawn from ethnographic analogy or from processual analysis. A very common and very dangerous one is that models sometimes work their way into the literature and become very hard to dislodge--not as models but as a species of historical reality. One that I currently find very bothersome is the assumption by some writers that one or the other of the southwestern peoples (usually the Serrana groups and sometimes the Gila-Salt Indians) had "chiefdoms," in the redistributional sense employed by Service (1962) and by such later writers as Helms (1979). As I have pointed out both for the Sonoran and the old Hohokam areas (1979, 1980a), such shallow-rooted paradigms can do a great deal of damage and should be avoided except for presentation in the most tentative way (see also Earle 1977).

Interactions with the Greater Southwest

That the Greater Southwest formed a clear-cut interaction area is perhaps most dramatically demonstrated by the fact that the Spaniards in 1540 reached every section of it within a matter of a few months and never went beyond it, with the one planned exception of the Quivira expedition. In other words, the Spaniards were operating within a closed universe which was delineated for them partly by natives and partly by their own observations and insights. One need only compare the neatly packaged expedition of Coronado with that aimless wanderung of the De Soto party. Aside from Quivira, Coronado was interested in the Greater Southwest, and he intended to organize and govern it for the glory of Spain. He certainly knew what and where it was.

Coronado and his advance party reached the southern edge of the Greater Southwest in May of 1540. In the period May through July 1540, Coronado overran the Zuni country, established contact with Pecos on the far eastern edge of the region, and sent an expedition to Hopi on the far northwest side. Meanwhile Alarcón, coming by sea, arrived at the mouth of the Colorado River in August 1540 and remained there for several weeks. Shortly after he left, Melchior Díaz from the Sonoran area marched by land to the lower Colorado River, and García López de Cárdenas was sent, starting from Hopi with Hopi guides, to go down the Colorado River. Neither of these two expeditions came to anything. Díaz was accidentally killed, and Cárdenas insisted on (or was tricked into) following a waterless route somewhere between the San Francisco Mountains and the Grand Canyon, the expedition hugging the south rim of the canyon, at least during part of the journey.

Another of Coronado's captains, Hernando de Alvarado, reached Pecos and Taos in the late summer or early fall of 1540 and penetrated to the edge of the Buffalo Plains. Later that fall Coronado explored the Piro area. By the end of 1541, Coronado or his exploring parties had reached all parts of the Greater Southwest, perhaps with the exception of the Tompiro (Salinas) country and some of the Serrana valleys. It is inconceivable that the Spaniards would have lacked good information on any area, explored or not. None of Coronado's parties went beyond the Greater Southwest (as I use the term here) except for the Quivira adventure of 1541. Even Cárdenas' exploration of the Grand Canyon was on an alternative route from Tusayan-Hopi to the lower Colorado, although apparently an infrequently used one. Certainly all later Spanish parties, utilizing Hopi or Zuni guides, followed a much commoner route via the upper Verde Valley.

Not only did Coronado concentrate on the Greater Southwest but he also tried to garrison or otherwise control all parts of it. A major military post was established in the Corazones-Señora area. Hernando de Alarcón, who failed to meet and provision Coronado's armies in 1540, was commissioned in 1541 to launch a second expedition to support Coronado, to trade with the lower Colorado natives, and to begin a colony there (Hammond and Rey 1940:121). The general Spanish plan for the Greater Southwest is indicated by the reading of the requerimiento at various places, two of which, Cibola and Tusayan, are specifically mentioned in the accounts (pp. 168, 214).

The Spanish plan for the Greater Southwest was laid out in the document that appointed Coronado commander of the Cibola expedition. As of the time of this proclamation (January 6, 1540), the specificities of the Southwest were not very well known, the Spaniards having only the Vaca and Marcos information to go on: "We appoint you anew as captain general of . . . the lands and provinces of Acus and Cíbola, and the seven cities and the kingdoms and provinces of Matata [Marata] and Totonteac, and of all their subjects and dependents" (p. 84).

The speed and ease with which Coronado moved through this very large area indicated a firm knowledge of it, a knowledge that grew by leaps and bounds in the summer and fall of 1540. The reason is clear. The people of the Greater Southwest knew about each other. Information on the Zuni and Hopi given to Díaz by the Serrana people was both detailed and correct. Alarcón, in the lower Colorado the following year, also received basically correct information on Cibola. At Cibola and at Tusayan Coronado learned enough information about the lower Colorado area to send both Díaz and Cárdenas on expeditions to penetrate the lower reaches of that river. Pecos and Tiguex Indians at Zuni guided Alvarado to Acoma, Tiguex, Pecos, and Taos. Coronado had "experienced guides" in Castañeda's words (p. 220) when he went from Cibola-Zuni to Tutahaco (the Piro and possibly Tompiro area). These guides, as I have suggested in Chapter X, may well have been Cibolan. Even the trip to Quivira which led the Spaniards out of the Southwest was planned by Caddoan and Pecos Indians to rid themselves of the invaders.

The Coronado party also discovered a complicated series of sociopolitical interrelationships throughout the Southwest. Cibola was in touch with parts of the Serrana province during the Díaz visit of 1539 and offered military help against the Spaniards. The entire eastern part of the Southwest was involved in the long drawn-out battle of the Spaniards with Tiguex in the winter of 1540-1541. We have no record of either Cibola or Tusayan helping the beleaguered Tiguex although they must have kept close track of events in the Rio Grande Valley. It was, perhaps, no coincidence that the Sonoran statelets rebelled about this time. The Spaniards blamed the flare-up at San Gerónimo on excessive brutality by Diego de Alcaráz, Coronado's commander there, but troubles in Tiguex and a knowledge of the Bigotes plot may have been factors. The peripheral lower Colorado groups seem to have taken no part in the Tiguex War, but judging from the speed with which Alarcón received word of Cibola the previous year, the Yuman groups probably knew all about it.

The lower Colorado area was very much on the minds of the Spaniards. Every major party--except those of Castaño who never got beyond the Rio Grande Valley and Chamuscado who reached Zuni in bitter weather--pushed out an expedition in a westerly direction. Most of them failed to reach the lower Colorado proper. García López de Cárdenas had Hopi guides who (I suspect, deliberately) took his party over the scenic route via the Grand Canyon. Hopi guides escorted the smaller (and therefore less threatening) Espejo party to the Jerome area well south of the rugged and largely waterless Grand Canyon route to the lower Colorado. Some fifteen years later, Hopi guides also led Oñate's captain, Marcos Farfán de los Godos, to the Verde River area, where Farfán got clear information on the lower Colorado people. Vicente de Zaldívar made a trip to central Arizona during the year 1599, a journey for which there is very little information (Hammond and Rey 1953:814-815) except that Zaldívar may have contacted Piman groups at some point on his route (p. 829; Forbes 1960:92-93). Parenthetically, Forbes (p. 93) suggests that Zaldívar may have followed the Verde River to Pima country. An expedition to the Verde was made by another of Oñate's captains, Gerónimo Márquez, in 1603 or 1604 (p. 103).

The Vizcaino expedition in 1602 also made connection with the lower Colorado peoples, perhaps in the area of San Diego (Bolton 1916:88, 118). Zárate Salmerón, writing a number of years later, states that Oñate, in 1604-1605, had with him a soldier

> who had gone with Sebastian Vizcaino to California; he said that he went in search of the Tizon River, and I believe that had he reached it he would not have returned, as he did, for lack of food, because there is much here (p. 273).

The Oñate expedition left the headquarters at San Gabriel on October 7, 1604, and reached the lower Colorado via Zuni, Hopi, the upper Verde, and the Bill Williams River areas. Oñate's plan, like that of Coronado, was to give the projected Spanish settlement a sea outlet. Coronado had been forced to retreat, and Oñate had no better luck. His followers underwent severe hardship in New Mexico, and the leader himself was eventually ordered back to Mexico. At one point there was even a plan to discontinue the colony of San Felipe de Nuevo Mexico, but because of the large mission potential, Spain decided to hold on. The operation was minimal, however, and throughout the seventeenth century New Mexico was both underpopulated and underfinanced. After Oñate, the Spaniards gave up any serious plan to supply the province by sea, utilizing the Gulf of California.

Nevertheless, the attempt of Oñate to reach the Gulf of California and the continuing (though increasingly feeble) attempts of Franciscan friars

and others to penetrate the Gila-Salt and the Serrana regions in the early seventeenth century indicate continued Spanish understanding of the former unity of the Greater Southwest. That unity was already passing. The Serrana region, so important to the total Southwest in the sixteenth century, underwent some sort of cultural and demographic disaster toward the end of that century. By Oñate's time, the Serrana influence on the upper Southwest was very much on the wane.

Spanish religious politics contributed finally to breaking up the southwestern entity. The northwest coast of Mexico had been given to the Jesuits as a mission area, and Jesuit movement into the Serrana region was complete by about A.D. 1630. After that time the New Mexican government was uninterested in a Gulf of California presence because in Spanish eyes Sonora, the Gila-Salt, and the lower Colorado areas were Jesuit territory. Even though it was not till the end of the century that the Jesuits actually established themselves in the lower Colorado and Gila River valleys, such actions had been in the planning stage for some time. In fact, by the end of the seventeenth century Jesuit pressures were so strong that there was even talk of Jesuit missionization of the Tusayan area. In any case, the division of the Southwest into its upper and lower components, so familiar to us today, had begun in the first decades of the seventeenth century and was complete a half century later.

I have discussed in the body of this report the considerable sociopolitical, religious, and economic interaction in the Greater Southwest. The weakest cohesion was political; even the provinces (except for Pecos) were not political entities in any significant sense. On the other hand, rather similar culture extended over large areas, and, as pointed out earlier, there was a series of traits that appeared among all the people of the Greater Southwest. These included an agricultural base with maize, beans, and squash; considerable importance of hunting with a strong ceremonial component; use of pottery and cotton; a propensity for warfare utilizing the bow and arrow, shield, and the mace; a solar and astral religion with strong interest in birds, especially brightly feathered ones; special religious houses (though data for the lower Colorado are not very clear in this regard); a taste for luxury goods, especially shell, coral, and turquoise; and dependence on bison hide for certain manufactured items (robes, shields, and headgear). These general traits and others blanket the Greater Southwest. The unity of the Southwest and its debt to Mesoamerica are, as pointed out elsewhere in this book, by no means new ideas. See for example the brilliant paper of W. Duncan Strong (1973; originally published in 1927).

The inhabitants of the Greater Southwest not only traded with each other but also had an interest in each other's lifeways. To take one example, from the lower Colorado, the Serrana, and the Gila-Salt Basin, the earliest Spaniards received accounts of the distinctive pueblo stone and mud apartment-type houses (the "skyscrapers" of the sixteenth century), accounts that were often accurate even in small details.

As discussed in considerable detail throughout the book, the major integrative mechanism within the Greater Southwest was that of trade. Figure 1 shows the important trade routes as of the beginning of the Spanish period. In addition to the primary and important secondary trails shown on the map, there were numbers of smaller ones that branched off to settled areas throughout the region.

Evidence for the trade is very clear since the actual finds of objects, sometimes identifiable as to provenience and often as to date, appear in site after archaeological site. Evidence also comes from the documents of the period, for, from the time of Diego de Guzmán and Cabeza de Vaca, the Spaniards were very sensitive to the trading situation. Although it is clear that much of the trade material was transshipped, we also know that individuals and groups went long distances to carry specific trade materials and to obtain others. Examples in which trade was the certain or probable reason for travel include trips by Pecos and Tiguex individuals to Cibola-Zuni, expeditions by Tusayan and Cibola Indians to the lower Colorado River, trips by Sonoran Indians to the lower Colorado River and to Cibola-Zuni, and voyages of Tusayan Indians to Acoma. From the frontier centers in the Serrana, in the lower Colorado, at Cibola, and at Pecos, goods from outside the Greater Southwest came flooding in—shell and coral from the Pacific, bison products from the High Plains, parrots and macaws from Mexico. This was added to the riches of the Southwest, especially turquoise, pottery, cotton, pigments, semiprecious stones, and salt, and much of it was shipped out again. Some of the trade goods peregrinated, as demonstrated by the archaeological or historical record, or both, for many hundreds (in some cases thousands) of kilometers.

The Mesoamerican Stimulus to Trade

I have recently outlined a model for the development of the extensive southwestern trade routes:

I suggest that the Greater Southwest,

slowly picking up cultural baggage (e.g., techniques of maize agriculture) from the Mesoamerican heartland, but lagging behind that heartland in sophistication, became very early an area of exploitation by Mesoamericans. The process was initiated and encouraged by a strong demand for certain kinds of luxury, rare, and exotic materials in the Mesoamerican heartland and the development of trade networks and trading organizations to meet this demand . . . .

Since trade networks are sensitive to changing political situations one would expect a fluctuation on the frontier as conditions changed in the heartland. Indeed, as far as the Southwest is concerned this likely does happen, the ending of two great contact phases seeming in a broad way to relate to events at the ends of Classic and Post Classic times in Mesoamerica. The third contact period was ended by the Spaniards (1980b:16).

Pailes and Whitecotton (1979; see also Weigand 1978; Pailes 1980) have suggested a model based on the world system idea of Wallerstein (1974). According to this model, the Southwest represents a peripheral area to the mesoamerican world system, developed as such by trade contacts, with the two areas tied by economic rather than political bonds. This, in a somewhat less formalized way, is the concept of Ferdon (1955), Di Peso (1974), Kelley (1966), Reyman (1980), and Riley (1980b), among others.

The data presented in this report certainly point to strong mesoamerican influence, not only in the sixteenth century but for many hundreds of years before the coming of the Spaniards. The Southwest and Mesoamerica were probably not involved in "heavy" trade. In fact, the only basically mesoamerican products traded into the Southwest for which we have clear evidence are parrots and macaws, their feathers, copper (mostly in the form of tinklers), and some pottery. There may, indeed, have been other things; some of the shell perhaps came from western Mesoamerica, and there is some reason to think that peyote had entered the trade picture before Spanish times (Riley 1976b:40). What Mesoamericans got from the Southwest is only partly known. Turquoise is one item for which there is considerable evidence of trade southward. Slaves may have been traded from the Serrana or perhaps transshipped from the upper Southwest through the Serrana centers. I should stress that there is no clear evidence for trade of slaves except within the Serrana province. However, both Di Peso (1968a:30, 1968b:50, 52) and I (1976b:41) see a good possibility for the trade of slaves to Mesoamerica. There is also evidence that some sort of green emerald-like stone was being traded southward from Cibola through the Serrana; this was likely peridot (p. 40). Salt is a trade possibility, as is pottery. Apropos of the latter, a few examples of Rio Grande glaze pottery have been found in Nayarit. The extensive trade in bison hide objects reached into the Serrana region and over to the Sonoran coast of the Gulf of California, but we are uncertain if it went farther south. Interestingly, the Serrana people seem to have been one of the major distributors of coral, getting it from the "South Sea," according to Vaca (p. 11), and trading it to the lower Colorado and perhaps to Cibola-Zuni (Bolton 1916:279). It is not known how much, if any, of the coral went south to western Mesoamerica.

The two most massive items of trade in the Greater Southwest in terms of actual weight were likely bison products and shell. Mesoamerica was probably only peripherally involved in the movement of either of these categories of goods. In other words, even though southwestern trade was stimulated by the mesoamerican connection, and as suggested above, Mesoamericans may have set the trade mechanism in motion, much of the southwestern trade in the sixteenth century originated and stayed well north of Mesoamerica.

As indicated above, an important class of ceremonial items, the richly colored feathers of parrots and macaws, did come from Mesoamerica. It is interesting that of the approximately 150 macaw skeletons found in southwestern sites and analysed by Hargrave (1970:52), about two-thirds are identified as Ara macao (scarlet macaw) whose natural habitat begins in southern Tamaulipas and extends southward from there through the tropical lowlands into South America (Olsen and Olsen 1974:67). The finds date from around A.D. 1000 through the early Spanish contact period. In his paper on macaws, Hargrave (1970:52) definitely identified only one bird as Ara militaris (military macaw), which has a more western and northern range, extending into southern Sonora. Hargrave's count did not include Casas Grandes which is described in Di Peso (1974:Vol. 2, 599-600) and in Di Peso et al. (1974:Vol. 8, 272-274). Di Peso found 322 Ara macao, 81 Ara militaris, and 100 macaws that could not be identified by species. There were far fewer parrots at Casas Grandes, but both the thick-billed parrot (Rhynchopsitta pachyrhyncha) and the lilac-crowned parrot (Amazona finschi) appear. The native habitat of both the latter birds includes the northern Sierra Madre (p. 279). Macaws were bred at Casas Grandes over a number

of human generations, but, of course, the Casas Grandes area was in ruins and could not have met the southwestern demand for macaws during the sixteenth century. Parrot and macaw feathers continued to be popular throughout historic times, at least in the Pueblo area, and feathers from these birds are used today as components of costume as well as for other ceremonial purposes.

Influences Other Than Trade

Kelley and Kelley (1975) have made a good case for actual mesoamerican traders of the trocador, or pochteca, type at Chaco Canyon in the eleventh and twelfth centuries A.D. One of the things that interested these traders (accepting for the moment the Kelley and Kelley model) was clearly turquoise, and they seem to have furnished macaws and parrots to the Chacoans. One suspects that they were purveyors of important esoteric knowledge as well. Di Peso (1968b:49-53) believes that large increments of mesoamerican religion, including specific deities, were brought to the Southwest at various times through what were fundamentally trade contacts. Ellis and Hammack (1968:41-42) also outline a diffusion into the Southwest of specific mesoamerican gods (see also Ellis 1976). By the sixteenth century this religion had been reinterpreted so that obvious mesoamerican elements such as human sacrifice had been removed, except for echoes in the mythology (see Parsons 1939:185, 220, 241 ff.). However, if I understand Frisbie (1978:213, 1980:62) and Reyman (1978:255) correctly, they believe that human sacrifice was practiced at Chaco Canyon as late as the eleventh or twelfth century. In any case, the religion of the Pueblo Indian area in the fifteenth and sixteenth centuries was strongly impregnated with mesoamerican elements, as indicated by the mural paintings at Kuaua (Dutton 1963b), at Awatovi (Smith 1952), and at Pottery Mound (Hibben 1960, 1966). The extensive use of flageolets in the sixteenth century and the popularity of the hunchback flute player have led me to suggest (1975b:147) that there was an attenuated form of the Tezcatlipoca cult in the upper Southwest. For further discussion of the Kokopelli (flute player) figure see Hawley (1937), and for possible mesoamerican connections see Miller (1975) and Farmer (1980).

Comparative ethnographic work strengthens the evidence for this generalized mesoamerican flavor of southwestern religion (Parsons 1939, 1974; Riley 1963). In this regard it is interesting to point out that Nahuatl may have been spoken or understood in the sixteenth century Southwest (Riley 1971:304).

The extent to which trade relationships stimulated the introduction of new sociopolitical organizations is unclear. Although the Kelleys think in terms of a pochteca model, as does Di Peso (1974:Vol. 2, 328-331), others are somewhat reluctant to use this particular paradigm. Weigand, in a discussion of trading operations in Zacatecas, remarks:

> The Aztec model of long-distance trade and exploitation, i.e. the puchteca, has been most often utilized for pre-Aztec, even Teotihuacan, times. I believe that this model is not appropriate for the following reasons: (1). the concept puchteca as an institution is fairly well defined . . . for the Aztec-specific situation, as the puchteca were in tight social and ceremonial association with the feather-workers, and seem to have emerged from a common background with them, and (2). the puchteca were oriented toward trade with southern Mesoamerica, and in general the Aztecs had been effectively blocked from access to the north by the development of the Tarascan kingdom . . . . No known trading or exploitative organization engaged in the north is documented for the Aztec period, though certainly neither Teotihuacan nor the states of the early Postclassic period (i.e. Tollan, Culhuacan) had difficulties acquiring the produce of the northern frontier. If we must postulate an institution for the exploitation of the north prior to the Aztecs, I suggest, in analogy to the puchteca-feather workers (with their southern orientation), the tulteca-stone workers (1980:3).

I also have some hesitation in drawing too liberally from the historic Aztec situation. In a paper primarily concerned with the Serrana area, I make the following points:

> We have some fairly good descriptions of what was traded and some indications of the intensity of trade, but almost nothing of the mechanisms of trade. Was there, for example a barrio of foreign traders in the various towns, a sort of "pochteca?" We cannot rule out the possibility, but from the evidence at hand it would seem that trade was largely in local hands. In the upper Southwest, for example at Pecos and Cíbola, what I call an "entrepreneurial redistribution" situation existed in which privately organized groups within the pueblo conducted trading operations. Trade parties were led by particular experts, perhaps members of the Bow Priesthood. The entire pueblo doubtless benefited by this trade through the crossties of kinship, but the pueblos, as entities, were probably not redistributive in the political sense . . . . Whether the leaders of the Sonoran statelets had political control over the lucrative trade that passed through their territory . . . is not clear. Whatever the specific situation, I personally suspect that trade was somewhat more centrally organized than was the case among the Pueblos (1979:37-38).

The Cultural Importance of Trade

Regardless of the mechanisms of trade, some scholars feel that the actual contact, as indicated by trade goods found in the Greater Southwest, was quite minimal. For example, Haury, speaking of trade from Mesoamerica, says:

> If all the Mexican goods recovered from precontact sites are brought together . . . the combined weight would not exceed a few kilograms, barely enough to make it worth a trader's time and effort to pack it northward over an arduous trail . . . . The evidence we do have does not support the idea of large scale importations by the pochtecas (1976:347).

Haury recognizes that much of the trade may have been in perishable materials (feathers, textiles, etc.). Even so, he obviously does not find the mesoamerican trade impressive.

I have a somewhat different evaluation of known trade to the Southwest, especially since I consider it necessary to think of trade entering the Southwest from all sides. If all trade goods recovered from southwestern archaeological sites were put together, it would amount to considerably more than "a few kilograms," and if those items going from one side of the Southwest to the other are added in, we are dealing with a considerable aggregate of goods. In other words, we are dealing with a flow, not a trickle. Add to this the statements of early Spanish explorers about the movement of trade goods, and the flow becomes something of a flood.

I believe, however, that even this misses the

point.   As Tolstoy points out in a recent review of a book on pre-Spanish central Mexico:

> Like sex, foreign trade here is the flow of information more than it is the flow of energy. To minimize it because few kilocalories are involved seems absurd. Moreover, negligible increments of energy are quite sufficient to upset certain equilibria, and feedback, once triggered, borrows energy in its neighborhood and need not import it over long distances (1980:313).

Other Considerations

This is a very preliminary study.   I do not expect the major outlines of the work to change, but the details will unquestionably do so. Perhaps one of the most important questions that must be answered in the future is the role of disease in the sixteenth century Southwest.   In fact, the really basic question is at what point in time the onrush of Spanish disease had a significant sociocultural and demographic effect on the Southwest.   There are students of southwestern demography such as Henry Dobyns (personal communication) who believe that, even before Coronado, there had been a decided lessening of southwestern energies due to the spread of disease coming up the trade routes.   My own belief, as discussed above, is that the Southwest retained its vigor and organization through at least the first half of the sixteenth century.   As late as the 1560s the Serrana area seems to have been fully functioning.   Clearly, the last few decades of the sixteenth century saw drastic things happening in Sonora, with population decline and simplification of the sociopolitical organization.   When the Jesuits invaded Sonora, they had a very different situation to deal with than did Coronado and Ibarra.

In the upper Southwest there is considerable evidence that the Tiguex area never really recovered from Coronado's depredations (Riley 1981a).   Cibola and Tusayan also seem to have suffered some decline. One indication comes from Escobar, who in October 1604 arrived with the Oñate expedition on its way to the lower Colorado: "We came to the province of Quini [Zuñi], which has six pueblos, four of them almost completely in ruins, although all inhabited" (Hammond and Rey 1953:1013-1014).

A few days later Escobar remarked of Hopi: "It had only five pueblos, four of them half in ruins and destroyed" (p. 1014).   The downward spiral of the pueblos during the seventeenth century has been

discussed above.   The role of disease in breaking up the native Southwest was unquestionably very significant, but as yet it has not been completely evaluated.

Given the very great importance of trade in the sixteenth century Greater Southwest, the question of some medium of trade, some primitive "money," has been raised.   Frisbie (1975:124-127) suggested that hishi (shell beads) may have been used as a form of currency in the aboriginal Southwest, and I have tentatively advanced the idea that turquoise may also have served that purpose (1975b:138-139).   Much more work needs to be done on this subject.

Another approach to the sixteenth century Southwest that has not, as yet, been used to any great degree is locational analysis.   While I agree with Chang (1972) that one must proceed with caution when applying models taken from Western culture to non-Western situations, the particular distribution of towns, especially in the upper Southwest, may lend itself to this kind of analysis.   Pailes has made a preliminary evaluation of the Sonora River settlements in terms of their hierarchical arrangements. According to Pailes:

> The settlement pattern data tend to indicate that there was no central place hierarchy within each of the valley segments, but that the large sites served all other sites with no intermediate sites functioning as secondary centers (1980:29).

It is likely that in the sixteenth century Hawikuh functioned as a major focus for trade for the Cibola group of towns, but Matsaki may mave been the major ceremonial center--at least this was the tradition given Stevenson (1904:424) in the late nineteenth century and still repeated at Zuni today (Riley fieldnotes;   see also Ferguson et al. 1977:16-17).   However, there is uncertain and conflicting evidence from Cibola that suggests a kind of lattice arrangement during the sixteenth century in which each of the more or less equidistant towns had its own particular and interdigitating religious functions, which each town in turn performed for the whole group (Parsons 1939:872-881;   Huff 1951:120, 127;   Frisbie 1980:65).   In any case, it must have been very much of a situation of primus inter pares. Though the details may have differed, the same kind of cooperative autonomy among towns was probably practiced in the Tusayan area and in the Rio Grande Valley.

The whole question of the sociopolitical and economic interplay of towns and provinces throughout the Greater Southwest is one that has been, though much speculated upon, very little investigated. It obviously will differ from one area to another; for example, the situation at Tiguex in the middle Rio Grande Valley was likely not quite the same as at Cibola. All too little is known about the extent and direction of the difference(s).

Work on carrying capacity has not advanced very much for the sixteenth century Southwest. For one thing, there is no real agreement on population size and no great certainty as to the amount of raw materials that could be or were processed with the technology available to the natives. In Chapter VI, I made a crude preliminary attempt to establish population in the Serrana area on the basis of food availability and historic population density. For other work that touches on this problem in the Southwest see Bronitsky (1975) and Zubrow (1975).

- - -

A final comment on the question of southwestern-mesoamerican relationships is appropriate. Archaeology and ethnohistory are no more immune to fashions in research orientation than are other fields. In the latter part of the nineteenth century, work in the archaeology, ethnohistory, and ethnology of the Greater Southwest had as its goal (stated or unstated) the demonstration of the Southwest's place in a larger framework of American Indian civilization. Only from about the time of World War I did the idea of an autonomous upper Southwest become paramount, and this isolationism was maintained for several decades. However, beginning about the time of the Second World War, scholars again became interested in the Southwest as part of a larger setting. Even though in the 1960s there was a fresh wave of archaeological isolationism (which, for theoretical and methodological reasons, insisted on internal explanations for change and growth of southwestern cultures), a belief in the "mesoamerican connection" was never lost (Riley 1978a).

The decade of the 1970s has seen a wave of interest in southwestern-mesoamerican contacts. A new generation of archaeologists, ethnohistorians, and historians are working out explanations, often at the level of broad cultural generalizations, which deal with the Southwest as part of some mesoamerican "world system." The 1980s should bring us closer to this goal of understanding the Southwest as a clearly defined part of the cultural polity of Mesoamerica.

REFERENCES CITED

Adams, E. Charles
  1981 The view from the Hopi mesas.   In The protohistoric period in the North American Southwest, A.D.
    1450-1700, edited by D.R. Wilcox and W.B. Masse, pp. 321-335.   Arizona State University Anthropological
    Research Papers 24, Tempe.

Adams, Eleanor B., and Angelico Chavez, O.F.M. (translators and editors)
  1956 The missions of New Mexico, 1776, a description by Fray Francisco Atanasio Domínguez.   University of
    New Mexico Press, Albuquerque.

AGN
  1593- Añuas; memorias para la historia de la provincia de Sinaloa.   Archivo General de la Nación, México
    Historia (Tomo 15). Bancroft Library copy.

Aiton, Arthur S., and Agapito Rey
  1937 Coronado's testimony in the Viceroy Mendoza residencia. New Mexico Historical Review 12(3):288-329.

Alegre, Francisco Xavier
  1841-1842 Historia de la Compañía de Jesús en Nueva España.   3 vols.   Edited by C. María de Bustamante.
    J.M. Lara, México.

Alexander, Hubert G., and Paul Reiter
  1935 Report on the excavation of Jemez Cave, New Mexico. University of New Mexico, Bulletin 278, Albuquer-
    que.

Arregui, Domingo Lázaro de
  1946 Descripción de la Nueva Galicia.   Edited by F. Chevalier.   Publicaciones de la Escuela de Estudios
    Hispano-Americanos de la Universidad de Sevilla, no. general 24, serie 3, no. 3.

Bandelier, Adolph F.
  Journals--See Lange and Riley 1966 and 1970.

  1890-1892 Final report of investigations among the Indians of the southwestern United States, carried on
    mainly in the years from 1880 to 1885.   Part 1, 1890; Part 2, 1892.   Papers of the Archaeological Insti-
    tute of America, American Series 3 and 4, Cambridge, Massachusetts.

Bandelier, Adolph F., and Edgar L. Hewett
  1937 Indians of the Rio Grande Valley. Handbook of Archaeological History 3. Albuquerque. Reprinted 1973
    by Cooper Square Publishers, New York.

Barnes, Thomas C., Thomas H. Naylor, and Charles W. Polzer
  1981 Northern New Spain: a research guide. University of Arizona Press, Tucson.

Bartlett, Katharine
  1942 Notes upon the routes of Espejo and Farfán to the mines in the sixteenth century. New Mexico Histori-
     cal Review 17(1):21-36.

Beals, Ralph L.
  1945 The contemporary culture of the Cáhita Indians. Bureau of American Ethnology, Bulletin 142.

Beaumont, Fr. Pablo
  1932 Crónica de . . . . Michoacán. Publicaciones del Archivo General de la Nación, 17, 18, and 19.   Tall-
     eres Graficos de la Nación, México.

Beers, Henry P.
  1979 Spanish and Mexican records of the American Southwest.   University of Arizona Press, in collaboration
     with The Tucson Corral of the Westerners, Tucson.

Benavides, Alonso de, O.F.M.
  1945 Fray Alonso de Benavides' revised memorial of 1634.   Translated and edited by F.W. Hodge, G.P. Ham-
     mond, and A. Rey. Coronado Cuarto Centennial Publications, 1540-1940 (Vol. 4).   University of New Mexico
     Press, Albuquerque.

  1954 Benavides' memorial of 1630. Translated by P. P. Forrestal, with an historical introduction and notes
     by C. J. Lynch. Academy of American Franciscan History, Documentary Series 2. Washington, D.C.

Benson, Lyman
  1969 The cacti of Arizona. University of Arizona Press, Tucson.

Bliss, Wesley L.
  1948 Preservation of the Kuaua mural paintings. American Antiquity 13(3):218-223.

Bloom, Lansing B. (editor)
  1936 Bourke on the Southwest, IX. New Mexico Historical Review 11(2):188-207.

Bohrer, Vorsila L., Hugh C. Cutler, and Jonathan D. Sauer
  1969 Carbonized plant remains from two Hohokam sites,   Arizona BB:13:41 and Arizona BB:13:50.   The Kiva
     35(1):1-10.

Bolton, Herbert E.
  1916 Spanish exploration in the Southwest, 1542-1706. Charles Scribner's Sons, New York.

  1964 Coronado: knight of pueblos and plains. University of New Mexico Press, Albuquerque.

Bolton, Herbert E. (translator and editor)
   1948   Kino's historical memoir of Pimeria Alta.   2 vols. in 1.   University of California Press, Berkeley and
      Los Angeles.

Bourne, Edward G. (editor)
   1904   Narratives of the career of Hernando de Soto.   2 vols.   Trail Makers Series, New York.

Bradfield, R. Maitland
   1971   The changing pattern of Hopi agriculture.   Royal Anthropological Institute of Great Britain and Ire-
      land, Occasional Paper 30, London.

   1974   Birds of the Hopi region, their Hopi names, and notes on their ecology.   Museum of Northern Arizona
      Bulletin 48, Flagstaff.

Brand, Donald D.
   1936   Notes to accompany a vegetation map of northwest Mexico.   University of New Mexico Bulletin, Biologi-
      cal Series 4(4), Albuquerque.

   1937   The natural landscape of northwestern Chihuahua.   University of New Mexico Bulletin, Geological Series
      5(2), Albuquerque.

   1973   Aboriginal trade routes for sea shells in the Southwest.   In The Classic Southwest, edited by B. C.
      Hedrick, J. C. Kelley, and C. L. Riley, pp. 92-101.   Southern Illinois University Press, Carbondale and
      Edwardsville.

Braniff, Beatriz C.
   1978   Preliminary interpretations regarding the role of the San Miguel River, Sonora, Mexico.   In Across the
      Chichimec Sea, edited by C. L. Riley and B. C. Hedrick, pp. 67-82.   Southern Illinois University Press,
      Carbondale and Edwardsville.

Bronitsky, Gordon
   1975   Jemez and Tiguex: a test of an ethnological inference.   In Collected papers in honor of Florence Haw-
      ley Ellis, edited by T.R. Frisbie.   Papers of the Archaeological Society of New Mexico 2:22-46.

Burrus, Ernest J., S.J.
   1971   Kino and Manje: explorers of Sonora and Arizona.   With an appendix of thirty documents, a map of the
      area, and a placefinder by R. L. Ives.   Sources and Studies for the History of the Americas (Vol. 10).
      Jesuit Historical Institute, Rome and St. Louis University.

Bushnell, G.H.S.
   1954   Some Pueblo IV pottery types from Kechipaun, New Mexico, U.S.A.   XXXI Congresso International de Amer-
      icanistas 2:657-665, São Paulo.

Bustamante, Carlos María de
  See Alegre 1841-1842.

Cabeza de Vaca, Alvar Nuñez
  1555 La relación y comentarios. Published in Valladolid.   This publication is now generally known as Naufragios.

Castetter, Edward F.
  1943 Early tobacco utilization and cultivation in the American Southwest.   American Anthropologist
  45(2):320-325.

Castetter, Edward F., and Willis H. Bell
  1942 Pima and Papago Indian agriculture.   University of New Mexico, School of Inter-American Affairs,
  Inter-American Studies 1, Albuquerque.

  1951 Yuman Indian agriculture: primitive subsistence on the lower Colorado and Gila rivers. University of
  New Mexico Press, Albuquerque.

Castetter, Edward F., and Ruth M. Underhill
  1935 Ethnobiological studies in the American Southwest II.   The ethnobiology of the Papago Indians.   University of New Mexico Bulletin, Biological Series 4(3), Albuquerque. Reprinted AMS, 1978.

Caywood, Louis R.
  1966 Excavations at Rainbow House, Bandelier National Monument, New Mexico. U.S. Park Service, Globe, Arizona.

Chang, K.C.
  1972 Settlement patterns in archaeology. Addison-Wesley Modular Publication 24.

Chauvet, Fr. Fidel de J. (editor)
  1947 Relación de la descripción de la Provincia del Santo Evangelio . . . por Fr. Pedro Oroz, Fr. Gerónimo
  de Mendieta, y Fr. Francisco Suárez.   Anales de la Provincia Franciscana del Santo Evangelio de México
  4(2).

Chavez, Angelico, O.F.M.
  1968 Coronado's friars. Monographs of the Academy of American Franciscan History (Vol. 8).   William Byrd
  Press, Richmond, Virginia.

Chavez, Angelico, O.F.M. (translator and editor)
  1972 The Oroz codex. Publications of the Academy of American Franciscan History, Documentary Series (Vol.
  10). William Byrd Press, Richmond, Virginia.

Colton, Harold S.
   1945   The Patayan problem in the Colorado River Valley.   Southwestern Journal of Anthropology 1(1):114-121.

Colton, Harold S., and Lyndon L. Hargrave
   1937   Handbook of northern Arizona pottery types.   Northern Arizona Society of Science and Art,   Flagstaff,
      Museum of Northern Arizona, Bulletin 11.

Correll, Donovan S.
   1962   The potato and its wild relatives.   Texas Research Foundation, Renner, Texas.

Cortés, Hernán
   1971   Letters from Mexico.   Translated and edited by A.R. Pagden.   Grossman Publishers, New York.

Crampton, C. Gregory
   1977   The Zunis of Cibola.   University of Utah Press, Salt Lake City.

Cuevas, Mariano
   1924   Historia de los   descubrimientos antiguos y modernos de la Nueva España,   escrita por el conquistador
      Baltasar de Obregón, año de 1584.   Departamento Editorial de la Sría. de Educación Pública, México.

Curtis, Edward S.
   1926   The North American Indian (Vol. 16).   Edited by F.W. Hodge.   Plimpton Press, Norwood, Mass.

   1930   The North American Indian (Vol. 19).   Edited by F.W. Hodge.   Plimpton Press, Norwood, Mass.

Cushing, Frank H.
   1883   Zuni fetiches.   In Second annual report of the Bureau of Ethnology, 1880-1881, pp. 9-43, Washington
      D.C.

Day, A. Grove
   1940a   Coronado's quest.   University of California Press, Berkeley.

   1940b   Mota Padilla on the Coronado expedition.   The Hispanic American Historical Review 20(1):88-110.

Di Peso, Charles C.
   1951   The Babocomari village site on the Babocomari River, southeastern Arizona.   Amerind Foundation Publi-
      cation 5, Dragoon, Arizona.

   1953   The Sobaipuri Indians of the upper San Pedro River Valley.   Amerind Foundation Publication 6, Dragoon,
      Arizona.

1956   The Upper Pima of San Cayetano de Tumacacari: an archaeohistorical reconstruction of the Ootam of Pimeria Alta. Amerind Foundation Publication 7, Dragoon, Arizona.

1968a   Casas Grandes, a fallen trading center of the Gran Chichimeca. The Masterkey 42(1):20-37.

1968b   Casas Grandes and the Gran Chichimeca. El Palacio 75(4):45-61.

1974   Casas Grandes: a fallen trading center of the Gran Chichimeca.   Vols. 1-3 contain the narrative description of the Casas Grandes project, paged consecutively.   Amerind Foundation Publication 9 and Northland Press, Dragoon and Flagstaff, Arizona.

1979   Prehistory: southern periphery. In Handbook of North American Indians (Vol. 9), edited by A. Ortiz, pp. 152-161. W. C. Sturtevant, series editor. Smithsonian Institution, Washington, D.C.

Di Peso, Charles C., John B. Rinaldo, and Gloria J. Fenner
   1974   Casas Grandes: a fallen trading center of the Gran Chichimeca (Vols. 4-8). Amerind Foundation Publication 9 and Northland Press, Dragoon and Flagstaff, Arizona.

Dobyns, Henry F.
   1963   Indian extinction in the middle Santa Cruz River Valley, Arizona.   New Mexico Historical Review 38(2):163-181.

   1966   Estimating aboriginal American population. Current Anthropology 7(4):395-416.

   1974   The Kohatk: oasis and Ak Chin horticulturalists. Ethnohistory 21(4):317-327.

   1976   Brief perspective on a scholarly transformation: widowing the "virgin" land.   Ethnohistory 23(2):95-104.

Doelle, William H.
   1976   Desert resources and Hohokam subsistence: the Conoco Florence project.   Arizona State Museum Archaeological Series 103, Tempe.

   1981   The Gila Pima in the late 17th century.   In The protohistoric period in the North American Southwest, A.D. 1450-1700, edited by D.R. Wilcox and W.B. Masse, pp. 57-70. Arizona State University Anthropological Research Papers 24, Tempe.

Domínguez, Francisco A.
   See Adams and Chavez 1956.

Doolittle, William E.

1979 La población serrana de Sonora en tiempos prehispanicos: la evidencia de los asentamientos antiguos. Memoria, IV Simposio de Historia de Sonora. Instituto de Investigaciones Historicas, Hermosillo, México, pp. 1-16.

1980 Aboriginal agricultural development in the valley of Sonora, Mexico. Geographical Review 70(3):328-342.

Douglas, Charles L.

1972 Analysis of faunal remains from Black Mesa: 1968-1970 excavations. In Archaeological Investigations on Black Mesa: the 1969-1970 seasons, edited by G. J. Gumerman, D. Westfall, and C. S. Weed, Appendix 3, pp. 225-238. Prescott College Studies in Anthropology 4, Prescott, Arizona.

Doyel, David E.

1976 Salado cultural development in the Tonto basin and Globe-Miami areas, central Arizona. The Kiva 42(1):5-16.

1977 Excavations in the middle Santa Cruz River Valley, southeastern Arizona. Arizona State Museum Contributions to Highway Salvage Archaeology in Arizona 44, Tempe.

Dozier, Edward P.

1954 The Hopi-Tewa of Arizona. University of California Publications in American Archaeology and Ethnology 44(3):259-376. Berkeley and Los Angeles.

DRH

1650 Documentos relativos a la historia de las provincias y misiones de las Indias Occidentales, P. Pastells, comp., c. 1650 Entrada de . . . Almendez Chirinos hasta el Río del Yaquimi. Est. 138, caj. 5, leg. 23, tomo 40, pp. 510-514, AGI, from copy at Pius XII Library, St. Louis University.

Dunbier, Roger

1968 The Sonoran Desert. University of Arizona Press, Tucson.

Dutton, Bertha P.

1963a Friendly people: the Zuni Indians. Museum of New Mexico Press, Santa Fe.

1963b Sun father's way: the kiva murals of Kuaua. University of New Mexico Press, School of American Research, and Museum of New Mexico Press, Albuquerque and Santa Fe.

Earle, Timothy K.

1977 A reappraisal of redistribution: complex Hawaiian chiefdoms. In Exchange systems in prehistory, edited by T. K. Earle and J. E. Ericson, pp. 213-229. Academic Press, New York.

Ekholm, Gordon F.
1942 Excavations at Guasave, Sinaloa, Mexico. Anthropological Papers, The American Museum of Natural History 38(2):23-139.

Ellis, Florence Hawley
1974 The Hopi: their history and use of lands. Garland Publishing Company, New York.

1976 Datable ritual components proclaiming Mexican influence in the upper Rio Grande of New Mexico.   In Collected papers in honor of Marjorie Ferguson Lambert, edited by A. H. Schroeder. Papers of the Archaeological Society of New Mexico 3:85-108.

Ellis, Florence Hawley, and Laurens Hammack
1968 The inner sanctum of Feather Cave, a Mogollon sun and earth shrine linking Mexico and the Southwest. American Antiquity 33(1):25-44.

Ezell, Paul H.
1961 The Hispanic acculturation of the Gila River Pimas. American Anthropological Association, Memoir 90.

1963 Is there a Hohokam-Pima culture continuum? American Antiquity 29(1):61-66.

Farmer, Malcolm F.
1935 The Mojave trade route. The Masterkey 9(5):154-157.

1980 Dwarves and hunchback figures in the prehistoric cultures of southern North America.   Anthropological Journal of Canada 18(2):2-6.

Ferdon, Edwin N., Jr.
1955 A trial survey of Mexican-southwestern architectural parallels.   School of American Research, Monograph 21, Santa Fe.

Ferguson, T.J., William A. Dodge, and Barbara J. Mills
1977 Archaeological investigations at Kyaki:ma.   Zuni Indian Reservation, McKinley County, New Mexico. Zuni Archaeological Enterprise, Pueblo of Zuni. National Park Service, Contract No. PX 7029-7-0586.

Fernández de Oviedo y Valdés, Gonzalo
See Oviedo y Valdés.

Fewkes, J. Walter
1896 Pacific Coast shells from prehistoric Tusayan pueblos. American Anthropologist 9(11):359-367.

Fontana, Bernard L.
1976 The faces and forces of Pimeria Alta. In Voices from the Southwest: a gathering in honor of Lawrence Clark Powell, pp. 45-54. Northland Press, Flagstaff.

Forbes, Jack D.

1960 Apache, Navajo, and Spaniard. University of Oklahoma Press, Norman.

1965 Warriors of the Colorado: the Yumans of the Quechan nation and their neighbors. University of Oklahoma Press, Norman.

Ford, Richard I.

1972 Barter, gift, or violence: an analysis of Tewa intertribal exchange. In Social exchange and interaction, edited by E.N. Wilmsen. University of Michigan Museum of Anthropology, Anthropological Papers 46:21-45.

Ford, Richard I., Albert H. Schroeder, and Stewart L. Peckham

1972 Three perspectives on Puebloan prehistory. In New perspectives on the Pueblos, edited by A. Ortiz, pp. 19-39. University of New Mexico Press, Albuquerque.

Forde, C. Daryll

1931 Ethnography of the Yuma Indians. University of California Publications in American Archaeology and Ethnology 28(4):83-278.

Frisbie, Theodore R.

1975 Hishi as money in the Puebloan Southwest. In Collected papers in honor of Florence Hawley Ellis, edited by T. R. Frisbie. Papers of the Archaeological Society of New Mexico 2:120-142.

1978 High status burials in the Greater Southwest: an interpretative synthesis. In Across the Chichimec Sea, edited by C. L. Riley and B. C. Hedrick, pp. 202-227. Southern Illinois University Press, Carbondale and Edwardsville.

1980 Social ranking in Chaco Canyon, New Mexico: a Mesoamerican reconstruction. In New frontiers in the archaeology and ethnohistory of the Greater Southwest, edited by C.L. Riley and B.C. Hedrick. Transactions of the Illinois State Academy of Science 72(4):60-69.

García Icazbalceta, Joaquín

1866 Colección de documentos para la historia de México (Vol. 2). 2 vols. Antigua Librería, Portal de Agustinos, México.

Garcilaso de la Vega

1951 The Florida of the Inca. Translated and edited by J.G. Varner and J.J Varner. University of Texas Press, Austin.

Gasser, Robert E.

1976 Hohokam subsistence: a 2000 year continuum in the indigenous exploitation of the lower Sonoran Desert. U.S.D.A. Forest Service, Southwestern Region, Archaeological Report 11, Albuquerque.

Gifford, E.W.
1931   The Kamia of Imperial Valley. *Bureau of American Ethnology, Bulletin* 97.

Gladwin, Winifred, and Harold S. Gladwin
1930   The western range of the Red-on-buff culture. *Medallion Papers* 5, Gila Pueblo, Globe, Arizona.

1934   A method for designation of cultures and their variations.   *Medallion Papers* 15, Gila Pueblo, Globe, Arizona.

Glass, John B.
1964   *Catálogo de la colección de códices.* Museo Nacional de Antropología, Instituto Nacional de Antropología e Historia, México.

Gómara, Francisco López de
1922   *Historia general de las Indias.* 2 vols. Calpe, Madrid.

Gonzaga, Fr. Franciscus
1587   De origine seraphicae religionis Franciscanae eiusque progressibus, de regularis observantiae institutione, forma administrationis ac legibus, admirabilique eius propagatione. Rome.

Goode, George B.
1903   *American fishes.* New edition completely revised and largely extended by T. Gill. L.C. Page, Boston.

Grinnell, Joseph
1914   An account of the mammals and birds of the lower Colorado Valley.   *University of California Publications in Zoology* 12(4):51-294.

Guitéras, Eusebio (translator)
1951   *Rudo ensayo: by an unknown Jesuit padre, 1763.* Originally published as vol. 2, no. 2 of the Records of the American Catholic Historical Society of Philadelphia, June 1894.   Republished by Arizona Silhouettes, Tucson. See also Pradeau and Rasmussen.

Gumerman, George J.
1970   Black Mesa: survey and excavation in northeastern Arizona, 1968.   *Prescott College Studies in Anthropology* 2, Prescott, Arizona.

Gumerman, George J., and Emil W. Haury
1979   Prehistory: Hohokam. In *Handbook of North American Indians* (Vol. 9), edited by A. Ortiz, pp. 75-90. W. C. Sturtevant, series editor. Smithsonian Institution, Washington, D.C.

Gumerman, George J., and Patricia M. Spoerl
1980   The Hohokam and the northern periphery. In Current Issues in Hohokam prehistory: proceedings of a symposium, edited by D. Doyel and F. Plog, pp. 134-150. *Arizona State University Anthropological Research Papers* 23, Tempe.

Gunnerson, Dolores A.

1974 The Jicarilla Apaches: a study in survival. Northern Illinois University Press, DeKalb.

Hack, John T.

1942 The changing physical environment of the Hopi Indians of Arizona. In Reports of the Awatovi expedition, Peabody Museum, Harvard University, Report 1. Papers of the Peabody Museum of American Archaeology and Ethnology 35(1). Cambridge, Massachusetts.

Hackett, Charles W.

1915 The location of the Tigua pueblos of Alameda, Puaray, and Sandia in 1680-81. Old Santa Fe 2(4):381-391.

Hackett, Charles W. (editor)

1923-1937 Historical documents relating to New Mexico, Nueva Vizcaya, and approaches thereto, to 1773. Collected by A. F. Bandelier and F. R. Bandelier. Carnegie Institution of Washington Publications 330; Monograph Series (Vols. 1-3).

Hallenbeck, Cleve

1940 Álvar Núñez Cabeza de Vaca: the journey and route of the first European to cross the continent of North America, 1534-1536. Arthur H. Clark, Glendale, California.

Hammond, George P., and Agapito Rey (translators, editors, and annotators)

1928 Obregón's history of 16th century explorations in western America . . . 1584. Wetzel, Los Angeles.

Hammond, George P., and Agapito Rey (editors)

1940 Narratives of the Coronado expedition, 1540-1542. Coronado Cuarto Centennial Publications, 1540-1940 (Vol. 2). University of New Mexico Press, Albuquerque.

1953 Don Juan de Oñate, colonizer of New Mexico, 1595-1628. 2 vols. Coronado Cuarto Centennial Publications, 1540-1940 (Vol. 5). University of New Mexico Press, Albuquerque.

1966 The rediscovery of New Mexico, 1580-1594. Coronado Cuarto Centennial Publications, 1540-1940 (Vol. 3). University of New Mexico Press, Albuquerque.

Hanson, Jeffery R.

1980 The destruction of Awatovi re-examined through Hopi culture history. The Journal of Anthropology 2(1):1-21.

Hardy, R.W.H., Lt., R.N.

1829 Travels in the interior of Mexico in 1825, 1826, 1827, and 1828. Henry Colburn and Richard Bentley, London.

Hargrave, Lyndon L.
1938 Results of a study of the Cohonina branch of the Patayan culture in 1938.   Museum Notes 11(6):43-49. Museum of Northern Arizona, Flagstaff.

1970 Mexican macaws: comparative osteology and survey of remains from the Southwest.   Anthropological Papers of the University of Arizona 20. University of Arizona Press, Tucson.

Harrington, John P.
1911 The ethnography of the Tewa Indians.   In Twenty-ninth annual report of the Bureau of American Ethnology, 1907-1908, Washington, D.C.

Haury, Emil W.
1945 The excavation of Los Muertos and neighboring ruins in the Salt River Valley,   southern Arizona. Papers of the Peabody Museum of American Archaeology and Ethnology 24 (1). Harvard University, Cambridge, Massachusetts.

1976 The Hohokam: desert farmers and craftsmen. University of Arizona Press, Tucson.

Havens, Y. Harmon, et al.
1973 Landscaping with native Arizona plants. Natural Vegetation Committee. Arizona Chapter, Soil Conservation Society of America. University of Arizona Press, Tucson.

Hawley [Ellis], Florence M.
1937 Kokopelli, of the prehistoric southwestern Pueblo pantheon. American Anthropologist 39(4):644-646.

Hayes, Alden C.
1974 The four churches of Pecos. University of New Mexico Press, Albuquerque.

Hayes, Alden C., Jon N. Young, and A. H. Warren
1981 Excavation of Mound 7, Gran Quivira National Monument, New Mexico.   National Park Service, Publications in Archaeology 16. Washington, D.C.

Hedrick, Basil C., and Carroll L. Riley (translators)
1974 The journey of the Vaca party. Research Records of the University Museum, University Museum Studies 2. Southern Illinois University, Carbondale.

1976 Documents ancillary to the Vaca journey. Research Records of the University Museum, University Museum Studies 5. Southern Illinois University, Carbondale.

Heiser, Charles B., Jr.
1951 The sunflower among the North American Indians.   Proceedings of the American Philosophical Society 95(4):432-448.

Helms, Mary W.
  1979 Ancient Panama: chiefs in search of power. University of Texas Press, Austin.

Henderson, Junius, and John P. Harrington
  1914 The ethnozoology of the Tewa Indians. Bureau of American Ethnology, Bulletin 56, Washington, D.C.

Herrera y Tordesillas, Antonio de
  1944 Historia general de los hechos de los castellanos, en las islas, y tierra - firme de el mar occeano.
        Editorial Guaranía, Asunción del Paraguay.

Hewes, Leslie
  1935 Huepac: an agricultural village of Sonora, Mexico. Economic Geography 11(3):284-292.

Hewett, Edgar L.
  1904 Studies on the extinct pueblo of Pecos. American Anthropologist 6(4):426-439.

Hibben, Frank C.
  1955 Excavations at Pottery Mound, New Mexico. American Antiquity 21(2):179-180.

  1960 Prehistoric paintings, Pottery Mound. Archaeology 13(4):267-275.

  1966 A possible pyramidal structure and other Mexican influences at Pottery Mound, New Mexico. American
        Antiquity 31(4):522-529.

Hill, James N.
  1970 Prehistoric social organization in the American Southwest: theory and method. In Reconstructing pre-
        historic Pueblo societies, edited by W. A. Longacre, pp. 11-58. University of New Mexico Press, Albuquer-
        que.

Hodge, Frederick W.
  1896 Pueblo Indian clans. American Anthropologist 9(10):345-352.

  1920 Hawikuh bonework. Indian notes and monographs. Museum of the American Indian, Heye Foundation,
        3(3):69-151.

  1924a Pottery of Hawikuh. Indian notes. Museum of the American Indian, Heye Foundation, 1(1):8-15.

Hodge, Frederick W.
  1924b Snake-pens at Hawikuh, New Mexico. Indian notes. Museum of the American Indian, Heye Foundation,
        1(3):111-119.

1937   History of Hawikuh, New Mexico: one of the so-called cities of Cíbola.   Frederick Webb Hodge Anniver-
sary Fund Publications (Vol. 1), Los Angeles.

Hodge, Frederick W. (editor)
1907   The narrative of Alvar Nuñez Cabeça de Vaca and the narrative of the expedition of Coronado,   by Pedro
de Castañeda.   In Spanish explorers in the southern United States, 1528-1543,   edited by F.W.   Hodge and
T.H. Lewis, pp. 1-126, 273-387. Charles Scribner's Sons, New York.

1907-1910   Handbook of American Indians north of Mexico.   2 vols.   Bureau of American Ethnology,   Bulletin
30, Washington, D.C.

Hodge, Frederick W., George P. Hammond, and Agapito Rey (editors)
See Benavides 1945.

Hoffmeister, Donald F., and Woodrow W. Goodpaster
1954   The mammals of the Huachuca Mountains,   southeastern Arizona.   Illinois Biological Monographs 24(1).
University of Illinois Press, Urbana.

Hofman, Jack L.
1978   An analysis of surface material from the Little Deer site,   34 Cu-10,   of western Oklahoma: a further
investigation of the Wheeler complex.   Bulletin of the Oklahoma Anthropological Society 27:1-109.

Holden, Jane
1955   A preliminary report on Arrowhead Ruin.   El Palacio 62(4):102-119.

Holmes, W.H.
1912   Report to the chief.   In Twenty-eighth annual report of the Bureau of American Ethnology,   1906-1907,
pp. 7-22. Washington, D.C.

Hooton, Earnest A.
1930   The Indians of Pecos pueblo: a study of their skeletal remains.   Phillips Academy and Yale University
Press, Andover, Massachusetts, and New Haven, Connecticut.

Housewright, Rex
1946   A turquoise bead necklace.   The Record, Publications of the Dallas Archaeological Society 5(2): title
page and 10.

Hrdlička, Aleš
1904   Notes on the Indians of Sonora, Mexico.   American Anthropologist 6(1):51-89.

Huckell, Bruce B.
1979   The Coronet Real project: archaeological investigations on the Luke Range, southwestern Arizona.   Contributions by J. C. Rose, M. G. Million, D. M. Fournier, B. L. Brandau, L. W. Huckell, C.   Bass.   Arizona
State Museum Archaeological Series 129.

Huckell, Lisa W., and Bruce B. Huckell

1979 Marine shell from AZ Y:8:3, the Lago Seco site. In The Coronet Real project, edited by B. B. Huckell, Appendix 3, pp. 151-166. Arizona State Museum Archaeological Series 129.

Huff, J. Wesley

1951 A Coronado episode. New Mexico Historical Review 26(2):119-127.

ICC

1544 Información contra Francisco Vásquez de Coronado, AGI Justicia legajo 1021, pieza 4. From transcription in Bancroft Library.

Ives, Ronald L.

1936 Melchior Díaz--the forgotten explorer. Notes and Comments, Hispanic American Historical Review 16(1):86-90.

1959 The grave of Melchior Díaz: a problem in historical sleuthing. The Kiva 25(2):31-40.

Ives, Ronald L. (translator and editor)

1939 Sedelmayr's relación of 1746. Bureau of American Ethnology, Bulletin 123, Anthropological Papers 9, pp. 97-117.

Jelinek, Arthur J.

1967 A prehistoric sequence in the middle Pecos Valley, New Mexico. University of Michigan Museum of Anthropology, Anthropological Papers 31, Ann Arbor.

Jennings, Francis

1971 Goals and functions of Puritan missions to the Indians. Ethnohistory 18(3):197-212.

Jernigan, E. Wesley

1978 Jewelry of the prehistoric Southwest. School of American Research Southwest Indian Arts Series, University of New Mexico Press, Albuquerque.

Johnson, Alfred E.

1963 The Trincheras culture of northern Sonora. American Antiquity 29(2):174-186.

1965 The development of western Pueblo culture. Unpublished Ph.D. dissertation, Department of Anthropology, University of Arizona, Tucson.

Johnson, Jean B.

1971 The Opata: an inland tribe of Sonora. In The north Mexican frontier, edited by B.C. Hedrick, J.C. Kelley, and C.L. Riley, pp. 169-199. Southern Illinois University Press, Carbondale and Edwardsville.

Johnson, Ross B.

1969 Pecos National Monument, New Mexico: its geologic setting. Contributions to General Geology, Geological Survey Bulletin 1271-E, United States Department of the Interior, Washington, D.C.

Jones, Volney H.

1936 A summary of data on aboriginal cotton in the Southwest. In Symposium on prehistoric agriculture, pp. 51-64. University of New Mexico Bulletin, whole number 296, Anthropological Series 1(5).

Kearney, Thomas H., Robert H. Peebles, and collaborators

1960 Arizona flora. Second edition, with supplement by J. T. Howell, E. McClintock, and collaborators. University of California Press, Berkeley and Los Angeles.

Kelley, J. Charles

1966 Mesoamerica and the southwestern United States. In Handbook of Middle American Indians (Vol. 4), edited by G.F. Ekholm and G.R. Willey, pp. 95-110. University of Texas Press, Austin.

1971 Archaeology of the northern frontier: Zacatecas and Durango. In Handbook of Middle American Indians (Vol. 11), edited by G.F. Ekholm and I. Bernal, pp. 768-801. University of Texas Press, Austin.

Kelley, J. Charles, and Ellen Abbott Kelley

1975 An alternative hypothesis for the explanation of Anasazi culture history. In Collected papers in honor of Florence Hawley Ellis, edited by T. R. Frisbie. Papers of the Archaeological Society of New Mexico 2:178-223.

Kelly, William H.

1977 Cocopa ethnography. Anthropological Papers of the University of Arizona 29. University of Arizona Press, Tucson.

Kent, Kate Peck

1957 The cultivation and weaving of cotton in the prehistoric southwestern United States. Proceedings of the American Philosophical Society 47(part 3):457-732.

Kessell, John L.

1979 Kiva, cross, and crown: the Pecos Indians and New Mexico 1540-1840. National Park Service, United States Department of the Interior, Washington, D.C.

Kidder, Alfred V.

1924 An introduction to the study of southwestern archaeology with a preliminary account of the excavations at Pecos. Published for Phillips Academy by Yale University Press, New Haven, Connecticut.

1931 The pottery of Pecos (Vol. 1). Phillips Academy, Andover, Massachusetts.

1932   The artifacts of Pecos.   Phillips Academy and Yale University Press, Andover, Massachusetts,   and New Haven, Connecticut.

1958   Pecos, New Mexico: archaeological notes.   Papers of the Robert S. Peabody Foundation for Archaeology (Vol. 5).   Andover, Massachusetts.

Kidder, Alfred V., and Anna O. Shepard
  1936   The pottery of Pecos (Vol. 2).   Phillips Academy and Yale University Press, Andover,   Massachusetts, and New Haven, Connecticut.

Kino, Eusebio F., S.J.
  See Bolton 1948 and Burrus 1971

Kniffen, Fred B.
  1931   Lower California studies III: the primitive cultural landscape of the Colorado Delta.   University of California Publications in Geography 5(2):43-66.

  1932   Lower California studies IV: the natural landscape of the Colorado delta.   University of California Publications in Geography 5(4):149-244.

Koster, William J.
  1957   Guide to the fishes of New Mexico.   University of New Mexico Press in cooperation with the New Mexico Department of Game and Fish, Albuquerque.

Krieger, Alex D.
  1946   Culture complexes and chronology in northern Texas.   University of Texas Publication 4640.   University of Texas Press, Austin.

Kroeber, Alfred L.
  1925   Handbook of the Indians of California.   Bureau of American Ethnology, Bulletin 78.   Republished 1976, Dover Publications.

  1928   Native culture of the Southwest.   University of California Publications in American Archaeology and Ethnology 23(9):375-398.

Lambert, Marjorie F.
  1954   Paa-ko, archaeological chronicle of an Indian village in north central New Mexico.   Monographs of the School of American Research 19, parts 1-5.   Santa Fe.

Lange, Charles H.
  1959   Cochiti: a New Mexico pueblo, past and present.   University of Texas Press, Austin.

Lange, Charles H. (editor)
1968   The Cochiti Dam archaeological salvage project, part 1: report on the 1963 season. Museum of New Mexico, Research Records 6. Museum of New Mexico Press, Santa Fe.

Lange, Charles H., and Carroll L. Riley (editors)
1966   The southwestern journals of Adolph F. Bandelier: 1880-1882. The University of New Mexico Press, The
School of American Research, and the Museum of New Mexico Press, Albuquerque and Santa Fe.

1970   The southwestern journals of Adolph F. Bandelier: 1883-1884. University of New Mexico Press, Albuquerque.

Las Casas, Fr. Bartolomé de
1967   Apologética historia sumaria. 2 vols. Edited by E. O'Gorman. Universidad Nacional Autónoma de México, Instituto de Investigaciones Históricas, México.

Lawrence, Barbara
1951   Mammals found at the Awatovi site. Papers of the Peabody Museum of American Archaeology and Ethnology
35(3), part 1. Harvard University, Cambridge, Massachusetts.

Lawton, Sherman P.
1968   The Duncan-Wilson bluff shelter: a stratified site of the southern Plains. Bulletin of the Oklahoma
Anthropological Society 16:1-94.

LeBlanc, Steven A.
1976   Mimbres archeological center: preliminary report of the second season of excavation 1975. Journal of
New World Archaeology 1(6):1-23.

1977   The 1976 field season of the Mimbres Foundation in southwestern New Mexico. Journal of New World
Archaeology 2(2):1-24.

LeBlanc, Steven A., and Ben A. Nelson
1976   The Salado in southwestern New Mexico. The Kiva 42(1):71-79.

Lewis, Theodore H.
1907   The narrative of the expedition of Hernando de Soto by the Gentleman of Elvas.   In Spanish explorers
in the southern United States, 1528-1543, edited by F.W. Hodge and T.H. Lewis, pp. 127-272.   Charles
Scribner's Sons, New York.

Lipe, William D.
1978   The Southwest. In Ancient Native Americans, edited by J. D. Jennings, pp. 327-401. W.H. Freeman, San
Francisco.

Lister, Robert H.
  1978 Mesoamerican influence at Chaco Canyon, New Mexico. In Across the Chichimec Sea, edited by C. L.
  Riley and B.C. Hedrick, pp. 233-241. Southern Illinois University Press, Carbondale and Edwardsville.

Lombardo, Natal
  1702 Arte de la lengua Teguima. Bancroft Library copy no. 1506013.

Longacre, William A.
  1970 A historical review. In Reconstructing prehistoric Pueblo societies, edited by W.A. Longacre, pp.
  1-10. University of New Mexico Press, Albuquerque.

Lopez, David R.
  1973 The Wybark site. Bulletin of the Oklahoma Anthropological Society 22:11-126.

López de Gómara, Francisco
  See Gómara, Francisco López de

López de Velasco, Juan
  1971 Geografía y descripción universal de las Indias. Edición de Don Marcos Jiménez de la Espada. Biblioteca de Autores Españoles (Tomo 248). Ediciones Atlas, Madrid.

Lorenzana y Butrón, Francisco Antonio, arzobispo de México
  1770 Historia de Nueva España escrita por su esclarecido conquistador Hernán Cortés. Aumentada con otros
  documentos y notas. Impr. del superior gobierno, J.A. de Hogal, México.

Lumholtz, Carl
  1902 Unknown Mexico. 2 vols. Charles Scribner's Sons, New York. Reprinted 1973 by Rio Grande Press, Glorieta, New Mexico.

Mackey, James
  1977 A multivariate, osteological approach to Towa culture history. American Journal of Physical Anthropology 46(3):477-482.

Martin, Paul S., and John B. Rinaldo
  1950 Turkey Foot Ridge site: a Mogollon Village, Pine Lawn Valley, western New Mexico. Fieldiana:
  Anthropology 38(2). Chicago Natural History Museum.

  1960a Excavations in the upper Little Colorado drainage, eastern Arizona. Fieldiana: Anthropology 51(1).
  Chicago Natural History Museum.

  1960b Table Rock pueblo, Arizona. Fieldiana: Anthropology 51(2). Chicago Natural History Museum.

Martin, Paul S., William A. Longacre, and James N. Hill
  1967 Chapters in the prehistory of eastern Arizona, III. Fieldiana: Anthropology 57. Field Museum of Natural History.

Martin, Paul S., et al.
  1962 Chapters in the prehistory of eastern Arizona, I. Fieldiana: Anthropology 53. Chicago Natural History Museum.

Martin, Paul S., et al.
  1964 Chapters in the prehistory of eastern Arizona, II. Fieldiana: Anthropology 55. Chicago Natural History Museum.

Masse, W. Bruce
  1975 The Peppersauce Wash Project: excavations at three multicomponent sites in the lower San Pedro Valley, Arizona. MS. in author's possession.

  1980 Excavations at Gu Achi: a reappraisal of Hohokam settlement and subsistence in the Arizona Papagueria. Western Archeological Center, Publications in Anthropology 12. National Park Service, Tucson.

  1981 A reappraisal of the protohistoric Sobaipuri Indians of southeastern Arizona. In The Protohistoric period in the North American Southwest, A.D. 1450-1700, edited by D.R. Wilcox and W.B. Masse, pp. 28-56. Arizona State University Anthropological Research Papers 24, Tempe.

  1982 Hohokam ceramic art: regionalism and the imprint of societal change. In The development of southwestern ceramic patterns: a comparative review, edited by A. Schroeder. The Arizona Archaeological Society, Phoenix. In press.

McDougall, W.B.
  1973 Seed plants of northern Arizona. Museum of Northern Arizona, Flagstaff.

McGimsey, Charles R., III
  1980 Mariana Mesa: seven prehistoric settlements in west-central New Mexico. Papers of the Peabody Museum of Archaeology and Ethnology 72. Harvard University, Cambridge, Massachussetts.

McGregor, John C.
  1943 Burial of an early American magician. Proceedings of the American Philosophical Society 86(2):270-298.

Mecham, J. Lloyd
  1926 The second Spanish expedition to New Mexico. New Mexico Historical Review 1(3):265-291.

Mendieta, Gerónimo de, O.F.M.
  1945 Historia eclesiástica indiana. 4 vols. Edited by S. Chávez Hayhoe. México. Reprint of Mendieta, 1870.

Mendoza, Antonio
  1542 Carta Mendoza al Rey, 10 de Marzo.   Biblioteca de Autores Españoles, Cartas de Indias (Tomo 1, Vol. 264). Ediciones Atlas, Madrid, 1974.

Mera, Harry P.
  1939 Style trends of Pueblo pottery. Memoirs of the Laboratory of Anthropology (Vol. 3). Santa Fe.

Merriam, C. Hart
  1890 Results of a biological survey of the San Francisco mountain region and desert of the Little Colorado, Arizona. U. S. Department of Agriculture, Division of Ornithology and Mammalogy, North American Fauna 3.

Miksicek, Charles H.
  1979 From parking lots to museum basements: the archaeobotany of the St. Mary's site. The Kiva 45(1-2):131-140.

Miller, Jay
  1975 Kokopelli. In Collected papers in honor of Florence Hawley Ellis, edited by T. R. Frisbie. Papers of the Archaeological Society of New Mexico 2:371-380.

Miller, Joseph, and Henry G. Alsberg (editors)
  1956 Arizona the Grand Canyon State: a state guide. Hastings House, New York.

Montgomery, Arthur
  1963 The source of the fibrolite axes. El Palacio 70(1-2):34-48.

Montgomery, Ross G., Watson Smith, and John O. Brew
  1949 Franciscan Awatovi: report no. 3 of the Awatovi expedition. Papers of the Peabody Museum of American Archaeology and Ethnology Harvard University (Vol. 36). Cambridge, Massachusetts.

Montoya, Joan de
  1602 Relación del descrubimiento del Nuovo Mexico. Bartholame Bonfadino, Roma.

Moore, Bruce M.
  1979 Pueblo isolated small structure sites. Unpublished Ph.D. dissertation, Department of Anthropology, Southern Illinois University, Carbondale.

Morris, Earl H.
  1919 The Aztec ruin. Anthropological Papers of the American Museum of Natural History 26(1):1-108.

Mota Padilla, Matías de
  See Day 1940b.

Motolinía, Toribio (Fr. Toribio de Benavente)
  1541 Historia de los indios de la Nueva España. Barcelona.

Nabhan, Gary P.
  1978 Chiltepines: wild spice of the American Southwest. El Palacio 84(2):30-34.

Navarro García, Luis
  1967 Sonora y Sinaloa en el siglo XVII. Publicaciones de la Escuela de Estudios Hispano-Americanos de Sev-
        illa 176. Sevilla.

Nelson, Nels C.
  1914 Pueblo ruins of the Galisteo basin, New Mexico. Anthropological Papers of the American Museum of Nat-
        ural History 15, Part 1.

  1916 Chronology of the Tano ruins, New Mexico. American Anthropologist 18(2):159-180.

  1917 Archaeology of the Tano district, New Mexico. Proceedings of the 19th International Congress of Amer-
        icanists, pp. 114-118. Washington, D.C.

Nentvig, Juan
  1971 Descripción geográfica de Sonora. Edición preparada . . . por Germán Viveros, segunda serie, numero
        1. Publicaciones del Archivo General de la Nación, México.

Northrop, Stuart A.
  1959 Minerals of New Mexico. Revised edition. University of New Mexico Press, Albuquerque.

  1973 Turquoise. El Palacio 79(1):3-22.

Obregón, Baltasar de
  See Cuevas 1924 and Hammond and Rey 1928.

Olsen, Stanley J.
  1960 Post-cranial skeletal characters of Bison and Bos. Papers of the Peabody Museum of Archaeology and
        Ethnology, Harvard University 35(4). Cambridge, Massachusetts.

  1978 Bones from Awatovi, northeastern Arizona, no. 1, the faunal analysis: report no. 11 of the Awatovi
        expedition. Papers of the Peabody Museum of Archaeology and Ethnology, Harvard University 70(1):1-34.
        Cambridge, Massachusetts.

Olsen, Stanley J., and John W. Olsen
  1974 The macaws of Grasshopper Ruin. The Kiva 40(1-2):67-70.

Oviedo y Valdés, Gonzalo Fernández de
  1959 Historia general y natural de las Indias. 5 vols. Biblioteca de Autores Españoles. Vols. 67-71,
      Ediciones Atlas, Madrid. See also Hedrick and Riley 1974.

Pacheco, Joaquín F., and Francisco de Cárdenas (editors)
  1864-1884 Colección de documentos inéditos relativos al descubrimiento, conquista y colonización de las
      posesiones españoles en América y Oceania. 42 vols. Madrid.

Pailes, Richard A.
  1972 An archaeological reconnaissance of southern Sonora and reconsideration of the Rio Sonora culture.
      Unpublished Ph.D. dissertation, Department of Anthropology, Southern Illinois University, Carbondale.

  1976 Relaciones culturales prehistóricas en el noreste de Sonora. In Sonora: antropología del desierto,
      edited by B. Braniff and R. Felger, pp. 213-228. Colección Científica 27. Instituto Nacional de Antropo-
      logía e Historia, México.

  1978 The Rio Sonora culture in prehistoric trade systems. In Across the Chichimec Sea, edited by C. L.
      Riley and B. C. Hedrick, pp. 134-143. Southern Illinois University Press, Carbondale and Edwardsville.

  1980 The upper Rio Sonora Valley in prehistoric trade. In New frontiers in the archaeology and ethnology
      of the Greater Southwest, edited by C.L. Riley and B.C. Hedrick. Transactions of the Illinois State Acad-
      emy of Science 72(4):20-39.

Pailes, Richard A., and Joseph W. Whitecotton
  1979 The Greater Southwest and mesoamerican 'world' systems: an explanatory model of frontier relation-
      ships. In The frontier: comparative studies (Vol. 2), edited by W. Savage and S. Thompson, pp. 105-21.
      University of Oklahoma Press, Norman.

Parsons, Elsie Clews
  1939 Pueblo Indian religion. 2 vols. The University of Chicago Press.

  1974 Some Aztec and Pueblo parallels. In The mesoamerican Southwest, edited by B. C. Hedrick, J. C. Kel-
      ley, and C. L. Riley, pp. 131-146. Southern Illinois University Press, Carbondale and Edwardsville.
      First published in 1933.

Peabody, Charles
  1904 Explorations of mounds, Coahoma County, Mississippi. Papers of the Peabody Museum of American Archae-
      ology and Ethnology 3(2). Harvard University Press, Cambridge, Massachusetts.

Pearce, T.M. (editor)
  1965 New Mexico place names. University of New Mexico Press, Albuquerque.

Pennington, Campbell W.

1963   The Tarahumar of Mexico: their environment and material culture.   University of Utah Press, Salt Lake City.

1969   The Tepehuan of Chihuahua: their material culture.   University of Utah Press, Salt Lake City.

1980   The Pima Bajo of central Sonora, Mexico, volume 1:   the material culture.   University of Utah Press, Salt Lake City.

Pennington, Campbell W. (editor)

1979   The Pima Bajo of central Sonora, Mexico,   volume 2:   vocabulario en la lingua Névome.   University of Utah Press, Salt Lake City.

Pérez de Ribas, Andrés, S.J.

1944   Historia de los triunfos de Nuestra Santa Fe.   Editorial Layac, Mexico, D.F., pp. 77-346.   Originally published in 1645.

Pfefferkorn, Ignaz

See Treutlein 1949.

Polzer, Charles

1972   The evolution of the Jesuit mission system in northwestern New Spain, 1600-1767.   Unpublished Ph.D. dissertation, Department of History, University of Arizona, Tucson.

Polzer, Charles W., Thomas C. Barnes, and Thomas H. Naylor (editors)

1977   The documentary relations of the Southwest: Project manual.   Arizona State Museum, University of Arizona, Tucson.

Pradeau, Alberto F., and Robert R. Rasmussen (translators and annotators)

1980   Rudo ensayo: a description of Sonora and Arizona in 1764.   Written by Juan Nentvig, S.J.   University of Arizona Press, Tucson.   See also Guitéras.

PSM

1541- Punctos Sacados nos. 3 and 4, vol. 25, Misiones, Archivo General de la Nación, México.   Testimony of Martin Pérez and Antonio Ruíz.   Taken from Sauer 1932 appendix of unpublished documents.

Ramusio, Giovanni Battista

1556   Delle navigationi et viaggi . . . volume terzo.   In Venetia appressi i Guinti.

Reed, Erik K.

1943   The southern Tewa pueblos in the historic period.   El Palacio 50(11):254-264; 50(12):276-288.

1950 Eastern-central Arizona archaeology in relation to the western Pueblos. Southwestern Journal of Anthropology 6(2):120-138.

1958 Review of Charles C. Di Peso, the Upper Pima of San Cayetano del Tumacacori. American Antiquity 23(3):316-317.

Reiter, Paul
1938 The Jemez pueblo of Unshagi, New Mexico. University of New Mexico, Bulletin 326.

Reyman, Jonathan E.
1978 Pochteca burials at Anasazi sites? In Across the Chichimec Sea, edited by C. L. Riley and B.C. Hedrick, pp. 242-259. Southern Illinois University Press, Carbondale and Edwardsville.

1980 The predictive dimension of priestly power. In New frontiers in the archaeology and ethnohistory of the Greater Southwest, edited by C.L. Riley and B.C. Hedrick. Transactions of the Illinois State Academy of Science 72(4):40-59. With a note on solar and lunar cycles by Harold J. Born (p. 55).

Riley, Carroll L.
1963 Color-direction symbolism: an example of Mexican-southwestern contacts. América Indígena 23(1):49-60.

1971 Early Spanish-Indian communication in the Greater Southwest. New Mexico Historical Review 46(4):285-314.

1972 Blacks in the early Southwest. Ethnohistory 19(3):247-260.

1973 Las Casas and the Benavides Memorial of 1630. New Mexico Historical Review 48(3):209-222.

1974 Mesoamerican Indians in the early Southwest. Ethnohistory 21(1):25-36.

1975a Pueblo Indians in Mesoamerica: the early historic period. In Collected papers in honor of Florence Hawley Ellis, edited by T.R. Frisbie. Papers of the Archaeological Society of New Mexico 2:454-462.

1975b The road to Hawikuh: trade and trade routes to Cibola-Zuni during late prehistoric and early historic times. The Kiva 41(2):137-159.

1976a Las Casas and the golden cities. Ethnohistory 23(1):19-30.

1976b Sixteenth century trade in the Greater Southwest. Mesoamerican Studies 10, Research Records of the University Museum. Southern Illinois University, Carbondale.

1978a Pecos and trade. In Across the Chichimec Sea, edited by C. L. Riley and B. C. Hedrick, pp. 53-64. Southern Illinois University Press, Carbondale and Edwardsville.

1978b Retrospect and prospect. In Across the Chichimec Sea, edited by C. L. Riley and B. C. Hedrick, pp. 3-8. Southern Illinois University Press, Carbondale and Edwardsville.

1978c The Sonoran statelets in the sixteenth century. Paper presented at the twenty-sixth annual meeting, American Society for Ethnohistory, Austin, Texas, 1978.

1979 Casas Grandes and the Sonoran statelets. Paper presented at the Chicago Anthropological Society, 1979.

1980a Mesoamerica and the Hohokam: a view from the 16th century. In Current issues in Hohokam prehistory: proceedings of a symposium, edited by D. Doyel and F. Plog, pp. 41-48. Arizona State University Anthropological Research Papers 23, Tempe.

1980b Trade and contact in the prehistoric Southwest. In New frontiers in the archaeology and ethnohistory of the Greater Southwest, edited by C.L. Riley and B.C. Hedrick. Transactions of the Illinois State Academy of Science 72(4):13-19.

1981a Puaray and Coronado's Tiguex. In Collected papers in honor of Erik K. Reed, edited by A.H. Schroeder, pp. 197-213. Papers of the Archaeological Society of New Mexico 6.

1981b Sonora and Arizona in the protohistoric period: discussion of papers by Sheridan, Reff, Masse, and Doelle. In The protohistoric period in the North American Southwest, A.D. 1450-1700, edited by D. R. Wilcox and W. B. Masse, pp. 123-128. Arizona State University Anthropological Research Papers 24, Tempe.

Riley, Carroll L., and Basil C. Hedrick
  1976 La ubicación de Corazones. In Las fronteras de Mesoamerica (Vol. 1), pp. 243-248. Fourteenth Mesa Redonda, Tegucigalpa, Honduras. Sociedad Mexicana de Antropología, Impresos Rosete, México.

Riley, Carroll L., and Howard D. Winters
  1963 The prehistoric Tepehuan of northern Mexico. Southwestern Journal of Anthropology 19(2):177-185.

Robbins, Wilfred W., John P. Harrington, and Barbara Freire-Marreco
  1916 Ethnobotany of the Tewa Indians. Bureau of American Ethnology, Bulletin 55.

Roberts, Frank H.H., Jr.
  1931 The ruins at Kiatuthlanna, eastern Arizona. Bureau of American Ethnology, Bulletin 100.

  1932 The Village of the Great Kivas on the Zuñi Reservation, New Mexico. Bureau of American Ethnology, Bulletin 111.

Rogers, Malcolm J.
  1945 An outline of Yuman prehistory. Southwestern Journal of Anthropology 1(2):167-198.

Rosenthal, E. Jane, et al.
  1978 The Quijotoa Valley project. Cultural Resources Management Division, Western Archeological Center, National Park Service, Tucson.

Rouse, Irving
  1962 Southwestern archaeology today. In An introduction to the study of southwestern archaeology with a preliminary account of the excavations at Pecos, by Alfred V. Kidder, pp. 1-53. Yale University Press, New Haven, Connecticut.

RSC
  1546-1548 Relación sacada de la probanza . . . que trata con Dn García Ramirez de Cárdenas. AGI Justicia, legajo 1021, pieza 3. From transcription in Bancroft Library.

Ruby, Jay, and Thomas Blackburn
  1964 Occurrence of southwestern pottery in Los Angeles County, California. American Antiquity 30(2), part 1: 209-210.

Russell, Frank
  1975 The Pima Indians. Reedited with introduction, citation sources, and bibliography by B. L. Fontana. The University of Arizona Press, Tucson. Originally published in Twenty-sixth annual report of the Bureau of American Ethnology, 1904-1905.

Sauer, Carl O.
  1932 The road to Cibola. Ibero-Americana 3.

  1934 The distribution of aboriginal tribes and languages in northwestern Mexico. Ibero-Americana 5.

  1935 Aboriginal population of northwestern Mexico. Ibero-Americana 10.

Sauer, Carl O., and Donald D. Brand
  1931 Prehistoric settlements of Sonora, with special reference to Cerros de Trincheras. University of California Publications in Geography 5(3):67-148. University of California Press, Berkeley.

  1932 Aztatlán: prehistoric Mexican frontier on the Pacific Coast. Ibero-Americana 1.

Saxton, Dean, and Lucille Saxton (compilers)
  1969 Dictionary: Papago & Pima to English; English to Papago & Pima. The University of Arizona Press, Tucson.

Schaafsma, Polly, and Curtis F. Schaafsma

1974 Evidence for the origins of the Pueblo katchina cult as suggested by southwestern rock art. American Antiquity 39(4), part 1: 535-545.

Scholes, France V.

1930a The supply service of the New Mexican missions in the seventeenth century. New Mexico Historical Review 5(1):93-115.

1930b The supply service of the New Mexican missions in the seventeenth century, part II, 1631-1664. New Mexico Historical Review 5(2):186-210.

1930c The supply service of the New Mexican missions in the seventeenth century, part III, 1663-1680. New Mexico Historical Review 5(4):386-404.

1935a Civil government and society in New Mexico in the seventeenth century. New Mexico Historical Review 10(2):71-111.

1935b The first decade of the Inquisition in New Mexico. New Mexico Historical Review 10(3):195-241.

1936-1937 Church and State in New Mexico, 1610-1650. New Mexico Historical Review 11(1):9-76; 11(2):145-178; 11(3):283-294; 11(4):297-349; 12(1):78-106.

1937 Troublous times in New Mexico, 1659-1670. New Mexico Historical Review 12(2):134-174.

1949 Mission chronology. Manuscript distributed by Dr. F.V. Scholes for use of students, University of New Mexico, Albuquerque.

Scholes, France V., and Lansing B. Bloom

1944-1945 Friar personnel and mission chronology, 1598-1629. New Mexico Historical Review 19(4):319-336; 20(1):58-82.

Schroeder, Albert H.

1955-1956 Fray Marcos de Niza, Coronado and the Yavapai. New Mexico Historical Review 30(4):265-296; 31(1):24-37.

1957 The Hakataya cultural tradition. American Antiquity 23(2):176-178.

1960 The Hohokam, Sinagua, and Hakataya. Archives of Archaeology 5. Society for American Archaeology.

1964 The language of the Saline Pueblos: Piro or Tiwa? New Mexico Historical Review 39(3):235-249.

1968 Birds and feathers in documents relating to Indians of the Southwest. In Collected papers in honor of Lyndon Lane Hargrave, edited by A. H. Schroeder, pp. 95-114. Papers of the Archaeological Society of New Mexico 1.

1972 Rio Grande ethnohistory. In New perspectives on the Pueblos, edited by A. Ortiz, pp. 41-70. School of American Research and University of New Mexico Press, Santa Fe and Albuquerque.

1974 A study of Yavapai history. In Yavapai Indians, pp. 23-127. Garland Publishing Co., New York.

1977 Of men and volcanoes: the Sinagua of northern Arizona. Southwest Parks and Monuments Association, Globe, Arizona.

1979a History of archeological research. In Handbook of North American Indians (Vol. 9), edited by A. Ortiz, pp. 5-13. W. C. Sturtevant, series editor. Smithsonian Institution, Washington, D.C.

1979b Pecos pueblo. In Handbook of North American Indians (Vol. 9), edited by A. Ortiz, pp. 430-437. W. C. Sturtevant, series editor. Smithsonian Institution, Washington, D.C.

1979c Prehistory: Hakataya. In Handbook of North American Indians (Vol. 9), edited by A. Ortiz, pp. 100-107. W. C. Sturtevant, series editor. Smithsonian Institution, Washington, D.C.

1979d Pueblos abandoned in historic times. In Handbook of North American Indians (Vol. 9), edited by A. Ortiz, pp.236-254. William C. Sturtevant, series editor. Smithsonian Institution, Washington, D.C.

Schroeder, Albert H., and Dan S. Matson
  1965 A colony on the move: Gaspar Castaño de Sosa's journal: 1590-1591. School of American Research, Santa Fe.

Sedelmayr, Jocobo
  See Ives 1939

Sellers, William D., and Richard H. Hill (editors)
  1974 Arizona climate 1931-1972. Revised second edition. The University of Arizona Press, Tucson.

Service, Elman R.
  1962 Primitive social organization: an evolutionary perspective. Random House, New York.

Sharrock, Floyd W.
  1959a Preliminary report on the Van Schuyver site. Bulletin of the Oklahoma Anthropological Society 7:33-40.

1959b Test excavations at the Willingham site, M1-5, McClain County, Oklahoma. Bulletin of the Oklahoma Anthropological Society 7:41-50.

Shea, John G.
   1882 The expedition of Don Diego Dionisio de Peñalosa . . . as described by Father Nicholas de Freytas, O.S.F. Includes the Spanish text. Privately printed, New York. Republished 1964, Horn and Wallace, Albuquerque.

Shreve, Forrest
   1934 Vegetation of the northwestern coast of Mexico. Bulletin of the Torrey Botanical Club 61:373-380.

Shreve, Forrest, and Ira L. Wiggins
   1964 Vegetation and flora of the Sonoran Desert. 2 vols. Stanford University Press, Palo Alto.

Sigleo, Anne M. Colberg
   1970 Trace-element geochemistry of southwestern turquoise. Unpublished M.A. thesis, University of New Mexico, Albuquerque.

Smith, Buckingham
   1861 Grammatical sketch of the Heve language, translated from an unpublished Spanish manuscript. Cramoisy, New York. Reprinted 1970, Shea's Library of American Linguistics, AMS Press, New York.

Smith, Watson
   1952 Kiva mural decorations at Awatovi and Kawaika-a, with a survey of other wall paintings in the Pueblo southwest: report no. 5 of the Awatovi expedition. Papers of the Peabody Museum of Archaeology and Ethnology, Harvard University (Vol. 37). Cambridge, Massachusetts.

   1971 Painted ceramics of the western mound at Awatovi: report no. 8 of the Awatovi expedition. Papers of the Peabody Museum of Archaeology and Ethnology, Harvard University (Vol. 38). Cambridge, Massachusetts.

Smith, Watson, Richard B. Woodbury, and Nathalie F.S. Woodbury
   1966 The excavation of Hawikuh by Frederick Webb Hodge: report of the Hendricks-Hodge expedition, 1917-1923. Museum of the American Indian, Heye Foundation, Contributions 20.

Snow, David H.
   1973 Prehistoric southwestern turquoise industry. El Palacio 79(1):33-51.

   1975 The identification of Puaray pueblo. In Collected papers in honor of Florence Hawley Ellis, edited by T.R. Frisbie. Papers of the Archaeological Society of New Mexico 2:463-480.

Spicer, Edward H.
   1962 Cycles of conquest. University of Arizona Press, Tucson.

Spier, Leslie
   1917 An outline for a chronology of Zuñi ruins.   Anthropological Papers of the American Museum of Natural History, 18 (part 3):207-331.

   1924 Zuni weaving techniques. American Anthropologist 26(1):64-85.

   1933 Yuman tribes of the Gila River. University of Chicago Press.

Spoerl, Patricia M.
   1979 Prehistoric cultural development and conflict in central Arizona.   Unpublished Ph.D. dissertation, Department of Anthropology, Southern Illinois University, Carbondale.

Stacy, V. K. Pheriba
   1974 Cerros de Trincheras in the Arizona Papagueria. Unpublished Ph.D. dissertation, Department of Anthropology, University of Arizona, Tucson.

Stebbins, Robert C.
   1954 Amphibians and reptiles of western North America. McGraw-Hill, New York.

Steck, Francis B., O.F.M.
   1943 A tentative guide to historical materials on the Spanish borderlands. The Catholic Historical Society of Philadelphia, Philadelphia.

Stevenson, Matilda Coxe
   1904 The Zuñi Indians: their mythology, esoteric fraternities, and ceremonies.   In Twenty-third annual report of the Bureau of American Ethnology, 1901-1902. Washington, D. C.

   1915 Ethnobotany of the Zuñi Indians.   In Thirtieth annual report of the Bureau of American Ethnology, 1908-1909. Washington, D.C.

Strong, William D.
   1973 An analysis of southwestern society. In The Classic Southwest, edited by B. C. Hedrick, J.C. Kelley, and C.L. Riley, pp. 110-152. Southern Illinois University Press, Carbondale and Edwardsville. First published in 1927.

Strout, Clevy L.
   1971 Flora and fauna mentioned in the journals of the Coronado expedition.   Great Plains Journal 11(1):5-40.

Stuart, L.C.
   1964 Fauna of Middle America.   In Handbook of Middle American Indians (Vol. 1), edited by R.C. West, pp. 316-362. R. Wauchope, series editor. University of Texas Press, Austin.

Stubbs, Stanley A., and W.S. Stallings, Jr.
1953 The excavation of Pindi pueblo, New Mexico. School of American Research and Laboratory of Anthropology, Monograph 18, Santa Fe.

Stubbs, Stanley A., Bruce T. Ellis, and Alfred E. Dittert
1957 The "lost" Pecos church. El Palacio 64(3-4):67-92.

Swanton, John R.
1942 Source material on the history and ethnology of the Caddo Indians. Bureau of American Ethnology, Bulletin 132.

1946 The Indians of the southeastern United States. Bureau of American Ethnology, Bulletin 137.

Sykes, Godfrey
1937 The Colorado Delta. American Geographical Society, Special Publication 19, W.L.G. Joerg, editor. Carnegie Institution and the American Geographical Society, Washington and New York.

Tamayo, Jorge L., in collaboration with Robert C. West
1964 The hydrography of Middle America. In Handbook of Middle American Indians (Vol. 1), edited by R.C. West, pp. 84-121. R. Wauchope, series editor. University of Texas Press, Austin.

Tello, Antonio, O.F.M.
1891 Libro segundo de la crónica miscelanea . . . . Imprenta de "La Republica Literaria," Guadalajara.

1942 Crónica miscelanea de la Sancta Provincia de Xalisco (Book 3). Edited, with an introduction, by J. Cornejo Franco. Guadalajara.

Tichy, Marjorie Ferguson [Lambert]
1939 The archaeology of Puaray. El Palacio 46(7):145-163.

Tidestrom, Ivar, and Sister Teresita Kittell
1941 A flora of Arizona and New Mexico. The Catholic University of America Press, Washington, D.C.

Tolstoy, Paul
1980 Review of The basin of Mexico by William T. Sanders, Jeffrey R. Parsons, and Robert S. Santley. American Scientist 68(3):312-313.

Torquemada, Fr. Juan de
1723 Monarquía Indiana. 3 vols. Nicolas Rodriguez Franco, Madrid.

Toulouse, Joseph H., Jr.
1949 The mission of San Gregorio de Abó. Monographs of the School of American Research 13, Santa Fe.

Toulouse, Joseph H., Jr., and Robert L. Stephenson
1960 Excavations at Pueblo Pardo. Museum of New Mexico Papers in Anthropology 2, Santa Fe.

Tower, Donald B.
1945 The use of marine mollusca and their value in reconstructing prehistoric trade routes in the American Southwest. Papers of the Excavators' Club 2(3), Cambridge, Massachusetts.

Treutlein, Theodore E. (translator and annotator)
1949 Sonora: a description of the province. Written by Ignaz Pfefferkorn. University of New Mexico Press, Albuquerque.

Turner, Christy G., II, and Nancy T. Morris
1970 A massacre at Hopi. American Antiquity 35(3):320-331.

Undreiner, George J.
1947 Fray Marcos de Niza and his journey to Cibola. The Americas 3(4):415-486.

Varner, John G., and Jeannette J. Varner
See Garcilaso de la Vega 1951

Vázquez de Espinosa, Antonio
1948 Compendio y descripción de las Indias Occidentales. Smithsonian Miscellaneous Collections 108, Washington, D. C.

Vetancurt, Agustín de, O.F.M.
1698 Teatro Mexicano: descripción breve de los sucesos exemplares, historicos, politicos, militares, y religiosos del nuevo mundo occidental de las Indias. 2 vols. México.

Villagrá, Gaspar Pérez de
1933 History of New Mexico. Translated by G. Espinosa. First published in 1610. Quivira Society, Los Angeles.

Vivian, Gordon
1932 A re-study of the province of Tiguex. Unpublished M.A. thesis, Department of Anthropology, University of New Mexico, Albuquerque.

Vivó Escoto, Jorge A.
1964 Weather and climate of Mexico and Central America. In Handbook of Middle American Indians (Vol. 1), edited by R.C. West, pp. 187-215. R. Wauchope, series editor. University of Texas Press, Austin.

Vogt, Evon Z., and Ethel M. Albert (editors)
1966 People of Rimrock: a study of values in five cultures. Harvard University Press, Cambridge, Massachusetts.

Wagner, Henry R.
  1937 The Spanish Southwest. 2 vols. The Quivira Society, Albuquerque.

Wagner, Philip L.
  1964 Natural vegetation of Middle America. In Handbook of Middle American Indians (Vol. 1), edited by R.C.
      West, pp. 216-264. R. Wauchope, series editor. University of Texas Press, Austin.

Wallerstein, Immanuel
  1974 The modern world system: capitalist agriculture and the origins of the European world-economy in the
      sixteenth century. Academic Press, New York.

Ward, Albert E.
  1972 The tree-ring dating of the Black Mesa project: 1968-1971. In Archaeological investigations on Black
      Mesa: the 1969-70 seasons, edited by G. J. Gumerman, D. Westfall, and C. S. Weed, Appendix 2, pp.
      211-223. Prescott College Studies in Anthropology 4, Prescott, Arizona.

Warren, A. Helene
  1969 Tonque. El Palacio 76(2):36-42.

  1974 An archaeological survey of the Occidental Minerals Corporation proposed mining project area in the
      Cerrillos district, Santa Fe County, New Mexico. Conducted for the Rocky Mt. Center for the Environment.
      Manuscript on file, Laboratory of Anthropology, Santa Fe.

Wedel, Waldo R.
  1959 An introduction to Kansas archeology. Bureau of American Ethnology, Bulletin 174.

Weigand, Phil C.
  1976 Rio Grande glaze sherds in western Mexico. Pottery Southwest 4(1):3-5.

  1978 La prehistoria del estado de Zacatecas: una interpretación. In Zacatecas: anuario de historia (Vol.
      1), pp. 203-248. Departamento de Investigaciones Históricas, Universidad Autónoma de Zacatecas, México.

  1980 Mining and mineral trade in prehispanic Zacatecas. In Zacatecas: anuario de historia (Vol. 3),
      edited by C. Esparza Sanchez. Departamento de Investigaciones Históricas, Universidad Autónoma de Zacate-
      cas, México.

Wendorf, Fred, et al.
  1953 Salvage archaeology in the Chama Valley, New Mexico. Monographs of the School of American Research
      17, Santa Fe.

Wernstedt, Frederick L.
  1972 World climatic data. Climatic Data Press, Lemont, Pennsylvania.

Whipple, A.W.
   1856   Report of explorations for a railway route near the thirty-fifth parallel of north latitude, from the Mississippi River to the Pacific Ocean. U. S. War Department, Department of Exploration and Survey 3-4. Washington, D.C.

White, Leslie A.
   1935   The pueblo of Santo Domingo, New Mexico. Memoirs of the American Anthropological Association 43.

   1942   The pueblo of Santa Ana, New Mexico. Memoirs of the American Anthropological Association 60.

Wilcox, David R.
   1981   The entry of Athapaskans into the American Southwest: the problem today. In The protohistoric period in the North American Southwest, A.D. 1450-1700, edited by D.R. Wilcox and W.B. Masse, pp. 213-256. Arizona State University Anthropological Research Papers 24, Tempe.

Winship, George P.
   1896   The Coronado expedition, 1540-1542. In Fourteenth annual report of the Bureau of Ethnology, 1892-1893, part 1, pp. 329-613.

Winter, Joseph
   1973   Cultural modifications of the Gila Pima: A.D. 1697-A.D. 1846. Ethnohistory 20(1):67-77.

Witte, Adolph H.
   1947   Certain archaeological notes on the High Plains of Texas. Bulletin of the Texas Archaeological and Paleontological Society 18:76-82.

Work Projects Administration
   1945   New Mexico: a guide to the colorful state. Compiled by workers of the writer's program of the Work Projects Administration, second edition, University of New Mexico Press, Albuquerque.

Yarnell, Richard A.
   1978   Domestication of sunflower and sumpweed in eastern North America. In The nature and status of ethnobotany, edited by R. I. Ford, pp. 289-299. University of Michigan Museum of Anthropology, Anthropological Papers 67.

Zubrow, Ezra B.W.
   1975   Prehistoric carrying capacity: a model. Cummings, Menlo Park, California.